SECOND EDITION

HUMANITIES ONE
Interactive

A CUSTOMIZED VERSION OF
LECTURES IN WESTERN HUMANITIES, 2ND EDITION, BY EMMANUEL X. BELENA
DESIGNED SPECIFICALLY FOR HUMANITIES 201 AT HAMPTON UNIVERSITY

Edited by **DR. KAREN TURNER WARD**
Introduction by **DR. JOY HENDRICKSON** AND
DR. STEPHEN MAGU

Kendall Hunt
publishing company

D1285800

On the cover: John Biggers, Four Sisters, 1986, Oil and Acrylic on Board, 36″ × 42″.
Copyright © Hampton University Museum. Reprinted by permission.

Kendall Hunt
publishing company

www.kendallhunt.com
Send all inquiries to:
4050 Westmark Drive
Dubuque, IA 52004-1840

CONTENTS

INTRODUCTION

Dr. Joy Hendrickson and Dr. Stephen Magu

Hold on to your seats. We are about to embark on a mind-bending journey through time and space in search of possible answers to enduring questions. Who are we? Where did we come from? How did we get here? Where might we be headed?

On our trip together, we will sift through the earliest evidence so far unearthed of the very beginnings of humanity's existence. Archaeologists will be our guides as we ponder the question of our own creation. How did the human race begin? When did we become human?

We will hear the echoes of stories told to explain our origins as we crawl through cracks in rock formations to openings where we can stand upright. In the darkness, with the help of a torch, we will encounter images on the walls of these caves. We will stand face-to-face with human creations. Here is the irrefutable evidence that the arts are fundamental. They have existed as long as the human race itself has existed. Our ancestors created these works of art. We shall learn that some of their art was created for religious purposes, to honor the gods, spirits, and ancestors. And through the ages, in every corner of the world humans continued this tradition of expressing themselves through the arts: painting, sculpture, storytelling, theater, music, dance, etc. Over the course of humanity's travel through time, we shall witness the shift from cave art to writing—on tokens, tablets, and ultimately paper, telling their tales of being: of creation, of their origins in the heavens, expressed in heroic poems, odes, epics, and timeless classics.

Of special importance, a theme that we shall return to time and time again, is the interconnectedness of societies, and of how we have all learned from each other. We shall stand in awe of the great wonders of the world—no less epitomized by the burial monuments in Egypt—the pyramids; through the Greek and Roman architectural marvels—busts, statues, columns, tombs, roads, arches, coliseums, Olympic games—to the more modern expressions of the human experience such as Dante's *Commedia,* Shakespeare's great literary works to Michelangelo's works—icons that have continued to inspire us all.

HUMANITIES

The study of the Humanities begins with the recognition that humans did not create themselves. Some supernatural entity created the universe and all that is in it including human beings. A need to comprehend the spiritual realm leads to diverse explanations of the mystery of creation. Ancient narratives have been passed down from generation to generation as myths inform the development of religious dogmas and rituals. We explore these ideas in order to know how different cultures develop reasons to live and die.

Nature itself is created by this metaphysical force but humans create their own artificial products. Anthropologists will use the metaphor of raw versus cooked to explain the distinction between natural versus artificial. Humankind must meet their physical needs. The raw materials of nature are transformed by human creativity into food, clothing, housing, furniture, etc. All are decorated with a taste for what each culture considers to be beautiful.

We study the evidence of our immense diversity primarily in order to find what we have in common. Besides our relationship with the spiritual realm, there is our relationship with each other, the worldly realm. The comparative examination of political, social, and economic ideas expressed in patterns of behavior called institutions will bring us to a recognition that our most important question in the twenty-first century remains, how do we live together in peace and harmony with justice?

In our conversations over time with the ideas of the past we also find out that the underworld is another sphere which captures the attention of all humans. Every human is born into this world and is also buried when they depart. The burial sites are some of the oldest evidence of human constructions. The customs of how to deal with the human remains varies widely. What is our relationship with those who have passed on from this world to the next? Each culture answers this question differently. The mystery endures.

In this text, we will mine the Ancients for their wisdom. The legacy of past civilization will be examined beginning with the Mesopotamians, Egyptians, Greeks, Romans. The beginnings of their engagement with, and attempt to understand, the world they lived in: the seasons, animals, plants—and the beginnings of philosophy, starting with the understanding of matter around them, through to contemplating knowledge. Here we meet iconic philosophers such as Socrates, Plato, and Aristotle, mathematicians such as Archimedes of Syracuse, Euclid, Pythagoras of Samos, and with historians such as Herodotus, Thucydides, and Cicero and statesmen—such as Julius Caesar, Octavian Augustus, Alexander the Great, and even tragic figures such as Cleopatra and Mark Antony—all whose contributions to our modern appreciation of government, empire, drama, arts, music, love, and other related concepts cannot be gainsaid.

To illustrate the parallel developments of different civilizations, to acknowledge and recognize that while Western civilization and its predecessors—the Greek civilizations—are instrumental in how we view and understand the world today, there were other civilizations in other parts of the world. In Africa, we trace the continental migrations that led to the early African Kingdoms including, for instance, Mali, Songhay, Benin, and the famed trades (Trans-Saharan) routes and centers such as Timbuktu, and the Old Zimbabwe Kingdom in the South. Further east, we shall acknowledge the Xia, Shang, Zhou, and the most famed Qin dynasty, and the Han dynasty and their contribution to modern China. In the West, albeit later, we shall engage with the rise of the Maya, Inca, and Aztecs, who built great civilizations in Mexico and in Central and South America between 2,500 and 500 years ago. After engaging with the contributions of the African civilizations, detouring to the East and West—primarily to demonstrate the interconnectedness of humanity—we shall return to review the decline of the Hellenes, Hellenists, and Romans, bringing us to the medieval period and the renaissance primarily in the West.

World religions occupy a special place in man's history, present and future. Religion has been asserted as part of the human experience from as far back as man's symbols on cave walls, and continues to have significant impact on societies today. We shall trace the beginnings, the foundations, the major teachings, influential figures, and the spread of the three major world religions: Judaism, Christianity, and Islam. We shall review other religions, for instance, Hinduism, and other perhaps less discussed religions such as African traditional religions—all to illustrate the rich heritage of religion. Through the dark ages and into the early enlightenment, we shall review the major figures and works that have continued to have a major impact on modernity, and to how we conceive of ourselves today, through poetry, literature, and the arts.

CULTURE

Culture is the way of life of a people. It encompasses a plethora of material and immaterial objects without which a society cannot survive. In order for life to continue, all of humankind needs food, shelter, and clothing. Over time, each particular group of people devises their own method of meeting these needs. Life together requires some form of communication, therefore languages, customs, rituals, beliefs, patterns of behavior all develop over time.

- Why do we study the Humanities?
- We study the Humanities to develop an appreciation for the beauty of the world and humanity itself.
- We study the Humanities so that we may know ourselves and know others. Becoming cognizant of the multitude of creations of humankind will help us to recognize those things which are universal and those which are particular to our specific origins in place and time.
- We study the Humanities because it is fundamental to our common identity as fellow human beings.
- We study the Humanities to become aware of the destruction of cultures over time by dominant groups who conquer peoples of different cultures.
- We should study the Humanities because it will help us to develop a critical stance. Our own fundamental beliefs may not coincide with the beliefs of others, but we must look and see, listen and hear, what others believe in order for us to be a contributing part of the global world in which we live.

Humanities makes us think. It helps us to envision a better world. It helps us to act in a manner to bring that vision into reality in our own time.

Chapter 1: Mesopotamia

One tool we shall use to explore the Humanities is our textbook. The text is divided up into ten chapters. Chapter 1 begins with the early civilizations of Mesopotamia, which emerged between two rivers, the Tigris and Euphrates, which flow through modern day Iraq. In this area of the Middle East, various empires rise and then fall to allow others to dominate the land: Sumerians, Babylonians, Assyrians, and Persians emerge as all powerful for a time. In this mélange of cultures and civilizations, we will find some of the earliest city states, law codes, step pyramids, as well as evidence of written language and the oldest surviving record of an epic entitled *Gilgamesh*. It is the narrative of the journey of a hero who searched for the secret of immortality.

Chapter 2: Ancient Egypt

This chapter takes us to Ancient Egypt, the oldest continuous civilization of the ancient world. Located on the African continent on the banks of the Nile River, the ancient Egyptians have left us evidence of magnificent sculptures, temples, and pyramids as well as written records of their religious and moral beliefs written in hieroglyphics on papyrus scrolls and painted on the walls of their tombs.

Chapter 3: Ancient Greek Civilization

Our journey continues on to the islands in the Aegean Sea. We examine the culture of the Minoans, the Mycenaeans, and the Greeks. The philosophy, literature, and poetry of the Greeks will be examined in order to better comprehend the complexity and variety of Greek ways of thinking about the world as it develops from the archaic to the classical period of Greek civilization. The surviving examples of Greek art and architecture as well as Greek ideas of democracy and freedom are also discussed in detail.

Chapter 4: The Hebrew Civilization

In this chapter we will explore the history of the Hebrew people. Hebrew law and literature and especially the monotheistic religion of the Hebrews, Judaism, is examined in-depth. An emphasis on how these early civilizations contributed to the development of modern Western culture is discussed at length in the text.

Chapter 5: Roman Civilization and Byzantium

We next find ourselves on the Italian peninsula as we search for the site and story of the founding of Rome. Our travels take us through periods of history to places that are interrelated. As the Hellenic world gave way to the Hellenistic Age, Rome was growing in power and dominance. Romans contributed their own innovations in architecture but the Romans greatly admired Greek architecture, philosophy, and religion. In fact they adopted the Greek panoply of gods and goddesses giving them their own names (i.e., Zeus becomes Jupiter and Aphrodite becomes Venus).

The events around the founding and existence of Rome can be found in both myth and legend: the Romans tell the tale of *Romulus and Remus*, twins nursed by a she-wolf, who are the founders of Rome.

The second myth on the origin of the Romans is contained in *Aeneid*, written by Virgil. In this version, Aeneas traveled from Troy to Italy and became the ancestor of the Romans. Of course students know already that Aeneas was a character in Homer's *Iliad*. This is important, not only in learning about Rome and the Romans, but also in seeing the threads of the Humanities: often, each society—from the well-known Hellenes, to the Romans, to the Maasai, to the Incas—have myths and legends of their coming into being. It is one of the landmarks of our human origins, often developing independently among the different civilizations.

More conventionally, ancient Rome is thought to have begun in the Italian Peninsula about 753 BCE when Rome was founded. With the overthrow of the last Etruscan king, Rome established a Republic that lasted between 509 BCE and 27 BCE. Aspects of the United States political system—at least at its founding—mirrored Rome's: the Senate was comprised of "nobles"—patricians while the representatives were elected from the plebeian population. We will see that class divisions did not begin with the United States: Rome's population consisted of 10% patricians and 90% plebeians. And before Julius Caesar, we will note that the *Imperium*—power over Rome—was held by two consuls, while other instruments of the state—the Centuriate Assembly, tribune, and Senate helped give the Roman Republic political guidance and somewhat of stability.

The chapter will introduce you to the likes of Julius Caesar, his dictatorship, his peer but critic Cicero, and his nemesis, Brutus; the struggle for power in Rome after the death of Julius Caesar, between Gaius Octavian and Mark Antony who was rather enamored with Cleopatra, one of the well-known Pharaohs of Egypt. You will learn about *pax romana* and how some of the issues that Rome solved—for example, military service in exchange for citizenship—have bedeviled us in modern times. The challenges of administering Rome will become apparent—from corruption, to political intrigue and assassinations, to the challenges within the state, for example, such as wrought by the works of Jesus and his disciples in "challenging the Roman empire."

The Roman Empire lasted through 476 AD. Over time, the Romans, with superior weapons (and maybe better fighting spirit) would expand throughout the Italian peninsula, North Africa—Egypt, Carthage, and all the way to Algeria and Morocco, the Iberian Peninsula—Spain and Portugal, and all the way through Europe to Great Britain. By 230 AD, right about the time Christianity was beginning to take hold in the Empire, Rome controlled territory that made it the largest empire of its day.

Eventually, Emperor Constantine would stop the persecution of the Christians throughout the Roman Empire (with the Edict of Milan in 313 CE and convert to Christianity. Eventually, as perhaps all empires do, Rome did begin to decline—the decline wrought on by a multitude of reasons. From the invasion by the Germanic tribes that the Romans called the **barbarians** to the invasions by the Vandals, internal corruption to the war with the Goths (Visigoths, Ostrogoths, and the like).

While Romans did not concern themselves with philosophy, they were admirers of the stoics, the epicureans, and the skeptics. Neo-Platonism would also become quite important. The Romans made other significant contributions such as to law (the Twelve Tables, rules of criminal and civil law and subsequently *case law*); they also gave us architectural marvels, such as the rounded arch (the Etruscans), vaults, domes, amphitheaters, baths, paved roads, and sculptures that have survived to-date. The contributions of Rome to the modern arts, politics, government, literature, and other aspects is evident, even as it collapsed under the weight of problems it was unable to solve. Importantly, it eventually tolerated Christianity, which is discussed in Chapter 6 of your book.

Chapter 6: The Middle Ages

The Middle Ages is a term used to generally describe the period between the fall of the Roman Empire (remember, 476 AD/CE) and about 1500 CE, marking the Renaissance period. Some scholars separate this period into early and late Middle Ages. Some of the key landmarks of this era include the reorganization of social, economic, political, cultural, and religious systems, accompanied by landmarks and popular concepts, people, and events. These include, for example, the gradual Christianization of Europe, and the growth of monasticism.

This, the early- to middle-Middle Ages, was the time of Charlemagne and the Carolingian dynasty, in effect the first emperor crowned head of the Church by Pope Leo. The split of the Catholic Church occurred in this time, and it is also a period that marks the rise of the feudal society (where lords who owned land and other resources allowed the not-so-rich to work on their farms in return for payments of taxes, forty fighting days and paying ransom in the event of a lord being captured—and thereby providing the first forms of organized local government). This is also the age when the Vikings swept through Northern Europe, and William of Normandy landed in Britain, establishing himself through several battles, some of which are represented in different landmarks. Later changes in this High part of the Middle Ages (from about 1000 AD) also saw the population of Europe increase due to technological, agricultural, and trade activities, and the changes in organization of peasants, giving rise to Manorialism: labor services for rent.

The Middle Ages also feature the controversial Crusades, the rise and importance of Gothic art and architecture. While the educational system—particularly the University—may have been more organized in Europe, and the founding of the University of Bologna in Italy in 1088 is testament to this, we must recall that the oldest existing, and continually operating, educational institution in the world is the University of Karueein (Morocco, 859 AD—*Guinness World Book of Records*). In England, the University of Oxford was founded in 1096 while in France, the University of Paris (Sorbonne) came into existence between 1160 and 1250. These institutions were the stomping grounds for such famous figures as the theologian Thomas Aquinas (author of *Summa Theologica*), the painter Giotto, Dante Alighieri, Italian poet, Chaucer, Christine de Pisan, France's first woman of Letters, among others. It was also a time of revisiting Aristotle and the contest between faith and reason.

The Black Death marks one of the gloomy periods of the history of Europe: the Black Death is believed to have decimated Europe's population by about 25–30%. On the religious front, this was the era of the Inquisition: those who disagreed with the church found themselves at great peril: burnt, broken at the wheel, subjected to the inquisition, and other atrocities. At the same time, the population of Europe was becoming more socially distinct and classes arose: the clergy, the nobility, and the commoners. In the arts, even as religious leaders shunned the earlier expressionism of the Hellenic and Hellenistic eras, there was attention paid to a mix of the Greco-Roman world, to the Germanic peoples and to the emerging arts and literature inspired by the church; buildings such as the Hagia Sophia, the Gothic churches, and so on dotted the European landscape. Here, we also find the Romanesque churches and decorative arts that often borrowed from the art of the populations in which they were built.

These churches—and Cathedrals—were not only monasteries and worship places; they were also built regally to demonstrate the authority of the church and the importance of religion in everyday life, decorated by emerging classes of artists, poets (for example the *chanson de gestes*), and artists such as the troubadours whose art crossed over into the secular. It bears mention that one of these works was Dante Alighieri's *Commedia Divina* (Divine Comedy)—he of the Dante's Inferno fame. The Late Middle Ages are also characterized by the explosion of literature that was the beginning of the Northern Italian Renaissance: the early works of diplomats such as Francesco Petrarch (writer of *Canzoniere*), Giovanni Boccaccio (author of *Decameron*—on the conditions of the Black Death), Geoffrey Chaucer, writer of *The Canterbury Tales* and Christine de Pizan (Pisan) who wrote the *Book of the City Ladies* (1405), were some of the notable laureates.

Chapter 7: How Christianity Led to Freedom, Capitalism, and Western Success

The next chapter in the book, Chapter 8, begins rather controversially: as we journey through the long road from pre-history to modern society, we have seen how different societies have endeavored to organize their affairs: from the arts, to religion, commerce, culture, language, literature, government and politics, affairs with their neighbors and within their own societies—and how sometimes, other cultures have borrowed from one another, no doubt each proposing to improve over that which they conquer, but always moving *forward*. Humanities and humanists have not argued that there is any one society that proposes to become less successful; progress is the glue that binds all societies together; all societies are in constant pursuit of self-improvement, and the absence of one technology in one society does not instantly convey it into the unfortunate dustbin of such terms as "backward" or "uncivilized." After all, who defines these terms?

Even though now we critique certain activities that the previous societies or sections thereof did, although we might frown upon the Greek gods and their amorous relations with humans, leading us to define new ways in which religion brings about meaning to our lives, we must be cognizant, indeed aware, of normative judgments about our—but particularly other—societies. This is why a title such as "How Christianity Led to Freedom, Capitalism, and Western Success" can be controversial: it may imply that other societies are less successful precisely because they were not Western, or Christian. One has to be judicious in how they see other societies; it is particularly important to insure that narratives of "success" and "backwardness" are carefully evaluated and challenged by students of the humanities, the interconnectedness between cultures, the cross-cultural pollination and borrowing appreciated, and the non-linearity of cultures appreciated.

The post-Middle Ages era in the West was one in which religion and philosophy interacted to produce (eventually), the contours of the modern state and modern society. Christianity was at the center of this progress. As the chapter points out, Christianity "embraced reason and logic as the primary way to religious truth." The European/Western society did benefit greatly from science and technology that stemmed from as far back as Greece. The Greeks taught us how to move from the physical to the metaphysical, to question logic, to begin experimentation; after all, such philosophers, scientists, and mathematicians as Democritus (matter made of atoms), Pythagoras of Samos (Pythagorean Theory), Archimedes of Syracuse's work on geometry, pi, calculating area, innovating machines, screws, and pulleys—all contributed to Western technology.

Coupled with philosophy and the writings of such religious figures as St. Augustine (writing of free will to act), St. Thomas Aquinas (freedom to make moral choices), and the further scholarship of individuals such as Thomas More led to the growth of literature and philosophy on society, government, and related concepts. With the growth of constitutionalism and change in governance, there was subsequent change in the rights and responsibilities of the individual, of the church, and of the state. At the same time, conflict between the church and the political authorities saw the beginnings of schisms between the two. Henry VIII separated from the church about the time when Europe was about to embark on years and years of civil strife, some of it connected to the disagreements over the role of the state in the church. In this chapter, students will further engage with such concepts as capitalism, and consider its impact in the development of Western society.

Chapter 8: The Renaissance

At the end of the Middle Ages, Europe was ready for a rebirth—yes, the renaissance—a cultural period and movement lasting from the fourteenth to seventeenth century, whose key highlights included revisiting classical learning, and was particularly centered around Italy and later spread to other areas. In particular, Florence, Italy, and the ideas of Dante Alighieri (yes, he of the *Commedia Divina* fame) and his compatriot, Francesco Petrarch as well as Giotto di Bondone's paintings. Other major occurrences of the period included improvement in navigation and coming into the knowledge of other continents, decline of the feudal system and early innovations such as paper (as opposed to parchment, calfskin, and sheepskin), improvement of the printing press (first invented by the Chinese in the twelfth century). The knowledge base brooked by the intellectual movement is generally referred to as "humanism." One peculiarity of the Renaissance that students should keep in mind is well illustrated by one of its best known prodigies: Leonardo da Vinci, who combined painter, sculptor, architect, poet, musician, and scientist into one.

Italy, as the center of this Humanist movement of the beginning of the Renaissance had many other such figures as Manetti, Bruni, Ficino, Pico della Mirandola, Lorenzo Valla, and Salutati. Events elsewhere, such as the fall of Constantinople in 1453 released quite a bit of literature, manuscripts, and other troves of examination of materials to the West: this included prior Hellenic scholarship—and these could for the first time be re-examined by the humanists, and thus re-interpret perhaps for the first time, the original manuscripts. Other features of the humanism movement included: study of human nature as its subject, unity and compatibility of the truth in philosophy and theology and emphasis on the dignity of man.

The Renaissance spread North with aid of the new Humanists and their inventions or improvements to inventions—such as the printing press, enabling more people to read. As the Renaissance spread from southern Europe—Italy—to the North—Germany, the Netherlands and France, we began to see the writings of philosophers such as Desiderius Erasmus, whose *Praise of Folly* (1509) is widely celebrated. Overall, enlightenment figures—including painters such as Leonardo da Vinci, Masaccio, the Lorenzeti brothers, Boticelli, Raphael, and sculptors such as Pisano, Donatello, Verrochio, Ghiberti, and Michelangelo, and architects including Alberti and Brunelleschi redefined the notion and importance of the human as the focus of arts and paintings. Other conditions peculiar to parts of Europe were favorable to commissioning of the Arts: Florence, with the Medici Family, was one of those that commissioned great works of art.

You will become familiar with the names of Raphael's paintings, *The Madonna*, Michelangelo's *Last Judgment* (in the Sistine Chapel in Rome), among others. You will hear about *The Prince,* a political treatise written by Niccolò Machiavelli and quoted widely by political scientists. Albrecht Dürer will become known to you for his wood-cuts (Dürer was a Da Vinci-esque painter, printmaker, mathematician, and theorist); Pieter Brueg(h)el The Elder will become part of your conversation, as will William Shakespeare, Sir Thomas More, John Milton, Francis Bacon, Michel de Montaigne, and Caterina de' Medici will be some of our compatriots on this journey into the Italian and later Northern Renaissance.

Chapter 9: Original Source Readings of Western Civilization

Periodically during our journey we will turn to this chapter to unearth selected primary sources from the Mesopotamian, Greek, Roman, Hebrew, and Christian writings. We shall dip into the works of the poet Homer; philosophers like Plato and Aristotle; playwrights like Euripides. We will read selections from the epic of *Gilgamesh,* passages from the Bible; Roman documents about slave labor and slave revolts; Caligula and the Jews. To hear the words, as they were written by luminaries from the past, is to experience first-hand the events, thoughts, and feelings of fellow human beings. It is to reconnect with the origins of our own happenings in the world we live in now. Let us embark on this thrilling journey into our past, so as to better understand our present and make our future brighter than ever before.

The collection of reference maps will help us navigate our way on our travels. Then we have a comprehensive outline of the chapters in the book and sample exercises composed of short answer quizzes and essay questions for reviewing and sharing with one another what we have learned on our journey.

Practical Matters: Interactive Web Learning

In this digital age, it is important for students and their instructors to utilize all tools available to them that make learning interactive, informative, and also fun. The new, customized Humanities course-book is accompanied by an innovative, user-friendly website that will augment your learning. With the companion website whose access code is available with the purchase of every new book, students will have access to materials such as interactive games to test your knowledge of the humanities, chapter summaries, study guides, multiple-choice and true/false assessments and if your instructor so chooses, tests can be administered on the course site or they can be imported into Blackboard. Students will have access to collaboration tools such as an interactive discussion board, suggested topics for group projects, and other free humanities-related content on the site. Other materials on the site will include links to project sites, depositories of artistic material that includes photographs, pictures, famous paintings and drawings, videos, articles, and other humanities learning support materials. Instructors will set these sites up. The goal of availing these materials to the students and instructors is to provide for a better learning experience. We hope that your journey through the humanities will be fun, full of excitement, will give you tools which, at the end of the course, will equip you with the knowledge, skills, experience, and aptitude to appreciate the interconnectedness of the human experience.

CONCLUSION

The content of this Humanities course is based on shared communications sent across time and space within a community which is global. We can appreciate these past examples of human creativity best when we compare and evaluate them to contemporary expressions. Besides the textbook, students as fellow travelers on our journey together are expected to visit museums, galleries, music, dance, and theater performances in order to experience the ongoing activity of the communal expression of humankind. These activities will allow us to stretch our consciousness in ways that we have not dreamed were possible.

What will YOU do? We must continue to express our own versions of the human imagination to be fully human. The study of the creative outpourings of humanity over the centuries makes us think, makes us change, makes us move, literally dance. This is the way to actually break out of the box. To transcend the limits of one's time, one's particular place in the world, the circumstances under which one lives is to freely express oneself as a member of the human race.

It is up to you. This journey, which is the embracing of all humanity in its infinite diversity, will affect you depending on the extent to which you are open to it. Life is what YOU make it. Let us continue on this journey together with eyes and ears wide open to the beauty around us.

CHAPTER 1

MESOPOTAMIA

Roots of Western civilization are found in the Middle East (Turkey, Palestine, and Mesopotamia). **Mesopotamia,** in Greek, means the land between two rivers, the Tigris and Euphrates in modern Iraq (Figure 1.1).

In the Neolithic era, 10,000 years ago, a new civilization and culture developed.

Why did this extraordinary event happen? The reason was man's change from hunting and gathering to cultivation. The discovery of agriculture was the reason for great changes and progress.

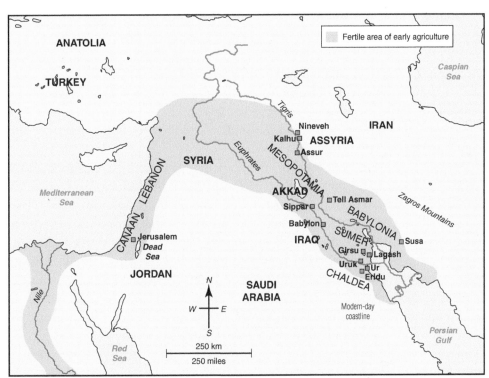

Figure 1.1 Mesopotamia between the Euphrates & Tigris. *Image Copyright Kendall Hunt Publishing Company.*

CULTIVATION: CULTURE AND CIVILIZATION

In the Neolithic era about 8000 B.C. (10,000 years ago), a new civilization and culture developed. The reason for this development was the change from hunting and gathering to **cultivation** or **agriculture.** Agriculture was the cause for the great changes and progress. As hunters and gatherers, early man had to live a nomadic life, organized in primitive tribes or clans, living at the mercy of nature and nomadic animals.

When man learned to farm and domesticate animals, he became free from a nomadic life and was able to **settle down permanently.** Drought, floods, and disease have plagued farmers and domesticated animals, but man was much better able to survive and feed himself than as a more primitive hunter/gatherer. The surplus food he produced through agriculture allowed man to overcome periods of famine, and barter what he had in excess for what he lacked which later developed into full-fledged commerce of crops, animals, and household goods. As commerce increased, the villages with the market centers grew into towns and later these towns into cities, and some cities became city-states with a well developed urban center. Also the surplus food would allow for a portion of the population to be free from dedicating themselves to produce the food they need and thus be able to devote themselves to other activities such as weaving, making leather items, making tools and weapons, jewelry, pottery, art crafts, defense, government, etc.

The new agricultural societies settled in villages would be able to develop many innovations. Living in a permanent place, man can now spend some of his time and efforts to create objects that satisfy his needs. Man will have needs he did not have when he had a nomadic life. These new needs will require that man invent ways to satisfy them; therefore, the phrase "necessity is the mother of invention" will apply.

Once there are permanent agricultural communities man will need to create permanent housing; pottery items for daily use such as pots, jugs, and dishes; weaving to make clothes; furniture for his house; tools for farming, building, and carpentry; math to count crops and animals, to barter and measure land that now is private property; writing to keep records of goods, land, and taxes; calendars to predict rains, floods, planting, and harvesting seasons; organization of government to have the larger population living in an organized manner; laws to regulate human behavior, commerce, and private property; organized defense to protect the property and settlements from raids by other human groups which creates armies, weapons, and building of walls and fortifications to protect the cities; city-states which are a large urban center with the surrounding countryside and villages and towns, which have become the centers of commerce and government, etc.

Therefore, these material necessities to survive, improve living conditions, organize and protect are what put in motion new ideas that resulted in the creation of these inventions to meet society's needs. Without agriculture there would not exist permanent settlements and the inventions and organization of society that came out of them which brought progress for mankind. This progress brought a relatively advanced stage of social, political, and cultural development which is known as **civilization.** The new civilizations will each develop their own socially transmitted behavior patterns, beliefs, institutions, laws, arts, and other creations; in other words, they will develop their own **culture.** Thus, culture and civilization can have the same meaning.

New agricultural societies were able to develop many innovations. These innovations were due to newly created needs. Therefore, the phrase "***Necessity*** *is the Mother of invention*" applies.

(Examples of innovations are: pottery, weaving, housing, markets, calendars, math, writing, records, and organized communities (government).)

Once you have a permanent agricultural community you need:

- Permanent housing
- Settle in villages
- Pottery—daily use (pots, containers, dishes)
- Weaving—cloth (wool)
- Calendar—predict rain, floods, planting, harvest, seasons
- Math—count crops, land, barter
- Markets—exchange surplus goods and buy necessities (commerce)
- Tools—farming, carpentry, building

- Organization—government
- Laws—regulate behavior, commerce, and private property
- Records—writing/math—to record land, crops, trade
- Defense—weapons, walls, armies to protect community and land
- Cities—centers of commerce and government then become city-states

It was in Sumer, located in modern Iraq, where a loose confederation of city-states united political and economic power into one of history's earliest dynasties. Here and in Egypt about the same time a high civilization developed which are the roots of our Western civilization.

Sumer—in Mesopotamia was the first loose confederation of city-states to unite political and economic power into a kingdom.

Sumer—3000–2350 B.C. (5,000 years ago) that began at the same time as ancient Egypt, invented the first written language CUNEIFORM (wedge writing made up of wedge-like characters or symbols). It was used to record water flow of rivers and astronomy to determine the seasons and be able to manage agriculture by predicting floods and the planting and harvest seasons.

Early Religion—They had a practical religion and believed the gods controlled natural phenomena such as floods, storms, earthquakes, rain, etc. Emphasis was on daily survival in an unpredictable harsh environment with devastating floods and raids by hostile neighbors.

Polythestic Religion—belief in many gods. Gods had powers and were immortal, but had human attributes such as they were selfish, frivolous, quarrelsome, etc.

Not a religion of ethics or morals, the focus was on pleasing the gods by prayers, incantations, and magic to gain their favor. So it did not improve ethical behavior.

Kings were the servants and representatives of the gods. His government presumed that the gods were in control. Thus, people obeyed the king and his priests because they communicated with the gods and could attain the gods' favor and protection.

Ziggurats were terraced pyramids built to ascend toward heaven so the king and priests could praise the gods.

Art—The Sumerians made sculpture by adding carved parts of different materials, such as stone, wood, and metal, reaching a high level of skill.

Important contributions were the foundations of mathematics, science, engineering. For example in math the Sumerians invented division, multiplication, the square and cube roots, 60 seconds in a minute and 60 minutes in an hour, and the 360 degree circle.

Other important inventions were the plow, wheeled vehicle, metal, sailing ships, city-states (government) and writing.

The Epic of Gilgamesh—was the first literary story with a protagonist with a name and personality, and earliest written record of the discovery of death. Gilgamesh is a king whom the gods propose to chastise. To humble the arrogant monarch they create a foil called *Enkidu* of a strong body but with a simple heart. Before encountering Gilgamesh, Enkidu is civilized by the gods who provide him with a courtesan to instruct him in the erotic arts. This humanizing process enables Enkidu to overcome his brutish nature and gain wisdom. Gilgamesh and Enkidu meet in combat as the gods intended, and end in a draw. They become friends and both will go through a series of exciting adventures. A misadventure provokes the wrath of the gods and Enkidu dies in the arms of

Gilgamesh, who is left alone facing the reality of death. This makes him ponder over the meaning of life and death. Gilgamesh then learns that a legendary hero possesses the secret of eternal life, so Gilgamesh tracks him down and finds the thorny plant that guarantees immortality. Full of happiness with his acquisition, Gilgamesh decides to celebrate by bathing in a nearby pool. While he enjoys his bath a snake snuffed (put out) the fragrance of the plant and carried it away. Going back the snake shed its skin. Thus, Mesopotamians consider the snakes immortal because they annually shed their skins and continue living. The snake stole Gilgamesh's immortality. Thereupon Gilgamesh weeps because he lost immortality. This confirms the pessimistic and *fatalistic attitude* of the Mesopotamians that life ends in nothingness or death. This epic story was told by many of the Mesopotamian civilizations.

The origins of epic poetry can be dated back to the 20th and 10th century B.C. Originally the poems were performed orally in front of large audiences. Epics were formulaic. The poems were often taken from established myths, containing acts of heroism, unimaginable challenges often in the form of wild beasts, damsels in distress waiting to be saved, all while numerous Gods and Goddesses watch on, amused by their intervention in human affairs. Aside from its subject matter, the language of an epic is unique. Unlike most poems, the poems often contained lengthy reserved speeches, highlighted by beautiful language. Epics were usually saturated with similes, metaphors, and epithets.

Similes

A figure of speech involving the comparison of one thing with another thing of a different kind, used to make a description more emphatic or vivid.

Metaphors

A figure of speech in which a word or phrase is applied to an object or action to which it is not literally applicable.

Epithets

An adjective or descriptive phrase expressing a quality characteristic of the person or thing mentioned.

AKKADIAN—2350–2150 B.C.

Were barbarians (less civilized people, but usually strong enough to invade and take over) that took over Sumer. Introduced new concept of divine monarchy supported by force of arms. Absolute control by monarch.

Babylonia—1900–1500 B.C.

Took over by force. King Hammurabi introduced **HAMMURABI**'s Code of Law that established the rule of law from the Persian Gulf to the Mediterranean Sea. It was the most practical legal standard up to that point in time. Its goal was to establish order by regulating private property, trade, other business affairs, and human behavior in society (Figure 1.2).

Its 282 regulations regulated commerce, land tenure, marriage and divorce, perjury, theft, inheritance, adoption, hire of labor, slaves, etc. There is no mention of taxes, but that does not mean taxes did not exist. Justice was administered by the principle of retaliation in kind—"eye for an eye, tooth for a tooth." So, if someone hit another individual and broke a tooth, a tooth would also be broken on the guilty perpetrator. The code did have some retaliation in fines and money compensation, that was a progressive element. The code worked for the society of its time.

The major contribution of the code to progress was to establish order, protect society, protect the weaker members, and it had the principal that all were equal before the law, a principle modern legal systems embrace.

Figure 1.2 Detail from the Code of Hammurabi stela. Babylonian laws—Cuneiform writing. *Image Copyright John Said, 2009. Used under license from Shutterstock, Inc.*

HAMMURABI'S CODE FACTS

- Slaves were not protected under the code at all
- Women were inferior and wives were considered the personal property of husbands
- Women were protected from neglectful and abusive husbands
- Punished violence or injustice of one person upon another.
- Fathers could not disinherit their sons unless the son had committed a severe crime
- Incest was forbidden
- Trade and property rights were given great importance in the Code
- The Hammurabi Code established the rule of the land for a millennium
- Few exceptions could be made to the rules
- The law was less subjective and left very little room for arbitrary interpretations

Assyrian Empire—1076–612 B.C.

They were warlike. First militaristic state in history. They were extremely cruel with the captured people and controled them by fear. They would cut off the hands and feet of subversive subjects in front of their families and leave them to bleed to death. The Assyrians practiced the removal of entire populations from their homeland and forced them to resettle in other lands to control dissent. Sargon II dispersed the Israelites producing the ten lost tribes of Israel.

Art was to serve the king by glorifying and showing his hunting and military abilities. Its themes were power and conquest (Figure 1.3).

Figure 1.3 Relief of an Assyrian god with cougar head. *Image Copyright Quintenilla, 2009. Used under license from Shutterstock, Inc.*

The Chaldean (2nd Babylonian Empire)

They conquered Jerusalem and many Jews or Hebrews were forced to resettle in Babylon to serve their new master. This became known as the Babylonian captivity. This civilization became decadent with internal struggles which brought it to great weakness and were conquered by Persians.

Persian Empire-539–331 B.C.

Covered a great area, the largest empire up to that point in history, and spanned from Greece to India, Russia to the Indian Ocean. They were tolerant, allowing other people to keep their customs and religions. This was a necessary means to gain the adherence of the many people that were under the empire, and avoid rebellions. They had these features:

Figure 1.4   Ruins of ancient city of Persepolis-Persia (Iran). The figure is of a man's head (face has been destroyed) on a body of an animal. Persian architecture places its emphasis on secular buildings.) *Image Copyright javarman, 2009. Used under license from Shutterstock, Inc.*

- Network of imperial roads—1,600 miles, that allowed armies to move more quickly providing greater security and communication needed in a vast empire.
- Absolute monarchy, autocratic rulers.
- Eclectic culture—that was not original, and borrowed from other cultures.
- Architecture was secular, and not religious putting their focus on places and not temples, because Zoroastrianism required no organized religion with priests and temples (Figure 1.4).

The Persian empire was taken over by Alexander the Great in the 4th century B.C.

CHARACTERISTICS OF THE MESOPOTAMIAN CIVILIZATIONS

The culture of Mesopotamia was one of survival, floods, droughts, and innovations. Had no lasting stability or balance as contact and invasions by other people and civilizations brought new ideas. It had mainly periods of adaptations or adjustments. Tended to go from one crisis to another. Little concern for ideals (truth, good, beauty) and focused on palpable reality that they needed to survive. Were pragmatic, trying to please the gods, and with an authoritarian government.

ZOROASTRIANISM

Most important contribution of the Persian culture was the new religion of Zoroastrianism. It was created by **Zoroaster,** born about 660 B.C. Some interpret his new religion as *monotheistic* (one god), while others as *dualistic* (two gods), but all see it as ethical.

In Zoroaster's work, the Holy Spirit, who is the principle of truth, created the world and existed before the world was born. The evil one, the twin of the Holy Spirit, was created so that people would appreciate goodness through its struggle with evil.

There is a debate over whether the evil one was created by the Holy Spirit, thus having **monotheism,** or created simultaneously as the evil twin of the Holy Spirit, and therefore **dualism**. For Zoroastrianism, all life became *a contest between good and evil,* truth versus error, light versus darkness.

In its original form—Zoroastrianism:

- was a personal religion—anyone could pray to god directly without the need of kings and priests
- focus on ethical moral living
- excluded institutionalized religion, priests, temples, and rituals
- was open to all men
- spoke of coming of a savior, who would resurrect the dead for judgment
- had Heaven as reward, and hell as punishment
- ultimately the Holy Spirit would triumph over the evil one, ending the conflict between good and evil.

The people did not quite understand all the abstract ideas of Zoroastrians and over time the practitioners put emphasis on sacrifices, liturgy, and priests. Ancient pagan gods were introduced, such as Ishtar (fertility goddess) and Mithra (god of light).

So Zoroastrians incorporated polytheism and institutionalized religious practices which Zoroastrianism originally attempted to eradicate. Therefore, in part it went back to the old beliefs it had tried to supplant.

Zoroastriasm became strong in Persia and spread in Mesopotamia, Asia Minor, and Egypt, and was incorporated by later religious movements. Alexander the Great's invasion brought the downturn of Zoroastriasm, and the Muslim conquest of Persia suppressed it. There was a migration of its followers to India and later revival has kept Zoroastriasm alive and practiced in India by descendants of Persian exiles.

CONTEXT

Mesopotamian Gods and Goddesses

Name	Symbol	Role
An/Anu	 Horned cap	Father of the gods, god of the sky.
Enlil	 Horned cap	God of the air and storm; later replaces Anu as father of the gods.
Utu/Shamash	 Solar disc	Sun-god lord of the truth and justice.
Inanna/Ishtar	 Star	Goddess of love and war.
Ninhursag/Belitili	 'Omega' symbol	Mother Earth.
Enki/Ea	 Goat-fish	God of water, lord wisdom, magic, art.
Marduk	 Spade	Chief god of Babylon.

Figure 1.5 Mesopotamian Gods and Goddesses. *Image Copyright Kendall Hunt Publishing Company.*

SUMMARY

The roots of our Western civilization go back to the Middle East where Mesopotamia is located. Part of the history of Western Civilization begins in Mesopotamia with its early agricultural settlements that unleashed a series of inventions, one after another. This developed into a complex civilization with its division of labor, greater productivity and wealth, government and the capacity for organized warfare. The history of Mesopotamia is characterized by civilizations that become established but not for a long period of time due to invasions that begin a new civilization. Therefore, none of the Mesopotamian cultures achieve a truly stable period of balance. Adjustment prevailed over balance from the Sumerians to the Persians. Their outlook in life was largely determined by geography and climate, in a harsh and unpredictable environment without geographical barriers to keep invaders out.

Its polytheistic religions and authoritarian governments did not inspire any move toward personal excellence in contrast with the excellence the Greek civilization will achieve during antiquity. Pleasing the gods and the authoritarian monarchs was apparently more important than striving for excellence to live a good life. They understood reality as a harsh visible world with its constant threats of invasions where their major concern was survival, and therefore their pragmatic attitude toward life. On the positive side their artistic and architectural achievements are a testimony to the remarkable accomplishments. They left us many contributions in the fields of law, mathematics, writing, religion, literature, and astronomy.

The **Sumerian civilization** developed organized polytheism and ziggurats with temples on the top of the pyramid. They made discoveries in math, writing, and astronomy. The first major literary work, *The Epic of Gilgamesh* was composed. The **Akkadians** improved and refined the arts of the Sumerian culture. The **Babylonian Empire** and the monarch Hammurabi gave us the written legal code of Hammurabi that encompassed principles that form part of the Western legal systems that still are prevalent today. The **Assyrian Empire** was the first militaristic state in history governed by ruthless warrior monarchs. Their art was to serve the king illustrating his warrior skill and power. The final apex of Mesopotamian culture came under the **Chaldeans** with one of the wonders of the ancient world the Hanging Gardens. The last were the **Persians** with the greatest empire the world had up to that date. Their culture was eclectic, encompassing diverse cultures within a vast territory and Zoroastrianism was its original contribution. Finally Mesopotamian culture that began in 3000 B.C., as well as Ancient Egypt, succumbed to Alexander the Great in 331 B.C. with his European Greek culture. It will take another 1000 years with the expansion of Islam for the Middle East to have an impact upon the West.

ANCIENT EGYPT

Egypt is the "gift of the Nile" because it is located in the Sahara desert, the largest and driest in the world. The only reason why life could be sustained in abundance was due to the water and silt (soil with decayed vegetable matter) deposited by the Nile River when it flooded and irrigated the Nile Delta. The Nile was a predictable river that flooded every year at the same time, so the farmers could prepare their fields accordingly. All cities are located along the Nile. Egypt has a "gentle" climate (relative warm winters) that paired with fertile soil and plentiful water was able to produce two crops per year, double compared to most parts of the world. The desert and seas formed a natural barrier that kept Egypt isolated and therefore free from invasions and raids by hostile neighbors (Figure 2.1).

Egypt had a more peaceful and consistent (continuous) development than any other ancient civilization. The isolation kept foreign ideas and influences from disrupting their cultural balance and they were free of foreign invasion throughout most of their history. Egypt was a homogeneous nation, a unified country with one people, one language, and one religion. Not much changed in Egypt over the centuries, and this can be seen in its art where the style and fashions and beliefs remained constant for well over 2,000 years. Thus, they viewed nature and life as immutable and the afterlife as a continuation of the good life on Earth.

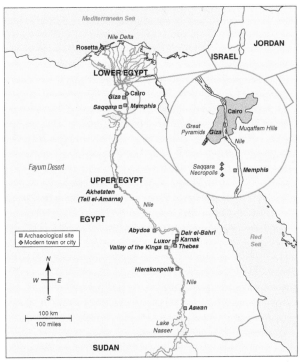

Figure 2.1   Egypt is located in the Sahara Desert.
Image Copyright Kendall Hunt Publishing Company.

Egypt	Mesopotamia
Balance **Maat** was the will of the gods that contained Order/truth/justice/righteousness, which were their **ethics**	*Adjustment* Survival was main focus in life
Mythical Thinking/Agriculture Stable-continuity; religion was ethical; beliefs remain constant and preoccupied for the after-life	*Mythical Thinking/Agriculture* Unstable-balance is disrupted in cycles. Religion is pragmatic and self-serving, to solve problems Belief changes. They are preoccupied with present reality.
Homogeneous One people, language, religion & culture	*Heterogeneous* Many people, languages & cultures

Figure 2.2

Egypt was a **theocracy** (government whose authorities are considered divine or also are the authorities of the religious establishment). The **pharaoh** (title means "great house," term originally applied to king's court and residence) was considered a living god. The pharaoh and the state were one, divine and indivisible. He was responsible for life, safety, and prosperity. Ancient Egyptians believed he controlled the Nile River, the source of life. Pharaoh was the source of the good life, the basis of his power and authority over his people.

Egyptians put emphasis on ethical living or right actions. Proper ethical conduct prepared the individual for continuing the good life after death. Ethical behavior resulted in reward after life (Figure 2.2).

COMPARISON WITH MESOPOTAMIA

Egyptians adhered to their traditions, political system, and culture. They saw their world as stable and beneficial. For ancient Egyptians their world was unchanging and eternal. Stone was used as it is a long-lasting, stable material that represents their long-lasting culture. Because Egyptians were content with their existence and saw it as beneficial without any other ideas to challenge this view of reality, so religious beliefs and art remained constant for almost 3,000 years. Little change was an Egyptian cultural reality.

Their gods personified nature: Amon-Re—god of the sun, Osiris—god of Nile and underworld. Art was mainly sacramental that gave it a massive and solemn characteristic. Art paintings and reliefs show people with face and legs in profile, eyes, and torso viewed from front which is not the natural look of real persons. They developed written language, **hieroglyphics,** and pictographic symbols for words (Figure 2.3). Their ancient written language was lost until a French scholar that came with Napoleon Bonaparte's expedition to Egypt in 1799 discovered this stone from 196 B.C. The text in the stone was written in three languages, two in Egyptian, hieroglyphics and Demotic, and the third in classical Greek. Knowing classical Greek, English

Figure 2.3 Egyptian hieroglyphs were known as the formal writing system in Egypt. Egyptian writing on stone wall.

Figure 2.4 Inside of Luxor temple. Ancient Egyptian culture. This large statue is an example of Egyptian rigid rectangular pose. *Image Copyright Pavel K, 2009. Used under license from Shutterstock, Inc.*

Figure 2.5 Statue of Ramses II in Karnak temple in Luxor, Egypt. Example of large, solemn sculpture that denotes the importance and greatness of the pharaoh that Egyptians had to acknowledge and serve. *Image Copyright DDCoral, 2009. Used under license from Shutterstock, Inc.*

and French scholars in 1822 were able to decipher the principles of ancient Egyptian hieroglyphics writings by comparing it with the text in Greek. This has allowed modern scholars to read and understand better this ancient civilization.

From 5000–3100 B.C. Egypt had no central government. In 3100 B.C. the first dynasty began with King Narmer who united the two kingdoms of Lower Egypt (Delta) and Upper Egypt.

Egyptian sculptures have the characteristics which express an impassive calm and enduring serenity that indicates eternal existence. Egyptian statuary has a monumental frozen solemn quality. The rulers are depicted as massive, bigger than the subjects. Symbolizing the total control of the god-ruler, this immobility is a visual counterpart of Egyptian belief in immutable laws that govern people and nature. This reflects the idea that the gods rule, they are in control, stability and an immutable reality or life. Also characteristic of Egyptian portraiture is the rectangularity of the figures, as if they were standing within a rectangular box that reinforces the impression of a composed immobility (Figure 2.4). The figures have a rigid look. Also it is common to find art ignoring perspective of the individuals depicted and scaling them according to their importance. Thus the pharaoh will be larger than a scribe and a scribe larger than a simple peasant or slave. It is not realistic art (Figure 2.5).

EGYPTIAN ARTS

While Egypt's allure is usually reserved for its golden treasures and lore, its true treasures are its works of art. Egyptian art includes architecture, pottery, paintings, and sculptures. Egyptian artwork holds a prevalent place in every aspect of Egyptian culture. Egypt's most popular architectural contributions, the pyramids, are not only art work, but as also serve as tombs for Egypt's great pharaohs and royalty (Figure 2.6). These tombs are usually decorated with paintings, sculptures, jewellery and pottery with the belief that the Pharaohs would enjoy them in the afterlife (Figure 2.7). Egyptian artwork also serves as the foundation of communication in Egypt. The Hieroglyphs are known as Egypt's sophisticated writing system (Figure 2.8).

During the Middle Kingdom, the Egyptians achieved the greatest standard of living of that period (2135–1786 B.C.) and greater decentralized authority from the Pharaoh.

The Second Intermediate Period was marked by the Hyksos or "Rulers of Foreign Lands" (1780–1550 B.C.) who were Palestinian invaders that disrupted the Middle kingdom and brought deep changes on the course of Egyptian history. By the end of the 1600s B.C. the rulers of southern or Upper Egypt began a revolt against the Hyksos which eventually drove this foreign dynasty out of Egypt. The changes from a pacific and isolationist state policy to one of aggressive imperialism brought about the beginning of the Egyptian Empire, because it induced the Egyptian rulers into imperial conquests from 1560 to 1087 B.C. during the New Kingdom or three successive dynasties, Eighteenth to Twentieth. From this period onward ancient Egypt will begin to look beyond its borders for conquest that will end its isolation. Government became more autocratic. The Pharaoh relied more on military might.

Figure 2.6 Bust of Queen Nefertiti in the Egyptian Museum in Berlin, Germany.

1379–1362 B.C. was the period of conflict between the pharaoh Akhenaten (Amenhotep IV) and the priests and the religious beliefs of that period. Egyptian religion had become seriously debased and its ethical foundations reduced to superstition and magic. This resulted in a great increase in the power of the priesthood that preyed on the fear of the masses. Priests were selling magical charms that were supposed to prevent the heart of the deceased from alerting Osiris to his or her true character, and avoiding to be judged for the faults committed during the life of the deceased. Priests also sold formulas that allegedly facilitated the passage of the dead to celestial realms. Thus, good deeds and a clear conscience were becoming a thing of the past. Therefore, Akhenaten dealt with the problem head-on by driving the priests from their temples and confiscating their property. He ordered the name of traditional gods be removed throughout all of Egypt and commanded his people to worship Aten, the sun disk, a new god. Only he as pharaoh spoke for and to Aten. Thus Akhenaten exercised total control over religion having all prayers directed to the pharaoh. This was a drastic change of balance returning to the old idea that the king was identified with God. Akhenaten began the Amara style in art when

Figure 2.7 Ancient Egyptian gods engraved in the stone wall of the Temple of Sobek.

Figure 2.8 Columns with ancient hieroglyphics.

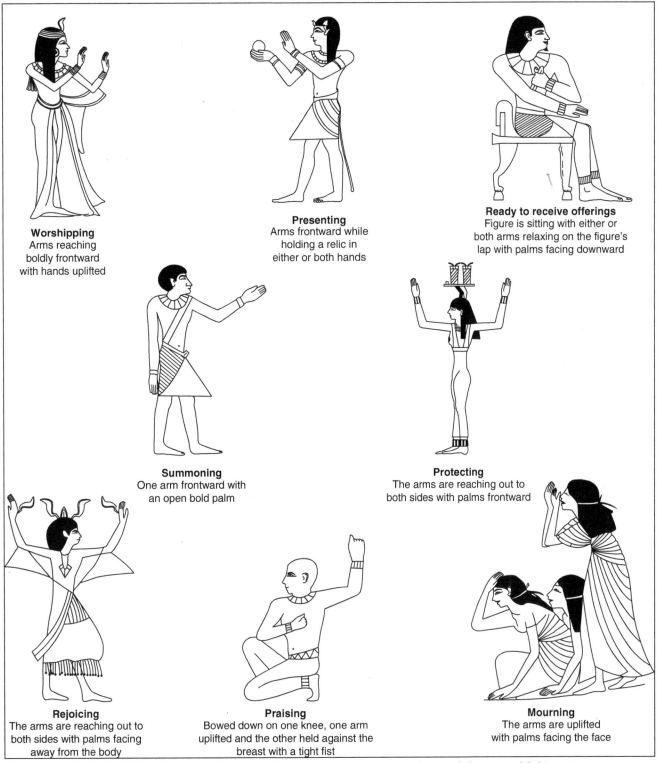

Worshipping
Arms reaching
boldly frontward
with hands uplifted

Presenting
Arms frontward while
holding a relic in
either or both hands

Ready to receive offerings
Figure is sitting with either or
both arms relaxing on the figure's
lap with palms facing downward

Summoning
One arm frontward with
an open bold palm

Protecting
The arms are reaching out to
both sides with palms frontward

Rejoicing
The arms are reaching out to
both sides with palms facing
away from the body

Praising
Bowed down on one knee, one arm
uplifted and the other held against the
breast with a tight fist

Mourning
The arms are uplifted
with palms facing the face

Figure 2.9   Stylized Forms of Egyptian Poses and Gestures. *Image Copyright Kendall Hunt Publishing Company.*

artistic styles became more naturalistic than any other time in Egyptian history. His expenses on a new city and his projects imposed heavier taxes on his people which brought him unpopularity. After his death, the priests regained their status and Egyptians returned to their traditional religion (Figure 2.9).

The Egyptian temples were the first buildings in the ancient world to be built entirely of stone and use the **post and lintel construction** that other cultures used on a small scale (Figure 2.10). These temples with their imposing, thick row of columns were visual symbols of the wealth of the pharaoh, authority of the priests, and power of the gods. Because Egyptian temples were symbols of divine royal authority, most of them were built on the flat banks of the Nile, the eternal source of Egyptian power (Figure 2.11). Temples like Amon-Mut-khonsu illustrate the nature of Egyptian religious architecture. These temples were designed as a succession of spaces of increasing holiness as the individual entered from the main portal. Ordinary worshipers assembled in the sequestered interior court surrounded by a forest of columns that darken the inner sanctuaries that were the exclusive preserve of the priesthood from where the all-powerful priests administered the temple of these gods.

After 1085 B.C., Egypt gradually declines in power. When it began to conquer other lands in Palestine their isolation was broken and other kingdoms had knowledge of Egypt's wealth and Egypt became later a kingdom to be conquered as it weakened. Egypt then falls to the Cushites, Assyrian, Persian, and Alexander the Great's innovations By 30 B.C. it became part of the Roman Empire.

Egyptian civilization and culture had the longest existence in ancient time, almost 3,000 years.

Conclusion: Egypt was the first national state where the whole people and territory became one nation, united in culture, language, religion, and government. Ancient worlds' most homogeneous society.

Her history for the most part was continuous from the first Dynasty in 3100 B.C. (over 2,000 years!). This continuity and prosperity was due to the safety provided by geographical natural barriers and consistent agricultural production. Not many changes in Egyptian culture occurred

Figure 2.10 Temple of Philae at Aswan, Egypt. An example of the post and lintel construction where the row of columns are the posts and lintel are place above them. *Image Copyright WH CHOW, 2009. Used under license from Shutterstock, Inc.*

Figure 2.11 The interior of Temple of the Pharaohs. Today ancient Egyptian ruins are colorless, but the Egyptians painted their buildings and sculptures. *Image Copyright Andreas Meyer, 2009. Used under license from Shutterstock, Inc.*

through time. This is reflected by its art where the artistic styles remain the same. Their *monumental* buildings and tombs, and their sculpture have the characteristics of *solemnity* (formal, deeply serious), *impassiveness* (unemotional), and *serenity* (calm, peaceful).

Theocratic government pharaoh and state were one, divine and indivisible (Figure 2.12). After the invasions of the Hyksos, the Egyptian rulers turned to the Empire building and began to conquer outside Egypt's borders ending the long period of isolation. The Hyksos (meaning "rulers of foreign lands" in Egyptian) were a Syro-Palestinian people from the region of Palestine, whose domination was resented by the native Egyptians. The Hebrews mentioned in the Bible that came to Egypt and settled there for a time, were allowed to do so by the Hyksos dynasty that was ruling Egypt. When the Hyksos dynasty was overthrown the new native Egyptian rulers did not welcome this foreign people with their different religion, and exploited them until the coming of their leader Moses.

The period of *balance* that predominates during most of Egypt's history as an ancient civilization had two periods of adjustments. Its society with its central government was very *stable*. It had rigid class structure with almost no social mobility. But it was the most stable society with the greatest amount of stability and security for the entire Egyptian society. For the average Egyptian of that period, they knew their food supply would remain constant and plentiful, their land and family were secure, and they would keep their positions in society and properties. For them it was a good life without knowledge of a better one, and most were content with their culture, religion, and government. Egyptian life was generally safer and more pleasant than in Mesopotamia, but the masses functioned as cogs (the teeth of a gear or wheel) in the splendid state machine. This is why they have no incentive to change things that remain constant generation after generation and is seen in their art that remains the same over many centuries. Each of the Three Kingdoms (*Egyptian history is divided into the Old Kingdom—2686–2181 B.C. that launched the brief Pyramid age and the* Sphinx; *the Middle Kingdom—2135–1786 B.C.; New Kingdom—1570–1085 B.C. marked by invasion of Hyksos and rise of Egyptian Empire*) can be viewed as an extended period of balance, with only two short periods of adjustment between the Old and Middle Kingdoms, and the Middle and New Kingdoms (Figure 2.13). With a central government, their society was very structured and so stable that it could stand up against any inter-

Figure 2.12   Abu Simbel statues, Egypt. Their monumental size communicates to the observer the idea that the pharaoh is all-powerful and divine, and that he is a plain, humble being in the service of the king and the gods. This monument cut into the cliff has an entrance in the center leading to manmade tunnels. *Image Copyright Iullabi, 2009. Used under license from Shutterstock, Inc.*

Figure 2.13   Sphinx and the great pyramid of Giza, Egypt, from the Old Kingdom. *Image Copyright Maksym Gorpenyuk, 2009. Used under license from Shutterstock, Inc.*

nal disruption at least after 1085 B.C. when there were some sporadic civil wars and later arrival of invaders. No other people have had a longer or more distinguished record. Egyptian cultural achievements were monumental and influenced Minoan, Mycenaean, Greek, and Roman civilizations.

Its religion had an ethical component, the "**maat**" that established a moral order and code of law that functions as a kind of natural law. It is a synthesis of four ideas: order, truth, justice, and righteousness. For peasants, this entailed hard work and honesty, and for officials to be just. This concern for the maat and the belief the gods would judge you according to your behavior in the afterlife, coupled with the highest standard of living in a land with abundant agriculture production, helped Egypt to have a cheerful and confident life for its society, and for the wealthy wonderfully elegant.

SUMMARY

Egypt was the ancient world's most homogeneous society. From 3100 B.C. to 1780 B.C. Egypt remained isolated by its natural barriers and, therefore, its culture remained in a state of balance. Its prosperity and continuity were due to security from invaders and great agricultural production that was the "gift of the Nile." There was little evolution of artistic styles, but the basic conventions remained the same through Egypt's history. Egyptians had the notion that life was immutable because the Nile River and environment were predictable and stable. Their life did not change. Its government was a Theocracy.

The invasion of the Syro-Palestinian Hyksos ended the isolation of Egypt about 1780 B.C. From 1570 to 1085 B.C. was the imperial period with military conquests outside Egypt. After 1085 B.C. Egypt begins to decline in power. Egypt enjoyed a balanced culture, with a rigid class structure that made social mobility very difficult. But it had a great stability and life was relatively safe with an abundant food supply. A major reason why its inhabitants did not demand changes was because they were content with the life they had. Eventually with the end of isolation, when Egypt was conquered by foreign civilizations, it gradually lost its cultural balance to foreign influences and domination.

Egyptian religion had the maat or its moral code for the Universe. Acting according with this code of ethics the person was in harmony with the gods. Egyptian cultural achievements influenced the Minoan, Mycenaean, Greek, and Roman civilizations.

ANCIENT GREEK CIVILIZATION

THE CHARACTER OF GREEK CIVILIZATION

Although Mesopotamians and Egyptians offer successful models of civilization, the tradition of Greece is often the first in which Westerners feel they can recognize themselves, because the Greek or Hellenic culture most clearly exemplified the spirit of our Western society. They were the culture that we can identify most, and have a feeling of greater familiarity with. We can perceive that their ideas about government, architecture, art, individualism, and philosophy are the most similar to ours, of all these ancient cultures of the Mediterranean and Middle East. What ties most modern westerners to ancient Greece is the Greeks' vision of humanity, for they were the first to place human beings at the center of the universe. The Near Eastern cultures focused on deities and godlike rulers, paying little heed to the strivings of humanity. The Greeks, on the other hand, no longer saw mortals as the inconsequential objects of divine whim. Men and women assumed some importance in the scheme of things, thus they were seen as having some control over their destinies and some moral responsibility for their actions. By the 5th century B.C., the Greek philosopher Protagoras could proclaim, "Man is the measure of all things."

The ancient Greeks, with their new way of thinking, surged forward in all areas of creativity, ultimately reaching heights that some think have never been equaled. Because of their grandeur and noble appeal, Greek poetry, sculpture, and architecture became the standard against which later works were frequently judged. From the Greeks the Western tradition has inherited many of its political forms and practices, its views on human behavior, its insistence on philosophical rigor, and its approach to scientific inquiry. In essence, through their human-centered consciousness and their cultural achievements, the Greeks laid the foundation of Western civilization.

Our idea of democracy originates with the ancient Greeks. Many buildings, especially government buildings, in our country are inspired by Greek classical architecture. Sculpture of life-size figures with human form, emotions, and gestures were copied from the Greeks by Western artists. Compare Greek architecture and art with Mesopotamian and Egyptian. Which art and architecture is most similar to our own? Which of these names are you more familiar with? The Mesopotamian Hammurabi and Zoroaster, or the Egyptian Aten, Akhenaten, Amon-RE, Osiris, or is it the Greek Socrates, Plato, Aristotle, Zeus, Venus, Neptune, Homer, and Hercules? More than likely you would answer the Greek. If you had to choose which of these three civilizations to live in, which one would you choose and why?

Therefore, compared to the other surrounding ancient civilizations the Greeks had the strongest devotion to liberty, had a firm belief in the nobility of human achievement, glorified humanity as the most important creation in the universe; had a secular and rationalistic attitude refusing to submit to dictation of priest and despots; supported the spirit of free inquiry; and made knowledge supreme over pagan religion. For all these reasons the Hellenic culture was the most advanced that the ancient world achieved.

The term **Ancient Greece** refers to the period of Greek history lasting from the Greek Dark Ages c. 1100 B.C., to 146 B.C. and the Roman conquest of Greece after the Battle of Corinth. The historical development of this extraordinary civilization spans across the *Archaic* (c. 9th–6th centuries B.C.), *Classical* (c. 5th–4th centuries B.C.), and *Hellenistic* (c. 3rd century B.C.—2nd century A.D.). It is predated by the Minoan civilization (c. 2600–1100 B.C.) and the Mycenaean civilization 1600–1100 B.C. (Figure 3.1).

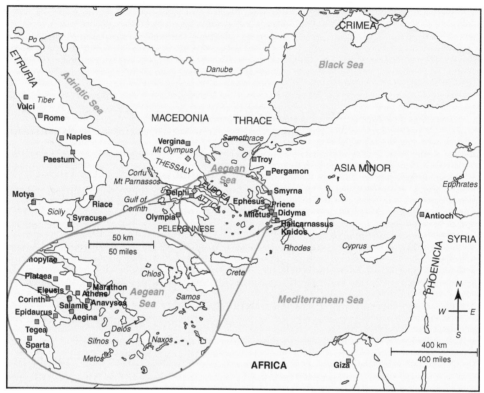

Figure 3.1   The city states of ancient Greece. *Image Copyright Kendall Hunt Publishing Company.*

AEGEAN CIVILIZATIONS

The Minoans, the Mycenaeans, and the Greeks of the Archaic Age

Greek culture developed in the basin of the Aegean Sea. On rocky coasts and rugged islands and peninsulas, these ancient people managed to obtain a subsistence living from the thin, stony soil, fishing, and turned to the sea for trade, conquest, and expansion. During the Bronze Age, the inhabitants of the island of Crete and the Greek peninsula traded with the Egyptians and the Hittites of Anatolia (modern Turkey). The early Greeks borrowed and adapted a writing system from the Phoenicians. They were indebted to the Egyptians for sculptural techniques in working with metal and clay, for music and mathematics, and for elements of their religious system.

The people referred to as the Greeks were not the first to thrive in the Aegean basin. Two other distinctive civilizations, the Minoan and the Mycenaean, established centers of culture in the areas and left their mark on the Greeks of the archaic age.

The *Minoan civilization* originated out of Neolithic settlements on the island of Crete in the Mediterranean Sea. Around 2000 B.C. a prosperous and stable civilization engaged in trade emerged. Between 1700 and 1100 B.C. it reached its high point in sophistication, wealth, and power. Its name Minoan is derived from the legendary King Minos. It had a complex class system made up of nobles, merchants, artisans, bureaucrats, and laborers. The Minoans seem to have had a tranquil existence as no walls have been found to protect their cities and no weapons have been excavated. This all suggests that the cities lived in peace and the sea offered protection against invading sea raiders. The palace at Knossos revealed that this was a sophisticated civilization with plumbing and drainage systems, *friezes* (decorative band of designs and figures) that decorated the walls, and *frescoes* (paint applied on wet plaster) of ocean creatures. Minoan trade dominated the eastern Mediterranean until about 1380 B.C. when Crete was devastated by a natural catastrophe, which most likely was a large volcanic eruption on a nearby island. They were weakened by Mycenaean incursions and quickly fell to raiders from the Greek mainland. During the last three centuries, until 1100 B.C., they became a blend of Cretan and Mycenaean elements, with an obvious decline economically and in artistic quality. This peaceful civilization vanished suddenly and mysteriously.

The *Mycenaean civilization* developed on the rugged lower Greek peninsula called Peloponnesus. They were an aggressive warrior people from Mesopotamia or southern Russia that arrived on the peninsula around 1900 B.C., and by 1500 B.C. they ruled the entire Peloponnesus. The Mycenaean political system was made up of local kings in their fortified cities and their warriors controlling the surrounding countryside. These local rulers through alliances and truces made up a confederation of small kingdoms. They achieved a high level of artistic skill on the artifacts and weapons they made. They also traveled and traded on a wide range. By 1380 B.C. they extended their raiding and trading through the eastern Mediterranean. Around 1250 B.C. trading conflicts with the city of Troy on the western coast of modern Turkey brought the Mycenaeans to carry on a long invasion and conquest of this city. This exhausted them. They became weaker in the end that aided other more vigorous tribes to conquer the Mycenaean. The siege of Troy probably inspired the sagas of the *Iliad* and the *Odyssey* attributed to **Homer.** By 1100 B.C. the Dorians from the north took over this civilization which faded away. But the Mycenaeans, unlike the Minoans, continued to live for the Greeks of the Archaic Age through literature, the *Iliad* and the *Odyssey,* two epic poems whose events occurred during the Mycenaean Age. These stories furnished the Greeks with many of their heroes, such as Achilles and Odysseus, the esteem of honor and courage, the appreciation of excellence and cunning and crafty intelligence, and the Greek pantheon of sky gods, in the Greek language of the Mycenaean. From the Mycenaean and the Homeric epics, poems originated the core of ancient Greek tradition that united all the Greek or Hellenic people.

Then followed a period known as the **Dark Ages** from 1100 B.C. to 800 B.C. During this period life reverted to simpler forms and people lived in relative isolation. Many Mycenaeans fled to the coast of Asia Minor (modern Turkey) that later became known as *Ionia* and extended the Greek community around the Aegean and Mediterranean Seas. The Greeks went from the Bronze Age to the Iron Age. Political power of the kings was shifting to the heads of powerful families, thus changing toward an **oligarchy** (government by a few, who have concentration of wealth and political power). From this period of stagnation the Greeks moved into an era of innovation and experimentation in politics and culture around 800 B.C. This period from the 9th to the 6th century B.C. is known as the *Archaic Age.* The Greeks were scattered and isolated among the mountains and valleys of the mainland and the islands and distant colonies through the Mediterranean and the Black Sea. This relative isolation did not keep them from having a shared sense of identity based on their common language, heroic stories, and folk tales, their myths and religion, and their commercial and trading interests. In their mythology they claimed a common mythical ancestor, **Hellen,** who was the father of three sons and each commenced his own tribe, thus becoming the ancestor of the major Greek tribes, the Ionians, the Aeolians, and the Dorians, from which the Greeks called themselves *Hellenes* and their land *Hellas.* During the next three centuries the Greeks reconstructed their political and social systems, in which kings were deposed by oligarchies of wealthy warriors, and the emergence of the **polis** or *city-states* occurred. Each polis will develop its own history and individual traits, but all will share the same features of an **acropolis** (a fortified hilltop) that served as the city's citadel (stronghold), and the **agora,** an open area where the populace gathered to conduct public and private matters. The different scattered poleis that constituted the Greek world played a crucial role molding its citizenry into an organic body with a collective identity, by controlling the religious, cultural, and psychological components of its relative closed community. These Greeks will develop new styles of art and architecture, new literary genres, and make the first philosophical inquiries into the nature of the universe and human behavior. Therefore, during the Archaic period the foundations for a new world that would give Western man rational thought, democracy, and high standards of the arts was established.

ANCIENT GREEK RELIGION

From 1150–800 B.C., after the fall of the Mycenaean civilization, came the "Dark Ages" when written records disappeared and culture retreated to simpler forms. During this period religion to the Greeks meant most of all a system for:

1. Explaining the physical world in a way to remove its mysteries and give people a feeling of intimate relationship with nature.
2. Explaining the tempestuous passions that sized human nature.
3. Obtain benefits such as a good harvest, long life, good health, good fortune, etc.

For the ancient Greeks there was no sin, commandments, dogmas, or sacraments. So they were at liberty to believe what they chose and follow their lifestyle without fear of divine wrath or punishment.

They were indifferent to life after death. The soul went to Hades after death, under the Earth. It was not heaven or hell. There were no rewards or punishments. Without religious dogmas to control their lives the ancient Greeks had more freedom to observe nature and human life and come to their own rational explanations. They had more freedom to think and question on their own, which allowed them to develop philosophy and rational thinking, than any other civilization.

Religion was *polytheistic,* made up of many gods (Figure 3.2). There was little superiority of one god over another god. Worship consisted mainly of sacrifices to please the gods to grant favors, not to atone for sins. Religious practice was external and mechanical, not a matter of spiritual internal life and morality. Professional priests were not necessary, nor elaborate religious institutions. Any man could perform religious rites, sacrifices, and hope for the best. This allowed the Greeks more independence from all powerful and dominating priestly class and dogmas that controlled what man thought about his life and the world he lived in.

Greek temples were a shrine for the god, for his or her honor, where the god may occasionally visit and use as a temporary house. It was not a "church" or place to assemble to worship. Most of the sacrifices and rituals were done outside the temples.

The Greek deities had human qualities, in other words they were *anthropomorphic.* The gods of the early Greeks' religion were conceived merely as human beings, but above the average mortal. They were like men, just that they had more power and were immortal. These "human" gods inspired security, feeling at home with religion. The Greeks did not want gods with great

Figure 3.2 Triumph of Dionysus and the Seasons sarcophagus. Image of anthropomorphic gods, with proportionate bodies that are permanently young. *Image Copyright Vladimir Korostyshevskiy, 2009. Used under license from Shutterstock, Inc.*

power, but deities you can bargain on equal terms as they are "similar to men." Therefore, the gods had human characteristics such as a human body, human desires, human weakness, but the gods were immortal and humans were not. The gods dwelled close to mankind by living on Mount Olympus, the highest mountain of the Greek mainland. Thus, the Greeks believed the gods to be located in a determined geographical area where men can go to honor them and demonstrate how good men can be. These were not gods who were in remote places such as the sky or the underworld. In their human likeness the gods quarreled among themselves and mingled freely with mortals, even had children by mortal women such as the case of Hercules whose father was a god and mother a mortal woman.

The ancient Greeks had a very different conception from oriental religions such as Egypt and Mesopotamia. In these oriental religions the gods were:

- Remote—the gods dwelled in the sky or underworld places where men could not go to.
- Omnipotent—gods had absolute power and authority. These were conceived as overbearing gods who controlled all aspects of life and men were just low creatures who must serve and obey them.
- These gods did not have human form or bodies.
- They inspired respect, fear, but not a sense of security.
- These gods and the religious practices to appeal to these gods required priest and kings to communicate and interact with humans to gain the god's favor. This brings about the creation and need for institutionalized religion, that is a dominant priestly social class that has been trained in the elaborate rituals and beliefs with its large and expensive temple buildings.

In these ancient societies the average man had less freedom from religious dominance and imposing thought, so men did not live in an environment that allowed them to be independent and creative, free to analyze and meditate on life in general and thus invent philosophy. Quite the opposite with the ancient Greeks who had a different concept of the gods and were free from dominating institutionalized religion with authoritative priestly class that controlled men's mind and life. Therefore, the Greeks were much more independent and free to observe, think, question, and experiment, which eventually led them to determine their own lifestyle, break out of mythical thinking, and become rational thinkers that invented philosophy.

With the Greeks there was no struggle between good and evil. The gods were not obsessed with combating evil and triumph of morality. Their rewards were based on whim rather than what is morally correct. No need to repent and correct injustices.

Social Ideals

Since the end of the Dark Ages the Greeks began on the path of social ideals that would be followed for centuries later, reaching the highest point during the classical period. The ancient Greeks were:

- Optimists—who believed life was worth living for its own sake, and death was not seen as an end to sufferance or as a release from a life of toil. The Mesopotamians on the other hand had a more pessimistic view of life, one of struggle, toil, and insecurity. For them death was an end to this existence.
- Egoists—the Greeks were geared to a life of self-fulfillment, rejecting self-denial and penance. Avoiding anything that would be frustrating in life.
- No sense of humility or forgiveness. They were proud and arrogant, with a competitive attitude of trying to be the best over all others.

- Humanists—they worshiped the natural and the world surrounding them, what was of this world, rather than otherworldly or sublime. This is why they did not endow their gods with great reverent qualities, and they did not conceive humans as lowly or depraved and sinful creatures.

Their focus was on understanding and pleasing human nature. Improving their life and serving their personal interests. Not in serving omnipotent gods with their dogmas, laws, and expecting men to be their servants. They were not interested in gods that inspired fear of their wrath in this life and the afterlife. The Greeks' culture strove for individualism and did not accept submitting to a theocracy like the Egyptians. (Theocracy: A government ruled by or subject to religious authority such as divine kings, priests, or religious leaders. Ancient Egypt was a theocracy where authority, both political and religious, resided on the pharaoh and priestly class. In the modern West, the Vatican in Rome, Italy, is an independent state and a theocracy ruled by the pope.)

All this religious belief and practice will lead the ancient Greeks on a path to feel free to analyze nature and men, to come to their own logical and natural explanations of the reality they observe, create their own philosophy, and look for self-fulfillment of life and more freedom for the common man.

From these individualistic Greeks a civilization that brought about a wave of creativity, progress, and democracy was able to flourish in the ancient world without equality in any other part of the entire world for that time and influenced the Western culture to our 21st century.

To **summarize,** the Greeks created a religion of mystical gods to explain natural forces and life, and get benefits from these immortal deities. Thus, inventing a very creative Greek mythology, where the human gods were gods that were immortal, powerful, beautiful, and permanently young. They constituted a superior race apart from men. Greek religion allowed their culture to be free to think, question, analyze, and experiment, like no other in the ancient world. This religion allowed them to live life passionately to the fullest and have a humanistic culture that put humans at the center of life. It glorified humanity and gave a comfortable relationship between human beings and the world they live in. The Greeks with their mythology are mythical thinkers, but through time they move out of this way of thinking to become the rational thinkers of ancient times and influence Western culture. Even if the Greeks invented philosophy and thought in a rational manner, society in general kept their polytheistic religion until the coming of Christianity.

LITERATURE

Epic Poetry

The term epic poetry comes from the ancient Greek adjective "epikos" for epic and "epos" for story or poem, is a lengthy narrative poem, ordinarily concerning a serious subject containing details of heroic deeds and events significant to a culture or nation. The originator of the major conventions of **epic poetry** is traditionally believed to be **Homer**, or the poet who sang his verses while accompanying himself on a stringed instrument. Not much is known about Homer's life. Thus when he lived is unknown and open to debate. Most modern researchers believe he lived in the eighth or seventh century B.C. Homer was a blind poet and recitation of poetry was a common occupation for the blind during Homer's day. He is revered as the greatest of ancient Greece's epic poets that composed the two most famous Greek epic poems the *Iliad* and the *Odyssey*. It is probable that the *Iliad* was composed around 750 B.C. during Homer's maturity and the *Odyssey* around 710 B.C. during his old age. Homeric poems have their origins in the oral tradition. These stories of the Mycenae heroes were told orally from one generation to another and Homer wove these oral stories and phrases into his epic poems. In the *Iliad* and the *Odyssey,* Homer sang of the events before, during, and after the Trojan War, stories that had circulated among the

Greeks since the fall of Mycenae. Homer entertained an aristocratic audience eager to claim kinship with the Mycenaean past. For many years, his poems were transmitted orally by other famous national poets, and they probably did not exist in written versions until the middle of the seventh century B.C. Homer's authorships and even his very existence are established solely by tradition because nothing is actually known about them. By 350 B.C. consensus was established that Homer was the author of the *Iliad* and the *Odyssey*. But this has been debated by some who believe these two epics were not composed by the same author, while others argue that the stylistic similarities are too consistent to support the theory of multiple authors. This issue has never been settled in a definite way, but traditionally and historically most experts believe Homer is the sole author. By the end of the Archaic Age, the appeal of Homer's poetry had embraced all social levels.

The basic appeal of the Homeric epics lies in their well–crafted plots, filled with dramatic episodes and finely drawn characters. Set against the backdrop of the Trojan War, the *Iliad* describes the battle of Ilium, another name for Troy, and the *Odyssey* recounts events after Greeks defeat the Trojans. The earlier of the epics, the *Iliad,* focuses on Achilles, the epitome of heroic Greek manhood. In contrast to the battlefield heroics of the *Iliad,* the *Odyssey* narrates the wanderings of the Greek warrior Odysseus after the fall of Troy on his return voyage to his home. Moreover, the *Odyssey* celebrates marriage, for Odysseus, despite some amorous adventures, remains fixed on thoughts of his wife, Penelope, who waits for him in Ithaca.

The **Iliad** is about the legendary ten-year war between the city-state of Troy located at the entrance of the Dardanelles (straight to enter the Black Sea) and the coalition of Mycenae Greeks states from the Greek peninsula or mainland that has been determined to have historically taken place. The city of Troy is sieged by the Greeks. In Homer's epic poem the story takes place during the last weeks of the last year of the war. The events and battles that take place are centered over the quarrels between the leader of the Greek coalition, King Agamemnon and the Greek warrior Achilles. In the epic, the reader gets a broader picture of this war because it mentions many of the Greek legends about the war that include the cause of the war, earlier events, and the events that are prophesized to occur in the future such as the destruction of Troy. Thus, a complete tale is given of the ten-year siege.

The legendary cause of the Trojan War is the kidnapping of Helen, the beautiful wife of king Menelaus of Sparta. Menelaus was the brother of Agamemnon, king of Mycenae and husband of Helen's sister Clytemnestra. Paris, one of the sons of Priam, king of Troy, takes Helen to Troy. When Menelaus and Odysseus fail to get Helen back by diplomatic means, Menelaus asks Agamemnon to keep his oath and he agrees. Agamemnon then forms a coalition with all the Achaean kings and sails to Troy setting off the war. The *Iliad* is set during some weeks toward the end of the siege of Troy where Agamemnon takes Achilles' Trojan female captive Briseis in compensation for a disagreement. This sets off the anger of Achilles as his honor as warrior is deeply offended and has violated the serious rule that warriors treat each other with respect. Achilles then declares he and his men will no longer fight for Agamemnon and return home. Agamemnon attacks the Trojans but things do not go well for the Greeks and Achilles' help is needed. Agamemnon then sends an embassy to Achilles offering him wealth and to return Briseis if he returns to fight on his side, but Achilles rejects the offer. The battle continues between Agamemnon's Greeks and the Trojans. Achilles allows his dearest friend Patroclus to go and defend his ships from Trojan attack and warns him not to pursue the Trojans. Patroclus routes the attacking Trojans from the ships and then pursues them and reaches the gates of Troy. There, Hector, brother of Paris and leader of the Trojan forces kills Patroclus in battle. Achilles becomes mad with grief over his friend's death and vows to take revenge on Hector. Agamemnon then appears and gives Achilles gifts including Briseis to get him to continue the fight and Achilles accepts with indifference. There is prophecy that Achilles is fated to die young if he kills Hector. With rage and grief Achilles battles the Trojans who flee back into their city leaving Hector behind. Achilles faces Hector who refuses the shame of leaving the battleground in spite of the pleas of his parent to take refuge inside the city walls and a duel begins ending in Hector's death by Achilles' hand. Before Hector dies he reminds Achilles that he is also fated to die in the war. Achilles in his *hubris* or excessive arrogant pride, then dishonors Hector's body by tying it to his chariot and dragging it around Patroclus' grave for twelve days before all the Trojans to see. Priam, unnoticed, enters the Greek camp and grasps Achilles by the knees begging him to return his son's body. Achilles, thinking of his own father, is moved to tears, and both weeping lament the losses during this war. They have a meal and then Priam takes Hector's body for burial to Troy and the city mourns. Although Achilles' death is not presented in the *Iliad,* other sources concur that he was killed near the end of the Trojan War by Paris, who shot him in the heel with an arrow that caused Achilles to fall from his chariot causing his death. Later legends state that Achilles was invulnerable in all of his body except for his heel. Because of his death from a small wound in the heel, the term *Achilles' heel* has come to mean a person's point of weakness. During all these events the gods have been active intervening some in favor of the Greeks and others of the Trojans, only Zeus remained neutral.

The sequel to the Iliad is Homer's second epic poem the **Odyssey.** It is about the Greek Odysseus, a name that means "trouble" in Greek, alluding to giving as well as receiving of trouble, and he is also known by his Roman name Ulysses. Odysseus is a character in the *Iliad* and after the fall of Troy he begins his ten-year voyage back home to Ithaca, an island west of the Greek peninsula or mainland. Odysseus has been away from home for ten years fighting in the Trojan War, and because he insulted the gods, they will create difficulties during his return voyage to Ithaca that will take another ten years to complete. He has been away so long from Ithaca that it is assumed he is dead. Odysseus, king of Ithaca, left his wife Penelope and his very young son Telemachus to fight the Trojans. Now his son is twenty years old and there are 108 boisterous young men who, believing that Odysseus is dead, aspire to marry Penelope. These suitors are coming to Penelope, enjoying and abusing of the hospitality of Odysseus' household and consuming his wealth. The goddess Athena protectress of Odysseus urges Telemachus to search for news of his father. Telemachus departs for the Greek mainland and finds Menelaus and Helen reconciled back in Sparta, and learns of Agamemnon's murder by his wife and her lover when the Mycenae king returned home. Telemachus is informed that on the island of Pharos Menelaus met the old sea god Proteus who told him that Odysseus is captive by the nymph Calypso. This is when the story of Odysseus is told.

Calypso has fallen in love with Odysseus and he has spent seven years captive in her island. Odysseus has rejected her advances and Calypso is persuaded by the god Hermes, who is Odysseus' great-grandfather to let him go free. Odysseus then leaves the island on a raft he built with food, drink, and clothing provided by Calypso. When Poseidon learns of Odysseus' escape, he wrecks the raft in his anger toward Odysseus. Helped by the nymph Ino, Odysseus swims to shore and, exhausted, falls asleep. Next morning he sees a group of young women who go to the seashore to wash their clothes and appeals to Nausicaa for help. Nausicaa tells Odysseus to ask her parents, rulers of the island for hospitality. Odysseus is welcomed by the Phaeacians and does not inform his hosts who he is. He participates in the entertainments, but when he listens to the blind singer tell the story of the Trojan War, not being able to resist the emotions it brings to relive these events, Odysseus reveals his true identity and tells the story of his return from Troy.

Odysseus then narrates a series of adventures up to this point of his voyage, so the readers get a complete picture of what the protagonist has gone through with his crew and ships heading back to Ithaca from Troy. Driven off course by storms Odysseus and his men visit the island of the Cyclopes or one eye giants and searching for food they find the cave of the Cyclops Polyphemus son of the god Poseidon. They are gathering provisions for their ships when Polyphemus returns to his cave and finds them. Polyphemus captures them by placing a huge boulder blocking the entrance to the cave and threatens to eat them. Odysseus and his men cannot overcome physically the size and strength of the Cyclops, thus cunning is Odysseus' only weapon. Odysseus tells Polyphemus that they will make for him the elixir of the gods, wine, which is unknown to the one eye giant. They crush the grapes and produce wine which

Polyphemus drinks without knowing its effects becoming drunk and falls asleep. Then Odysseus and his men blind Polyphemus by piercing his only eye with a sharpened stake. The now blind Polyphemus attempts to catch these Greek warriors but is unable because he cannot see them. Odysseus and his men cannot remove the huge heavy boulder blocking the entrance thus they are imprisoned inside the cave. Polyphemus has to let his sheep go out to the field to graze. He removes the boulder so the sheep can go out and with his hand he touches the sheep's back to be sure they are the sheep and not the Greeks escaping. Odysseus and his crew get under the sheep and crawl with them as they go out the cave and Polyphemus is unaware of the trick, thus the Greeks are able to escape from the Cyclops. When Polyphemus becomes aware of their escape he comes out of the cave and screams his pain of loss of sight and of his captives. He is asked by the other Cyclops why he is screaming and his reply is "Nobody is hurting me," referring to Odysseus. When asked by Polyphemus what his name was, Odysseus answered his name was "nobody." Therefore, the other Cyclops assumed nobody was hurting Polyphemus and they did not come to his aid. Finally Odysseus and his men went aboard their ship and in his hubris or prideful arrogance the Greek warrior as he sails away foolishly shouts at Polyphemus identifying himself with his true name and boasts that nobody can defeat the great Odysseus. Polyphemus, on top of a cliff, throws a large rock in the direction of Odysseus' voice in an attempt to sink the vessel but misses. Then the blinded giant prays to his father Poseidon informing the sea god that Odysseus blinded him which angers the deity who will curse and frustrate his return voyage to Ithaca for ten years losing his ship and crew. He finally returns home with the help of other men and gods.

Odysseus continues to narrate his many other adventures obtaining the sympathies of the Phaeacians who as able mariners decide to help him return home. They deliver him at night to a hidden harbor of Ithaca. The goddess Athena disguises Odysseus as a wandering beggar. This allows him to see what is actually occurring in his household while he is absent. Meanwhile Telemachus returns to Ithaca from Sparta, eludes an ambush by Penelope's suitors, and father and son meet in the hut of a poor servant of the household. Odysseus reveals only to his son his true identity. Father and son go back to their home where Penelope resides. Odysseus arrives as a beggar and is ridiculed by the suitors in his home. The next day Athena has Penelope convince the suitors to have an archery competition among them to decide who will marry her, and they all agree. The challenge is to string Odysseus' bow and shoot an arrow through twelve axe heads aligned in a row. The suitors do not have the strength necessary to bend and string the bow. Finally Odysseus asked to try and meets the challenge. Then he identifies himself as Odysseus to the suitors, and with the help of his son and servants he kills all the suitors using his bow. Finally Odysseus identifies himself to his wife Penelope and she accepts him, bringing a happy ending to this epic poem.

The historical importance of Homer's epic poems lies in that it was a major influence upon all of ancient Greek culture, giving a cultural unity to the many independent city-states that composed ancient Greece and its colonies. His epics helped shape the Greek spirit and religion. Homer is the earliest molder of Greek outlook and character, as his protagonists become famous role models for later generations to imitate as ideals. For several centuries Greek youth recited Homeric epics and admired its heroes that behaved with honor and were courageous in their willingness to suffer and die if necessary. These ideals for excellence as warriors and wives, and their role models became a centerpiece of Greek education, giving the Greeks a common code of behavior and what to aspire to as Greeks. The gods and goddesses who intervened in human affairs provided the Greeks with their rich mythology. These elements combined with the poetic language from which phrases were quoted by Greek thinkers to illustrate moral truths, provided all the independent ancient Greeks with a common cultural heritage that united them as a people or ethnicity, in a similar manner that the Scriptures (Old Testament) united the ancient Hebrew tribes.

Earlier works of mythology dealt with the hero's actions, but Homer also deals with his thoughts and feelings, giving its characters a more complete and humane personality. Homer reveals his character's deepest thoughts, feelings, and conflicts about his behavior. Their motives are complex expressing powerful human emotions of wrath, grief, vengeance, love, guilt, remorse, and compassion that will inspire ancient

Greek writers as well as Western writers to the present century. This can be easily seen in Achilles' wrath with Agamemnon over his captive Briseis, his grief over Patroclus' death, desire for vengeance by killing Hector and mutilating his body, and the compassion he feels for Priam as a father. In the *Odyssey*, Odysseus' love for his wife and son is constant and he even refuses the offer of a deity to live with her and attain immortality, preferring to go back home with his family to eventually grow old and die like all mortals.

Homer possesses several qualities that have made him one of the greatest literary figures of ancient Greece and of Western civilization. He focuses his attention on human characters, demonstrating that Greek quality of interest in humanity or human nature. Even the gods are anthropomorphic, that is their personalities and physical bodies resemble those of humans. So the gods are powerful and immortal human beings. Human love and compassion is displayed in Odysseus' reunion with his wife Penelope, and in Achilles weeping with Priam over the death of friends and family due to war. The poet glorifies the warrior and victory, but at the same time acknowledges the grief that war brings to its victims. He is not a warmonger, nor a pacifist. Homer also has an intense curiosity and contagious love of life. Odysseus personifies Homer's curiosity about humans and their creations, when he goes into the cave to see what kind of creature inhabited the island of the Cyclops. Therefore, Homer embodies the *humanistic outlook* shared by ancient Greeks. His descriptions are very vivid and he keeps the interest of his audience by creating suspense as he discloses the plot by increments. Last of all, the unique and the universal are combined. The unique quarrel between Achilles and Agamemnon is at the same time a universal theme because their foolish quarrel caused the death of many. This is a situation that is constantly repeating itself throughout history and from this the universal appeal it has over Homer's generation and all those that followed to modern times.

The themes of the *Iliad* are heroism, the pursuit of glory, exhilaration of war, and the sensitivity to suffering due to war's tragic character. The idea of achieving full human potential is found in the excellence of the aristocratic warrior who must demonstrate bravery and skill in combat to gain glory and honor. This passion to demonstrate his worth is *arête*, the passion for excellence. This is why Hector refuses the pleas of his parents to enter the city walls even when defeat seems certain, and continues combat with Achilles instead of dishonoring himself before his family, his city, and the Greek enemy. The epic poem illustrates the constant competition of proud warriors for glory and the suffering it brings. It also encloses the origin of what will become later a larger conception of human excellence applied in many fields and endeavors. Thus with Homer the beginnings of *Greek humanism* consists of a concern with human beings and their achievements.

The central theme of the *Iliad* is the wrath of Achilles which brings about great suffering to Greeks and Trojans. This quarrel with Agamemnon reveals a universal principle that wicked wrath and arrogance bring about suffering and death in the end. Homer understands that actions have their consequences, therefore, men and gods operate within a determined unchanging framework or laws that impose their fate. This is an important fundamental aspect of the Greek mind in that this civilization is aware that there exists a **universal order** to things in life, which will be later expressed in philosophical terms.

In the *Odyssey*, the themes focus on the intelligence, ingenuity, cunning, patience, self-control, curiosity, and the loyalty of Odysseus. It has a more favorable image of the poor and a concern with ethics. Common men play a larger role in the plot, and rules of Greek hospitality are stressed, such as the god Zeus allowing Polephemus to be blinded as punishment for violating hospitality to strangers. Hospitality was a necessity among the Greeks due to the increasing trade that required travel, becoming a rule of proper etiquette. Women are portrayed in a favorable light, with Penelope as the role model of the loyal Greek woman who performs her duty as wife and mother and looks out for the welfare of the household while her husband is absent. The epic demonstrates how the Greeks admired the exercise of cunning and crafty intelligence when Odysseus intoxicates the one eye giant blinding him to escape from his cave, and when he returns home disguised as a beggar.

In both poems, the deities merrily intrude into the lives of mortals, changing and postponing the fate of friend and enemy alike. Homer's stories of the gods and goddesses became the standard that circulated wherever Greek was spoken, although not completely replacing other versions of the deities' lives. His roguish portraits of the deities remained indelibly imprinted in the minds of the general populace. Homeric humanism is present in the mythology of the deities. Homer envisions the gods and humans as having similar nature and thus members of the same family which leads the Greeks to believe that men are capable of godlike actions. In his epics the gods intervene and have the last word, but in-between human action takes place that are subject to human standards of justice. Men also contribute to fate because their actions and personality play important roles having a considerable independence of will. Men decide what actions to take which bring about certain consequences. Mesopotamians and Egyptians saw the gods were the main reason why good or evil occurred to humans. But to the Greek mind humans played a major role having great responsibility for the final outcome.

Homer's importance in creating a common unifying culture among the Greeks was his greatest contribution to the ancient Greek civilization with its outlook on an eternal order of nature and achieving the goal of human excellence. Homer served as a guide to behavior for the Archaic Greeks. Because he became part of the Greek educational curriculum, his poems acquired an ethical function. A young man who took Achilles or Odysseus for a model would learn to maintain his well-being, to speak eloquently in company with other men, to give and receive hospitality, appreciate songs of bravery, and to protect his reputation as a man and warrior. Penelope, the patient and faithful wife of Odysseus, learned to weave at the loom, to manage a household, to cultivate her physical beauty, and to resist the advances of other men. Homer's poetic expression also gave texture to the Greek language. Homer's images also provide a rich repertory of ready phrases and metaphors, known as **Homeric epithets**. It can be stated that Homer shaped the Greek language. His poems left an immense literary legacy that shaped the works of later Greek and Roman poets and Greek drama, as well as famous modern literary writers to our present day. It is no wonder that the great writer of tragedy Aeschylus described his plays as "crumbs from the great table of Homer." Homer's epics contained the universality of the human condition that never changes and thus some say no new plots have been invented after Homer, only the particulars have changed. For example Homer's influence upon popular culture can be seen with the *Odyssey* that can be compared with the original *Star Trek* television series of the 1960s where in both cases a captain leads his ship and his crew into many adventures with unfamiliar creatures and expendable characters.

Lyric Poetry

Verses sung to the music of the **lyre** (a stringed instrument) or lyric poetry, became the dominant literary expression in the late Archaic Age, and lyric verses have dominated Western poetry ever since. Lyric poetry, which originated later than the epic, expressed an author's personal, private thoughts, though the muse (poet's inspiration), Euterpe, was credited with the inspiration. The shift from epic to lyric poetry in the 6th century B.C. coincided with changes in the polis, where the rising democratic spirit encouraged a variety of voices to be heard. The ancients, however, regarded *Sappho* (c. 600 B.C.) as the greatest of the writers of solo lyrics.

Her work is addressed to a small circle of aristocratic women friends on her native island of Lesbos in the Aegean Sea. She was deeply personal in her interests, writing chiefly about herself, her friends, and their feelings for one another. In her elegant but restrained verses, Sappho sang mostly about moods of romantic passion, with themes of longing, unrequited love, absence, regret dead feelings, jealousy, and fulfillment.

Greek Thought

Systematic speculation about the nature of the universe was a Greek innovation. (Systematic *is the arrangement of reality into a unified whole, which connects all knowledge into a* system *in a methodical and orderly manner.* For example, our solar system, as a system, includes all knowledge of its parts such as the sun, the planets, satellites or moons, gases, etc., the laws of physics that explain how it operates, the distances of the different bodies, etc. All this knowledge is integrated to explain and understand the solar system. Another example would be the nervous system of our bodies that would include the brain and all its tissues, the spinal cord, the nerves, the chemical processes to transmit messages, etc., all put together in an organized manner. In all these examples you try to get the "whole picture" to understand that aspect of reality or the universe.) The Greeks thought systematically about the entire world and how man related to it. Therefore, this ancient civilization in the quest to find answers to every conceivable question about the nature of the universe, the problem of what is truth, the meaning and purpose of life, was led to invent philosophy. In this search for answers to these questions lies the essence of their philosophy, so important a contribution to civilization, that philosophy ever since has been a debate over its validity. *They* began to think *about the natural world in a more abstract and general perspective, which led them to invent an explicit theoretical and abstract view of nature.*

This systematic *and abstract or theoretical* thinking led them to pioneer into the fields of science. The essence of this endeavor is to pursue objective knowledge about the world that surrounds mankind. They develop theories and gain knowledge in many different scientific fields that focused in a systematical manner to attain as much knowledge as possible about each scientific discipline. Math and medicine are good examples of these fields or disciplines.

Other ancient civilizations, like the Egyptians, made astronomical observations to predict natural events such as floods, or the Babylonians to predict the future, but not in a systematical way that allowed for objectively understanding reality in its entirety. Before the ancient Greeks, the ancient Egyptians and Mesopotamians made great advances especially in astronomy, engineering, mathematics, and medicine. The Greeks learned from these civilizations. The Greek historian Herodotus gave credit to the Egyptians for inventing geometry and dividing the year into twelve parts. Egyptian geometry resulted from the need of the pharaoh to survey the land after inundation by the Nile in order to calculate an accurate tax assessment. Greeks who studied the sciences, such as Aristotle, acknowledged the invention of the mathematical arts to the Egyptians. Herodotus recognized that the Greeks borrowed from the Babylonians the sundial, the gnomon that is the part of a sundial that casts the shadow, and the division of the day into 12 hours. Babylonian astronomy was remarkable in some ways but it was subordinated to the unscientific need to discover omens and predict the future. These ancient achievements were very important for man's progress but they did not come about from a scientific and rational attitude toward the world. Mesopotamian and Egyptian learning was practical because it was limited to solving immediate problems and serving a short-term, utilitarian interests. These and other civilizations still remained under religious mythological beliefs and thinking, while the Greeks developed rational explanations independent of religion and myths. Therefore, pure thought about the nature of things was uniquely Greek. Even if other civilizations had their thinkers such as Confucius or Buddha, only the Greeks developed systematic thinking in their pursuit of supplying a purely naturalistic interpretation of the universe as a whole. Here lies the big difference in that the Greeks began a constant search for natural rather than supernatural explanations, while the rest of the world, except the ancient Hebrews, had their official mythologies explaining how the world began and how it operates transmitted by priestly class with their elaborate religions and ceremonies.

The Greeks conceiving knowledge in an abstract and theoretical manner led them to think about seriously and demonstrate why and how something should be true, and seek the underlining causes of a phenomena. Such is the case of the Pythagorean theorem which was known to the Babylonians and Egyptians, but they never worked out a proof that the square of the hypotenuse of a right-angled triangle is equal to the sum of the squares of the other two sides. The Greek concern with rational demonstrations and explanations created a tradition of building upon the work of previous philosophers and scientists and improving them with the contribution of new ideas and better answers. This created a tradition of knowledge. A tradition toward finding the best explanations and adequate theories made the

Greek philosophers and scientists examine past knowledge, the evidence and arguments that support their explanations and theories, and the weaknesses of their opponents' theories. This critical debate is a necessary precondition for progress in philosophy and science. This keeps men's minds constantly understanding more and better the world in which they live that allows man to improve and change life for the better. Without this debate, knowledge will fall into purely utilitarian needs, religious and superstitious beliefs, and the authority of the ruling classes.

This freedom to think was partly the result of a loose and non-authoritarian character of religion with no mandatory creeds or dogmas and no priestly class to enforce them. The Greeks were skeptical of religious explanations, and open to questioning and observations to arrive at the objective truth or reality. *Removing the gods and spiritual forces from explaining what men observed in nature forced them to stand before nature with nothing but their own mind. Arriving at their own conclusion in a natural manner, excluding myths, gave them the ability to think critically.* A good example is the Greek Herodotus, who on his travel to Egypt visited a temple where he observed that food was placed at the foot of a statue of a god in the evening as offering to the deity. The Egyptian explained to Herodotus that the god consumes the food offered and the food eventually is gone in the morning which is proof that the god accepts the offering and therefore the god exists. For Egyptian mythical thinkers all this makes sense and confirms their belief in this myth. Herodotus with his Greek rational mind does not accept this explanation without questioning. Herodotus makes observations and sees fat rats running around the temple and finds this as the explanation of why the food is consumed. It would be even logical for a Greek thinker to also do an experiment to prove his explanation by leaving poisoned food in the temple and then if he found dead rats the next morning it would prove the rats eat the food and not the god, so therefore the existence of this god would be very doubtful. The interesting point of this story is that it demonstrates how the Greek mind thought. It observed nature and then attempted to discover rational explanations for the observed phenomenon. These explanations could be tested by experimentation, and once they found an explanation that was demonstrated to be correct, all other explanations were excluded. Thus the Greeks were in the pursuit of objectively understanding the world that surrounded them, leaving mythical explanations out. *This ability to take the responsibility to think critically arriving at their own conclusions, to seek knowledge for its own sake, for the pleasure of learning is part of being fully human. Only humans have this quality.*

This Greek rationalism did not mean that mythology or divine intervention no longer played a part in their progress. Mythical ideas about the gods and divinity of nature influenced Greek thinking even into the height of their rationalism in the 5th century B.C. It is made clear when the philosopher Anaxagoras, a friend of Pericles, left Athens to avoid problems when a decree was proposed that "anybody who did not believe in the gods or taught about celestial phenomenon should be liable to prosecution." This legislation went against those natural philosophers who were accused of diminishing the powers of the gods by explaining nature operating under natural laws. It is obvious that at least the general population believed in their mythological gods. Many Greek thinkers held a religious dimension to their thoughts. For example, Pythagoras believed in reincarnation and promoted the study of mathematics to unlock the divine mystery of the universe and to purify the soul. Socrates claimed that "god is only wise." But the critical spirit of Greek speculation was able to put aside explaining natural phenomena, such as thunder, as an activity of the gods and introduced naturalistic explanations.

Greek Philosophy

The first Greek philosophers were from the Ionian city of Miletus around 636 B.C. Greek philosophy had its origin in the 7th century B.C. with the **Milesian School.** The leading thinker of this school was **Thales** (636–546 B.C.) who founded the school. He was an engineer and a philosopher amateur. He began a philosophy that was scientific and materialistic. The problem resided in discovering the nature of the physical world. They believed that all things could be reduced to a basic element substance that made up each item or thing. They were searching for the "main ingredient" of the universe. From their observations of nature, Thales reasoned that as all things contain moisture, then *water* is the basic element that all things need to exist.

This conclusion that water is the essential element in the universe is not important in itself, the importance lies in that with Thales the Greeks broke away from mythical thinking in Greek philosophy and logical approach. They began to make informed guesses that were entirely **naturalistic,** without any reference to supernatural powers. This philosophy was of major significance because it broke with the mythological beliefs the Greeks had about the origin of the world substituting them with purely rational explanations.

The Greeks began to think logically, using mostly intuition, to explain the universe, and not relying on religion, myth, or legends. The opposite is true with the surrounding civilizations such as the Babylonians, where their creation myth had the world as all water, then the god Marduk made a mat and piled dry dirt on it to make dry land. Thales also thought everything was water, but he left the gods like Marduk out of his explanation. So mythical thinking is excluded from Greek philosophy. Here an objective logical approach is established over an irrational way of thinking based on myth.

The Milesian School (Ionian School) stated:

1. The universe is the same everywhere. The same rules apply everywhere.
2. Natural Laws: There are *causes* that cause everything man observes. They are objective. Even if appearances are different, reality is the same and is behind all appearances.

Now the Greeks have discovered a *unifying explanation* (the causes) behind all phenomenon. Here we have logical thinkers who want less details. When mythical thinkers on the other hand love details and diversity, thus avoiding objectivity, and accepting all sorts of subjective and contradicting explanations.

At this stage Ancient Greek reason is almost intuition that is worked in an orderly succession. You think in a *systematic* way. They do not use modern scientific methods to experiment at this point. It is intuition with a free rational form of thinking.

With the Greeks we come to the ***principle of exclusion:*** there is *only one* explanation, only one explanation is correct, is true. This correct or true explanation excludes all other explanations or possibilities. Now one argument can tear down another argument. With the Greeks there is *exclusion,* the opposite of *coexistence* of different and even contradicting explanations of mythical thinkers. An example of this would be if we observed that heat evaporates water from Earth and then condenses into clouds that cause rain. In this case we cannot accept that a god in the sky brings water as rain to Earth, and therefore it would make sense to have a cult to gain the favor of this god to produce rain for our crops. The explanation of heat and condensation producing rain, repeatedly confirmed when we observe that this phenomenon produces rain, excludes all other explanations that do not satisfy. Thus, we are able to arrive at the real explanation of why it rains that allows us to better understand reality. So we could make observations becoming aware that at certain times of the year the conditions exists to produce rain and therefore know the best time to plant crops. With this understanding we can better attempt to make changes that are favorable and in this manner achieve real progress.

Early in Greek thought the distinction between science and philosophy appeared. *Scientists* trust their senses and measure reality with instruments. They are more objective. *Philosophers* depend solely on their minds to reach the truth. Pure philosophers cannot trust their senses that can perceive the same reality in various ways, so what is true and therefore does not change can only be known with the mind. Philosophers are more intuitive and for this reason they are subjective, but they can also be very logical.

The Milesian School had another famous philosopher student of Thales, *Anaximander* (611–547 B.C.) who posed the second important question: How do specific things emerge from the basic element? The answer that he came up with was that it could not be a specific thing or substance, like water or air, but a something that was uncreated and imperishable, which he called "Boundless" or "Indefinite." Man cannot perceive it with its senses. Anaximander never determined what this Boundless consisted of which makes up all the things we perceive with our senses, such as the trees, rivers, animals, metals, etc.

Herakleitos (535–475 B.C.) expanded with a third major question: What guides the process of change? This philosopher-scientist accepted the idea of a basic element but there had to be a controlling force to keep the process of constant change in motion and following a natural order. This controlling force kept the process of universal change orderly, and this is why a fig tree always produces figs and not nuts, and a dog a dog and not a fish.

Everything is in a constant motion, in continuous change. The universe is not static, but a constant process of flow, or eternal flux. For example, a river and a flame are realities that can remain over time but appear to be the same, but in reality are ever changing. If you go into a river and come out of it and immediately jump into the river again, the water and bank have changed in these two intervals. Nothing is exactly the same. But what is the guiding force that gives order and direction? Herakleitos proposed the idea of the **logos** as the guiding force. Logos in Greek means "word," originating from the root of the Greek verb lego, "to say." For Herakleitos, logos is a great intelligence, universal in nature that guides all things. It is the greatest of the mysteries of the universe. (This concept of a universal guiding intelligence can be considered similar to the present-day concept of "intelligent design" that many scientists – sustain as the explanation to what created the universe and guides all its phenomenon. Contradicting the theory of evolution.)

The concept of logos is also applied to humans in respect to "reason" or "rational discourse" that men use to think, talk, and understand the constant changes of reality.

The **Eleatic School** under Parmenides (514 B.C.) did not accept Herakleitos' idea that nothing remains the same and reality is always changing. Their idea is based on what is real is permanent and unchanging. The mind is the only sure guide to truth, and not man's five senses (sight, hearing, touch, smell, and taste).

The Atomists

The Greek material philosophy which focused on explaining the physical world begun at Miletus, reached its high point with **Democritus** (460–370 B.C.). This philosopher with his intuitive mind invented the Greek **atomic theory.** He was the first to devise the idea that the smallest particles that make up all material reality are atoms, called *atoma* from the Greek for indivisible. These atomas or atoms exist in space and combine or separate conserving matter and energy because the same number of atoms always exists. Atoms are indestructible. Only the combination of these minute particles change and differ. The number and arrangement of atoms is what makes things different from others, such as a cat from a tree. Democritus atomic theory was verified in the 20th century and nuclear physics hold the strict conservation of matter and energy. It is astonishing how the ancient Greek mind came up with these ideas, with no prior scientific knowledge in these scientific fields they were pioneering and no instruments and experiments to confirm if they were true.

Pythagoras

In the late 6th century, Greek philosophy took a *metaphysical* turn. It stopped being solely occupied with problems of the physical world and shifted to more abstract or purely philosophical issues about the nature of being, the meaning of truth, the role of the divine in the universe.

Pythagoras (582–507 B.C.) established a religious brotherhood in southern Italy. His philosophy was linked with religion. There is a sharp distinction between spirit and matter, good and evil, harmony and discord; therefore, he founded *dualism* in Greek thought.

Speculative life was the greatest good. Reflection on intellectual issues—political and religion—was encouraged. They put emphasis on ethics. Thus, the focus was on matters that went beyond the purely physical. Pythagoras:

1. Discovered pure mathematics. The number was the essence of all things, just like for other philosophers the essence was water, air, or Boundless.
2. Development of mathematical proofs such as the Pythagorean Theorem.
3. Rejected the geocentric theory of our planetary system, that conceived the Earth to be at the center of our system and that the sun revolved around the Earth from east to west. He thought that our planet Earth revolved around the fixed point of a central fire.
4. He believed in the transmigration of souls; in other words, that the souls reincarnated in a series of lives as they struggled to ascend to an ideal existence to enjoy a divine bliss. So salvation was attained only after the soul achieved its final escape from the cycle of intermediate births (reincarnations).
5. He advocated for a humane society living in harmony and friendship. The brotherhood that he founded was forced to flee from southern Italy (Magna Graecia) or be killed by hostile neighboring tribes that saw them as a threat to established religious practices.

ANCIENT GREEK MUSIC TODAY

Our major scale in music owes its origins to the Ancient Greeks, especially to Pythagoras. One day he approached the members of his cult with a onestring guitar, plucked the open string, and called that his starting note. Pythagoras pointed out that by pressing a finger on the middle of the string (cutting its length in half) and plucking only half, a new sound would be eight steps higher than the starting note. Since only one half of the string was sounding, he called it a 1:2 ratio. He tried other ratios by pressing his finger at various points on the string to get ratios such as two thirds of the string (2:3), three fourths of the string (3:4), and four fifths the string (4:5). With each new note he added, he constructed what we know today as the standard major scale—do-re-mifa-sol-la-ti-do—a scale founded on simple whole number ratios. Did Pythagoras invent the major scale, or did he just discover that there were simple whole number ratios contained in the music of his time? No one now knows, but one of the important legacies of the Ancient Greeks to music today is their Dorian scale (now called the Ionian or major) scale. We still use it in as many musical pieces as you can name. We could not have jazz, pop, background music for films, or even elevator music without using the Ancient Greek (Dorian) major scale.

In conclusion, these extremely individualistic Greeks, with no organized religion, broke away from mythical thinking and began a rational system of thought in search of the nature of the physical world, and speculative philosophy with questions such as: What is man, what is good and evil, and who directs the universe?

Intellectual Revolution of the SOPHISTS

Around 450 B.C. an intellectual revolution began in Greece. Some Greek philosophers turned away from the study of the physical universe and turned to subjects related to the individual. Their focus was on man and ethics. The Sophists were the first to begin this tendency. Their leader was **Protagoras** (481–411 B.C.). Protagoras' main dictum was "man is the measure of all things." This phrase expresses the essence of the Sophist philosophy. By this phrase he meant that goodness, truth, justice, and beauty are relative to the needs of man and his interests. For this way of thinking there are *no absolute truths* or *eternal standards of right and of justice*. Therefore, without any conviction that absolute truths or eternal standards exists, this philosophical school developed a way of thinking that was completely relative. *Total relativism* was a major characteristic of the Sophists.

The Sophists concluded that everything was relative because they believed:

- Knowledge comes from our sensatory perception (our five senses), thus as men perceive reality in different ways, there can only be particular truth valid for a given time and place. Reality is perceived in different ways by different people, so there are no absolute standards and all standards change in time and from individual to another individual.
- Morality likewise varies from one people to another, so there are no absolute canons of right and wrong that are eternal, or from god, that fit all cases.

Being *individualistic* was a main characteristic of Protagoras' thought.

The individualism implicit in Protagoras' teachings was manipulated later by Thrasymachus into a doctrine which stated that all laws and customs are merely expressions of the will of the strongest and shrewdest for their own advantage. The "wise" man, or the man who is in control and leads society in government, ideology, and its laws is an unjust man who is above the law and is concerned to satisfy his own interest.

The danger of this philosophy was that it led to complete relativism which created skepticism and doubt about authority and government that could undermine the cohesion of society. A stable and harmonious society cannot be maintained if society distrusts its religion, morality, and its governing institutions and political authorities.

The contribution of the Sophists who shifted toward the welfare of the individual at the expense of the welfare of the state, included a healthy questioning of old traditions. Also they condemned slavery, became the champions of liberty and the rights of common man, they broadened philosophy to include ethics and politics rather than physics and metaphysics which had been the focus of previous philosophers.

The relativism, skepticism, and individualism of the Sophists brought strong opposition. Conservative Greeks saw that Sophist doctrines lead straight to anarchy and atheism. With no final truths, and if goodness and justice were entirely based on the whims of the individual, then all social institutions were undermined. This reaction brought about a new philosophical movement grounded upon the theory that truth is real and absolute standards do exist. The leaders of the new movement were **Socrates, Plato,** and **Aristotle.**

SOCRATES

SOCRATES—469–399 B.C., was from the city state of Athens (Figure 3.3). He became a philosopher mainly to combat the doctrine of the Sophists, and became a major critic of the Athenian government which had a direct democracy as their form of government, a Greek invention.

Socrates believed:

1. That there exists a stable and *universal valid knowledge,* that does not change with time and is valid for all of mankind.
2. You can obtain this knowledge by the *right method*.
3. The end of the good life is *happiness*.
4. In advocating the acquisition of knowledge. Man through education should put great emphasis in acquiring knowledge, which is an important goal in an individual's life.
5. Knowledge leads to virtue. Virtue is to have the right knowledge and make the right choice using this knowledge.

Now the issue was: how does man attain this valid universal knowledge that in the end would allow man to achieve happiness? Socrates then proposed his method to attain this knowledge by means of a logical and rational process known as the **Socratic Method,** or also known as the **dialectic** that comes from the word for "discuss." From Socrates' disciple Plato who recorded his philosophy, dialectic was a dynamic process of question and answer that challenged and analyzed man's knowledge of a specific concept to render an explanation of it in a logically coherent manner that would withstand scrutiny. The goal is to arrive at the truth of a concept by means of a rational discussion for the true definition of an idea. Unlike Plato, Socrates did not believe that the dialectic could be used to arrive at the pure truth, because his method usually finalized at a dead end, where Socrates confessed his own ignorance. The dialectic has the merit for exposing false opinions and unclear thinking. Even if it cannot arrive at the ultimate truth, at least men can use the process to expose falsehood, and be aware of their limitations. Socrates said that true wisdom was the understanding of the gods alone, but he has the merit of pursuing rational inquiry and not relying on religion or traditional ideas as the means to know the truth.

Figure 3.3   Bust of Socrates. *Image Copyright Album/Prism /Album/ SuperStock.*

The Socratic or Dialectic Method consisted of:

- You ask a question about a specific issue and you get an answer.
- Take away the part of the answer that is false. You eliminate or exclude the false part.
- Continue asking questions, getting more answers and then eliminating the parts that are false until you have as an answer the refined truth, and only what is true. All that is false has been excluded.

An example of the dialectic would be the theme of justice. One can ask the question: what is justice? An answer to the question can be: justice is to protect natural rights of men. But if we analyze the answer it means justice must protect all natural rights of human beings including the right to property. In ancient Greece there were slaves and women had no property rights by themselves. Slaves were considered property of other men, and had no property. But slaves and women are human beings, and therefore, their rights must also be protected to have real justice, including the right to freedom and property. The original answer is partly true but it has a false element. It is true that justice must protect all natural rights of man including freedom and property, but it cannot include property over slaves and prohibit women from owning property, because it would violate the concept of pure justice. We would have to exclude the part that is false; that is, protect men's right to property over slaves, and prohibition of women to own property and have an answer that is all true. Then we can conclude the justice is to protect all natural rights of men as long as it does not violate or conflict with the rights of other human beings. Here we have an answer that is true arrived at by Socrates' dialectic.

Once you arrive to the refined truth it will constitute the essence of truth recognized by all men. This universal recognized truth will be used to establish universal enduring principles of right and justice independent of the selfish desires of human beings. These found rational principles of conduct would prove an unmistakable guide to virtue because Socrates believed that all men when they know what is good will not choose what is evil. Once man attains virtue he will make the right decisions or choices that will lead him to life—the good life that will allow him to achieve happiness.

Socrates created problems for those in power because he used the agora or market place to ask embarrassing questions to politicians and those in power in Athens. All matters discussed in the agora were taken seriously by Athenian society. He described himself as the gadfly that stung the rump of the Athenian body politic. Socrates was a critic of the Athenian republic with its populist majority and democracy as its form of government. He preferred the rule of an enlightened aristocracy because these men were educated and would have the right knowledge to make the correct choices and decisions to lead society to a good life that would achieve happiness. The masses are not educated enough and can be easily mislead by shrewd and unscrupulous politicians. Socrates was finally sentenced to death on trumped charges by the politicians of Athens on charges of religious impiety and corrupting the youth in 399 B.C. He was forced to take hemlock poison.

PLATO

Plato was the most distinguished of Socrates' pupils who lived from 429–347 B.C. His objectives were most similar to Socrates but broader:

1. To combat the theory of reality as a disorderly flux.
2. Substitute the nature of the universe as essential, spiritual, and purposeful.
3. To refute the Sophist doctrines of relativism and skepticism.
4. To provide a secure foundation for ethics. Since ethics is the principle of what is right and good conduct, and a system of moral values, it requires for its existence a belief in fundamental permanent truths and standards to allow man to distinguish what is right from what is wrong.

To achieve these goals Plato developed his *doctrine of Ideas or Forms* (Figure 3.4). Through this doctrine Plato stated that:

1. Relativity and change are characteristic of the physical world we perceive through our senses. But this physical world does not make up all of reality. There exists another world or dimension.
2. There is an existence of a higher spiritual realm. It is made up of eternal forms or ideas which only the mind can conceive. These forms or ideas have no material substance or physical attri-butes. For Plato these ideas are realities in a spiritual dimension, and not mere abstractions invented by the mind. This realm of ideas existed eternally and were not originated by God.

Figure 3.4   Statue of Plato.
imagedb.com/Shutterstock.com.

The idea exists eternally in the spiritual dimension even before man becomes aware of its existence. The idea of a man, a tree, color, proportion, beauty, justice, etc., all exist and have existed for a very long time, and then man perceives their existence only with his mind. The idea of the Good is the highest, being the active cause and guiding purpose of the universe. Plato believed there is a hierarchy in the realm of ideas that started at the bottom with plants and animals and ended at the top with the idea of the good. The physical things we perceive with our senses are merely imperfect copies of the supreme realities or ideas. Therefore, the chair we sit on is merely a physical and imperfect copy of the idea of a chair that only exists in the spiritual dimension.

Closely related to his doctrine of ideas was Plato's *ethical and religious philosophy*. As Socrates did, Plato believed that true virtue is based on knowledge. This knowledge comes from the rational apprehension of the eternal ideas of goodness and justice. True virtue comes from the rational apprehension of the eternal ideas of goodness and justice, and does not come from the senses that perceive knowledge in a limited and unreliable manner. The rational aspect of man's life, and the ideas are what are highly valued in Plato's view, and not the physical reality which is relegated to an inferior place. Thus, the rational part of man's nature is noble and good, and the body (physical) is considered a hindrance to the mind. This gives an ascetic tinge to his philosophy. Emotions and bodily appetites are not denied but strictly subordinated to reason. Mind over the body was important for Plato. Plato's *religious beliefs* held that the universe is spiritual in nature and governed by intelligent purpose. He rejected materialism, and did not make clear his conception of God. Plato believed in the immortality of the soul that preexisted through all eternity.

Political Philosophy

Plato's ideal was a state whose ends were *harmony and efficiency,* not democracy and liberty. He was for a state free from turbulence and self-interest of individuals and social classes who tended to be self-serving and corrupt. In his *Republic,* Plato proposed a plan for society that consisted in dividing the population into three classes according to the functions of the soul or their inclinations in life. Each class would perform those tasks which it was best fitted. These three classes were:

1. The lowest class that represented the appetitive function or had the desire for the material wealth, would include farmers, artisans, and merchants whose major role in society was the production and distribution of goods.
2. The second class represented the spirited element. This class had the strong will. Their function was defense and they constituted the soldiers.
3. The highest class that represented the function of reason, those with education would constitute an intellectual aristocracy or philosopher kings. They possess the ability for philosophy which would allow them to attain the knowledge necessary to make the right decisions. This class would have the monopoly on political power because they were the best prepared to make wise political policies and decisions.

An individual entered a class by merit, and not by birth or wealth. Merit is demonstrated by education. Those with the least intellectual capacity went to the lowest class and with the greatest capacity entered the highest class.

Plato and Christianity

Plato's thought has philosophical repercussions later with Christianity. The most important one was the separation of the soul from the body, coinciding with the Christian belief that the soul is imprisoned in the physical body during the individual's life. Saint Augustine (5th century A.D.) borrowed heavily from Platonism to write his Christian theology. Even if Plato never came in contact with Hebrew beliefs and lived before the coming Christ, many of his ideas are in harmony with Christian beliefs, such as Plato's highest Idea of the Good that early Christian theology converted into the concept of God as the highest and best ideal and goal for all of mankind.

ARISTOTLE

Aristotle (384–322 B.C.) was the last champion of the Socratic tradition (Figure 3.5). He was tutor to the famous Alexander the Great. He wrote more than Plato and about many subjects such as logic, metaphysics, ethics, natural sciences, and politics. His philosophy and writings has influenced greatly the course of Western thought to the present date.

Aristotle was as interested as Socrates and Plato in absolute knowledge and eternal standards. He differed from Plato and Socrates in that Aristotle had a higher value for the concrete and the practical aspects of life. He was an empirical scientist who had interest in experimentation and was concerned about the changes he observed in nature. The mind was not the only guide to truth for Aristotle.

Aristotle agreed with Plato that ideas or forms are real and knowledge from the senses is limited and inaccurate. On the other hand, instead of Plato's dualism which views reality as two different worlds made up of the spiritual realm of ideas and the physical world, Aristotle tried to reconcile the two. He did not agree with Plato's independent existence of ideas and material items. For Aristotle, the abstract idea or form could not be separated from the substance or matter. The two must come together as different aspects of the same thing. Therefore, ideas or forms and matter are of equal importance, both are eternal and cannot exist without the other. The two united is what makes reality and gives the universe its character. For example, a brick can only exist when the idea of a brick and the clay composing it come together. The same for the idea of a house becoming only a reality when the bricks are put together to make the house, and the ideal of a town when the houses that

Figure 3.5   Bust of Aristotle. *Image Copyright Superstock/SuperStock.*

make up the town are grouped together. Thus, for Aristotle, ideas or forms are the causes of all things, being the force that shapes the world of matter into objects and living organisms. The interaction of form and matter is what produces changes and evolution. In this case the form of man in the human embryo molds and directs its development into a human being.

Aristotle's theory of **enteleche** (having a purpose) accounts for the process of change. This theory states that all things have an inner goal or destiny to fulfill. Thus, a seed has as its enteleche to become a plant and clay to become a brick or become a pot for a different enteleche. Aristotle's concept of the universe was **teleological,** that is the universe is governed for a purpose. Here the universe has an enteleche or purpose which is an upward movement that makes it more complex and leading all things toward their own perfection. This movement toward perfection is God the First Cause, who moved all things but nothing or no one moved. God is the "Unmoved Mover."

Aristotle conceived **God** primarily as the **First Cause** that began the universe and original source of all purpose. God's nature was *pure intelligence,* not a personal God. It was not a personal being with a strong will as in Judaism, or loving and merciful as Jesus Christ. It was more like an "impersonal major computer" that runs the universal system. This is not a God like in Judaism and Christianity that is loving and compassionate who you can pray to have a spiritual relation. For Aristotle God's motive is more of a cosmic yearning toward perfection, and that perfection by definition is God. God is pure form, with none of the weakness and imperfection of the physical world. God is separated completely from matter.

Aristotle's **ethical philosophy** was not as ascetic as Plato's and did not regard the body as opposed or a prison to the soul. The highest good was the self-realization which included the physical body, but guided by reason. When man controls his passions and physical desires with his reason he becomes human, otherwise he becomes more animalistic. The solution between excessive indulgence versus ascetic denial was the *Golden Mean.* This means nothing too much. He advises moderation. The good life is achieved by attaining the highest good (summum bonum), and this highest good is achieved when a person fulfills his enteleche or his natural inner destiny. When men are living in harmony, using their minds, functioning in family and state, and using his natural abilities to the fullest, then men will fulfill their enteleche or purpose. This will let men attain virtue and excellence to life, the good life. More important than the life of action is the life of contemplation. Contemplation is necessary to make the finest use of reason. Therefore, reading, talking, and thinking about the idea of excellence is essential to achieve man's high mindedness to live the good life.

INFLUENCES OF GREEK PHILSOPHY ON UNITED STATES GOVERNMENT

The *United States Constitution* and Declaration of Independence derive from writings of the Englishman, John Locke, who was infuenced by Aristotle. Thomas Jefferson paraphrased sentences from Locke's Second *Essay on Civil* Government in our *Declaration of Independence*. Thus, there is a direct link between the workings of our government and the ideas and practices of the Ancient Greeks; we now take for granted such things as rotating leaders, representative assemblies, importance of free expression and thought that originated in Ancient Greece.

In Aristotle's *Politics* he wrote his **political theory** that deals with the structure and function of governments. Aristotle saw man as a social animal, that is man by nature is a political animal that needs the state to live a civilized life. He rejected the position of the Sophists that the state was the invention of the few in power for their own advantage or the desire of the masses. On the contrary Aristotle considered the state as the supreme institution for the promotion of the good life. It is necessary to have a civilized life, and that is rooted in the instincts of man. He was concerned with the best form of the state to achieve the good life. Aristotle considered the best state a *polity* that was not a monarchy, nor aristocracy nor democracy. The polity was an intermediate government between an oligarchy (power and wealth is in the hands of a few) and democracy (consent and participation of the masses). The state should be controlled by the middle class. Middle class had to be large enough to avoid concentration of power and wealth in a few members of society.

Plato and Aristotle are the most influential philosophers in the history of Western civilization. Aristotle became the great authority and philosopher of medieval scholars, especially the scholastic philosophers Saint Thomas Aquinas.

The Greeks held that reason is what makes man human, the only rational animal, and that the rational mind has the capacity to control all the appetites and passions and therefore be able by itself to create psychological and social order. This absolute faith on human reason alone will be later challenged by Christianity which will declare that mankind needs faith and reason to control human passions and build a stable social order. But some Greeks during the climax of Greek rationalism recognize the limits of reason and the power of passion. The dramatist Euripides knew that the power of human passions is too great, and the power of reason too feeble. Thus he has little faith that virtue is knowledge, and that when man rationally understands the good, men will always practice it, which was Socrates' view. Clear examples in Euripides' plays are found in *Medea* when she is angered by her husband's infidelity, she takes revenge through murder, and as she agonizes over the decision to murder her children she cries out that passion is mightier than her reason, being the greatest cause of evil for mankind. Also in *Chrysippus*, when Oedipus' father, Laius rapes the boy Chrysippus, Laius later will explain it as his passion drove him on, even when his judgment indicated it was wrong.

In conclusion the Greek culture and its thinking was the first to be based on the primacy of the intellect or reason within a context of a great spirit of free inquiry. They had no fear to investigate all subjects, and no fear to use reason to solve all questions. As never before in history the Greek mind with its logic and science was supreme over superstition and myth. The rational mind was in control.

During the last four centuries B.C., Athens became the philosophical center of the Hellenistic world and philosophy students from the Greek world went to Athens to study in the various schools of philosophy that had high public visibility, and used this visibility to recruit students. A *philosophical school* normally began as a group of informal philosophers that shared certain interests and ideas under the nominal leadership of an individual such as Plato, Zeno, and Epicurus. It had no strong agenda that all members had to have an unquestioning allegiance. For example, in Plato's Academy (school) there was not any specific doctrine to teach, and Plato and other of his colleagues presented questions to be studied and solved by other members, with the probable use of the dialectic or Socratic Method. Once the founder of the school dies, the situation changes where his teachings are given a doctrinal status becoming unchallengeable. Any further progress is presented as a supplement or a reinterpretation of the founder's philosophical ideas, rather than a replacement. This provided the school with a "religious" reverence to the foundational writings that furnished the framework in which discussion were held by its members.

During the *4th century B.C.* Classical Greece has gone into decline with the wars between the Greek city-states which allowed the Macedonians to take over all of Greece. With the expansion of Alexander the Great into Asia and Egypt the combination of Greek and Asian cultural elements formed the **Hellenistic civilization**. The major movements of Hellenistic philosophy were Stoicism, Epicureanism, Cynics and Skeptics. The first two constituted the major trends and the latter the minor trends.

Stoicism and *Epicureanism* both originated around 300 B.C. and their founders both resided in Athens, Greece. These two philosophical movements had several features in common. Both were *individualistic,* concerned with the good of the individual and not the welfare of society. Both were *materialistic* because they denied the existence of the spiritual reality, and gods and souls were made of matter. Both had *universalism* considering all men the same regardless of their race, ethnicity and nationality. They regarded *reason* as key to solve human problems which was a Greek influence. But in all other aspects these two philosophies were different.

STOICISM

Stoicism was founded by the Greek philosopher **Zeno** of Citium in the early 3rd century B.C. and he taught in the Stoa, a public building in Athens and thus the name **Stoics**. The Stoics understood the universe to consist of matter that had its reasoning (logos), or a reasoning substance. This reasoning substance is known as god or nature and is made up of two substances, one is passive matter and the other is universal reason (logos) or fate. The latter is an intelligent force acting upon the former and governing it. This fate rules life as everything is subject to the laws of Fate, for the universe acts only according to its own nature. The universe is seen as a single pantheistic god. This god makes up all matter and the divine reason or logos that governs matter. Therefore, Stoics believed that the universe is an ordered reality, it forms part of a whole cosmos in which all contradictions are resolved for the ultimate good. The universe then follows a determined logical path that leads to a final perfection. Everything that happens in life, good and evil, is rigidly determined in accordance to a rational purpose. Nothing could escape or change this course of the universe. Therefore, no individual could escape or change his destiny, no one was master of his fate. The only freedom men have in life is to rebel or to accept their fate. Regardless if a person rebels or accepts he cannot overcome fate. Thus the *fatalistic* element of this philosophy. Their concern about the relationship between cosmic determinism and human freedom brought them the belief that a virtuous person accepts his fate in life by adapting his will to nature or the universal reality. Therefore, Stoics see their role or duty in life to submit to the order of the universe knowing that this order is good in the end, that is to resign themselves as graciously as possible to their fate. This *resignation* of the individual to his destiny will result in the highest happiness, which consists in *tranquility of mind*. The methods to obtain the self-discipline necessary to achieve an inner calm and clear judgment are logic, reflection, and concentration. According to the Stoics happiness derives from the individual who uses his reason to achieve a perfect adjustment of his life to the cosmic or universal purpose and has eliminated from his soul all bitterness and complaints against evil turns of fortune.

The Stoics developed their ethical and social theory that accommodated well with their philosophy. Believing that the highest good is the serenity of the mind, it was logical that they put emphasis on *duty* and *self-discipline* as main virtues. They were for participation in society as a duty, and not for withdrawal as the Cynics. Therefore the individual should get involved in politics, have a family, but do not let the world control him, remain serene and do not succumb to outside influences and his *emotions*. This constitutes the stoic person. Freedom from emotions was a goal to achieve because emotions were considered a corrupting element. The Stoics taught that destructive emotions resulted from errors in judgment, and that a person who is morally and intellectually upright would not allow himself to fall prey of those emotions. Emotions such as anger, envy, and lust that bring anguish or suffering are to be conquered by reason to enable the individual to achieve wisdom and self-control. Their goal was not to eliminate emotions but to transform them in a positive manner to achieve an inner calm and clear judgment or objectivity. Through peace of mind the individual became free from suffering because this peace brought about clear judgment and the maintenance of equanimity (calmness/composure) in the face of life's highs and lows. The only thing humans have complete control over is their mind and that is where man's freedom truly lies. The rest of the universe, even the human body is not under man's control, but under the control of destiny. They believed the consequences that might result from violent measures of social change would be worse than the evils they were meant to cure. Greater conflicts and chaos will result than order and stability. They did *not attempt to reform* the world or get *involved emotionally,* they just fulfilled their duty, accepted reality as it was, and did not let the troubles and worries of life get the best of them remaining serene in mind. *Serenity* of the soul, having a free mind, was the means to achieve serenity in this chaotic world. These were the teachings of the Stoics.

The stoics condemned slavery and war, but never preached or led any action against these evils. They taught equalitarianism, pacifism, and humanitarianism. They had a cosmopolitan view of society because all mankind came from one universal spirit or god, therefore rank, wealth, and ethnicity or nationality should not be obstacles to social relationships, and all men should live in peace with one another and be ready to help each other as brothers. Thus they urged clemency toward slaves. The movement had the most influence upon the Romans. Some Roman emperors were Stoics. Stoicism fits well with militaristic culture that puts emphasis on duty and self-discipline, which the ancient Romans considered essential virtues in Roman life. Later on Christianity will have some concepts in common with Stoicism even if the early Fathers of the Church considered it a pagan philosophy. It will reject Stoicism's pantheism, but will borrow and share certain terms as logos, virtue, and conscience, and maintain the beliefs in human brotherly love, freedom from lower passions, and attachment to worldly possessions. Stoic philosophy will be applied by some early theologians such as Saint Ambrose of Milan. A negative aspect of this philosophy in society is their resigned and deterministic outlook in life could and actually did lead many to apathy and unconcern, instead of believing changes for the better could be made in personal and public life. It was not a philosophy to enable society to change the course of events for the better. However, the ideal Stoic never became apathetic and he overcame Stoicism's fatalistic tendency by stressing his dedication to duty no matter how difficult or laborious.

Today, the modern use of the term stoic means a person who is indifferent to pain, grief, joy, and pleasure. It has been used since the late 16th century in a more simplistic manner than antiquity to describe a person who represses his feelings and suffers with patience. Thus the term has survived in common use from the Greco-Roman world to the present.

EPICUREANISM

Epicureanism is a philosophy founded by Epicurus in 307 B.C. They were as individualistic, universalistic and *materialistic* as the Stoics. Their universalism included women and slaves. Their materialism derived from the Greek physicist *Democritus' atomic theory.* Its founder believed that atoms moved in a mechanical and automatic way, but he also believed the atoms had the spontaneous ability change their movement and combine with other atoms. Therefore if human beings are made up of atoms and as atoms can move with certain freedom, therefore men can have human freedom, and are not tied down to a status of an automaton or mechanical behavior, thus are free from fatalism and have free will.

Epicurus' atomic materialism led him to be against divine intervention. He believed that the gods, the soul, and all matter is made up of atoms. He also believed there were gods, but they were unwilling and unable to eliminate evil. This was because the gods lived in a perfect state of tranquility and thus evil did not concern the gods, but it does concern man who suffers evil. These immortal and content gods, yet made of matter or atoms existed in the vastness of infinite space and were not concerned with mankind's affairs, and therefore did not intervene in human affairs. There was no use to worship and make sacrifices to the gods.

Epicurean's ethical philosophy was based on the doctrine that the highest good was pleasure. Their goal in life was to seek as much pleasure as possible and avoid pain as much as possible. Epicurus taught that what was important and ethical in life is to achieve as much individual pleasure as possible, nevertheless with moderation. Moderation is necessary to avoid the negative consequences and suffering of overindulgence in the pleasures that life provide. The way to pleasure was to become knowledgeable of how the world operated and of the individual's desires, living with modesty. The goal is to obtain a state of tranquility with freedom from fear and bodily pain. Thus tranquility and lack of pain make up the greatest happiness. The pleasures of the mind are emphasized over the pleasures of the flesh, thus for example there is more pleasure with the persons with whom we share a meal than the meal itself. The founder did not advocate sensuality nor lust, neither drinking bouts and gluttony. He advocated sober reasoning and thinking through all choices to pick the helpful ones and avoid the painful ones. Epicurus saw –marriage as an obstacle to peace of mind so he lived a celibate life but did not impose this restraint on others.

The pleasures of the flesh should be avoided because excesses of carnality bring great pain in the long run. But moderate satisfaction of bodily appetite can be convenient and thus permissible. For example excessive drinking brings about the pains of drunkenness. The greatest pleasure is mental pleasure. To retreat and meditate, to study, to ponder on the rational reasons to make the best choice to seek beneficial things and avoid others, to make mature reflections upon previous satisfactions enjoyed are the activities an individual should seek. The highest of all pleasures is the serenity of the soul, in complete absence of mental and physical pain. This can be achieved by eliminating fear. The worst fear is of the supernatural or from the gods that produces the greatest source of mental pain. For the gods do not care about men and the soul is material which cannot survive the body after death. So why bother worrying about the gods who do not reward or punish men, and life after death. Death should be seen as liberation from the toils and sufferings of life, and thus welcomed.

Their teachings and politics were based on utilitarianism. What was accepted as useful was what produced greater benefit and pleasure in life and were not concerned if it was the morally correct thing to do, and avoid all that produced pain and loss. The Epicurean judged an issue from this utilitarian perspective: will it produce more pleasure and benefits or pain and costs? If the former was the answer the individual should pursuit it, and if it was the latter it should be avoided. For example the only reason a person should be good is to increase his own happiness. Another, breaking the law is unwise because if caught by the authority it brought shame and the pain of punishment. Living with the fear of being apprehended takes away pleasure. Therefore, virtue for its own sake had no value unless it helped to gain happiness. Friendship and reciprocity is positive because they are beneficial, not because of being noble and fair. They also denied absolute justice existed arguing that laws and institutions are created to maintain security and order and not to achieve true justice. These rules and authorities are obeyed solely because it is to the benefit of everyone's advantage to do so. In other words, justice is a social contract based on mutual agreement among men to not harm nor be harmed. Laws and punishments serve to avoid being harmed and thus be able to pursue happiness. Just laws that promote happiness are just laws, and those that do not are unjust laws. The negative aspect of this philosophy is that it tends to lead to hedonism in its effort to seek pleasure. But the Epicureans did not include all pleasures in this pursuit.

Epicurus did not have a high regard for either political or social life, and recommended to stay away from them. He had no ideals to change things for the better and taught that the wise man should take no active part in politics. Learning about culture, as well as political and social involvement were discouraged because they could bring about desires and ideals that would be difficult to achieve and cause disturbance of a person's peace of mind. The state was a mere convenience. The state of happiness was basically *passive* and *defeatist*. He taught that the evils of the world cannot be eliminated by human effort. Thus the individual should withdraw to study philosophy and enjoy the simple pleasures of life like companionship of friends, a day at the theater, and not complicate his life by getting involved in reforming society or worrying about the world's evils which would only hinder the tranquility of the mind.

Epicureanism lasted for about seven centuries, until the 3rd century A.D. during the later Roman Empire. This philosophical school will become popular with Stoicism and Skepticism which were the three dominant schools of Hellenistic philosophy. It will be later revived in the 17th century. It had controversies with Platonism and it later opposed Stoicism. Today, modern use of the term epicurean can imply hedonism and/or the love and knowledge of good food and drink.

CYNICISM

The **Cynics** began around 350 B.C. and this philosophical school is better associated with its most famous teacher and practitioner ***Diogenes of Sinope***. Antisthenes is considered its traditional founder. Antisthenes was a pupil and follower of Socrates, lived during Plato's lifetime, and taught a life of poverty. Socrates' love of virtue and disregard for wealth and public opinion were a major influence upon Antisthenes. Later Diogenes took up Antisthenes' teachings and was well-known for his ascetic way of life that led him to live a life of self-sufficiency, austerity, and shamelessness. In art Diogenes is portrayed in his extreme asceticism sleeping in a large bathtub in the streets of Athens surrounded by dogs. There are stories of his shameless behavior such as eating raw meat.

In an age of uncertainty when Classical Greece was in decline and transition into the Hellenistic period or civilization began to take place the Cynics were frustrated with society in general. They were against the family, the polis (city), politics, religion, and Greek philosophers, in other words they were *antisocial*. They repudiated all that was conventional and artificial. Music and art were seen as artificial and thus manifestations of artificiality. The Cynics offered its followers in unstable times a possibility to attempt to achieve happiness and freedom from suffering. To achieve these ends the purpose of life is to be virtuous in agreement with nature. The goal of Cynicism is to arrive at a state of living well spiritually or happiness, and mental clarity. There needs to be freedom from ignorance and folly. Folly or acts of foolishness are caused by bad judgments of value that result in unnatural desires and vices. This happiness is achieved by means of living in harmony with nature understood in a rational manner. The Cynic's goal of happiness requires one to become self-sufficient (*autarky*), calmness to the unpredictable changes of life, a desire for excellence, and a love of humanity. The means to acquire this happiness and clarity of mind is through ascetic practices that free the individual of negative influences such as wealth, power, greed, and fame that do not have value in nature. The Cynic practices shamelessness in defiance of the norms and conventionalisms of society which foster a desire for social status, fame, wealth, and power. Therefore, a Cynic rejects ownership of property and conventional value of statues, wealth, fame, and power.

To live a life in harmony with nature, man only requires bare necessities that are needed to sustain life, free from any conventional necessities. In other words, a Cynic will need only the basic necessities such as food, clothes, and shelter. This leaves him free from the desires of having large properties, social status, and power, that bring the suffering caused by greed, envy, power struggles, and frustrations these states of mind impose on men. They argued for living a *"natural life"* which gave the movement its name because their idea was that men should *live as naturally as beasts,* and dogs behave in this manner. Therefore, the word "Cynic" comes from the Greek word for "dog". For them true freedom came from realizing that if one wants nothing, then one will never lack anything. Diogenes was referred to as "the dog" a nickname in which he took great pleasure, and as dogs behave he lived with indifference in the streets barefoot and slept in a tub.

Cynicism had the least impact on Hellenistic civilization of the four schools of thought and concentrated on ethics. It had an influence upon Stoicism. A good Cynic would attempt to convince his fellow men to abandon their conventional errors for virtue. The idea of cosmopolitanism is attributed to the Cynics who like Diogenes claimed to be citizens of the world and not from a city-state. Their ideas offended the educated members of society and its pessimism and scorn offered no hope to the masses. It declined by the 2nd and 1st centuries B.C., but came back with force during the Roman Empire in 1st century A.D. lasting until the 4th century A.D. Their emphasis on virtue and moral freedom that liberated man from his desires during antiquity was not made clear during the 18th and 19th centuries, but rather the negative scornful attitude, which changed the definition of cynicism as it is used today. They gave us a term that we use frequently which is "cynical" to describe a person who is very distrustful of the good intentions of others and thinks men only act out of selfishness. Also the Cynics had some resemblance to other movements that came up through the ages such as the hippie movement of the 1960s that was frustrated with the values, constraints, and goals of society, and therefore it rejected and rebelled against society in general with many of its followers opting to "drop out" of society.

SKEPTICISM

The **Skeptics** were a more radically defeatist philosophy than the Epicureans and were founded by *Pyrrho* of Elis (365–275 B.C.). Pyrrho travelled to India to study with men that were lovers of wisdom or Indian philosophers (Gymnosophists), and returned to Greece bringing with him the idea that nothing can be known for certain. As man's senses are easily fooled, he cannot be sure he knows exactly what is perceived by the senses. Reason follows easily what man desires. Therefore for the skeptics, how can men be completely sure they know the truth, the facts of life? They were at their height of popularity around 200 B.C. with *Carneades* (213–129 B.C.), who further developed this philosophy theoretically stating that conceptions of absolute truth and falsity are uncertain. Carneades was critical of the position of dogmatist as the Stoics, claiming that absolute certainty of knowledge is impossible. The stoic logical mode of argument was unsustainable according to this way of thinking because it relied on propositions which could not be said to be either true or false without relying on further propositions. The followers of Pyrrho founded Pyrrhonism, a school of skepticism in the 1st century B.C.

For the Skeptics their main source of influence was the *Sophist* teaching that all knowledge derived from the senses is limited and relative. This led them to conclude that man cannot prove anything is absolutely true. No truth can be certain. A philosophical skeptic does not assert that arriving at the truth is impossible. If he did make this statement it would consist in a truth claim that would contradict his philosophical tenets. Instead the Skeptic advises to *suspend belief*. So all that men state is that things *appear* to be in a certain manner, but man cannot know what they really *are*. Man cannot tell in absolute terms what is right from wrong. What is logical under this school of thought is the suspension of judgment which will lead to happiness. This happiness comes from abandoning the fruitless search for absolute truth and worrying about good and evil, allowing man to attain the peace of mind which is the highest satisfaction that life can afford. They were *relativist* like the Sophists. They were not concern with political and social problems. Their ideal was one of escape for the individual from a world that was not understandable nor capable of reform. This tendency toward escapism was typically Hellenistic. This movement had fewer followers than the Cynics. It faded after 129 B.C. but was revived during the Roman Empire and later passed into the mainstream of Western thought. Today, skepticism is a term used to indicate an attitude of doubt or incredulity in general or to a particular matter.

GREEK CULTURE

The achievements of the Greek civilization were some of the most remarkable in the history of the world. With limited resources they developed one of the most advanced and varied civilizations up to that point in history. But not all ancient Greeks were cultured and free as the citizens of Athens. For example, the Spartans were less cultured and their source of power was their militarism, discipline, and the fear they placed over their suppressed lower classes. The Spartans shunned culture in general to devote themselves entirely to the disciplined military life in which they excelled. From a very young age the boys were taken out of the home to live with other boys and begin their life of harsh training to become professional soldiers. The girls were raised to be physically fit to have healthy children and run the household. This military lifestyle was seen as the means to conquer and maintain under their control the lower classes that did the farm and menial labor that was necessary and thus permitted the Spartan to dedicate themselves entirely to the military life.

In ancient Greece there were many slaves, and women were denied many rights and participation in public life, even in democratic Athens. Racial discrimination such as Athens required both parents to be Athenians to be a citizen, denying political rights to the majority of the inhabitants. There was political persecution such as the case of Socrates who was sentenced to death. The philosophers Anaxagoras and Protagoras were forced to leave Athens due to its intolerance.

But besides its faults and defects ancient Greek Civilization, with limited resources, wealth, and cultural inheritance from the past to build upon, produced intellectual and artistic achievements which have served ever since as models or standards to be attained for our Western culture. For example, think of our modern Olympic games and many of our great buildings with their architectural designs inspired by Greek architecture.

The great influence the Greeks had in history is due to creating numerous ideals that are held to be central to the dignity and progress of humanity. This influence can be appreciated when compared to the cultures of Mesopotamia and Egypt. These two civilizations were dominated by absolutism, supernaturalism, and subjection of the individual to society, that is to the king and priestly class.

The typical political regime of the ancient Middle East had:

- Absolute monarch supported by a powerful priesthood
- Culture was at the service to magnify the power of the state and enhance the ruler and priests' prestige. Thus, the individual was at the service of the state and its ruling class.

The Greeks on the other hand had a humanistic civilization, whose best example was Athens, founded upon the ideals of:

- Freedom
- Optimism
- Secularism—did not allow religion and priests to control their intellect and morality
- Rationalism
- Glorification of the mind and body
- High regard for the dignity and worth of the individual
- Culture was bases on the primacy of intellect and spirit of free inquiry
- Intellect, science, and logic were supreme

The Greek's greatest tragedy was their failure to solve their political conflicts. The suspicion, fear, and rivalry of the city-states brought wars that caused their decline, especially between Sparta and Athens.

CHARACTERISTICS OF CLASSICAL GREEK CULTURE AND CIVILIZATION

ARÊTE

The Greeks had the notion that humans are worthy of the attentions of the gods. Thus, humans have great qualities that should be achieved and perfected. This is where the Greeks derive their notion of striving for human excellence. Arête is the diligence in the pursuit of excellence. It applied to everything the Greeks made or performed, from pots to temples, from music to theatre, from art to athletics.

In this pursuit of excellence the Greeks, especially the Athenians, became very competitive. This became their passion. With arête you pleased the gods that were excellent and valued excellence. Thus men by striving for excellence were worthy of the appreciation of their gods.

Idealism

The Greeks were **idealists** who envisioned the world as it should be. They had the notion of "perfection" or "excellence" and that was their goal. We can appreciate this in their sculptures whose figures had the perfect bodies. Perfect human form was the goal of the classical Greek artists. But at the same time they were realistic and saw themselves and their culture as it was in reality. This did not stop them from striving for excellence or arête.

Economy of Style

This was another of the Greek's characteristics. It consists of doing things in the simplest form. Any project done was reduced to its fundamental element. There is a basic structure to everything. The principle of exclusion is applied here and anything that is not necessary to what the Greeks want to express is excluded. This allowed the Greeks to express the "ideal" in their artistic works. If you look at their architecture you can see its simple but elegant style. There is nothing that is "heavy" or complicated. The opposite is true of a later artistic style of the 17th century A.D., the Baroque style. The characteristic feature of the Baroque was the elaborate, complicated, and heavily decorated style.

Amateurism

It derives from the word amateur. To practice an activity such as art, sports, or science, because you are attracted to it, and feel a great interest or passion for this activity. The amateur is not a professional or expert, and does not do it for pay. This was a requirement in the Olympics, where the athletes that were allowed to compete could never practice or compete in a sport for money. It forbade participation of professional athletes.

The Meaning of Greek Art

Above all the Greek art expressed humanism, the glorification of man as the most important creature of the universe. This humanism can be found in:

- Religion: The Greek deities existed for the benefit of man. When the Greeks glorified these gods in sculpture they were also glorifying themselves. This is clearly observed in sculptures of the gods all having human forms.
- Architecture and sculpture: Both embodied the ideals of *balance, harmony, order,* and *moderation.* Anarchy and excesses were abhorrent to the mind of the Greeks and also absolute repression (except for Sparta). Therefore, Greek art exhibits qualities of simplicity and dignified restraint. It is free of decorative excesses or extravaganzas on one hand, and from restrictive convention on the other. They had freedom within a spirit of moderation and simplicity.

Greek art was an expression of national life. It had an aesthetic purpose, but also a political one. The political aspect was to symbolize the pride of the people in their city, and to enhance their consciousness of unity. An example would be the Parthenon of Athens. This is the temple of Athena, the protecting goddess of Athens located on Athens' Acropolis. The Greeks believed Athena was looking over their city-state. By providing this temple, the goddess likely visited the site and provided the city with her protection. The Athenians were giving at the same time evidence of their love for their city and hope in continuing its welfare. Such beautiful buildings were also a way to show to themselves and all visitors how good they were, and that they were worthy of the attention of the gods, especially Athena.

The art of the Greeks was different from the arts of other people and eras in many ways. It was universal because the human beings depicted were human types, not individuals. It had an ethical purpose because it was a means for the ennoblement of humanity. Not for the mere decoration or expression of an artist's own ideas. Consequently, what was beautiful and ethically good were identical for the Greeks; both characteristics in the same artistic work of art.

The body was to express human ideal of perfection. They wanted to express the human ideals in their art, that is what was moral, which excluded all coarseness and obscenity, excessively large or fat, sensual excess, deformities, etc. They did not concern themselves with expressing nature or reality with its imperfections and defects, thus staying away from realism. Their art expressed their idealistic view of reality.

THREE PERIODS OF THE HISTORY OF GREEK ART
1. ARCHAIC PERIOD—9TH AND 6TH CENTURY B.C.

Architecture

The temple was the supreme architectural achievement of the Greeks. It became the fountainhead of the building components, decorative details, and aesthetic principles that together have largely shaped Western architecture down to Post-Modernism in the early 21st century. In its origins during the Archaic Age, the temple was a sacred structure designed to house the cult statues of the civic deities. The early houses of worship were probably made of wood, as the Archaic Age gathered economic momentum and wealth accumulated, each polis rebuilt its wooden sanctuaries in stone.

Generic Greek architecture is called **postbeam-triangle construction** (also known as **post-and-lintel construction**). *Post* refers to the columns; *beam* indicates the horizontal members, or *architraves,* resting on the columns; and triangle denotes the triangular area, called a **pediment,** at either end of the upper building. Other common features include the **entablature,** which is the name for all of the building between the columns and the pediment; the **cornice,** the horizontal piece that crowns the entablature; and **stylobate,** the upper step of the base on which the columns stand. A typical temple had columns on four sides, which in turn enclosed a walled room, called a **cella,** that housed the cult image. Each temple faced east, with the doors to the cella placed so that, when opened, they allowed the sunrise to illuminate the statue of the deity.

The earliest temple style in Greece was called **Doric,** both because it originated in the Dorian poleis and because the style's simplicity of design and scarcity of decorative detail reflected the severe Dorian taste. Doric columns have plain tops, or **capitals,** and the columns rest directly on the stylobate with any footing.

Eventually, after much experimentation, Greek architects overcame the awkwardness of the early Doric style by deciding that a temple's beauty was a function of *mathematical proportions*. The Temple of Aphaia, erected in 510 B.C. by citizens of Aegina, a neighbor of Athens, embodied this principle of proportion. The architect of this temple achieved its pleasing dimensions by using the ratio 1:2, placing six columns on the ends and 12 columns on the sides. They applied the principle of economy of style by reducing all the structures of the temple to three basic figures, a circle, square, and triangle. The circle forms the figure of the column, the square forms the figure of the cella (naos) or the innermost room containing the statue of the god, and the triangle forms the figure of the pediment under the gable of the roof.

Sculpture

During the Archaic period there is a clear Egyptian influence. The Greek's first sculpture was small so that it could be carried by the hands. Contact with the Egyptians taught the Greeks to quarry large stones and make life-size and large statues. The Egyptian influence is seen where the sculpture has a rigid pose, square bodies, in a position of "attention." Later there is a move toward **naturalism** which is sculpting figures that are more like they appear in real life. We see a more "natural look" in these figures.

Like the art of Mesopotamia and Egypt, Greek sculpture was rooted in religious practices and beliefs. The Greek sculptors fashioned images of the gods and goddesses to be used in temples either as objects of worship or as decoration for the pediments and friezes. Of greater importance for the development of Greek sculpture were the male kouros (plural, kourai) and the female kore (plural, korai), freestanding statues of youths and maidens. Before 600 B.C., these sculptures had evolved from images of gods, into statues of dead heroes, and finally into memorials that might not even relate directly to the dead person to whom they were dedicated.

What made the Archaic statues of youths and maidens so different from Egyptian and Mesopotamian art was the Greek delight in the splendor of the human body. In their representations of the human form, the Greeks rejected the sacred approach of the Egyptians and the Mesopotamians, which stressed conventional poses and formal gestures. Instead, Greek sculptors created athletic, muscular males and lively, robust maidens. For the Greeks, the health and beauty of the subjects was as important as the statues' religious purpose.

The first Archaic statues of youths owed much to the Egyptian tradition, but gradually Greek sculpture broke free of its origins moving toward naturalism.

ARCHAIC (CA. 800–480 B.C.E.)

Figure 3.6 *Kouros from Anavyssos* (ca. 530 B.C.E.), Attica, Greece. *Image Copyright DeAgostini/SuperStock.*

Figure 3.7 *Peplos Kore* (ca. 530 B.C.E.), Acropolis Museum, Athens. *Image Copyright Universal Images Group/SuperStock.*

Some of the early figures produced by the Ancient Greeks, called Kouros (koo – ros) figures (Figure 3.6), are reminiscent of Ancient Egyptian Pharaonic figures. Many of them are small votive-style offerings, but a number are very large; they all have a characteristic Egyptian stance—with one foot forward and arms held rigidly at thebody's side. Unlike the Ancient Pharaohs, however, the Kouros figures may depict athletes, who are known to have competed in the nude. Their faces are not individu-alized and many bear a stereotyped slight smile, setting them apart from later Greek works. They are typically tall, columnar, and possess the same block-like charac-teristics of the stone from which they are carved. Evidence shows that some of these figures were painted in bright, flat colors. The counterpart of the male Kouros was the female Kore (kor – ray) who was fully clothed (Figure 3.7).

Toward the end of the archaic period, Kouroi take on a naturalistic appearance and their bodies look more like those of an average person. There are several tran-sitional figures that illustrate this change.

The *Charioteer of Delphi* (Figure 3.8) was found at the site of the huge temple com-plex where the Delphic oracle issued her proclamations. He is standing in a chariot holding the reins of horses (now lost) in front of him. Notice that his face is ideal-ized, but his arms and the rest of his body look natural judging from the proportions of his chiton (k – eye – ton). The Chari-

Figure 3.8 *Charioteer of Delphi* (470 B.C.E.). Archaeological Museum, Delphi. *Image Copyright .VIZE/ Shutterstock.com.*

oteer's face is unlike the stereotyped smiles of the Kouros figures and there are more concessions to nat-ural reality in his posture and arms, but his chiton looks more like a fluted column than a naturalistic outfit. The Charioteer is a transi-tional figure from the old Archaic style to a later Classical style.

HELLENIC, "CLASSICAL" (CA. 480–300 B.C.E.)

The Ancient Greek Gods were said to be *anthropomorphic*, that is, they could take the shape of humans and reside temporarily in the body of a person. When an ath-lete won a contest at the Olympic Games, Apollo (the Sun God) was said to settle upon (or rather into) the winner; the athlete had attained god-like perfection. It is these athletically ideal types that are represented in the Hellenic, or Classical phase of Ancient Greek sculpture.

Since the Gods were *anthropomorphic*, one can often tell which god is represented in an Ancient Greek statue by the stance or pose. Zeus, head of the Gods, was known to take the form of an athlete throw-ing a spear and Heracles is usually shown shooting arrows. When viewing a Hellenic (or classical) Ancient Greek statue, the viewer sees an ideal, god-like type—an idea. The geometrical hairstyle, symmetrical fea-tures, and bodily proportions identify this style.

The Legacy of Archaic Greek Civilization

The Archaic Age in Greece was a precious moment in the story of the arts and humanities. Archaic Greeks developed a unique consciousness that expressed, through original artistic and literary forms, their views about the deities and themselves and how they interacted. A mark of the creative power of the

Archaic Greeks is that at the same time that they were inventing epic poetry, lyric poetry, the post-beam-triangle temple, the kouros and kore sculptures, and natural philosophy, they were involved in founding a new and better way to live in the polis.

The new way of life devised by the Archaic Greeks gave rise to what we call, in retrospect, the **humanities**—those original artistic and literary forms that made Greek civilization unique.

The Greeks' restless drive to experience life to the fullest and their deep regard for human powers was behind this cultural explosion. Archaic Greeks believed passionately that by simply employing these models, either through studying them or by creating new works, the individual became a better human being. In this way, the Archaic Greeks' arts and humanities were imbued with an ethical content, suggesting to its philosophers an alternative way of life to that offered by religion.

Early aesthetic efforts were fundamentally different from those of the earlier Near Eastern civilizations. The touchstone of the humanistic style developed by the Greeks was their belief in human powers, both intellectual and physical.

Homer, the most influential literary voice of this age, was quoted over and over for his claim that mortals and divinities are part of the same family. That is, men are similar to the gods except that they are mortals with less power. For the Greeks of this period, Homer meant that humans are capable of godlike actions. Thus, men must strive to be the best they can be, and by excelling in their achievements they would be worthy of admiration by their gods. The reverence of these Archaic Greeks had for all noteworthy deeds, whether in poetry, in art, in warfare, or in the competitive Olympic games, attested to their belief in the basic value of human achievement. They had an optimistic attitude that men have the ability for excellence.

2. CLASSICAL PERIOD 480–323 B.C.

During this period the Greeks reached full perfection of architecture and sculpture. The art was completely idealistic. During the late Classical period 400–323 B.C. architecture lost some of its balance and simplicity. Sculpture incorporated more realism, which reflected the artist's view, and the artist had less concern in expressing civic pride.

The Hellenic Age

A period that lasted until the death of Alexander the Great of Macedon in 323 B.C. During the more than 150 years of the Hellenic Age, the Greeks never wavered in their supreme confidence in the superiority of their way of life.

The Greek world consisted of several hundred poleis or city-states, located on the mainland, on the Aegean Islands and coast of Asia Minor, and in the lands bordering the Mediterranean and Black Seas. Athens was the cultural center, but many other city-states made their cultural contributions to the Hellenic civilization. The Hellenic Age was the first stage of Classical Greek civilization, the highest achievement of the ancient Greeks. Despite diversity among the poleis, the Greeks of the Hellenic Age shared certain characteristics. Competitiveness and rivalry were certainly dominant features, as was an increasingly urban lifestyle. Most Greeks still lived in the countryside, but the city now dominated politics, society, and economy.

The culture that flourished in Greece at this time is known as **Classic,** or **Classical,** a term with varied meanings. Classic means, first of all, "best" or "preeminent," and the judgment of the Western tradition is that Greek culture was in fact the highest moment in the entire history of the humanities. Classic also means having *permanent* and *recognized significance;* a classic work *establishes a standard* against which other efforts are measured. In this second sense, the aesthetic values and forms of Greek culture have been studied and imitated in all later stages of Western history. By extension, "the classics" are works that have survived from Greece and Rome.

Classic also refers to the body of specific aesthetic principles expressed through the art and literature of ancient Greece and Rome, which is a system known as **Classicism.** The first stage of Classicism, which originated in the Hellenic Age, emphasized simplicity over complexity; balance, or symmetry, over asymmetry; and restraint over excess. At the heart of Classicism was the *search for perfection,* for the *ideal form,* whether the ideal was expressed in the canon of the human anatomy molded in bronze or in a philosophical conclusion reached through logic. Hellenic Classicism found expression in many areas: theatre, music, history, natural philosophy, architecture, and sculpture.

Architecture

Of all the Greek art forms, architecture most powerfully embodied the Classical ideals of the Hellenic Age. The stone temple, the supreme expression of the Hellenic building genius, now received its definitive shape. Ironically, the Doric temple, which had originated in the Archaic Age, reached perfection in Ionian Athens. The versatile Athenians also perfected a new architectural order, the **Ionic,** which reflected more clearly their cultural tradition (Figure 3.9).

By the Hellenic Age, each polis had its own sacred area, usually built on a hill or protected by walls, which contained building and altars. This was a concept of a holy place set aside from the business of everyday life. Although each polis worshiped the entire pantheon of deities, one god or goddess was gradually singled out as patron, and a temple was erected to house the statue of that particular divinity; such as Athena was the patron god of Athens for which the Parthenon was built and housed her large statue.

Temples were rectilinear and of post-beam-triangle construction. Influenced by the Pythagorean quest for harmony through mathematical rules, the eastern builders had standardized six as the perfect number of columns for the sides. These balanced proportions, along with simple designs and restrained decorative schemes, made the eastern temples majestically expressive of Classical ideals.

The second order of Greek architecture was the *Ionic,* which originated in the late Archaic Age, and like the Doric reached full maturity in Hellenic times (Figure 3.10). The Ionic style has more freedom and is more graceful that the Doric. More decorated than the plain Doric,

Figure 3.9   Parthenon in Athens, Greece, dedicated to the goddess Athena. Classical Greek architecture. *Image Copyright krechet, 2009. Used under license from Shutterstock, Inc.*

Figure 3.10   Greek temple with Ionic columns, the cella in the interior that housed the statue of the god, the triangular tympanum with mythological sculptures, and decorative figures on the roof. Post and lintel construction. There is simplicity, elegance, proportion, and balance. *Image Copyright Baloncici, 2009. Used under license from Shutterstock, Inc.*

the Ionic columns have elegant bases, and their tops are crowned with capitals that suggested either a scroll's ends or a ram's horns. What solidified the Ionic temple's impression of elegance are its slender and delicate columns.

Sculpture

Believing that the task of sculpture was to imitate nature, the Greeks created images of gods and goddesses as well as of men and women that have influenced the Western imagination ever since. They not only forged a canon of idealized human proportions that later sculptors followed but also developed a repertoire of postures, gestures, and subjects that have become embedded in Western art.

During the Hellenic Age, Classical sculpture moved through three separate phases: the **Severe style,** which ushered in the period and lasted until 450 B.C.; the **High Classical style,** which coincided with the zenith of Athenian imperial greatness; and the **4th-Century style,** which concluded with the death of Alexander the Great in 323 B.C. (Figure 3.11).

Sculpture in the Severe style, inspired perhaps by its association with funeral customs, was characterized by a feeling of dignified nobility. The Kritios Boy that is showing a figure fully at rest, is an elegant expression of this first phase of Classicism, and the sculptor altered the frontality, a feature of the Archaic style, by tilting the head subtly to the right and slightly twisting the upper torso. The flat-footed stance of the Archaic kourai has given way to a posture that places the body's weight on one leg and uses the other leg as a support. This stance is called **contrapposto** (counterpoise), and its invention, along with the mastery of the representation of musculature, helped to make the Classical revolution. Thereafter, sculptors were able to render the human figure in freer and more relaxed poses. At this point *naturalism* (a natural human poise verses a rigid one) is achieved (Figure 3.12).

In contrast to the Severe style, which accepted repose as normal, the High Classical style was fascinated with the aesthetic problem of showing motion in a static medium. The sculptor's solution, which became central to High Classicism, was to freeze the action, resisting the impulse to depict agitated movement, allowing an ideal world to emerge in which serene gods and mortals showed grace under pressure. The Discus Thrower (discobolus) by the sculptor Myron is one of the best examples of sculpture with a "frozen action" movement.

Figure 3.11   Pediment with a tympanum with sculpture of mythological gods, Greece. *Image Copyright fafoutis, 2009. Used under license from Shutterstock, Inc.*

Figure 3.12   Ancient Greek statue showing a mythical muse with a natural poise. *Image Copyright Panos Karapanagiotis, 2009. Used under license from Shutterstock, Inc.*

The transition to 4th-Century style coincided with the disintegration of the Greek world as it passed into the Macedonian political orbit, when Philip of Macedon conquered the Greek city-states. Sculpture remained innovative, since each generation seemed to produce a master who challenged the prevailing aesthetic rules, and free expression continued as a leading principle of 4th-Century style. But sculptors now expressed such new ideas as beauty for its own sake and a delight in sensuality. Earlier Classicism had stressed the notion that humans could become godlike, but the last phase concluded that gods and mortals alike reveled in human joys. The sculptor Praxiteles achieved a new vision that influenced other artists, that sculptors in the Hellenistic Age became interested in more frankly sensual portrayals of the human figure, both male and female. A good example is Praxiteles' statue of Hermes with the Infant Dionysus.

This face of the *Discus Thrower* (Figure 3.13) pos-sesses the unique quality of Hellenic art—it is perfectly symmetrical. Who is this person? Is it Don, Lloyd, Jim, Rich, or Phil? It is none of them in particular. It is the best of them—it is the best of every man who ever was. This is an idea; the face is bi-laterally sym-metrical and there is not a wart, a mole, or a bump on this per-fectly smooth face. The locks of hair are carefully organized into geometrical spirals and the eye, the eyeball, and the eyelid con-tain sequences of parabolas. The face has the holy "gaze into infinity" associ-ated with priestly cults from the Middle East. This is not a person, it is an idea—or an *ideal*—the purpose of which is not to identify a single person, but rather generalities about the best in people and their proportions.

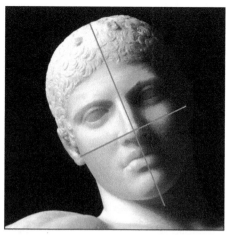

Figure 3.13 Detail, *Discobolus, Discus Thrower* (ca. 460–450 B.C.E.), Myron. Museo Nazionale Romano—Palazzo Massimo. Rome. *Image Copyright Araldo de Luca/Corbis.*

What makes a Hellenic statue "classical" is an inherent system of bodily measurement and pro-portion. The *Doryphoros* (do – ree – for – us) by Polykeitos (Figure 3.14) has perfect beauty. If one draws a line down this statue from head to foot and divides the line in half, it crosses the groin area of the statue. If the ver-tical line is bisected at .25 it crosses the knees, at .75 it crosses the chest, and at .62 (the Golden Section), it crosses the navel. Ancient Greek artists thought that the center of each person's universe was the navel, and that this spot had to be properly (mathematically) positioned on their statues.

Doryphoros includes mathematical proportions and ratios from top to bottom, which is why it is labeled, "classical." Some peo-ple think that the word "clas-sical" is defined as "that which lasts a long time." As an artistic term, however, "classical" is rooted in concepts of mathematics. As a style, it is not necessarily better or worse than any other, but its requirements are very specific. One can see the for-mula at work in other Ancient Greek statues such as *Apoxyomenos* by Lysippus (Figure 3.15).

Can you tell the difference between the characteristics and proportions of the two human figures shown in Figures 3.16 and 3.17? One is an outline of an ancient Greek statue and the other is an outline of a modern weight-lifter. Putting aside the obvious muscles on the weight lifter, the legs of the Greek statue on the left are proportionately longer. This is because Ancient Greek proportions follow a Pythag-orean geometrical formula requiring use of the Golden Section. The formula for locating the navel on any given classical statue is given below in the chart below, and summarized in Figure 3.17.

Figure 3.14 Roman copy of bronze original. *Doryphoros*, "Spear bearer" (ca. 450–400 B.C.E.), Polykleitos. Museo Archeologico Nazionale di Napoli, Naples. *Image Copyright Album/Prisma/Album/Superstock.*

Figure 3.15 Apoxyome-nos, "The Scraper" (ca. 330 B.C.E.),Lysippus, Vatican Museums, Rome. *Image Copyright Vanni Archive/ Art Resource, NY.*

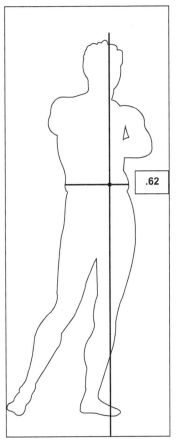

Figure 3.16 Outline of Apoxyomenos. *Image Source: Raechel Martin. Copyright Kendall Hunt Publishing Company.*

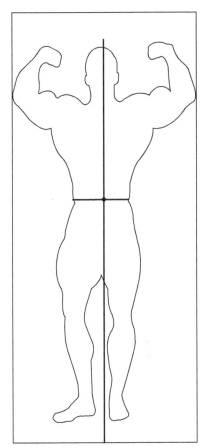

Figure 3.17 Outline of Modern Body Builde. *Image Source: Raechel Martin. Copyright Kendall Hunt Publishing Company.*

Point F divides the original line into two unequal segments (AF) and (FB). The rela-tion of (AF) to (FB) on the original line drawn on the statue is the Golden Section. It is sometimes referred to as the Golden Mean or Golden Proportion. There are other ways to derive the Golden Section, but it is defined here as a way of dividing a line into two beau-tiful (i.e., mathematical), but unequal parts. If this line (AB) is superimposed upon the vertical axis of a classical statue (Figure 3.16), the navel would fall at the Golden Section.

The Legacy of Hellenic Civilization

Athenian culture dominated the Hellenic Age. Tragic poets, comic playwrights, and natural philosophers made the Athenian dialect the medium of expression for poetry and prose. The buildings on the Acrop-olis expressed visually the purity and restraint of the Athenian style. Humanism, the other great creation of Athens, survived as a guide to refined living for the cultivated classes in the West. Athenian culture became the heart of the educational curriculum that was followed in Hellenistic civilization and was adopted by Rome and transmitted in the humanistic tradition to Europe. In time, the study and the prac-tice of humanistic learning, literature, philosophy, theatre, music, and the arts and architecture, became the crowning glory of Western civilization, affecting private individuals and entire societies.

Moreover, Classicism, the style of humanistic achievements in the Hellenic Age, had three impor-tant effects on the Western tradition. First, the principles of Greek Classicism, balance, simplicity, and

Figure 3.18   Modern University of Athens. Example of classical Greek architecture still used today. *Image Copyright Elpis Ioannidis, 2009. Used under license from Shutterstock, Inc.*

Figure 3.19   Parliament Building Vienna, Austria. Example of classical Greek influence in architecture and sculpture. *Image Copyright Nakic, 2009. Used under license from Shutterstock, Inc.*

restraint set the standard by which the styles of other times are often measured. Second, the actual works of Classicism became basic building blocks of Western culture, having an immense influence up until the second half of the 19th century. In the world of thought, the works of Plato and Aristotle quickly acquired a luster of authority and retained it until the 17th century A.D. Some of the Greek tragedies are thought by many to be unsurpassed.

Among Greece's accomplishments, architecture has had the most potent effect (Figures 3.18 & 3.19). Finally, the idealized statues of men and women, have inspired Western artists with their vision of noble beings that are searching for the rich possibilities of human life.

The third and perhaps most important contribution of Classicism to the Western tradition was a skeptical spirit that was rooted in democracy. Humanists declared war on all tyrants, hierarchical societies, and divinely ordered states—in other words, the prevailing order of the ancient world. However, the passion for questioning, for inquiry, which characterizes the skeptical spirit, is at the core of Western consciousness.

3. HELLENISTIC PERIOD—323–30 B.C.

This period is after the death of Alexander the Great when his empire was disintegrating and the emphasis of life was on survival in a world weighed with sectional strife in the territories Alexander conquered. This art was no longer concerned with ideals and classical harmony, and became increasingly interested in more realistic art work and the great variety of human nature and experience. It was the art of Hellenism, the international culture that Alexander left when the Greek culture merged and dominated over the conquered Eastern cultures.

The spread of classicism to the Hellenistic world continued the Greek tradition. The Hellenistic world to some extent rejected the simplicity, balance, and restraint that had characterized Hellenism and embraced a more emotional, theatrical view of culture. The expansiveness of Alexander's territorial conquests is reflected in the expansion of emotional and expressive content in the arts. As new energies, languages, and traditions from the East were poured into old artistic and literary forms, the seriousness of Hellenism began to give way to a Hellenistic love of playfulness along with an interest in ordinary, everyday subjects.

Hellenistic culture also reflected the tastes and needs of the period's diverse states. Greek tragedy lost its vitality but comedy appealed to sophisticated urban audiences who were seeking diversion. New philosophies and religions arose in response to the urban isolation and loneliness that many people experienced. Architecture was put to the service of the propaganda needs of autocratic rulers that demanded grandiose projects.

Realistic sculpture reflected the tastes of an increasingly urban, secular culture. Nevertheless, the values of Hellenistic culture did not replace the standards of Hellenic Classicism as they enriched and elaborated the older ideals. Like Hellenism, the Hellenistic style depicted the realities of the physical world rather than finding truth in fantasy or abstraction. And Hellenistic artists and authors agreed with their Hellenic forebears that art must serve moral purposes, revealed through content and formal order.

Architecture

As in Hellenic times, architecture in the Hellenistic Age reflected the central role that religion played in the life of the people. Public buildings served religious, ceremonial, and governmental purposes, and the temple continued as the leading type of structure. Hellenistic architecture modified the basic temple and altar forms inherited from Hellenic models to express the grandeur demanded by the age's rulers. Influenced by Alexander the Great's claim to divinity, Alexander's successors built temples and altars whose massive size and elaborate decoration manifested both their own earthly majesty and the divine authority of whatever deity with whom they claimed kinship.

The **Corinthian** temple came to embody Hellenistic splendor. The Corinthian column had first appeared in the Hellenic period, because it was taller, more slender, and more ornamented than either the Doric or the Ionic column. The Corinthian column was now used on the exterior of temples erected by Hellenistic builders for their kings. The major feature of the Corinthian column was the elaborate floral capital with tiers of acanthus leaves. The rest of the other constituent parts were borrowed from the Ionic order. Corinthian order later became the favorite of the Roman emperors, and it was revived in the Renaissance and diffused throughout the Western world, where it survives today as the most visible of Hellenistic influence. The most outstanding Corinthian temples combined grandeur with grace.

Sculpture

Like Hellenistic architects, Hellenistic sculptors adapted many of the basic forms and ideas of the Hellenic style to meet the tasted of their day. The Hellenistic sculptors perpetuated such Hellenic principles as *contrapposto* and *proportion,* as well as the Hellenic emphasis on religious and moral themes. But Hellenistic art increasingly expressed a secular, urban viewpoint, and Hellenic restraint often gave way to realism, eroticism, and violence, expressed and enjoyed for their own sake.

VENUS DE MILO

One of the most famous classical Ancient Greek statues, *Venus de Milo* (Figure 3.20), has perfect, mathematical proportions. Venus is the Roman name for the Greek goddess *Aphrodite*, or the goddess of love. *Venus de Milo* is French for *Aphrodite of Melos*. Aphrodite (af – ro – die- tee) is a goddess of beauty. *Milo* is French for the Greek island of Melos (me – losh) where the statue was found.

One can tell that this is a Hellenistic statue because the female form is partially nude; however, the *Venus'* physical measurements are clearly classical. If a line is drawn from her head to toe, the halfway point is located at the groin area and the Golden Section crosses the navel. One could verify the location of the navel by drawing a vertical line on top of the *Venus* pictured here and construct the Pythagorean triangle (Golden Section) as given above. *Venus de Milo*, like other Ancient Greek statues, has long legs as a result of her Golden Section proportions.

HELLENISTIC: INFLUX OF NEW IDEAS (CA. 300—20 B.C.E.)

In the final Hellenistic style of Greek art, the artist's concern for mathematical propor-tions is missing. Many of the subjects in Hellenistic sculpture include elderly women, or injured soldiers—intro-ducing pathos and theatricality into the art without math-ematical proportions; *Laocoön* (lay – ah – co – ahn) is one such statue (Figure 3.21).

One of the greatest pieces of statuary of all time, *Laocoön*, is not classical. *Laocoön* was a Trojan warrior who defied the wishes of the gods during the Trojan War. He understood that the Trojan Horse would contain soldiers and planned to advise his countrymen not to bring the giant horse into the city. However, the Gods sent a snake to kill him and his sons to avoid having him reveal the secret of the Trojan horse. Full of complex organic shapes, dense texture, and twisting bodies, the statue of *Laocoön* and his sons depicts the family wrestling with a snake. One can easily observe the expressions of pathos and turmoil on the faces of the figures and their disrupted hairstyles. These are people in trouble—very unlike the calm, cool, collected gods illustrated in the high classic period of Ancient Greek art. This statue is not classical and is not about mathematics, but it is dramatically exciting, theatrical, and full of visual interest.

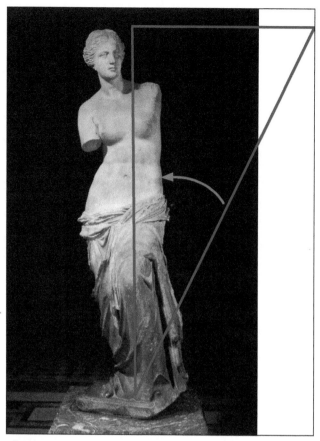

Figure 3.20   *Venus de Milo* (ca.130–100 B.C.E.) Louvre, Paris. *Image Copyright Bridgeman Art Library, London/SuperStock.*

Drama and Literature

In the Hellenistic Age, Greek comedy began to resemble modern productions. Comedies became a form of popular amusement, and Hellenistic playwrights developed a genre known as **New Comedy** to appeal to pleasure-seeking audiences. Avoiding political criticism and casual obscenity, New Comedy presented general scenes from middle-class life.

The plays were generally comic romances on such themes as frustrated first love or marital misunder-standings. The endings were inevitably happy and there was formula writing, similar to today's situation comedies on television.

A writer who stands apart in the Alexandrian school is the poet Theocritus (c. 310–250 B.C.), created a new poetic form, the **pastoral**, which would influence later Classical and modern European literature. These poems describe the lives of shepherds and farmers in a somewhat artificial, idealized way.

The Legacy of the Hellenistic World

In the Hellenistic Age, Athens and its culture achieved the status of an inspiring model to be honored and emulated. But the Hellenistic rules had no interest in democracy; indeed, their larger political interest often conflicted with the needs of local subjects. Nor did these kings want to further humanism, which they regarded as either irrelevant to imperial goals or subversive of them. What appealed to the Hellenistic kings was a narrow, lifeless humanism.

Figure 3.21 *Laocoön* (ca. 25 B.C.E.), Agesander, Athenodoros and Polydorus. Vatican Museums, Rome. *Image Copyright Lyubov Timofeyeva/Shutterstock.com.*

The Hellenistic monarchs wanted to do no more than create new cultural centers that rivaled the fame of the old Athens. The great Hellenistic centers of Pergamum and Alexandria, with their libraries, poets, scientists, artists, schools of philosophy, marble building, and monuments, were perceived as politically useful to these ambitious rules. In other words, they wanted to harness art to politics for propaganda purposes.

Artists brought to their genre sculpture an invigorating realism that expressed emotions and individualism. They introduced the portrayal of female nudity, a practice that persisted in Western art to the present day, with the exception of the Christian Middle Ages. Their emphasis on individualism influenced Roman sculptors, who, in carving many lifelike busts during the republic, preserved this tradition in Western art. The Corinthian temple, perfected in the Hellenistic era, set the standard in decoration and proportion for Roman temples.

A final legacy of the Hellenistic Age was its schools of philosophy—Stoicism, Epicureanism, Skepticism, Cynicism. Although contradictory of each other, these schools of thought had a common appeal:

the promise of a stable belief system and inner peace in the face of a hostile and chaotic environment. From Roman times to the present, these philosophies have attracted followers, but Stoicism has had the most enduring impact (on republican Rome, early Christianity, and the Enlightenment of the 18th century), with Epicureanism the next most influential (on the Scientific Revolution of the 17th century and the 20th century). With their advice to disengage oneself from either the world or one's own passions, these four schools have provided solace in every age marked by overwhelming events and social disorder.

Greek Theatre

The Greeks created tragedy (literary work where the character or main characters end with misfortune) where it reached a state of perfection: comedy (play that has a happy ending and its characters may be humorous), melodrama (has suspense, sensational episodes, and romantic sentiments), acting, ballet, costume and set design, stage machinery, and theatrical structure. Thus, theatre is a Greek invention. Greek drama (a play in prose or verse) is linked to music, dance, and to religion. During the Archaic Age, in the 6th century B.C., theatre in Athens had taken the form of a series of competitive performances presented annually during the Great Dionysia, a religious festival honoring the god Dionysos, god of wine and agricultural fertility celebrated in March. The first staging of the Great Dionysia festival in Athens was about 534 B.C. During the religious festival in March in Athens, participants danced and sang hymns to honor Dionysos. The hymns were performed by a group of singers called a chorus, that means

Figure 3.22 The Odeon of Herodes Atticus—theatre in Athens, Greece. Example of ancient Greco-Roman theatre still in use, based on the ancient Greek theatre. The seating area is carved into the hill, the circular space called the orchestra is where the chorus and actors performed, behind the orchestra was the skene, a long, low building with rooms at either end for dressing and storage, and a platform or stage between the rooms. *Image Copyright krechet, 2009. Used under license from Shutterstock, Inc.*

"dance." The hymns expressed many emotions such as courage, sorrow, solemnity, enthusiasm, etc. The themes of the early choric performance were about religious themes or mythology about Dionysos. At first, the chorus served as both the collective actor and the commentator on the events of the drama. Then, in the late 6th century B.C., according to tradition, the poet Thespis introduced an actor with whom the chorus could interact. Thus the first actor stepped outside the chorus having a dialogue. The theatre was born. Initially, the main function of the actor was simply to ask questions of the chorus. During the Hellenic Age, the number of actors was increased to three, and, occasionally, late in the 5th century B.C., a fourth was added. Now there was dialogue among individuals. In the 5th century B.C., the chorus achieved its classic function as mediator between actors and audience. As time went on, however, the role of the chorus declined and the importance of the actors increased. By the 4th century B.C., the actor had become the focus of the drama.

Theatres were semicircular stadiums cut into natural hills (Figure 3.22). These stadiums had good acoustics, and the audience seated at the top end could easily hear the performers down below. At the base of the hill was the orchestra or circular space (dancing place), where the chorus performed. In the center of the orchestra was a functioning altar, serving as a reminder that tragedy was a religious rite. Behind the orchestra was the stage or platform. In a typical Greek theatre, the audience sat around two-thirds under the open sky. The other third of the orchestra was backed by a wooden or stone building. Tragedies were performed on religious festivals and civic festivals.

By the 5th century B.C. the conflict between human will and passion was in full swing. The subject matter of Greek tragedies concentrated on themes of the human conditions such as struggles, sufferings, weakness, and triumphs of individuals. Dialogues between thinking individuals occurred when the dramatist first placed humans against gods and destiny, later human characters against each other. Thus, Greek tragedy evolved as a continuous striving toward humanizing and greater individuality of its characters, by making them active subjects responsible for their behavior and decisions. If the characters made bad decisions they were punished.

There was no censure in Athens, except for religion. So dramatists had freedom to express their thoughts and criticisms. Politicians, corruption, greed, hypocrisy, and politics were favorite targets of writers of Greek plays. Greek spectators felt intensively involved in the tragedies they saw and talked about them all year long. Theatre became an important part of Greek culture and a major contribution to our Western civilization.

GREEK DEMOCRACY

Democracy as a form of government is one of Greece's greatest legacies to the Western world. The original principles of our form of government were born in Classical Greece.

The idea of consensual government was unknown in the ancient Mediterranean world. The Greeks invented this idea that men should govern themselves according to laws, offices, and institutions that belong to the collective citizenry and not to an individual or elite group; that those in power when their tenure is over surrender peacefully the power they hold to those who are elected to office. This practice typical of contemporary stable and mature democracies, was atypical everywhere else in the ancient Mediterranean world. In Egypt, Israel, and Mesopotamia, power was in the hands of kings, aristocratic or plutocratic (wealthy) elites, priests, and castes. The masses did not have any participation in the political decisions of their societies. Hierarchical bureaucracies were an extension of the king's household, thus all government offices were at the service of the interests, ambitions, and whims of the kings, nobles and priests. Autocratic rule organized men into functioning kingdoms and empires that had order and accomplished great public works such as the Egyptian pyramids. But the common man was not free nor did they determine their fate. In typical Greek fashion the ancient Greeks made solving the problems of governing society, public order, and justice first objects of debate and criticism. In this manner the Greeks initiated a dialogue on human freedom which opened for the Western world to create forms of government that have been widely inclusive and respectful of the rights of mankind. And today this dialogue is still ongoing and has spread to non-Western societies.

HISTORICAL DEVELOPMENT OF DEMOCRACY

The Mycenaean kingdoms (1650–1000 B.C.) were divinely sanctioned by kings and their household bureaucracy controlled political, legal, economic, military, and religious aspects of life. Power was centralized and organized around the king and his bureaucracy. Thus, the Mycenaean resembled Near Eastern kingdoms that existed in antiquity. After the fall of the Mycenaean kingdoms, during the Dark Age (1100–800 B.C.), powerful, noble clans ruled smaller regions with the support of warriors and influenced by councils of aristocratic elders. The power of these rulers was more confined than was the case with the Mycenaean kings. The Greeks from this period apparently learned the dangers and faults of an overly centralized power.

By 650 B.C. the polis or city-state emerged from the Dark Age household and alliances of aristocratic clans with a major contribution of a new class of men in the "middle" who were not aristocratic powerful men but neither poor peasants dependent on wealthy landowners. This "middle class," most probably made up by small farmers who were able to create a certain amount of income with which they could afford to purchase warrior's armor and weapons and become the armored infantryman or hoplite. This hoplite soldier (who employed phalanx fighting highly disciplined units of hoplites with long spears well trained to maneuver in tight formations) depended on collective courage and group cohesion, where each soldier had to performed his duty in the phalanx. These men of the "middle," these hoplites, developed the government of the polis to protect their agrarian interests, promote justice, avoid the dangers of concentration of power and wealth in the hands of a few, as well as the dangers of clan alliances and conflicts. They wanted equality among land-holding citizens. Thus, these men of the middle class interests were in conflict with elites possessing large estates and wealth and who ruled and exploited the masses with little or no political and economical means. From them emerges a new consciousness that justice and rights are not only the prerogative of the few powerful and wealthy, but of all citizens.

ATHENIAN DEMOCRACY

Like other city-states, the Athenians until 750s B.C. had a monarchial form of government. The council of nobles, the Areopagus, gradually stripped the powers of the king. Then the power and wealth of a few grew tremendously resulting in an increasing concentration of wealth. The main agricultural products of that society were olives and vineyards which take a long time to grow and begin to produce. So a farmer must wait several years before he can begin to reap the fruits of his land. Thus, only rich farmers or landed nobility could afford to survive, and the rest had to go into debt to pay for living expenses while they waited to produce. Many lost their land due to debts and some were sold into slavery to pay for their debts. The rich became richer at the expense of the poor.

A crisis occurred and there were many complaints about this situation. So the urban middle class took up the cause of the peasants demanding liberating reforms.

In 594 B.C. all parties agreed to appoint the aristocrat Solon as chief magistrate with absolute powers to carry out reforms. Solon saw hubris, an excessive arrogance that comes from wealth and power, that leads men to be blind to just limits of his actions and this results in greed. Civic order is broken down when justice is perverted to serve the greed of the powerful, and the oppressed react with vengeance and in search of wealth for themselves. Solon found the solution in a political order based on moderation, avoiding the extremes of wealth and poverty which bring about tyranny and anarchy. Based on this idea of the ethic of the mean, Solon reformed the Athenian constitution. Reforms were made to cancel existing mortgages, prohibiting enslavement for debt, and limiting the amount of land one individual could own. His laws and ordinances were common to all men and did not favor nor threaten the wealthy, nor the masses. This focus on moderation reflects the Greek acknowledgement that all men, whether noble or commoners, are subject to powerful passions that can affect their sense of right and justice. The Greeks learned a political lesson, that humans must restrict the amount of power one man, family, or elite group wields, and place this power instead into institutions and offices regulated by law and custom. This may not be perfect, but it reduces the mischief due to the weakness of human character.

But still there was great discontent among the nobles, middle, and poor classes. This chaos brought the first Athenian tyrant in 546 B.C. Peisistratus, who was a benevolent despot making improvements. His successor, his son Hippias, was a ruthless oppressor. Many were unhappy with this tyranny and in 510 B.C. Hippias was overthrown by a group of nobles.

At this point, the Athenians had ended their rule by a king to then fall into a concentration of power and wealth in the hands of a few. They tried to solve this situation by giving power to individuals to make reforms, reforms that never solved the issues completely falling into tyranny.

Cleisthenes, an intelligent aristocrat with support of the masses, attained power and leadership of society bringing a reform of the government. He is known as the "father of Athenian democracy." His reforms consisted of:

1. Full rights to all free men (not including women and slaves) making them citizens, thus enlarging the citizen populations. Here is the idea of citizenship, a civic identity with equal rights and responsibilities and control over public and military authority, which was not dependent on birth, social status, or wealth. The state is identified with its citizens.
2. New council that was the chief organ of government with control over the executive and administrative functions. Members were chosen by lot. Any citizen over 30 years old was eligible to be voted into office.

Athenian democracy attained its full perfection or development with **Pericles** (461–429 B.C.). The main instruments of government of the Athenian democracy were the Assembly, the Council of Five Hundred, the law courts, and the magistrates. The assembly was made up of all the citizens who came to its meeting. During the meetings the most important matters of state were debated and discussed, and motions approved or rejected. Any citizen had the right to speak before the assembly. Therefore, all important decisions were determined or initiated by the votes of the citizens who attended the meetings. Under Pericles the assembly that had the power to ratify and reject proposals of the council, now acquired the authority to initiate legislation. The council determined the matters that were brought before the assembly for a final decision. The council was made up of five hundred citizens selected by lot to serve for a year paid by the state and it was representative of the whole citizenry. Councilmen, state officers, and any citizen could propose matters to the council. Nearly all magistrates were chosen by lot, except for the members of the Board of Ten Generals. The generals were chosen by the assembly for a term of one year and could be reelected indefinitely. Their policies were subject to review by the assembly which could recall their service at the end of one year or be indicted for malfeasance at any time during their service. The Athenian court system reached its maturity as the supreme court was no longer the only court to hear appeals of decisions of the magistrates. There was a large number of popular courts created to try all kinds of cases. Citizens were chosen by lot from different sections of the state to serve as jury for particular trials. Each of these juries constituted a court with power to decide by majority vote for each case. The court was presided over by a magistrate, but the magistrate did not have the authority of a judge. The jury itself had that authority, and the jury's decisions had no appeal. They were representative of all citizens. Each year six thousand citizens were enrolled to select those who would serve as judges and jurors. They heard the cases and decided guilt and innocence, interpreted the law and applied it, and imposed penalties. Most offices of state were opened to the majority of its citizenry by election and by lot. The important issue that we have here is that the citizenry elects its own officials and jury adhering to the principle of majority rule, and there is accountability of those in office to the government during their tenure in office. Decisions come out of rational debate and free choice. Power is not concentrated in the hands of a few or one individual. Equality of all citizens before the law is the best guarantor of justice. These are some of democracy's main characteristics that are part of modern democracies in the West. Adherence to the principle of majority rule showed the confidence in the political capacity of its citizens.

Athenian democracy *differed* from our modern democracies in that in Athens it practiced a **direct democracy.** A direct democracy is when the citizen votes directly on major decisions of government and its laws. It is not a **representative democracy** like our democratic system in which the citizenry vote for representatives who in theory will represent their constituencies by voting in the way their constituencies would vote for a particular issue. The Athenians did not want to be governed by a few men elected as their representative, which they distrusted. They wanted the citizenry to make the decisions; therefore, the assembly of all male citizens met most weeks of the year to vote on all major issues. A direct democracy was possible as a practical form of government in Athens because it was a small city-state that only the free male citizens had participation and voice. In our nation of over 300 million inhabitants, for example, it would be impractical, even impossible, for all citizens to participate with the necessary knowledge to make all our decisions. Thus, our founding fathers decided on creating a representative democracy. Athenian democracy also differed from our modern democracies in that citizenry was restricted only to free males forming a social class. This did not include the majority of the population of Athens that was made up of 230,000 inhabitants and only 40,000 were free males. Modern man owes to the ancient Greeks these ideas of the right to citizenship, hold public office, to debate and vote, and equality before the law, which today have expanded to all humans regardless of sex, ethnicity, and social status allowing to have a more just and free society.

At this point with Pericles the Athenians have solved the issue of unjust and oppressive rule by tyrants and powerful groups by evolving into a new form of government in which all citizens vote for candidates to hold office and on the policies they think are best. They have established the principle of majority rule, and political power has shifted to the common man, and not in the hands of one man or in a small powerful group.

The Greek characteristic of having a critical mind is demonstrated when, after inventing democracy, they also criticize it, searching for its weaknesses or faults. Their critique centers on the extreme egalitarianism of democracy which allows common people (who can be very ignorant, disordered, and wicked) to make up the majority of the votes that determine the decisions made by government. This criticism reflects the idea that some people are better prepared than others to govern, and thus deserve more political power—a position that the aristocratic class held. An example is Theognis of Megara who in the 6th century B.C. was upset with the ascendancy of wealthy non-nobles stating that those who knew nothing of laws, who lived in the countryside far from the city like wild deer are now considered great men and the former nobles rabble. These commoners have no innate wisdom and virtue, and only have money. Xenophon states that democracy allows the unworthy men in birth and character to tyrannize their betters, and more offices are assigned to popular types than to good men. The lyric poet Pindar wrote that "the splendor in the blood has much weight," in other words, that the wisdom and virtue needed to govern well are by nature the inherited qualities of a few due to their blood and family upbringing, while the common low classes lacks these qualities with the disadvantage of ignorance and vice. This critique is found also in the historians Herodotus and in Thucydides, the latter who did not trust the judgment of the masses, and commented that the masses are fine when led by a good leader like Pericles, but when influenced by unscrupulous leaders it ends all in disaster.

Socrates was the most famous Greek to scorn the opinion of the majority or masses without proper knowledge that only a few possessed. How can the uneducated masses incapable of rational arguments and decisions be competent to participate in government, especially through debate and discussion in the assembly? Can the masses, driven by emotion rather than reason, and therefore easily manipulated by orators and demagogues, see the truth and what is just? Thus, Socrates argues that the fundamental principal of Athenian democracy, that the many are capable of effective participation in government, is a folly. Plato and Aristotle rejected the radical egalitarianism of democracy that assumed that every citizen had the right to participate in government. This extreme egalitarianism denies the natural hierarchies of talent, virtues, abilities and upbringing that all societies have among its members. This imposition of equality to equals and unequals alike constitutes an injustice that corrupts the public life to the lowest denominator. Plato favors a more just equality that recognizes the natural differences of talent and achievement, which gives more to the best and less to the inferior in proportion to the nature of each. Thus, merit is the measure to determine how much power and participation a citizen may have in his government.

The orator Isocrates in the middle of the 4th century B.C. criticized democracy's radical egalitarianism because it trained the citizen to think that lawlessness equals freedom, disrespect, and arrogance as democracy, rude boldness of speech as equality, and license to do what they pleased as happiness. Therefore, this unnatural equality leads to licentiousness and disorder.

These Greek thinkers are all critical of Athenian radical democracy which leads to absolute freedom for the masses which is dangerous because human nature is subject to strong passions and appetites that are self-destructive, and promotes radical individualism that fosters an amoral relativism that seeks pleasure and wealth by any possible means. Thus the need for constant vigilance, and social and political constraints. These limitations need to be enforced by men of superior values and moral character belonging to an elite by either birth or superior education. Does our present modern Western society which has exalted both extreme egalitarianism and appetitive indulgence suffer from the defects that these ancient Greeks criticized in democracy and democratic man?

Both sides of this issue, favoring and criticizing the democratic form of government, have their merit. History demonstrates that concentration of power and wealth in the hands of a few allows for corruption, exploitation, and injustice, but power in the hands of the majority or common man to make decisions when the masses are not enlightened, with not enough education or moral fiber, especially when persuaded by demagogues can lead to corruption, mob rule, and tyranny. After all the fascist dictator Adolph Hitler was elected under a democratic government by the majority of the German citizens in 1932, and what was the result of it in the end? Therefore, both sides have their worth, and the best lies somewhere in the middle, or as the Greeks would have it the mean or moderation is best. The lesson we can draw from the Greeks and history is that democracy is a good and legitimate form of government, but it needs an educated and responsible citizenry with good moral character who is capable of making the best decisions at least most of the time. This is a main reason why modern democracies have a major interest in a good public system of education for all citizens that instills in its students critical thinking, and fosters the moral fiber of its citizens. These are very necessary elements for society to have an upright and responsible working democracy.

The legacy of the Hellenic or Classical Greek civilization, Athenian democracy, served as the exciting teacher of its citizens, and was the envy of most of the other Greek poleis. After the fall of Greece to Macedonia, however, the idea of democracy fell into disrepute. Almost 2,000 years passed before some in Europe were ready to give democracy a second chance.

GREEK FREEDOM

The ancient Greeks invented the idea of freedom. This is a major value the West tradition has inherited from the ancient Greeks. Its development through history has provided Western man today to have a level of personal and political freedom that has no precedent in history. This Greek invention was based on principle, that is, freedom as an ideal, versus de facto freedom that derives from simple societies that are not organized enough to impose limitations on males who have the use of arms. The latter consists of a society's independence from the dominion from another. This is typical of Homer's warriors such as Achilles and Hector who defend their freedom and protect their families and property by the force of arms. The Greeks conceived freedom in various dimensions. They distinguished between: **civic** freedom, the freedom of citizens to participate in public life and political institutions; **personal** freedom, the freedom of the individual to live as he pleases with a minimum of external restraint and; **philosophical** freedom, based on the use of reason in a suitable manner. It held that the rational control of man's passions and appetites creates the only true freedom. Reason allows man to choose what is best.

Personal freedom is a natural freedom enjoyed by male warriors who used force. Civic and philosophical freedoms were conceived only by the Greeks. Everywhere else in the ancient Mediterranean and

Middle East freedom was the privilege of elite classes with the king or pharaoh who enjoyed complete freedom. For this reason, many Greeks considered the masses under these ruling elites and autocrats as slaves. Civic freedom was derived from laws, constitutions, and institutions that determined the rules and procedures to govern and protect the individual citizen's autonomy. Democracy was based on the equal right to rule and participate in public life and government. The Greeks believed in the freedom of speech both in their personal and political life. Politically, it consisted of the right to address the assembly. They also valued freedom of expression which is clearly obvious in the liberty given to dramatists, especially those who wrote comedy, to be free to write about sensitive political issues and to criticize the polis, its policies and politicians, corruption, philosophy, and drama itself. Any public figure, whether political or not, was fair game for caricature and abuse. Something that was not allowed in ancient societies, and not even in some modern ones, was anyone who dared to criticize would be sent to jail or executed.

But the Greeks' inventors of freedom were also critical of its excesses, just as they were of the excesses of democracy. Socrates, Plato, Isocrates, and others criticize the idea of personal freedom to live as one likes because it fostered egocentric license and indulgence of man's passions, appetites, and whims to the detriment of society and body politic. They saw the danger of unrestrained freedom that will result in the slavery of tyranny when the masses attached to their anarchic freedom and disdaining the good advice of the wiser men, will sell their political rights to any demagogue who promises to suppress the better men or highly educated elites and leave the masses' appetites and passions unrestrained.

HELLENISTIC CIVILIZATION

The word **Hellenic** means Greek or purely Greek. **Hellenistic** means Greek-like or similar to the Greek. From the Hellenic or Greek civilization a new civilization spread from Greece into what was the entire Persian Empire from 323 B.C. to the 1st century A.D. or beginning of the Christian era.

The Greek civilization had weakened itself due to the continuous wars between the Greek city-states. These city-states with their arrogance, competitiveness, distrust of one another and ambitions had been at war from 431 to 338 B.C. that left them worn out from a military and political point of view. This permitted Philip of Macedon, a semi-barbarian chieftain from the north of Greece to move down in Greece and defeat the Athenian-Theban force in battle in 338 B.C. This left Philip as king of all of Greece with no opposition. Philip was then assassinated due to a family feud in 336 B.C. which left his son Alexander (356–323 B.C.) on the throne at the age of 20. Alexander took control and quickly established his autocratic rule over all Greece by putting to death all his rivals by 334 B.C. Then he was secure enough to leave Greece under a trusted deputy while he crossed into Asia with his army of 40,000 men. Alexander fought the Persian emperor and defeated him taking over his entire empire that included Asia Minor (today Turkey), Egypt, Syria, Mesopotamia, and Persia (today Iran). Then Alexander with his insatiable ambition to conquer the world marched into east into Bactria (today Afghanistan) and into India. Finally, his troops tired of fighting and far from home decided to return and Alexander had to return to Persia. He died in Babylon in 323 B.C. from an infectious disease not quite 33 years of age. Conquering such a vast empire, the largest of his day, in roughly a decade and leaving a new civilization behind earned him the title in history of Alexander the Great.

Alexander the Great laid the foundation of the Hellenistic civilization which was a hybrid of Greek and Asian culture. Alexander married and had his generals and troops marry local women of the lands he conquered. His policy was to merge different people and cultures in a single empire living in peace. This also became the Roman Empires ideal. Stoicism, Epicureanism, Cynicism, and Skepticism were the philosophies during this period that were discussed earlier. Greek philosophy and literature were cultivated in western Asia. Greek became the language of government in Egypt, Mesopotamia, and Syria. But Alexander and the Greeks wore oriental fashions and the Greek rulers had themselves adored as divinities which was an Asian tradition and not Greek. These are examples of the merging of cultures in this civilization that developed its own distinctive traits. After Alexander's death his vast empire was divided among his generals. Thus, the unity of the empire ceased and new kingdoms under Greek rulers continued with this Hellenistic culture, such as Egypt that came to be ruled by a Greek dynasty from which Cleopatra originated until Egypt was conquered by the Roman Julius Caesar.

In conclusion, we find one unique characteristic of the ancient Greeks that explains more than anything else their innovative brilliance and that is their critical spirit. They made all things they found in life an object of thought to be discussed and analyzed without the interference of pagan religion and the ruling class or monarchs. Their ability to think in an abstract and rational manner, to question, to discuss, to explain human existence rationally and with logical consistency is what allowed them to pioneer other intellectual achievements such as logic, physics, criticism, history, philosophy, rhetoric, dialogue, dialectic, analysis, tragedy, and many sciences. This critical consciousness and freedom to discuss it in public is what makes the Greeks different from the rest of the ancient world. We owe to these Greeks the invention of democracy, political freedom, free inquiry, the idea of the middle class, citizen militias, language of abstraction and rationalism, systematic thinking, literature separated from religion and theatre. The West owes to these ingenious Greeks a great influence in the arts and architecture, as well as in Olympic sports competitions.

The beginning of Western intellectual history is found in the Greek civilization. It achieved the triumph of philosophy to an extent with Plato and Aristotle in the 4th century B.C., which was its glory. Plato arrived an understanding in a speculative manner of the existence of god, the freedom of the will, and immortality of the soul. The idea of virtue that he defined as the order and harmony of the soul is essential to happiness, and makes up part of his ethical doctrines. Aristotle had the greatest influence upon Western civilization and is credited for providing the building blocks of the scholastic philosophy of the Middle Ages. His great range of learning formed the groundwork for studies in metaphysics, logic, ethics, psychology, rhetoric, botany, zoology, etc.

Yet the Greeks' speculative theories were never able to solve and overcome the final moral decay the Greek civilization succumbed to. Their philosophies never came to formulate any moral code to restrain the increasingly vice-ridden behavior of their citizens, nor did they arrive at the worship of God, the creator, giver of a moral code, as the Hebrews and later Christians did. This lack of moral code was an important missing element that may have helped the Greeks avoid or overcome their proud and quarrelsome character which led to constant conflicts that wore them out at the end, and their moral vices. Many historians see them as the main cause of the decay of Greek culture from the decline from the traditional institutions, especially a very basic one in any society, the family bond, who found their pleasure with women of the streets (Corinth was famous for its prostitutes or courtesans), and in many cases with other men. The practice of abortion and infanticide (newborns were inspected in Sparta and those found not fit for future military life (boys) or to raise a family (girls) were thrown off a cliff) further damaged family life. Whatever positive came out of Plato and Aristotle was obscured later by the Stoics, Epicureans, and Cynics of the 3rd century A.D. who did not solve the decadence Greeks fell into and did not attempt to correct the conflict between man's reason and his animal nature. Thus ancient Greece was an artistic success, with a certain amount of intellectual success, but a moral failure in the end.

SUMMARY

The ancient Greeks took a considerable amount of their cultural heritage from Mesopotamia and Egypt, but also absorbed much from the early Aegean cultures of the Cycladic, Minoan, and Mycenaean civilizations. Little is known about the Cycladic. The Minoans were a prosperous people who had the greatest trading empire of their time. It was a peaceful and sophisticated culture as demonstrated by its architecture and art. They had a secure good life with a high standard of living. Trade helped develop a well-off middle class. Their culture was one of enjoying life in a peaceful and refined manner and not one based on strength and warfare. Their period of balance was from 2000–1628 B.C. A volcanic eruption on the nearby island Thera (today Santorini) produced a tidal wave that devastated their civilization, and the Mycenaean invasion of 1450 B.C. ended it. Minoans then had to adapt to Mycenaean rule.

The Mycenaean city-states were a warrior society whose center of life was the heroic warrior. The heroic ideal was personified in Homer's warrior-aristocrat Achilles. The Mycenaean produced the traditional heroic tales that Homer (about 750–710 B.C.) wove into his famous epic poems the *Iliad* and the *Odyssey,* that later generations have romanced.

Religion was not organized; therefore, it had no hierarchical priests. Neither did they have divine kings. Consequently they had freedom from a centralized dominant religion like those in Mesopotamia and Egypt and this led to greater freedom than any other ancient culture, to think independently and to question and discuss all aspects of life. This freedom allowed the Greek to invent philosophy, the love of wisdom or the pursuit of truth, beauty, and justice. Religion during the Dark Ages was a means to explain the world, nature, and human nature with its passions. The gods and goddesses were seen as an imaginative way of representing the forces of nature and later as symbolizing abstracts ideas such as power, thought, civilized living, love, lust, anger, and fine craftsmanship. Greeks had no conception of sin and no code of ethics to follow and be judged by in the afterlife. This allowed them to decide freely their lifestyle, and they were highly optimistic and egotistic. Athenians valued optimism or the belief that anything and everything could be achieved or at least attempted. They were also the greatest humanists of their time placing man at the center of the universe; even their gods were anthropomorphic.

The most famous poet of Greek epic literature was Homer with his epic poems the *Iliad* and the *Odyssey* composed during the Archaic Age. The events and heroes belong to the Mycenaean Age. The *Iliad* is the story of Achilles and the Trojan War, the *Odyssey* of Odysseus and his return voyage home from the war with Troy. The historical importance of Homeric literature is due to its great influence upon all of ancient Greek culture. It provided the cultural unity of what was otherwise independent and quarreling Greek city-states. It helped shape the Greek spirit and mythology by providing stories and portraits of immortal deities that remained in the minds of the Greeks. Homer had a humanistic outlook that was characteristic of the Greek civilization in which he placed humans at the center of his poems with anthropomorphic gods that intervene in men's life. His characters provide role models for the Greeks and these two poems became centerpieces of Greek education, thus his major influence upon later Greek culture, and even upon modern writers to date. He even shaped the Greek language.

In the late Archaic Age lyric poetry became the dominant literary expression and it has influenced Western poetry ever since. In contrast to the epic, it expressed the author's personal view and feelings. Sappho was very famous for her solo lyrics.

Systematical thinking was a Greek invention. It consisted of understanding reality as a unified whole, analyzing all its parts and how they relate to one another in an orderly manner. This systematic, and abstract or theoretical way of thinking, with the application of the principal of exclusion will lead the Greeks to begin to develop science as the attempt to understand nature with objective knowledge and not relying on myths. Having great freedom due to the non-authoritarian character of their religion, and not having autocratic and divine rules, allowed the Greeks to question, discuss freely, and come to their own natural conclusions. This allowed the Greeks to invent philosophy and break out of the "mythical thinking box." They became rational, logical thinkers. Their search for natural explanations of the physical world led them to invent theoretical science.

The first philosopher was Thales of the Milesian philosophical school. His great contribution was to attempt to explain the physical world through natural explanation, and not employing any myths. The Greeks at this stage are using intuition in an orderly or systematical manner to arrive at explanations.

Herakleitos came up with the idea of the logos as the guiding force that kept the constant process of change following a natural order. Today this topic is, in a way, discussed in the modern concept of "Intelligent Design." Democritus came up with the concept of the atom as the smallest particle that make up all matter and that modern science has proven to be correct. Therefore, these ancient Greek were into topics that modern Western man still discusses and are debated today. With Pythagoras Greek philosophy takes a metaphysical direction, thus getting into what today we consider the field of philosophy. He was much involved with mathematics. The Sophists brought about an intellectual revolution with their highly individualistic and relativist philosophy that denied that men could know absolute truths, and that eternal standards exist. The threat they posed was that this way of thinking led to complete relativism and skepticism over all authority in society and government. This would lead to anarchy, consequently strong opposition arose from conservative Greeks. A new philosophical movement that stood upon the idea and belief that absolute standards exist began with Socrates, and continued with Plato and Aristotle, the three greatest Greek philosophers to influence the West from antiquity to the present.

Socrates believed in an eternal universal valid knowledge for all mankind. The Socratic or dialectic method of questioning was his means to attain this true knowledge so man could have the virtue to make the correct decisions that lead to happiness. Happiness is Socrates' goal of the good life. Socrates' student, Plato, followed his teacher and developed the doctrine of ideas or forms. This doctrine held that there exists a spiritual dimension made up of ideas or forms that man can only perceive with his mind, and the physical world that man perceives through his senses are imperfect copies of ideas or forms. Plato's political philosophy was written in his Republic where harmony and efficiency were the goals of the ideal state. He divided the population into three groups according to their inclination in life. The state should be governed solely by the highest class, an intellectual aristocracy or philosopher kings. This aristocracy had the proper knowledge so they could make the best decision that would lead to a happy society. Aristotle agreed with Socrates and Plato, but for Aristotle reality was made up of both the spiritual and physical dimensions. All physical objects and living beings are shaped by the ideas or forms, and both dimensions need each other to exist, and thus their unity and equal importance. Aristotle gave importance to both mind and the physical world that includes the human body. He conceived god as a first cause, as pure intelligence. In his *Politics,* Aristotle's political philosophy conceives man as a social animal that needs society and the state to be civilized and develop its full potential, thus the state is necessary to have a good life. The best state was a polity that is governed by a large middle class avoiding the extremes of an oligarchy that concentrates power in a few and a democracy that can turn into the tyranny of the many. Socrates, Plato, and Aristotle were critical of Athenian democracy because the masses that voted did not possess the sufficient knowledge to make the best decisions. The philosophies of Plato and Aristotle will be utilized later by Christian thinkers, thus preserving them and allowing them to influence the West.

The four major schools of philosophy during the Hellenistic civilization were Stoicism, Epicureanism, Cynics, and Skeptics. Stoics believed the universe consists of an ordered reality that works at the end for the ultimate good. This order is not escapable, it is destiny. The wise man understands this fate and knows what his duty is to this good universal order. Their goal is to attain serenity of the mind through self-discipline and fulfilling one's duty. It is not about reforming society which brings more chaos than good. Epicureanism believed that the highest good in life was to seek pleasure and avoid pain as much as possible. It had a utilitarian attitude to life and was not concerned about justice or to reform society to conform to true morality. Serenity of the soul is considered the highest pleasure. The cynics were critical and frustrated with society in general that led them to an antisocial attitude. True freedom was renouncing desires and their goal was self-sufficiency. The skeptics, similar to the relativist Sophists, believed no truth can be certain; therefore, no absolute concept of what is right or wrong can be attained by man. Happiness comes from not pursuing absolute truth, which allows man to not worry about good versus evil attaining peace of mind. These four philosophical movements did not offer any real solutions to the social problems of their era, nor how to change society for the better.

Even with all its flaws and limited resources, Greek civilization produced intellectual and cultural achievements that have served as models to imitate and set standards to be achieved by Western culture. They were also the greatest and most humanistic culture in that point in history that placed man at the center of life. They had the freedom to excel in a society that valued and rewarded excellence, which generated great motivation for achievement in many fields. Classical Greek culture had these characteristics, arête or the pursuit of excellence, idealism, economy of style, and amateurism. Greek art expressed humanism, glorifying and placing man at the center of the universe. It was an expression of national life, with a political goal of civic pride and unity among citizens of the city-state. Their art was universal depicting human types, not individuals. Its ethical purpose was to ennoble humanity, and to express the human ideal of perfection. Classical art was idealistic, not realistic.

The history of Greek art developed through three periods, the Archaic, Classical, and Hellenistic. Architecture is dominated by post-and-lintel construction. The three orders of styles were Doric, ionic, and briefly toward the end the Corinthian. Proportion of building was achieved using mathematical proportions. Greek sculpture was borrowed from ancient Egypt with its rigid, squared figures that have no expression of emotions in their faces. Through time the Greeks moved toward naturalism with sculptures that have more real life appearance or a "natural look."

The Greeks created theater with its tragedy, comedy, and melodrama. It began with religious festivals to honor the god Dionysius by dancing and singing hymns. The themes were about Dionysius and mythology. Then actors were introduced, and from mythology the themes dealt with humans and gods and finally humans and their lives. There was no censorship so subjects were open as long as religion was respected.

Athens invented democracy. Its small farmer was a middle class which made up the majority of free men who had a conflict of interest with the aristocratic wealthy elites. This conflict led to complaints and all parties agreed to appoint the aristocrat Solon to carry out reforms. Solon's reforms focused on moderation, restricting the power and wealth of the very rich, placing law above political and economic power. Still there was discontent, even with improvements by the benevolent despot Peisistratus. Then a popular aristocrat, Cleisthenes, reformed the government becoming the "father of Athenian democracy" by creating citizens with full rights given to all free men, and governed by a council whose members were chosen by lot and open to all citizens both poor and wealthy. Under the leadership of Pericles, Athenian democracy attained its full development with the Assembly, Council of Five Hundred, law courts, and magistrates. Their democracy functioned by the principle of majority rule and it practiced a direct democracy, not a representative democracy as modern democratic nations have today.

Some Greeks, such as Socrates, Plato, and Aristotle, criticized democracy's flaws that are found in its extreme egalitarianism because Athenian democracy is based on the principle of majority rule, and therefore an ignorant and poorly led majority can vote for bad decisions making big mistakes that affect the entire city-state. They argued better educated and virtuous men are better capable and should make the important decisions, or at least their voices or votes should have more weight. With the masses emotion prevails, with the educated reason prevails.

There are three kinds of freedom: personal, civic, and philosophical. The Greeks invented civic freedom, the freedom of citizens to participate in public life and political institutions such as in democratic Athens; and philosophical freedom, the freedom to learn and use reason to choose what is best and control man's passions. Philosophical freedom was the most critical freedom allowing for the unrestrained pursuit of knowledge in a society that valued learning for its own sake.

CHAPTER 4

THE HEBREW CIVILIZATION

HISTORY OF THE HEBREWS

The Hebrews had an extraordinary historical importance and legacy for Western civilization despite their political insignificance among the great empires of Mesopotamia and Egypt. The Hebrews exerted the greatest influence of any ancient peoples of the Middle East and Egypt on the thought and life of the modern Western world. The first time that the Hebrews appear in history they are in Mesopotamia and are members of the Semitic language family. They were originally a wandering pastoral people. Their nomadic beginnings make it difficult to locate their exact origin. According to the Bible, the Hebrew patriarch **Abraham** was from Sumer. From about 1900 to 1500 B.C., the Hebrews gradually migrated from Mesopotamia to southern Syria known as Canaan, and from there to Egypt. During this period of time a tribe of Hebrews who claimed decent from the grandson of Abraham, Jacob, began to call themselves **"Israelites"** after Jacob's alternate name. **Israel** means "soldier of God" and in the Book of Genesis in the Old Testament received the name Israel for wrestling with an angel for a whole night. Joseph, one of Jacob's younger sons who had the ability to foretell the future by interpreting dreams, was sold by his older jealous brothers to a caravan as a slave. The caravan took Joseph to Egypt. In Egypt Joseph's ability to interpret dreams reached the ears of the pharaoh who had a recurring dream that he nor anyone else could explain. Joseph explained to the pharaoh his dream about a coming future seven-year famine and the pharaoh placed Joseph in charge of the granary of his kingdom, a very important post. This allowed Joseph to prepare Egypt to face the future famine. During the period of famine the Hebrews moved to Egypt which had plenty of grain and stayed to live there, with the support of Joseph, thus uniting Joseph with his family. After the dynasty of the Hyksos, the Hebrews were then enslaved by the new native Egyptian dynasty that wanted to expand as an empire and needed slaves to keep the economy running. Around 1250 B.C. (some scholars disagree with this date and place it about 1500s B.C.) **Moses** becomes the leader and hero of the Hebrew people. Moses has to overcome the strong will of the pharaoh who wants to keep the Hebrews as forced labor building his monumental projects and rejects Moses' pleas to let his people leave Egypt. Moses warns the pharaoh of plagues that his God will send if he keeps the Hebrews in bondage and Egypt suffers various plagues that ultimately force the pharaoh to give in and allow the Hebrews to leave. Moses leads them out of bondage from native Egypt into the Sinai Peninsula (a desert territory between Egypt and Canaan) in what is known as the **exodus.** When Moses is leading his people out of Egypt they reach the Red Sea and they see the Egyptian army in chariots charging toward them. Moses then turns to God and the waters of the sea part to make a path and allow the Hebrew nation to escape to the other side. When the Hebrew reach the other side in safety and the chariots chase them through the parted waters Moses has the waters flow back to their normal course drowning the entire army. (Some have challenged the veracity of this event in the Old Testament indicating it is a fictional story or part of the Hebrew religious-national myth. In 1978, the explorer Ron Wyatt discovered at the bottom of the Red Sea numerous archaeological pieces—wheels of Egyptian carriages, armors, carriage parts, and human and equine (horse) skeletons incrusted on the corals—these findings demonstrate the passage of the Jewish people according to those who support the Biblical version of the exodus. Later immersions brought to light a greater quantity of objects, from the Egyptian side as of that of Saudi Arabia. Waytt showed his finds to the director of Antiquities of the Museum of Cairo, Dr. Nassif Mohammed Asan, who after an exhaustive analysis, came to the conclusion that these items were dated of the epoch of Ramsés and Tutmosis, that is to say, the XVIII and XIXth dynasties.) Moses persuaded his people to become worshippers of **Yahweh,** the name given to God of the Bible and later on written **Jehovah.** At this point the Hebrews become Israelites because Moses convinced them that Yahweh was the God of Abraham, Isaac, and Jacob, and therefore the God of Israel was the God now worshiped by them all.

After wandering in the Sinai deserts for about a generation, the Hebrews under **Joshua** moved back into the richer lands of Canaan that were occupied now by the Canaanites, another people of the Semitic language. The Canaanites were not willing to share their land with the newcomers so the Hebrews had to fight their way into Canaan. This was a long, difficult venture and after Joshua, the Hebrews lost their ability to pursue a united military action due to the revival of tribal rivalries. Therefore, they only gained some of Canaan's less fertile lands.

Then the Philistines, a non-Semitic people from Asia Minor who conquered most of Canaan about 1050 B.C., and gave the land the name of **Palestine** or Philistine country, invaded the Hebrew territory. Up to this point the Hebrews had been organized in a tribal form with **judges** or wise men who led their people during difficult times. The Hebrews under this new threat of the Philistines were faced with survival and they decided they needed a tighter national form of government to meet this external challenge. They saw how other nations around them had established kingdoms with their governments and military power, and the Hebrews wanted the same kind of political and military strength. The Hebrews demanded to have a monarchy. **Samuel,** a tribal judge and a prophet, that announced messages from God, with the force of personality to gain the adherence of all the Israelite tribes, selected for the Hebrews a king. Samuel anointed the first king, **Saul,** to indicate that the new sovereign was the prince chosen by God over His chosen people. Under King Saul the Hebrews became a united people marking the **beginning of national unity,** or the **United Monarchy.** Saul then attacked the Philistines using guerrilla tactics of ambush and deception obtaining victories. According to the Bible, confident due to his victories, Saul gave in to his arrogant and headstrong nature and became ungrateful and disobedient to God. He did not follow Samuel who expressed the will of God. Thus, Samuel became angered when his influence was disregarded by the king. Samuel totally abandoned Saul, and told the unrepentant king that because he rejected the word of God, God would reject him and give the kingdom to another king. Saul then suffered reverses against the enemy and with his melancholic temperament Saul began to suffer from bouts of depression and irritability. Samuel then travelled to Bethlehem to anoint secretly a young shepherd, thus establishing the royal seat of power in Judea from which later Jesus Christ will descend. **David** was the young warrior that Samuel supported energetically. David had musical abilities and was sent to the court of Saul to play music to soothe the increasing depression of the king (Figure 4.1). When Saul brought David with him to battle as his armor bearer, David was the only one who dared meet the challenge from the giant at the service of the Philistine. David killed him with his sling by sending a stone to his head and then decapitated the giant. The Philistines then left the battlefield. David's popularity and prestige rose as Saul's sank, falling deeper into his bad moods. Saul came to resent David and tried to kill him with a lance, and David fled from his court. David ran his own military campaigns achieving one victory after another, while Saul's forces were failing. In 1005 B.C. Saul was seriously wounded when he decided to confront the enemy in a pitched battle that was lost including the lives of his three sons. In despair Saul killed himself with his sword.

David then became king and initiated the most glorious period in Hebrew political history. He was able to unite all the 12 tribes into one kingdom and subdued the Philistines, the Syrians of Damascus and the troublesome Bedouin tribes. The crown of his military victories was the capture of Jerusalem, the last stronghold of the Canaanites. Jerusalem became the capital of the united kingdom of Israel. David was also a good administrator and under his rule the kingdom of Israel achieved its greatest extent of his power and its highest degree of organization it ever had in ancient times. The Canaanites had to recognize his rule and in the following generations lost their identity and merged with the Hebrew people. The Hebrews put aside pastoralism and took up farming or urban occupations. David as king obtained forced labor from his subjects and collected taxes after establishing a census. His goal was to build a splendid capital and religious center at Jerusalem and he began this large enterprise. But he died before it was completed in 972 B.C.

King **Solomon** succeeded David. He ruled from 973–933 B.C. becoming the last of the three great kings of the Hebrew monarchy. Solomon wanted to finish his father's work of building Jerusalem. He wanted a capital to be on the level as the other kingdoms which all had their capital, and he wanted to build a splendid temple to house the **"Ark of the Covenant"** that was the biblical chest that contained the tablets with the Ten Commandments that the Bible has Yahweh handing them down to Moses at Mount Sinai (Figure 4.2). The ark had been carried by the Hebrews in a "tabernacle" or tent when they wandered around, and now Solomon wanted a temple to house it. Solomon succeeded in his goal to build this lavish temple, but it created problems because Palestine was poor in building materials, gold and gems to adorn it (Figure 4.3).

Figure 4.1 King David, Jerusalem. *Image Copyright Colman Lerner Gerardo, 2009. Used under license from Shutterstock, Inc.*

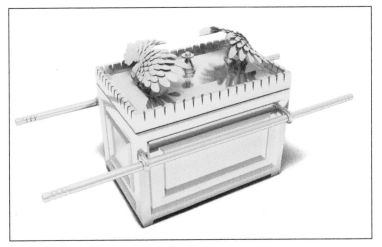

Figure 4.2 Ark of the Covenant. *Image Copyright Nip, 2009. Used under license from Shutterstock, Inc.*

Solomon had oppressive taxation to finance this expensive project, and not being able to pay the construction debts he ceded territory to his main supplier Phoenicia to the north and drafted and deported Hebrews to work in Phoenicia forests and mines.

Figure 4.3 Model of Jerusalem. Detail of the Temple finished by King Solomon. *Image Copyright Stasys Eidiejus, 2009. Used under license from Shutterstock, Inc.*

Figure 4.4 Sack of Jerusalem Temple by Rome. Arch of Titus. Romans carrying the Hebrew Menorah from the Temple as spoils of conquest. *Image Copyright Eduard Cebria, 2009. Used under license from Shutterstock, Inc.*

The tyrannical measures of Solomon provoked a bitter antagonism among his subjects. The northern part of the kingdom was the most affected by these harsh measures because this sector saw many young men sent to Phoenicia and were the least sympathetic to the building projects of Jerusalem that was located more on the southern part. While Solomon was alive his northern subjects remained obedient to the king, but after his death they revolted by refusing to pay taxes to his son Rehoboam. The northerners seceded from the united Hebrew state and set up their own kingdom of Israel, while the south became the Kingdom of Judah with its capital in Jerusalem. This split weakened the once united kingdom that never had the strength of surrounding empires. The Kingdom of Israel managed to exist for another two centuries, paying tribute to dominate neighbors until 722 B.C., when it was conquered by the Assyrians who had a policy of leveling all buildings and scattering populations of the conquered (Figure 4.4). Thus, the Kingdom of Israel was heard of no more. The Kingdom of Judah managed to exist until 586 B.C. when it was conquered by the Babylonians under Nebuchadnezzar, who burnt and plundered Jerusalem and the temple. The Babylonians deported the leading citizens to Babylon. The Judeans suffered the "Babylonian Captivity" for half a century, and from this point historians refer to them as **Jews.** In 539 B.C. Cyrus the Persian conquered Babylon and generously let the Jews return to their homeland ending the captivity.

The Jews returned to Palestine and were semi-independent under Persian overlordship. From 520 to 516 B.C. the Jews rebuilt the temple in Jerusalem and lived in relative peace under the Persians until 332 B.C. when Palestine was conquered by the **Greek, Alexander the Great** (Figure 4.5). After Alexander's death the Jews were under the rule of successive Greek-speaking overlords (Figure 4.6). The Seleucid Empire, a successor state of Alexander the Great's empire, ruled at the time over the Hebrews, and Antiochus IV Epiphanes was its emperor. He marched his army into Jerusalem and began the first religious persecution in the history of the Greco-Roman world. The Greek Antiochus Epiphanes in 168 B.C. attempted to destroy the Jewish faith, by desecrating the temple and prohibiting all worship in it. When he seized the temple an idol was set and dedicating the temple to this pagan deity with the sacrifice of a pig, thus mocking the Jews, who believed the pig to be unclean and therefore never to be used in sacrifice. Antiochus' soldiers went throughout the land setting up altars with idols and sacrificing pigs in all the towns and villages. People were ordered to participate in the sacrifice and eat the pig's meat. The death penalty was imposed on those who kept Hebrew worship and practiced it. Many Jews apostatized to their faith to avoid punishment and others did not heed and were

Figure 4.5 Alexander the Great immortalized in bronze relief. *Image Copyright Brigida Soriano/Shutterstock.com*

martyred. In 166 B.C. Greek army soldiers came to the town of Modein to set up an altar and sacrifice a pig. When the soldiers demanded all inhabitants to participate in the pagan ritual, a priest called Mathathias refused because he was loyal to God. A villager then offered to do the sacrifice. Mathathias would not allow this blasphemy to occur and attacked the villager, then turned on the commander of the soldiers. The villagers then rose up and killed the entire group of soldiers. Judas, one of the five sons of Mathathias, nicknamed Maccabeus (the hammer), took up the leadership of his people against the retaliation of the Greeks. The brothers became known as the *Maccabees*. Because the Jews were weak militarily, Judas fought a guerilla warfare. Under **Judas Maccabeus** the Jews attained many victories, and by 164 B.C. most of the Holy Land came under their control and they cleansed and reconsecrated the temple (Figure 4.7). In commemoration of this event an eight-day celebration called *Hanukka*

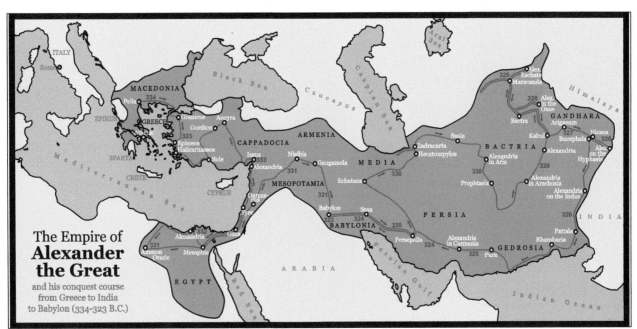

Figure 4.6 Egypt, Macedonia, Mesopotamia and Babylonia were some the regions conquered by Alexander the Great. *Image Copyright Peter Hermes Furian/Shutterstock.com*

would be kept every year. Later Judas and three of his brothers died in the struggle without a complete victory. After 20 years of struggle the Jews, under the leadership of the last Maccabean brother, Simon, managed to become independent of the Greeks in 141 B.C. The Jews then had Simon proclaimed leader and high priest, and enjoyed their independence under the Maccabean dynasty. Then in 63 B.C. the Roman general Pompey took advantage of the internal feuding of the dynasty to take over Palestine and turn it into a Roman protectorate. In 66 A.D. the Jews revolted against the Romans, but were unable to overcome the mightiest of all ancient empires and lost. The Jews, never content under the Romans who were pagans, revolted in 70 A.D. and Emperor Titus put down the uprising in

Figure 4.7   Judas Maccabeus Pursuing Timotheus - Picture from The Holy Scriptures, Old and New Testaments books collection published in 1885, Stuttgart-Germany. Drawings by Gustave Dore. *Image Copyright Nicku/Shutterstock.com*

a very harsh manner and razed the Temple of Jerusalem which has never been rebuilt. Many Jews were taken as slaves by the Romans who annexed Palestine to their empire. Many of these Jewish slaves were employed in building the Coliseum in Rome. Jews gradually left for other parts of the vast Roman Empire. This migration of Jews from Palestine to other countries through the centuries is known as the **diaspora,** becoming a central fact of Jewish existence from then until the 20th century when the modern state of Israel was created.

HEBREW CIVILIZATION

The Hebrews are important because they exerted the greatest influence of all people of the Middle East on the thought and life of the Western World. Think of the Old Testament, of the Ten Commandments. We find the basis of our morals, ethics, and laws of Western culture and legal systems in these commandments.

The **Hebrews** or **Jews** are Semitic people (related to the Arabs of today) who lived out of raising herds. They were pastoral and nomadic. They came out of city of UR in Middle East, and settled in Canaan under Abraham. The Hebrews were not united completely because they were divided into tribes who were related by kingship. Each tribe had a patron god. After the Egyptian Exodus with Moses, Monotheism is established as a native cult about 1250 B.C. It is obvious with the first of the Ten Commandments given to Moses by God that commands thou shall have no other gods but Yahweh.

HEBREW RELIGIOUS DEVELOPMENT

The religion of the Hebrews or Jews is *Judaism,* based on the Old Testament. Judaism is a product of a long process of change between the time of Moses to the time of Judas Maccabeus 1250 B.C.–150 B.C. Judaism has:

Four Stages of Growth

1. *Polytheistic stage* (pagan) Hebrews worshiped many gods, like other Asian people.
2. *National Monolatry*–1250 B.C. with Moses to 750 B.C. Monolatry is the exclusive worship of only one god, but without denying that other gods exist. With Moses the Jews worship exclusively "Yahweh," pronounced "Yahweh" and written "Yhwh" (Figure 4.8).

Yahweh was not omnipotent because his power was limited to the land occupied by the Hebrews. He had human-like characteristics, therefore the Hebrews conceived God in anthropomorphic terms. God could be good, or be angered and give harsh punishments. As an example is the priest Uzza, who was struck dead when he placed his hand on Ark of the Covenant to steady it as it was being transported to Jerusalem violating God's order of no man touching the Ark.

During this period the Hebrews made very important contributions to Western thought. The Hebrews believed:

- God was not part of nature, but entirely outside of it.
- Humans were part of nature, and humans rule over nature by divine will; therefore, humans can control and change nature.
    — God's command for humans to multiply and dominate over nature.
    — "Grow and Multiply." Humans can alter nature as they pleased.

Figure 4.8 Statue of Moses. *Image Copyright Jozef Sedmak, 2009. Used under license from Shutterstock, Inc.*

Idea of **Transcendence** (transcendent theology) meant that God can be understood in purely abstract or intellectual terms, and humanity had the potential to alter nature to its benefit. Thus, God is not in nature. He is outside nature. He is the Creator of Nature. Nature is a creation of God.

With this transcendent theology the ancient Hebrews break away from *mythical thinking,* break away from *natural myth.* They do not believe that nature has spirits (rivers, forests, animals, rains, etc.) There is no "magic" to influence the spirits or gods to benefit man and influence nature on man's behalf. **Immanism** the pagan belief that God is in nature, such as in animals and other objects, is discarded by the Hebrews.

Because now man is above all of God's creation, he can control nature to his benefit. This leads man to seek control, see nature as material reality he can understand and manipulate. This view of life helps man in the development of science and technology to understand and control nature which enables man to progress. This will be a major force in the progress of Western civilization.

The Hebrews believe that God is in control of history, because God intervenes in all reality and has a plan for mankind on Earth. Examples of this are when God opens the waters to allow the Hebrews under Moses to cross over to escape the persecuting Egyptian army, and when a Hebrew general prays to God to allow the day to last longer so that he can have a complete victory over the enemy during a battle and

God maintains the sun in the sky for several hours more than normal to allow complete victory. God is lord of history; thus, historical events are seen as God's will, such as victories, and invasions and captivity as God's punishments.

With the Hebrews comes the idea of the will of God and will of men, and how they can agree or oppose each other.

3. *Monotheism:* Belief in the existence of only one God for all mankind. This occurs during the era of the Judges when the Hebrews have settled in Palestine. By prophet the Hebrews meant preacher. They were inspired by God to preach to the Jewish nation God's will and to warn the people who behaved improperly of disasters as God's punishment. They were men like Amos, Hosea, Elias, Jeremias, Isaias, Daniel, and Ezekiel that lived between 722 to 586 B.C. The prophets criticized the ritualism of the Israelites, and those who were unfaithful by incorporating pagan gods into their worship. They spread a message of justice by relieving oppression and helping those in need. The basic doctrines of the prophets' teaching:

- *Monotheism*—Yahweh, only true God for all of mankind, thus all other gods are false.
- Yahweh is exclusively a God of **righteousness.** He wills only the good. Evil comes from men and their sins. Yahweh is a God of sin and reward, of justice to protect the weak.
- God demands **ethical behavior.** The Ten Commandments is the basis of a moral code. God's will extends to all mankind, His laws apply to all men.

4. *Post exilic stage* is the last stage of religious development (after the Babylon captivity in 539 B.C.) that lasted four centuries when they took the role of Jews into the divine plan for the world. The focus of post-exilic thinkers were *eschatological* doctrines that dealt with what will happen at the end of time.

MESSIANIC AND MILLENARIAN EXPECTATIONS

The Jews in Palestine under the Persian and Greeks, as well as during the Maccabean dynasty, began to wonder what their role in history would be, what role their small and weak nation would play in the divine plan for the world. The Jewish nation was weak politically, as well as economically and militarily.

They began to focus on messianic and millenarian expectations. God would send a Messiah who would lift up the Jews to greatness and spread the worship of YAHWEH to the entire world during a millennium (1,000 years) of peace and justice before the *end of time.*

For Christ's Jewish and Gentile followers, Christ is the Messiah. The Jews that denied that Jesus was the Messiah continued to expect the Messiah's coming. Most expected an earthly savior who would exalt the nation of Israel and rebuild the temple.

Now we will look into the new concepts that the Hebrews had about God and men. These concepts were entirely new religious ideas in antiquity.

GOD: ONE, SOVEREIGN, TRANSCENDENT, AND GOOD

With *Monotheism* as a central belief and force in Hebrew religion and culture, the Hebrews *broke* from near Eastern religious thought.

Yahweh was eternal; the only one; only one to be worshiped; *transcendent* above nature and not part of nature; so God is not identified with any natural force nor does He dwell in a particular place be it heaven or Earth. He is the creator of nature. The opposite was the concept of Eastern gods that were not free, limited in their power, many were created and even died, and they were subject to the negative human passions such as lust, frivolity, caprice, etc.

God was regarded as fully *sovereign*. Sovereign means completely free to do His will. God ruled all and was not subject to anything. He existed before all creation; he was eternal, never ending. His will is supreme and He is creator of the entire universe. He determined fate, and was not subject to it like the pagan gods. He governs the natural world as well as all human beings.

By removing the gods from nature, demystifying nature, the Hebrews paved an opening to the beginning of scientific thought. Now you see nature as purely physical reality with its own operating laws. It's a prerequisite of scientific thought.

The Hebrews did not create theoretical science. They were concerned with religion and morality. The Hebrews, unlike the Greeks, were not philosophical and scientific thinkers. They were not concerned with discovering nature's self-operating physical principle or natural laws. The natural phenomenon were seen as God intervening in an orderly manner in his creation. They saw God's handiwork.

The Hebrews were concerned with God's will, not the human intellect, with feelings of the heart, not the power of the mind, and with righteous behavior, not abstract thought.

Why worry about the origin of things, when God created all of nature? God's existence was based on conviction and revelation, not on rational inquiry and reason as the Greeks.

The **Hebrews as *religious* thinkers** and the **Greeks as *rational* thinkers** were the two civilizations of antiquity that broke away from mythical thinking opening the way to scientific and human progress for the West.

Christianity—retained this Hebrew view of transcendent God and the orderliness of his creation—concepts that would also accommodate Greek science and philosophy.

The Hebrews did not speculate about God's nature. They knew that God is :

- Good
- Made ethical demands on his people
- Is attentive to human needs

Individual and Moral Autonomy

With believing that God was one, sovereign, transcendent, and good the Hebrews made possible a new awareness of the individual.

As man confronted God, had a relationship with God, the Hebrews developed an awareness of self or the "I". The individual became conscious of his or her own person, moral autonomy, and personal worth. They knew man was created in God's image, had reason to understand and know God's will, had an immortal soul, and was put on Earth to worship God and attain salvation, not just be a servant or slave to powerful priests and kings. Man is an individual who has dignity and self worth. The Hebrews were the first in history to have these beliefs and ideas:

- God possessed the total freedom and He gave man **moral freedom,** the ability to choose between good and evil.
- God did not create men to be slaves. Men have freedom to choose to obey God and men should be free to live a life according to God's will.
- God made men autonomous and sovereign.
- Man is God's highest creation, on top of nature, and had reason to choose good from sin, and therefore is responsible for their choice.

Freedom—meant voluntary obedience to God's commands. Man's salvation and happiness on Earth depended on this obedience.

Disobedience brought evil, suffering, and death.

Man has freedom to obey or disobey God. The Hebrews conceived the idea of moral freedom that each individual is responsible for his or her moral actions.

These concepts of human dignity and moral autonomy are at the core of Western tradition and inherited by Christianity.

Social Justice—The classical prophets responded to problems that emanated from Israel's changed social structure from a tribal society to a kingdom with class distinctions and the rise of kings, government, commerce, and cities. By the 700s B.C. there was a big disparity between the wealthy and the poor. The prophets saw these social evils as religious sin. They denounced pomp, excessive wealth, heartless rich, and demanded justice. They insisted on God's compassion, and the obligation to care for the poor and needy. God demands righteous living individually and socially.

The Hebrew prophets brought:

- Hope that life on Earth could be improved, to overcome poverty and injustice.
- Individual could elevate himself morally and respect the dignity and rights of others.

Thus, the prophet's "social justice" teaching shaped a *social conscience* that has become a vital part of the Western Tradition. These were entirely new ideas in the ancient world and thus historians call this period the "prophetic revolution." The social reform movements in the West that since the 19th century struggled to end slavery, discrimination and child labor, defend the working class wages and working conditions, have as the origin of their convictions the teaching of the prophets.

Legacy of the Ancient Hebrews

The legacy of the ancient Hebrews to the Western World:

- Great value the Western World gives to the individual. Because men are created in God's image and possess free will and a conscience.
- Basis of Christianity—From which originates Western Civilization's view on God, human nature with free will, reason, individualistic, and social justice.
- Forms the basis and origins of the *Judeo-Christian tradition*.
- Hebrew vision of a future messianic age, a golden age of peace and social justice is at the root of the Western *idea of progress* that men can build a more just society. This gives man hope in the future.
- This perception of man and society has influenced modern reform movements.
- Judaism, Christianity and Islam are monotheist religions; thus, descendents in belief from Moses and Hebrew prophets.

Law and Literature

Ancient Hebrews were not great scientist, builders, or artists. Even Solomon's temple was not really a Hebrew construction or creation because Phoenician masons and artists were hired to handle the most difficult tasks of the project. In the field of art, no sculpture and no painting because the Hebrew religious code prohibited making images or "likeness" of anything from heaven or Earth (Exodus 20:4). Therefore, Jewish culture was profoundly shaped by the Second Commandment, which forbids the making of images or likenesses of God. In art, this meant that Yahweh would not, by definition, be depicted in any recognizable form. Furthermore, creation and creativity are considered the exclusive domain of God and reserved for him alone.

The consequence is that *law and literature* were the fields where the ancient Hebrews culture excelled and left us its most important influence to the Western civilization. Here lies their major accomplishments.

Hebrew Law: Major repository is the **Deuteronomic Code,** the core of the biblical book of Deuteronomy. This code from the time of the prophetic revolution has provisions more altruistic and equitable than other contemporary laws such as the Babylonian Code of Hammurabi. Examples of altruism: generosity to the poor and strangers; Hebrew slaves to be freed after six years of service with provisions to start his own life; after seven years all debtors to be released from their debts. Fairness: children should not be held responsible for guilt of parents. Judges should not accept gifts. Being just is God's command for the Hebrews.

Hebrew Literature: The Bible

The Jews enshrined their cultural developments in the Bible, their collection of sacred writings, or **scriptures.** Known as the Old Testament to Christians, the Hebrew Bible contains history, law, poetry, songs, stories, prayers, and philosophical works. Evolving out of the rich and long oral tradition, the Bible probably began to take its earliest written form during the United Monarchy in the 10th century B.C. By then the Hebrews had an alphabet, which, like that of the Greeks, was probably derived from the Phoenicians. Having acquired a written language and a unified political state, the Hebrews shared a consciousness of their past and desired to preserve it. They became the first five books of the Bible, known as the **Torah** or Pentateuch.

The final version of the Hebrew Bible is divided into three parts: the Law, the Prophets, and the Writings (Christians divide the Old Testament into four parts). The Law, also called the Torah (from Hebrew, "instruction"), recounts the story of God's creation of the world and the early history of the Hebrews. Most important, it details the establishment of the covenant and the foundation of the moral and ritualistic codes of personal and societal behavior that underlie Judaism.

The Prophets, canonized in the 1st century B.C., provide records about Israel and Judah and expand the Hebrews' ideas about God's nature and their relationship to him. They recount the conquest of Canaan, the events of the era of the Judges and the period of the United Monarchy, and the fate of the Kingdom of Judah after the Babylonian Captivity.

The Writings were not deemed canonical until A.D. 90, with the exception of Psalms, a collection of poems, which was given sacred status by 100 B.C. There is also a body of Jewish literature outside the canon. The Apocrypha are books written between 200 B.C. and 100 A.D. that include wisdom, literature, stories, and history, including the history of the Maccabees. Though not part of the Jewish canon, these books were included in the Septuagint, the Greek translation of the Hebrew Bible, and accepted by the Roman Catholic Church as part of the Christian Old Testament.

The Literature of the Hebrews is the finest of any ancient civilization of the Middle East. Found in the Old Testament and the books of the Apocrypha (ancient Hebrew works not recognized as scriptural because of doubtful religious authority), the Old Testament is God's revelation that explains origin and purpose of man's life, that God is the author of the universe, contains God's law and will and His moral code. It is also a record of Hebrew history, gives spiritual guidance and hope of salvation.

Early Hebrew Art and Architecture

The Second Commandment that forbids the making of images (Exodus 20:4). This is the reason why God was not represented in any form in art. Thus, there is no official Jewish sculpture or painting.

Because the early Hebrew had a nomadic existence, what sacred objects they had were transportable and kept in tents. These early works were not for public display because of the very holiness of Yahweh and the Hebrews' sense of their deity's power. Only a few persons were even permitted to see or be in the vicinity of these sacred objects. Once the tribes were united, however, Solomon enshrined the Ark of the Covenant and other ritualistic items in the splendid Temple that he built in Jerusalem. Solomon meant the Temple to be the central national shrine of the Hebrews and a symbol of his dynasty.

Solomon's Temple was destroyed by the Babylonians when they carried off the Jews in the early 6th century B.C. The description of the Temple in 1 Kings makes it sound similar to the "long-house" temples found in other civilizations of that time and probably indicated the influence of foreign neighbors. According to the Bible, Solomon's Temple was a rectangular building comprising three sections: a porch, a sanctuary or main hall, and an inner sanctum that housed the Ark of the Covenant. Artists and craftspeople decorated the interior with carvings of floral designs and cherubs, highlighting these with gold.

When the Jews were released from the Babylonian Captivity by the Persians, they returned to their homeland and reconstructed the capital city of Jerusalem and its Temple. The Second Temple, completed in the late 6th century B.C., exhibited a simpler design and decoration scheme than did Solomon's Temple.

Greek influences became apparent in Jewish architecture during Hellenistic times. John Hyrcanus (135–106 B.C.), constructed a fortress-place at present-day Araq el Emir in Jordan that shows this influence clearly.

During the reign of King Herod the Great from 37 to 4 B.C., architecture in Judea exhibited a further mix of Greek styles with Jewish motifs. The various buildings in Herod's complex contained many representative Greco-Roman features, including fluted Corinthian columns and marble facing. In Herod's palace, Classical patterned mosaics were combined with traditional Jewish decoration of flowers, fruits, and intertwined vines and branches.

Like the First Temple, this one contained many rooms, including the Holy of Holies where the menorah and the table where the prelists placed the consecrated, unleavened bread eaten during Passover, the festival that commemorates the exodus from Egypt.

When the Romans finally crushed the Jewish revolt in A.D. 70, the Temple, except for the Wailing Wall, was destroyed, and its sacred objects were transported to Rome.

In conclusion, the Hebrews with the Greeks broke away from a mythical world of pantheism where objects have a spirit or god. These civilizations developed an individual's dignity and freedom, and brought about a rational thought which allowed questioning, experimenting, and the development of science. All this allowed progress and individual freedom to develop in the Western world.

SUMMARY

The ancient Hebrews had an enormous historical impact on Western civilization. They exerted great influence upon the thought and religious belief of the Western world, creating the basis from which later Christianity will come. The history of the ancient Hebrews begins in Sumer, Mesopotamia, about 1900 B.C. They begin as a polytheistic people, same as the rest of mankind, departing from Sumer. They travel north to what today is Syria and then through Palestine into Egypt, which was ruled by the Hyksos, and later were forced to labor on the pharaoh's large projects. Moses will liberate the Hebrews from Egypt and lead them into the Sinai desert or wilderness for forty years, and establish the worship of one God with the Ten Commandments. The Hebrews then move into and conquer Canaan, what today is known as Palestine. They will develop from tribes ruled by judges into a kingdom ruled by kings. After King Solomon, due to internal antagonisms, the Kingdom of Israel splits itself into two kingdoms, Judah and Israel. Both kingdoms were later conquered by the Assyrians and the Babylonians. Many Hebrews were deported to Babylon during the "Babylonian Captivity," until liberated by the Persians who allowed them to return to Palestine and rebuild their temple in Jerusalem. Then they were conquered by Alexander the Great and ruled by a Greek dynasty until they were freed from Greek rule by the Maccabees brothers. They enjoyed a short period of freedom under the Maccabean dynasty until 63 B.C. when the Roman Empire took over Palestine. When the Jews revolted against the Roman rule in 70 A.D., the Romans brutally crushed the revolt and destroyed the temple in Jerusalem. Many Jews then migrated from Palestine to other countries in what is known as the diaspora (scattering). Since the diaspora they were without a homeland until the reestablishment of the state of Israel in 1948.

Hebrew religious development occurred in four stages of growth: polytheistic stage; national monolatry with Moses with the exclusive worship of Yahweh; monotheism, the belief in the existence of only one true God; and the post exilic stage when the Hebrews ponder their role in the divine plan for the world. During the period of national monolatry the ancient Hebrews begin to break away with mythical thinking with the idea of the transcendence of God, that God is not part of nature and He created nature. Also that man is the highest being in the creation of God and can control nature to satisfy his needs. With the teachings of the prophets or judges, Yahweh becomes the only true God, a God of righteousness with no flaws that only demands ethical behavior and holds all mankind accountable to His laws. During the post exilic stage the Hebrews begin to believe God would send a Messiah to raise the Hebrew nation and spread the worship of God to all mankind.

With the monotheistic stage the Hebrews have broken away completely with mythical thinking as religious thinkers. Their belief and idea of God is that He is one, sovereign, transcendent, and embodying perfect goodness. They also came to be aware through their concept of God that man has moral freedom to choose between good and evil, an entirely new concept of social justice with the hope that mankind's life on Earth could be improved overcoming injustice and poverty.

Religion was the main strength of the Hebrews. From the Hebrews came the first monotheistic religion of the Western World. Judaism gave these ancient people a covenant with God, Hebrew scripture, a way of life and hope based on faith. This faith sustained them through conquests by several ancient civilizations.

The legacy of the ancient Hebrews or Jews to the Western world has been in the fields of law and literature, with the Deuteronomic Code and the Old Testament (Torah) of the Bible. It forms the basis and origins of the Judeo-Christian religion and tradition.

ROMAN CIVILIZATION
AND BYZANTIUM

ROMAN CIVILIZATION

The great importance that the Roman Empire and its civilization has in the formation of Western civilization, derives from establishing a civilization that lasted over 600 years and reaching geographically from the Middle East to the Atlantic and from North Africa to Northern Europe (Figure 5.1). Rome was a builder of a great historical bridge between East and West, or the eastern Hellenistic, Egyptian, and Mesopotamian worlds, and Western Europe that in many places was still in the Iron Age.

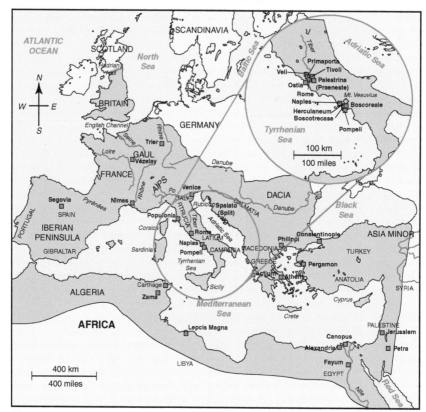

Figure 5.1 The Roman Empire at its greatest extent ca. 180 C.E. *Image Copyright: Kendall Hunt Publishing Company.*

Roman Legendary Origins

Two famous Roman legends about Rome's origin tell us the character and values of the ancient Romans. These legends are *Romulus and Remus,* and the one found in Virgil's epic poem the *Aeneid.* According to legend it all began with twin brothers Romulus and Remus who were the sons of the god of war, Mars, and a mortal woman Rhea Silva, daughter of King Numitor. Amulius, the wicked brother of King Numitor usurped the throne overthrowing his brother and made his daughter Rhea Silvia a Vestal Virgin. As a virgin she could not marry and have legitimate heirs to the throne. To secure his rule against future claimants, Numitor had Romulus and Remus placed in a basket set adrift on the Tiber River in today's central Italy. The infants were rescued by a female wolf which suckled them. Surviving in their natural environment the infants were then discovered by a shepherd couple and raised into manhood. Thus, they were nourished by nature, the she-wolf, and by hard working good humans connected to the land, the shepherd couple. The sculpture of a standing she-wolf with two infants suckling beneath her became an ancient symbol of Rome.

The twin brothers learned their true identity, and following their Roman nature, immediately killed Amulius and restored their grandfather Numitor to the throne. They set out to perform their destiny to found the city of Rome on the seven hills by the Tiber River. The serious Romulus quarreled with the lighthearted Remus when the latter made fun of the wall Romulus constructed. In his self-righteous wrath Romulus murdered his twin brother. Then Romulus raised an army, and having more men than women, he set off to supply his soldiers with wives by raping Sabine women who were their neighbors. Romulus founded Rome in 753 B.C., and received the first constitution from the gods becoming its first king.

The *Aeneid* is the epic poem about Rome's legendary beginnings written by the poet Virgil (70–19 B.C.) in 31 B.C. commissioned by Emperor Augustus. Virgil took his inspiration from the Greeks. The tradition that Homer's *Iliad* and *Odyssey* gave to Greek literature was admired by Virgil who desired to achieve that level of greatness; thus, he patterned his poem on these epics to give Rome the same kind of epic golden past the ancient Greeks had. Virgil's epic hero is Aeneas of Greek origin. It begins with the fall of the city of Troy in Asia Minor (modern Turkey) during the long siege of the Greeks lead by Agamemnon. Aeneas and his loyal band of warriors escape the fall of Troy and set sail on the Mediterranean Sea toward the west to fulfill their destiny. The wanderings of Aeneas are based on the Odyssey. Aeneas and his warriors are stranded on the North African shore after a sea storm and then arrive at nearby Carthage well received by Queen Dido who falls in love with Aeneas. She wants Aeneas to stay and live with her but the stern duty in the nature of the hero renounced the honors and the love of the queen and he abandons Dido to fulfill his sacred mission of founding Rome. Queen Dido represents the opposite of Aeneas by putting precedence of her desires and passions over duty. The despairing Dido, hoping Aeneas will return to her, at the last moment chooses suicide and Aeneas sails to Sicily and then to the Tiber River where he fights and defeats Turnus. War in Italy is based on the *Iliad.* The epic hero then marries Lavinia, the beautiful daughter of King Latinus, and faithful to his duty, founds Rome first among cities and home of gods. Thus, Virgil's hero founds an empire and launches a whole new civilization.

Aeneas represents a stoic Roman hero who is middle-aged with the wisdom that comes with maturity. In his sober austerity Aeneas coldly puts his passions aside to fulfill his destiny to found Rome. His will-power to carry out his destiny is his greatest virtue. It is clear in this poem that human actions are dictated by external forces when the hero fulfills his destiny, a stoic doctrine that states that people must follow the natural world because they cannot violate natural laws; thus, the cosmic determinism man is subjected to. Aeneas comes close to perfect freedom when he frees himself of all mundane desires, another stoic doctrine. The Roman hero achieves stoic virtue when he directs his will to the ends that coincide with nature, which in his case is to begin a great civilization. Following stoic philosophy, Aeneas is seen adhering to duty as the most noble of all human values. In Aeneas Romans found the best example of the superior qualities of the noble Roman that no other Roman individual in history and in fiction equaled. In his travels Aeneas mirrors Greek hero Odysseus in the *Odyssey* and in his struggle the Greek heroes of the *Iliad* Achilles and Hector. The *Aeneid* is literature but it is also propaganda for a great empire where society's most important reality was the state and therefore the principal aim of literature was to stir patriotism. It represents the best of the Roman ideal.

These two Roman legends tell us important traits about the Romans and what they thought about themselves. The Romans were practical, dedicated, hard working, thrifty, loyal to family and state, combative, and faithful to their duty as Roman citizens, the noblest of all virtues. They had little interest in theories or abstract ideas, and were practical at incorporating what worked and served their needs. This no-nonsense people who were resolute and combative conquered the largest empire of antiquity and established one of the most influential civilizations in history. They viewed themselves as virtuous, self-righteous, and superior people who had the right to conquer and exploit other people because they had the military ability and superior culture to accomplish this. Thus violence was a means to their goals. Romulus and Remus were sons of the god of war. Romulus murdered his brother in self-righteous wrath then he took the Sabine lands and women. Aeneas was a warrior who began the city-state that would grow to restore Trojan honor by conquering the Greeks. Aeneas was the ancestor of Romulus and Remus, therefore, Aeneas is also considered a founder of the Roman city-state. The murder of Remus leaves Romulus to take the credit for the founding of Rome. These legends were the version of history that Roman children heard of their origins, and were self-fulfilling prophesies in that Romans believed that they were fated to be warriors destined to grandeur, glory, and to rule the world. The Romans built a great civilization that had splendor, the highest standard of living of its time and achieved great building projects on a grand scale that the Western world inherited with its laws and Latin language. But it achieved this at the cost of exploitation, denigrating human value and the qualities of imagination and joy.

Roman morality and Roman law has a rural ethic by stressing the importance of nature and of living within one's means. This also applied to Roman literary culture that revered its rustic past, and when Rome became prosperous with its conquests, many writers criticized the corrupting power of luxury and looked up to the home-spun values of Rome's founders who were herdsmen and farmers. A very important value was the sanctity of the family and its reputation. Divorce was unheard of until the late republican era, and still family values continued to be praised by moralists and honored by its leaders. The Roman family was guided by the *paterfamilias,* or father of the family, which usually was reserved for the eldest male member of the entire family that could span to two or three generations. The *paterfamilias* exercised the legal power of life and death over his entire household which included family members, servants, and slaves. To get married you needed the consent of this family head regardless of age. The Roman matron had a freer and more influential role in family life than the secluded Greek wives, thus, seen more in public with her husband and supervising the education of her sons and daughters.

Rome's Origin

The Aeneas legend may have been based on the **Etruscans** who were a people that settled in northern and central Italy around the 9th century B.C. The Greek historian Herodotus wrote that the Etruscans originated from western Asia Minor, near Troy, and were advanced in culture. Modern historians agree with this view. They used letters derived from the archaic Greek alphabet. Thus, this legend may be based on actual historical facts.

The Etruscan civilization ruled Rome during the 6th century B.C. Etruscan civilization had a high standard of living and they originated the street plans for cities, the masonry arch, sophisticated sanitary and civil engineering, the triumphal processions, and gladiatorial combat. Rome borrowed many concepts from the Etruscans, making the cultural inheritance very strong. But the Romans did not accept all aspects of Etruscan culture. The Etruscans were not austere people; they valued what was pleasurable in life and pursued it. Their elaborate tombs of the members of the upper class demonstrate that the Etruscans were very concerned about life after death because the tombs looked like their luxurious homes with all the items that made life comfortable and pleasant; thus, they believed in a continuing afterlife and they wanted to keep enjoying it. Their tomb paintings portray men and women drinking wine together in a relaxed atmosphere. In contrast the austere Romans were not concerned with the afterlife and they frowned upon living life in the pursuit of pleasure. Romans did not give the same status to women as the Etruscans. Roman women would not socialize nor drink with men, and did not have the same rights and liberties as men. The battle of Lake Vadimon in 308 B.C. broke the Etruscan political and military control of central and northern Italy.

Greek Influence

Early in Rome's history during the 8th century B.C., the Romans came in contact with the Greek colonies in southern Italy known as Magna Graecia. The Greeks' culture in many ways was more sophisticated, and thus, Rome came under Greek influence. The Romans assimilated Greek architecture, sculpture, art, literature, theater, philosophy, and mythology. They looked up to the Greeks, but they were also suspicious of them. The Greek culture in many ways was the opposite of Roman values, and this created a hostile attitude toward the Greeks. The Greeks were urbane, artistic, intellectual, sophisticated, individualistic, and seeking the good life. Thus, the sober, austere, and warlike Romans that valued discipline, conformity, tradition, physical prowess, and duty to state and family looked down on their southern neighbors but recognized their cultural achievements. They had an ambivalent attitude toward the Greeks.

The Age of Kings, 753–509 B.C.

During the Age of Kings some of the basic elements of the Roman political, social, and economic structures were established. The small city-state was ruled by kings having a balance system of government in which a council of landowners took part in selecting the ruler and the entire people ratified its choice. This system came to an end when the Etruscans imposed their kings upon Rome around 600 B.C. Later on, this system of selecting rulers and voting for acceptance became the model for government under the republic. The Romans saw the Etruscans' kings as tyrants and eventually they were able to free themselves from their rule.

The Republic, 509–27 B.C.

Roman tradition has that the Republic began with the expulsion of the Etruscan king Tarquin the Proud in 509 B.C. Now that the Romans were free of foreign rule, they created a different way to govern themselves following their practical nature. They did not want another monarchy so Rome was under an oligarchy, which is the rule by the few who possess wealth and political power (Figure 5.2). The *oligarchy* became the basis of the new state. To be a member of the oligarchy required wealth, and in an agricultural economy land ownership was the source of wealth and political power. Thus, the oligarchs, the land-owning aristocrats, established a republic with full citizenship reserved only for their class. Oligarchs belong to the **patrician** class. This upper class that ruled over Roman society took its name from the Latin word "pater" or father. They had the authority in Roman society like a father has in his family. The patricians constituted 10 percent of the population. The remaining 90 percent were the **plebeians** from the Latin "plebs" or multitude. At this time a long-lasting aspect of Roman political and economic life takes roots and that is class conflict. When the aristocrats established the republic as their form of government and by denying citizenship to the plebeians they safeguarded their power. This policy of exclusion laid the groundwork for centuries of class conflict that would be a factor in the fall of the republic.

In contrast to the direct democracy of Athens, the republic was based on a system of representatives and separation of powers. In their pragmatic attitude, not being interested in political theories or abstract

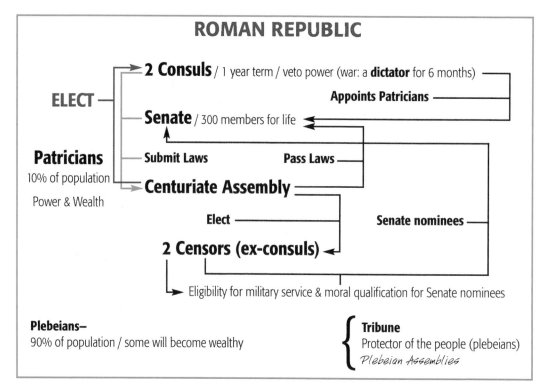

ROMAN REPUBLIC

ELECT

2 Consuls / 1 year term / veto power (war: a **dictator** for 6 months)

Appoints Patricians

Senate / 300 members for life

Patricians
10% of population
Power & Wealth

Submit Laws   Pass Laws

Centuriate Assembly

Elect   Senate nominees

2 Censors (ex-consuls)

Eligibility for military service & moral qualification for Senate nominees

Plebeians–
90% of population / some will become wealthy

{ **Tribune**
Protector of the people (plebeians)
Plebeian Assemblies

Figure 5.2   Roman Republic.

ideas about government, the patricians made the necessary adjustments to meet their needs developing the republican institutions and practices. They were the class that could participate and hold office in government, and be officers in the military. At the beginning the plebeians could not hold office and marry into the patrician class. But making money was not forbidden to this class. With time some plebeians became wealthy and were able to have adjustments made to have some representation in government and eventually marry into the patrician class. The patricians did not want to be ruled by one man or a very small group; therefore, one characteristic of the Republic is that during peace time political power is not in the hands of one person or group. It seeks to avoid concentration of power through the need of cooperation among the different bodies or institutions that govern. The Republic will have two heads of state with short terms and mutual veto power, and their legislative branch was made up of two legislative bodies that need to cooperate to pass laws.

The executive heads of state were two *consuls* who govern with full power for one year and each had the power to veto over the actions of the other consul. They were commanders of the army. Consuls were chosen from members of the senate by means of elections by patricians of Rome. The consuls had the functions of keeping the peace and order within Rome, raising armies and conducting foreign policy. Consuls appointed members of the patrician class to the Senate made up of 300 members who had life terms, and all were ex-magistrates. The Senate and the consuls submitted laws to the other legislative body the *Centuriate Assembly* which had less power than the Senate but it passed the laws, and elected the consuls. This assembly was organized around military units known as "centuries," and even if plebeians could be members in reality it was dominated by the rich patricians because military obligations were determined by a citizen's wealth. Also the Centuriate Assembly elected two censors among the exconsuls. The censors had the function of determining who was eligible for military service and who had the moral quality to become a nominee for the Senate. Military service was important in Roman society because service to the state was considered a mark of a true Roman who was fit to serve in government. Therefore, the Republic had built into it a mechanism of checks and balances with which to govern effectively and the consuls had to agree to cooperate because their mutual veto power could neutralize their acts and policies; the senators needed the appointment of the consuls to become Senate members; the Senate and consuls needed the approval of the Centuriate Assembly to make their legislation into law, and the consuls needed to be elected by this assembly as well as the censors; and those that wanted to serve in the military and become senators depended on being declared eligible by the censors. Thus, all governing bodies and offices depended on their mutual cooperation, and no one individual or group had absolute power and could act on his own. Most offices were held by patricians having the monopoly on power.

The risk that having two heads of state with mutual veto power and both being commanders of the army could jeopardize the state in case they disagreed or veto each other during times of war where the security and survival of the state was paramount, that led Rome to make another practical adjustment to government which was the office of the *dictator.* The word comes from the term to *dictate,* because this individual had the authority to dictate his decision and all had to obey him. The dictator became the supreme commander of the army and received his authority constitutionally for a term of six months. The short term was to avoid being under the absolute rule of one individual for a long time and not allow that person to get used to such great power or extend his term for a long period.

The plebeians, who were excluded from government, created a situation of abuse of power that became intolerable for this class and with their growing financial power were able to exert political influence to force the Senate to create the office of the *Tribune.* The tribune was the protector of the people, the plebeians. This office was created by a strike. In 494 B.C. when Rome was threatened by invading forces the plebeians went on strike and refused to fight, taking a position in the Aventine Hill. They created their magistrates called "tribunes of the people." Then the patricians had to recognize this office. It changed radically the balance of power between the patricians and the plebeians. Ten tribunes were elected annually by the plebs alone. Their function was to protect the plebeians from the abuse of power at the hands of government officials, especially consuls. Tribunes had the power of intervening physically if need be to defend a plebeian who was wrongfully punished or oppressed. They could prosecute any other magistrate and veto any proposed bill to prevent it from becoming law. Their veto could not be overridden. Their veto power meant that the only laws that could be enacted were those regarded as necessary by both patricians and plebs, in other words by practically everyone. Tribune had a protection in that any man who laid a violent hand upon the tribune could be executed without any trial by any citizen. Therefore, the two most important ruling magistrates were the consuls and tribunes. With time also the *Assembly of the Tribes* came to have power which allowed for plebeian participation in government. This new assembly could be attended by patrician and plebeians. The tribune convened the Plebeian Assembly (only for plebs). At first its votes served as a plebiscite that allowed for the Senate and consuls to measure the opinion of the majority of Roman citizens. By 287 B.C. the decisions of the Patrician and Plebeian Assemblies (both constituted the Assembly of Tribes) had the force of law binding all Roman society. Thus, with the office of tribune and the popular assemblies the Roman republic had evolved into "two heads," those of the Senate composed of the rich patricians and those of the Roman people.

Economics

The pragmatic Romans never resolved the issue of ownership of the land which held the key to Rome's economic health and wealth of its citizens. There were landlords that owned large estates with cheap slave labor, and controlled a large part of the agricultural market that left the small farmer struggling to stay in business. Competition from these large estates with lower cost due to labor from war-booty slaves, drought, and pestilence forced many farmers with small acreage into debt, bankruptcy, and some ended as slaves to pay their debt. The large estates grew larger at expense of small farms. Reforms were made to change the law and end debt-slavery and attempts to distribute the land, but many farmers still ended as urban poor who left the countryside to find work in the cities. This mass of poor country people could not find work in large estates because they could not compete with cheap slave labor and many could not find work in the cities because there were plenty of slaves there to work. Thus these urban poor became part of the permanent welfare program, receiving free bread from the state. By the 1st century B.C., 80 percent of the population of Rome was either slaves or living on the "panes et cirsens" or "bread and circuses," free bread and entrance to the spectacles of the Colosseum. This failure or lack of productive farms and urban jobs was a cause that contributed to the decline of the empire. The welfare program was a failure because many Romans lost their ethics of hard work and the decadent and sadistic entertainments of the Roman games diminished their moral fiber.

Military Might and Empire Building

Rome began its history as a small city-state governed by kings that was competing with neighboring city-states for power and control of the region of central Italy. Since its beginnings Rome was unique in that it had an open door policy of assimilating foreigners into its city-state, which was the opposite of its neighbors who were distrustful of outsiders. Its founder, Romulus, decided that Rome did not have enough population and therefore he decided to create an asylum, a free zone for anyone, whether it be runaway slaves and criminals, brigands, pirates, whoever wanted to come and join to be part of this great idea that is Rome. Thus, Rome had a very unique attitude, its openness to other people and ideas that were of use to their needs. To grow and become a stronger state, Rome became a safe haven for people who were desperate and were seeking a place to prosper and settle. This brought ambitious and ruthless individuals to populate this growing city-state. This aspect of Roman reality would influence the character of Roman people who were ambitious and inclined to use violence and ruthlessness to achieve their goals. This was a very important contributing factor, the use of violence, throughout the entire history of Rome. Since the story of Romulus and Remus, where Romulus murders Remus and becomes king of Rome, bloodshed became a means to produce a new Roman ruler. Civil war among the Romans is one of the defining features of the growth of the Roman state. Thus, the tradition of the murder of Romulus and Remus is one that reverberates or repeats itself throughout Roman history.

The openness of Rome to foreigners and ideas imported from other cultures encouraged a free exchange of ideas, among them engineering theories imparted from other cultures, especially from the Et-ruscans. The Romans will be masters in adapting, improving, and refining ideas and technologies to meet their needs, that will allow them to become a great empire with a high standard of living and achievement. Therefore, the Romans will make important contributions to Western civilization such as aqueducts, indoor plumbing, sewer systems, masonry arch, bridges, and paved roads, still in use today.

From 500 to 275 B.C. Rome gained control of the region of Latium in central Italy. It accomplished this in piecemeal fashion by means of a combination of diplomacy and war. Then it brought the rest of the Italian peninsula under its control. Initially the motivation for expansion was to gain more farming land due to the small farms of many peasants that were not large enough to sustain a large family. Also defending their territory was a motive. In 493 B.C. Rome joined an alliance with its Latin neighbors forming the Latin League to defend themselves from the invasion of central tribes of Volsci, Aequi, and the Sabines. Once they overcame this threat, Rome and its Latin allies turned on Etruria to the north. Some Etruscan cities came to peaceful terms while others were defeated and annexed. In 340 B.C. the city-state of Rome went to war against the Latin League and defeated it. By 290 B.C. Rome turned south and dominated the Samnites, thus controlling more territory. Now Rome was bordering with Magna Graecia, the Greek colonies in Southern Italy. Rome was conquering its neighbors through forced annexation, alliances, and conferring the privilege of citizenship and becoming absorbed in the Roman commonwealth. With this expansion the Latin language, customs, and culture of the Romans was gradually spreading throughout Italy. Loyalty to Rome was demanded upon all these forms of conquest and assimilation. Thus, Rome had a great supply of citizens and allies upon which to draw military manpower and enable Rome to make up its losses in battle and pursue its goals.

This period of conquest and expansion forged the character of resilience and discipline of the tough and unwavering Roman peasants and their leader, in whose work and struggles there was no place for comfort and self indulgence. In 280 B.C. the Greek city-state of Tarentum, fearing Roman expansion into its territory, called for military aid from Greece that came to their aid. By 275 B.C. Rome defeated the Greeks near Naples and gained control over all southern Italy. All the Italian peninsula was Roman territory (Figure 5.3).

Next was the conquest of the Mediterranean where Roma expands out of Italy. In the **Punic Wars** with Carthage, 264–146 B.C., Rome set out to conquer the World. Punic comes from the Latin word for Phoenician. The Phoenicians were from the Middle East, modern Lebanon, and they founded the city of Carthage in North Africa around 800 B.C. Carthage was a seafaring trading empire that by 265 B.C. had become the wealthiest and most culturally advanced city controlling the trading routes of the western Mediterranean. Their trading ports were in France, Spain, the islands of Sardinia and Sicily, and across North Africa. Sicily was a Carthaginian province where a war broke out among two cities. Carthage took the side of one city and Rome the other. This conflict escalated into a direct confrontation between Rome and Carthage for the control of Sicily. Rome only had an army but to win it had to weaken Carthage's control of the sea, thus Rome had to build its first navy. Rome seized a Carthaginian ship that ran aground in Italy and copied its design to build 100 warships with a new weapon, a rotatable spiked boarding bridge, to allow its soldiers to board and take over enemy ships. The Romans were victorious at sea after losing more ships to lack of experience than in naval action. After more than 20 years, Rome had its victory over Carthage.

To make up for losses of the islands of Sicily, Sardinia, and Corsica, in 238 B.C., the Carthaginians expanded their empire into Spain. Rome did not want their adversary to keep on expanding in Spain, and made an alliance with the city of Saguntum on the border of Carthage's expanding Spanish empire.

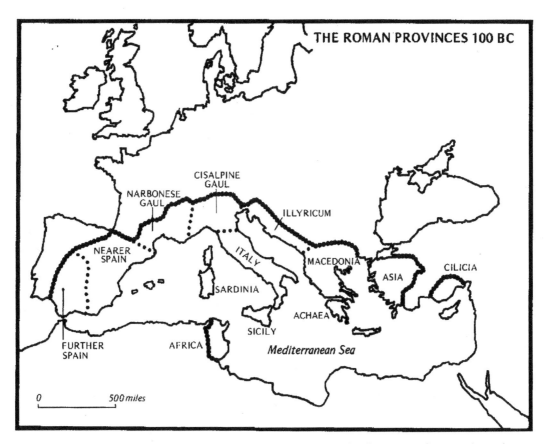

Figure 5.3 Roman Provinces in 100 B.C. *Source: Grant, Michael, History of Rome (1978), Charles Scribneis Sons, New York, page 180.*

When Saguntum became a threat to the Carthaginians towns, *Hannibal,* the Carthaginian general took over the city. Now Rome had an excuse to go to war in Spain and annex this wealthy territory. This sparked the second Punic War 218–201 B.C., the greatest between these two rival empires. Hannibal was a very able military leader and took his forces across Spain into France, then crossed the Alps into north Italy, a 1,000-mile journey. With his army and elephants Hannibal attacked Rome from the rear in its own backyard. Hannibal's determination and tactics defeated the larger Roman forces but did not take over the city of Rome, thus not having a complete victory. Rome was desperate and under the leadership of Scipio it attacked the vulnerable homeland of Hannibal, Carthage in North Africa. The leaders of Carthage called upon Hannibal who had to leave Italy and defend the capital of his empire. Scipio defeated Hannibal's forces in Africa in the battle of Zama in 202 B.C. ending the war with Rome's victory. Carthage lost its overseas empire forever.

The third and last Punic War, 149 B.C., was motivated by greed for Carthage's fertile soil and abundant harvest. Cartage had recuperated from the second Punic War but in no way had it means to be a threat to Rome. The senator, consul, and censor Cato after returning from a fact-finding mission to Carthage in 149, was able to convince the Senate that Carthage was a threat again. The Romans put many pressures and abusive demands upon Carthage and their goal of another war became a reality. This war resulted in the complete destruction and loot of the city in 146 B.C. Its male inhabitants were killed and its women and children sold into slavery. Salt was spread over the ground so nothing would grow after. The same year another Roman army applied the same treatment to the Greek City of Corinth. Greece was next to fall into Roman conquest. Now the Roman Empire extended all across the Mediterranean.

The recent conquests of Rome brought great wealth from the war booty into the empire which concentrated in the city of Rome. There was a massive injection of money into the capital, and Rome was flourishing. The city bulged with expenditures, imports and industry, new markets, slaves, more aqueducts were constructed, and large building projects sprang up. The new style with the most cachet was the Greek style. Thus, the wealthy élite made their luxurious villas with foreign influence, and also its public buildings. Greece's ancient civilization was what Roman aristocrats admired. Rome's population was approaching one million, which made the city crammed with people. There was an increase in the numbers of landless and jobless Romans. Despite Rome's new prosperity, its wealth was not distributed properly, thus not all sections of society shared in its wealth. Reform was long overdue.

Rome's success and wealth as an empire produced its dangerous consequence. The wealthy élite enriched by the empire's conquests fell into the practice of conspicuous displays of prosperity and success becoming the manifestation of a noble patrician's prestige and political standing. For example, if an aristocrat who was in command of the army and was successful at war returned to Rome with great honors and wealth, making a public display of this would incite other ambitious aristocrats to compete for prestige and political status with the wealth it brought. Now the other aristocrats had to play catch-up or lose status. The only way to catch-up and even outdo a successful opponent was to run for election and win an office such as a praetorship which could allow him to govern a province abroad and profit from it, or even better a consulship which offered the opportunity to command armies and gain by conquest. The family's status would rise which was also a very important concern of Roman noblemen. Thus, the prizes that the empire offered increased tremendously and the political élites competed in intensifying circles of rivalry that never ceased. By the 140s B.C. this common practice among the ambitious patrician class of self-serving competition was corrupting the republic. The new luxuries undermined the traditional Roman values of frugality, discipline, honesty, and respect for the law that were the virtues that made the Romans a strong people and on which the republic was built and depended. The ambitious aristocrats became ruthless to rise and profit to the point that vote-buying and ballot box stuffing became common practice. Roman proconsuls and tax collectors plundered the provinces they were in charge of to enrich Rome as well as themselves. Slaves were treated harshly which provoked several slave uprisings, the most famous by the gladiator *Spartacus* in 73–71 B.C. which was finally put down by the army and 6,000 rebels slaves were crucified along the Appian Way, south of Rome. The new class of merchants, tax collectors, moneylenders, and government contractors created by the empire's wealth were just as corrupt. The common people living under conditions of poverty and in slums became cruel and lazy. Thus, the "curse" of Roman conquest and empire building brought a moral decline that later would contribute to the republic's end and later to the empire's decline.

The gap between rich and poor increased as the wealth was unevenly divided. In the pursuit of status and wealth the Roman élite became blinder and heartless to the growing poverty in Rome. The land ownership issue was at the center of this unstable inequality that threatened the empire's social justice and harmony among its classes. Service in the army was an obligation of all Roman male citizens and most of the army was composed of smallholding farmers. As the empire's military campaigns of conquest became longer and farther away from Italy in faraway Spain, Greece, and North Africa, these small farmers had to stay in military service far away from their farms and some never returned. This left their families in danger of debt and starvation with the farms falling into disuse and neglect. The small farmer could not compete with the large-scale production by cheap slave labor of the large estates. Many were forced to abandon or sell their farms, and this allowed for aristocrats to gain more land. When they came to Rome to find sustenance they were forced to support the political interests of these aristocrats to be able to earn a living. Also the gap between political power of the patricians and plebeians widened when Rome grew from a village to the large center of a vast empire with over 750,000 inhabitants by the 2nd century B.C. The popular or plebeian assemblies could not function in the same manner before Rome became an empire due to their larger membership. Therefore, they could not make the swift decisions that the empire required. This increased the power of the senate and the aristocratic proconsuls who administered the provinces. The end result was the loss of the little power the plebeians had in government in which the patricians always had the upper hand. This troubled situation led many to believe that if the élites became more selfish and greedy and the frustrated poor became a mob that would run a riot, it would lead the republic to tear itself apart.

The senate became divided on the issue of land reform. There was the faction that saw land reform a threat to their large estates and wanted to keep the status quo, and the opposing faction that viewed the need for concord between the senate and the people. By 140 B.C. both factions came face to face in conflict. Land reforms were introduced in the senate but the majority were rejected. Two patricians brothers from an old prestigious family will take the cause of the landless poor. **Tiberius Gracchus** in 133 B.C. became tribune. He believed the means to restore the Roman values and the Republic was to restore the small farmer. His plan was to reenact an old law that limited the estates in public land rented out to any man to the amount of 300 acres and distribute the rest of the land to landless farmers. He proposed a compensation to the rich landowners for the excess land surrendered. The plebeians were with Tiberius. In 132 B.C. Tiberius was murdered by a group of senators and their followers and clubbed 300 of Tiberius' followers to death. Other followers of the populist tribune were exiled or executed without trial. The traditional reverence for law was giving way to unconstitutional acts and corruption. His brother **Gaius Gracchus** was elected tribune in 123 B.C. and he also took the cause of the commoners and had the goal to enforce Tiberius' agrarian law. Many came from Italy to Rome to support Gaius. The senate ordered the Italian supporters to leave the city and wanted Gaius murdered. Consul Opimius even placed a reward of gold for Gaius' head. The populist patrician was murdered and 3,000 of his followers were arrested and executed. This unresolved land issue with the wide gap between the have and have nots in Roman society ruined the integrity of the state, generating class warfare. The senate unknowingly lost the last opportunity to salvage the republic and set the stage for one-man rule.

The division between the aristocrats and the Populares who favored the poor opened the way to three civil wars in Rome. The concentration of wealth in a small section of Roman society and corruption brought about by the riches of conquest and greed, divided Rome into two political parties that were both corrupt and willing to use violence against the opposition, the *Populares* and *Optimates*. The Populares wanted to make changes to check the concentration of wealth and power the old constitution was unable to prevent, and opening opportunities for new seekers of wealth and power. The Optimates wanted to restore the old constitution and its checks on individual power with minimal changes. The first of the generals to seize power was Consul **Gaius Marius.** He came from a lower class, the equites (knights) and looked down upon the sophisticated senators who lived in luxury. Marius was successful in his campaigns in North Africa and against Celtic tribes in Europe. His major change and improvement was converting the army from amateurs loyal to Rome who farmed between campaigns and provided their military equipment to full-time professional soldiers equipped by and loyal to its commander. Marius was not of high birth and he acquired his consulship on his proven ability elected by the people not the Senate. The Senate had elected military commanders, but by 110s B.C. the populist faction in the Senate after the murder of the Gracchus brothers was able to pass anti-corruption laws that curbed the excesses of senators and provincial governors, and allowed for the people to select military commanders. Marius used the threat of armed force to overcome opposition in the Senate to the distribution of land in North Africa to his troops, which had not been done before. He was elected consul for six consecutive years (105–100 B.C.) that went against the law that prohibited consuls from holding office for two consecutive terms. He never seized Rome and retired.

In 88 B.C. King Mithridates led Greece and Asia Minor into rebellion against Rome's oppressive proconsuls and the existing corruption, killing 80,000 Italians in his territory. The Senate chose **Lucius Sulla,** leader of the optimates, as commander of the forces to put down the revolt, but the comitia tributa, one of Rome's three popular assemblies, chose Marius, leader of the populares, who was popular among the plebeian class. Sulla had served under Marius but now was his rival. An open struggle between Marius and Sulla for power with their respective factions broke out. Sulla failed to find and kill Marius who had fled to North Africa and left for the east to fight Mithridates' rebellion. Marius returned to Rome in Sulla's absence, looted the city and murdered some of his opponents including a consul. Maruis died of natural causes, and Sulla after defeating the rebellion in the east in 85 B.C. returned to Rome defeating Maruis' army in a civil war that caused many deaths, including many senators that reduced the Senate from 300 to 150 members. In 82 B.C. the Senate appointed Sulla as dictator and he replaced most of the government functions leaving the popular assemblies and the tribunes powerless—again, the ongoing struggle for power between the aristocrats and the people of Rome.

Sulla then went on a purge of his enemies and to restore the Senate to a dominant position. His troops killed 30,000 to 50,000 people, so a great number that the Senate had to beg him to stop. After serving as consul Sulla voluntarily retired to his rural estate and died in 78 B.C. Marius and Sulla had the scruple of not making themselves permanent dictators and the republic survived. The civil war accelerated the trend toward strong factions in the government and personal ambition.

In 70 B.C. **Gnaeus Pompey** and **Marcus Crassus** were elected consuls. Both had supported Sulla during his dictatorship, but now pursuing an opportunity to further their glory they changed to the side of the populists. They won the favor of the common people by repealing most of Sulla's laws, thus restoring power to the people from the aristocrats in the Senate. Pompey then was successful in campaigns against piracy at sea and in the east against another revolt from Mithridates and conquered southeast Asia Minor that included Judea and Syria. Pompey returned to Rome in 62 B.C. and disbanded his army quickly, thus losing his influence upon the Senate that refused to give the land he requested for his soldiers. In frustration, Pompey formed the **First Triumvirate** in 60 B.C. when he made an alliance with Crassus, the second wealthiest man in Rome after Pompey, the wealthiest Roman due to his eastern conquests, and **Julius Caesar.** Pompey gave money and popular support that Caesar needed to be elected consul, and Caesar agreed to propose laws that conservative senators refused so his army veterans could receive farmlands and the ratification of Pompey's treaties in the east. When Pompey's land bill was defeated in the Senate, Caesar, breaking with tradition, took it directly to the popular assembly and had it approved. Caesar's consulship demonstrated that at this moment the populists had the upper hand over the constitutionalist senators.

Caesar was a member of the oldest Roman aristocratic families (Figure 5.4). His family claimed to be descendants of the legendary Trojan hero Aeneas, founder of Rome, who was thought to be son of the goddess Venus. Thus Caesar was able to claim descent from the gods, which he took advantage of to have royal blood and status. A nephew of Marius, married to a daughter of Marius' allies, and sympathetic to the masses, he was not on Sulla's favorable side and was nearly banished in his youth by Sulla. Through the triumvirate Caesar was elected consul in 59 B.C. He then set out to conquer Gaul (today France, Belgium, southern Holland, Germany west of the Rhine River, and Switzerland), crossed into Britain, dominated a sector of Spain and Egypt where he had an affair with its queen Cleopatra and produced a son, Caesarion. With his victory in Gaul Caesar wrote *Commentaries on the Gallic War* which served to promote his popularity and became a masterpiece of the Latin language. In 53 B.C. Crassus was treacherously killed by the enemy when he attempted to conquer Parthia, in Persia east of the Euphrates River. Now only Pompey and Caesar remained on the triumvirate.

At home Caesar sided with the people and won their support. The plunder from his conquests made him very wealthy, and he used his fortune to gain favor with the masses of Rome putting on spectacular gladiatorial games and bribed Roman officials. Pompey and the Senate were jealous of Caesar's conquests and popularity. After Crassus' death as well as Julia's, Caesars' daughter who was married to Pompey, Caesar and Pompey began to drift apart. Riots in Rome between populists and the conservative élite produced a chaotic situation. Rome, having no police force, left the conservative senators to align with the only powerful man in Rome, Pompey, to gain security and peace. The Senate then granted Pompey sole consulship. This delighted Pompey who always

Figure 5.4 Julius Caesar. *Image Copyright Andrei Nekrassov, 2009. Used under license from Shutterstock, Inc.*

desired the acceptance of the senatorial establishment with the status and prestige it gave him. Pompey brought order to Rome with his troops, and now was siding with the conservative senators.

Caesar's conquest of Gaul brought more wealth for the empire. Now that he accomplished his mission Caesar was ready to return to Rome and to his enemies in the Senate. Caesar knew his power base was his army that was loyal to him because he had led them to victory and given them shares of the spoils of war, the only wealth with their salaries that the Roman soldiers could expect, and not farmland from the republic. Land grants for Pompey's veterans were the exception not the rule. Caesar managed with popular support to have a law passed extending his command in Gaul. The conservative senators attacked Caesar who they considered a dangerous and powerful man who was a threat to the republican power-sharing principal and could come to Rome with his army and tell everyone, including Pompey what to do. Pompey thus announced that Caesar should give up command the following year and sided with the Senate controlled by the conservatives. Caesar feared that if he disbanded his army and presented himself to the Senate, his political enemies could then prosecute him for his past actions. Therefore, Caesar disregarded the tradition and order to present himself in Rome without his loyal army, his sole protection against his enemies, and crossed the Rubicon River with his legions headed for Rome in 49 B.C. This began another civil war.

As Caesar marched to Rome, Pompey and most of the Senate fled the city. Pompey went to the east. Caesar defeated Pompey's forces in Spain and then went east to defeat Pompey. In the battle of Pharsalus, Greece, in 48 B.C. the outnumbered Caesar defeated Pompey forces. Pompey fled to Egypt. Upon arriving in Alexandria, Egypt, the Egyptian officials thinking they would be better off pleasing

Caesar, treacherously assassinated Pompey and sent his head to Caesar. When Caesar saw it he wept at the dishonorable death of the great Roman and ordered the assassins put to death. He then stayed in Egypt, met Cleopatra, and brought Egypt with its large supply of grain into the Roman domain. By 45 B.C. Caesar had triumphed in Italy, Spain, Gaul (France), Greece, Syria, North Africa, and Egypt.

Between 49 and 44 B.C. Caesar was voted four consulships and four dictatorships. He set out to honor his promises to the people by passing legislation granting land to veterans and urban poor in Italy and colonies abroad fulfilling the Gracchi brother's goal. He cancelled all interests on debts originating during the civil war inflationary period, reduced Rome's debt with better administration, put down street gangs, rebuilt the city, reduced unemployment to more than half with public works program, and decreed one-third of laborers in the large estates be free men, and removed corrupt officials and senators. Caesar rejected the title and crown of a king. But his enemies saw in him a threat to their interest and his social class, and as an autocrat when in February of 44 B.C. Caesar became dictator in perpetuity. Therefore Caesar became Rome's **first emperor.** Instead of sharing power and relating with the new senatorial élite working toward complete reform of the republic, Caesar pursued his patrician dignity, his honor and power rather than the liberty of the citizens. In March of that year a group of senators—about 60—came up to Caesar to make petition, and while having a conversation one of them pulled his dagger and stabbed the dictator and the rest followed suit. Caesar died of 23 wounds. The motive for his murder ranged from jealousy to patriotic concerns over constitutional violations, and the resentment of corrupt officials Caesar had interfered with their greed. The people who supported Caesar considered him a martyr. The conspiring senators thought they had restored the republic. In reality it was dead.

The Empire, 27 B.C.–476 A.D.

Augustus. Gaius Octavian was Caesar's adopted grandnephew and heir (Figure 5.5). When Caesar was murdered Augustus was 18 years old. Although young, Octavian reacted like a veteran politician. He formed a Second Triumvirate with Mark Anthony and Lepidus, and reignited civil war in 43 B.C. when he pursued power and to revenge his adoptive father's assassination. Octavian began to call himself Caesar to attach his adoptive father's fame to his person in the eyes of the Roman people. He joined Mark Anthony and went to war against Caesar's assassins defeating them and driving Brutus and Cassius to suicide. Even though Mark Anthony was a large and well-built man with experience serving with Caesar during his military campaigns, the more fragile and younger appearance of Octavian disguised his ruthless mind and cold-bloodedness by which he took violent measures against his rivals and enemies. Octavian is considered Rome's first emperor, but was actually the second after Caesar. Thus the term "Roman Empire" is often used to refer to the period from Octavian in 27 B.C. to 476 A.D., even if most of the conquered territory was accomplished under the republic. Constitutional government ended with Caesar, and under Octavian, or Augustus as he is better known, the Roman Republic

Figure 5.5 Roman statue of emperor Caesar Augustus. *Image Copyright Asier Villafranca, 2009. Used under license from Shutterstock, Inc.*

was transformed into an autocracy or one man rule, the emperor. This was the greatest revolution in all of Rome's history. To achieve this goal Octavian used many means. Sometimes force, other times the law, but he preferred the use of persuasion which he mastered to the point that the Roman people and senators willingly gave up their freedoms under the republic and handed them to Octavian.

The Second Triumvirate ruled the Roman Empire as dictator. The three heads divided the empire among themselves. Octavian ruling the western empire, thus having all of Italy with Rome, Mark Anthony had the eastern empire with the important province of Egypt, and Lepidus had North Africa. To secure an alliance between Octavian and Mark Anthony, the latter married Octavian's sister Octavia. In 36 B.C. Octavian forced Lepidus out of the triumvirate when Lepidus tried to take Sicily from Octavian and most of his troops deserted him for Octavian.

Mark Anthony fell in love with Cleopatra and both planned to take over the empire using Caesar's son, Ptolemy XV, as heir to Caesar and thus rule of the empire. Mark Anthony lived a lavish lifestyle with Cleopatra in Egypt and had sons with her. When he divorced Octavia, who was respected by the Roman people, and Mark Anthony's will was publicly revealed by Octavian, the shrewd politician was able to convince the Roman people that Mark Anthony was not loyal to Rome and waged a war against his rival. The will of Mark Anthony declared his sons by Cleopatra his heirs, gave control of three Roman territories to Cleopatra, and if he died in Rome to have his body sent to Cleopatra in Egypt. Octavian was clever to use the outrage of Roman society at the possibility of being ruled by men who were half Roman, and declared war only on Cleopatra, claiming that Mark Anthony was under the Egyptian queen's spell. After defeating the combined forces of Cleopatra and Mark Anthony in the naval battle of Actium off the coast of Greece in 31 B.C., Octavian trapped Mark Anthony in Egypt where before his defeat and thinking Cleopatra had committed suicide, he stabbed himself through the stomach, but lived to die in Cleopatra's arms. After her capture by Octavian, Cleopatra committed suicide in 30 B.C. using a poisonous snake smuggled in a basket of figs. She chose this means because she conducted many experiments on condemned prisoners that convinced her it was the least painful way to die. This demonstrates how the life of slaves and prisoners in antiquity had little value to those that ruled who had the power of life and death over other men. Octavian killed Caesarion, Caesar and Cleopatra's young son, due to the possibility of claiming to be the heir of Caesar which made him a dangerous rival.

Octavian returned to Rome victorious having great wealth provided by the breadbasket of Egypt. Octavian immediately proceeded to gain the loyalty of the people of Rome and the Roman Army. He spent this wealth by giving generous cash awards to his soldiers, and money to every Roman citizen. He secured Egypt's granary which became Rome's reliable source of grain. He brought the end of civil war and offered peace and order after a century of chaos and violence under the Roman republic. Now Octavian held all the power but he lacked legitimacy. To overcome this weakness became the most important goal in his life. To achieve legitimacy he prudently maintained the appearance of restoring the Republic. He was clever to dress his power in the clothes of the old republican offices.

Understanding the lesson of Caesar's assassination and aware of the distrust and hatred of the noble Romans toward monarchy and an all powerful individual who dominated the state, Octavian avoided exercising supreme power in an explicit manner and disguised it. When he met the Senate, Octavian renounced all his powers and territories he conquered handing them to the Senate and Roman people. The Senate, fearful of continual civil wars and of Octavian's power, responded by granting Octavian consulship which is what he wanted. On the surface the republic seemed restored with power in the hands of the Senate and assemblies of the Roman people. The Senate granted Octavian the provinces of Gaul, Syria, Egypt, and Cyprus for ten years. These important military provinces were governed by Octavian where most of the legions were located. Octavian had command of armies, a major source of power, and these wealthy territories. He also managed to acquire the power of a tribune and become the defender of the people's interest in the entire empire. This political move secured unrivalled popularity with the people.

Octavian gained complete power and political legitimacy with a resonant title in 19 B.C. He created the name "Augustus" that translates to sacred or revered but not calling himself a god in a direct manner. Accepting from the Senate the title of **Augustus,** the "revered one," and princeps civitatis or first citizen title which was granted to elder statesmen during the republic, the people thought of him as someone worthy of a special respect and somehow holy or religious. He was careful to avoid being named emperor or any title suggesting he was a monarch. Augustus kept the republic's tradition of letting senators speak in a specific order to appear that everyone had a voice in government. But in reality Augustus' wish prevailed and their opinions were merely role-playing the appearance of the old republic. An advisory body of consuls and senators was made that met in his imperial palace and not the Senate. Important information was kept from the Senate, so most senators did not know how the empire was really functioning. Augustus nominated the consuls and tribunes to be elected, and the list of candidates for office to be voted were all his yes-men senators that would not go against him. He transferred the judicial and legislative functions of the popular assemblies and courts to the Senate. As Augustus controlled the appointment to the Senate and the senators were fearful of the army under his control, they rubberstamped his will. An example of Augustus' power was when young senator Egnatius Rufus became very popular and refused to withdraw his name for the list of candidates for consulship, he was tried for conspiracy and executed. Therefore, Roman citizen's vote had no real power. To give stability to his regime Augustus reformed the army. This reformation gave stability to future emperors. He managed to nationalize the Roman army taking it out of politics. No longer were generals recruiting armies and gaining their loyalty by offering spoils of war and land. The loyalty was attached to the Roman state. Citizens were offered a professional military career with its benefits and promotions. The army became the empire's greatest expense, over half the entire annual budget.

From 27 B.C. to 14 A.D. Augustus achieved many accomplishments for the empire. First of all was peace and prosperity in an unprecedented way. He began the **Pax Romana** or "Roman peace" that lasted until the death of Emperor Marcus Aurelius in 180 A.D. For the first time in its history the Roman Empire enjoyed peace and a stable order for over two centuries. People were safe at home and when they traveled by land or sea. Increased trade produced prosperity and it was increased by establishing an efficient monetary system.

Efficient administration was another major accomplishment. Augustus appointed honest and efficient governors to the provinces. The policy of these provincial governors was to respect local customs and allow for provincial autonomy and local self-government. This pluralistic and pragmatic policy allowed Rome to influence and govern all its provinces holding together a vast empire composed of many ethnic groups each with their own customs and religions. Rome was very wise with this flexible policy of not imposing its religion and culture on conquered people, but allowing them to keep their traditional ways of life as long as they were loyal to Rome, paid taxes, and served in the military. It kept rebellions to a minimum and avoided an inefficient centralized bureaucracy. Only the province of Judea due to its monotheistic religion which only allowed for the worship of one true God and would not accept the emperor as god, did not have a peaceful relation with the Roman Empire that ruled this province, and had a rebellious attitude. The populations of all other provinces aspired to become Roman citizens and enjoy the benefits and higher standard of living that the empire offered. Augustus established a periodic census to keep track of changes in wealth and population and was thus able to shift tax burden from the poorest provinces to the more wealthy ones. He also reduced the number of taxes collected by the private tax collectors. A civil service based on merit was created and had a veteran's pension fund for the military. He rebuilt Rome, constructing another forum, created the first police and fire departments, and sponsored army construction of public works projects such as roads and bridges throughout the empire. Therefore, Augustus can be ranked as one of the most skillful and energetic administrators Rome had in all its history. He not only conquered territories for Rome but administered them properly, a feat that not all great conquerors like Alexander the Great achieved after devoting most of their energies and resources to conquest. The bureaucratic machinery he put in place continued to function under good, mediocre, and incompetent emperors.

Augustus lived according to Roman morality. He lived a Roman traditional frugal life in his modest house, ate frugally, and wore simple clothes made by his female relatives. He banished from Rome the poet Ovid for his lascivious poems and a scandal involving his promiscuous daughter Julia, who he also exiled for her adultery. To avoid a decline of Roman traditional values and depopulation, he passed laws rewarding those having legitimate children and penalizing adultery, bachelorhood and childlessness. For example, punishment of sex offenses in severe cases included loss of property and exile. Men still were permitted adulterous sex only with slaves or prostitutes, but respectable citizen women could not have sex outside marriage.

Augustus patronized poets, among the most famous Virgil (Publius Vergilius Maro) who wrote the epic poem the *Aeneid* to celebrate the victory at Actium and stir patriotism, the second greatest poet Horace (Quintus Horatius Flaccus), and the historian Livy (Titus Livius).

Augustus left a tremendous legacy to Rome. His very capable administration and popularity was essential to Roman society's acceptance of the imperial system of government. Imperial rule paved the way for despotic emperors such as Caligula and Nero. His political stability and enduring peace saved the Greco-Roman civilization from a complete downfall due to a continuation of civil wars, just as the Greek city-states declined due to their exhaustion produced by continuous rivalry and wars until taken over by the Macedonians. By restoring peace, prosperity, and order, Augustus saved an exhausted and demoralized civilization permitting it to endure over four more centuries that allowed for the development and spreading of this civilization into new territories along with the spread of Christianity to all parts of the Roman Empire which was a major influence upon Western civilization.

Augustus's Successors. Augustus created the **Julio-Claudians dynasty** (27 B.C.–68 A.D.) that ruled the solid political institutions he left to Rome. Members of the Julian and Claudian clans provided the next emperors of Rome. Tiberius and Claudius were able rulers and administrators, Caligula and Nero were weak and frivolous. This dynasty schemed against one another to gain and hold power. In this struggle for power and their immoral way of life involves among others ills, murder, forced suicide, adultery, bigamy, incest, and sexual promiscuity. Despite these decadent emperors, the empire prospered due to the governmental legacy of Augustus. The last emperor of this dynasty, Nero, who attained power through the scheme of his mother who murdered her husband emperor Claudius, was inept as a ruler. His excesses and faulty rule led to military rebellion and his suicide. Four men fought for the position of emperor and Roman armies marched to Rome to make their commanders emperor. The commander Vespasian came out of this civil war as the victor.

Vespasian began the **Flavians dynasty** (69–96 A.D.) and designated his sons Titus and Domitian to become his successors. This act turned the principate (from princeps or first citizen, is the position of emperor from the combination of his power as consul and tribune) begun under the Julio-Claudians into a monarchy. Vespasian increased the power of the emperor and did not solve the problem of the army involved in politics. He was responsible for putting down the Jewish revolts in Judea, which led to the destruction of Jerusalem and its temple that was plundered, and the enslavement of Jewish survivors who were forced to work on his grand project the Colosseum in Rome. The empire expanded its conquests of new territories under this dynasty that ended with the stabbing of the hated and cruel Domitian.

The **Antonine dynasty** succeeded the Flavians with the era of the **"five good Emperors,"** Nerva, Trajan, Hadrian, Antoninus Pius, and Marcus Aurelius (96–180 A.D.). The Roman Empire during this "golden age" of the good emperors had firmly established a monarchy with definite rights, powers, and prerogatives. The emperor was an *absolute monarch*. These emperors were not despotic and ran the empire efficiently with the aid of professional bureaucrats. Later rulers used the power built by these emperors in a despotic manner. The Roman army changed from the times of Augustus. From a mobile force it became a garrison force living in forts along the empire's borders. Under the five good emperors the army was a source of stability and Romanizing agent. The vast empire and the large army required to defend it effectively no longer could it be all recruited from Italy. Gradually the officers came from Italy and the Romanized provinces, but increasingly the legionaries were recruited from the provinces near the borders. Even though the Roman soldier was an element that brought Roman culture to the provinces of the frontier, exposing the local population to Roman traditions, habits, and way of thinking, by the 3rd century A.D. the increasing number of soldiers that were not from Italy and its Roman culture produced an army indifferent to Rome and its traditions. This would later turn to be a cause of Rome's decline as an empire because it created a military weak point in defending the empire's vast frontier from Barbarian invaders in the 3rd and 4th centuries A.D.

These were the last years of the Pax Romana that began under Augustus. The empire prospered during these years of peace and stability under these five fair rulers. Roman culture spread through city life, Rome being an urban culture, and the Roman army. The melding of culture can be clearly seen in the Romance languages that derived from Latin blending with native languages that resulted in the makings of Spanish, French, Italian, Portuguese, and Romanian and other minor tongues that are spoken in Europe today. The extensive network of roads and secure sea-lanes throughout the entire empire connected all regions and allowed for extensive trade as well as human travel and migration. Northern, central, and eastern Europe became connected with the cultural and economic life of the Mediterranean world. Rome became the grand capital with its large population of 500,000 to 750,000, its aqueduct and sewage system, the center of entertainment with its Colosseum and gladiatorial contests and more popular chariot racing. The emperors, continuing republican practices, provided free bread, and later wine and oil, to the citizenry of Rome avoiding bread riots and shortages. To noncitizens grain was provided at low prices. The emperor and even some very wealthy citizens entertained the Roman populace at great expense. The most popular were gladiators and chariot races. This free grain and entertainment is referred to as "bread and circus" which became a means to gain popularity with the masses and appease them.

The Pax Romana and its "golden age" came to an end with the death of Emperor Marcus Aurelius in 180 A.D. The success of the five god emperors was due in part that the first four designated capable young men as their successors, rather than their sons or close relatives. Marcus Aurelius did not continue this practice and made his son Commodus emperor. Commodus was a vicious and incompetent individual. He indulged in his perversities, had open contempt for the Senate and was so brutally despotic that he was strangled to death in 192 A.D. As the empire did not have clear law and tradition of succession the situation worsened as the generals of the empires' legions claimed the throne and went into civil war to gain power. The provincial general **Septimius Severus** (193–211 A.D.) came out victorious from this struggle for power. From this point on the provincial armies could meddle in imperial politics at will. Severus and other successors ruled as **military dictators** eliminating the rights of the Senate aggravating the problem. During this period until 235 A.D. Rome was under a military monarchy that was autocratic and that gave all free men in the empire Roman citizenship. As law yielded to the sword, any ambitious general could try his luck in fighting to attain the Roman throne. This led to an **endemic period of civil wars from 235–284 A.D.** where there were 26 emperors in 49 years known as the "barracks emperors" coming out of the army and only one managed to avoid a violent death. The political chaos and civil wars were the worst in Rome since its rise to world power and a cause of its final decline. The political institutions of the empire, its bureaucracy and ordinary lower officials protected by loyal soldiers were the only means that the empire avoided internal collapse. The beginnings of barbarian invasions that took advantage of the gaps on the frontier left by the armies that went to fight the civil wars became a major threat to the empire. In 251 A.D. the Goths broke through the border of the Danube River and defeated emperor Decius in battle and sacked Athens. Other Germanic tribes followed suit in different regions of Europe. In the east the Persians captured Emperor Valerian in battle in 260 A.D., enslaved and humiliated having to kneel as a footstool so King Saphur would step on his back to mount his horse. Valerian died in captivity and his body was stuffed and placed in a Persian temple as a warning to Roman ambassadors. The empire lost several European provinces when they succeeded and queen

Zenobia from Syria took control of Roman provinces in the east. Emperor Aurelian (270–275 A.D.) was able to recover these lost provinces in the east, repel the invading Germanic tribes, and restore the seceded provinces in Europe. He began a great building project of massive walls to protect Rome. The Roman Empire was at its all time low and vulnerable; therefore, it was logical that the Roman culture of the 3rd century A.D. was characterized by pervasive anxiety. Even the busts of the emperors of this period show the expression of worry with furrowed brow typical in portraits of this period.

Diocletian (284–305 A.D.) was the next emperor to rise and put an end to this chaotic period. He began to repair the damage done by civil wars which consumed most of his efforts but was not completely successful in this task. Gaius Aurelius Valerius Diocletianus or Diocletian was a low-born soldier from a provincial family who rose through the ranks of the army. He spent most of his time at the frontier which made him aware of the urgent need of the empire to reform if it were to continue in existence. His reforms improved and placed the army under central control. He made reforms to improve the economy by revaluing the coins, stopping inflation, and passed laws to ensure collection of taxes, thus establishing a regular budget to run the empire. To improve imperial administration Diocletian reorganized the provinces into smaller regions under new administration.

Diocletian's major reform that he is famous for in history was to recognize that the empire had become too large for one man to manage it; therefore, on March 1, 293, he created a college of four emperors to rule the Roman Empire. This new system of rule in known as the **Tetrarchy** or rule by four emperors. Under this system there were two senior emperors with the title of Augustus, with Diocletian ruling the eastern half of the empire and Maximian the western half. Each Augustus appointed a junior colleague with the title of Caesar. Thus Galerius joined Diocletian in the east and Flavius Valerius Constantius, father of the future Emperor Constantine, aided Maximian in the west. Diocletian was the senior partner and the final authority. These four emperors resided in different cities across the Roman world ensuring that the presence of the emperor of Rome was established in many different areas at the same time. The Roman Senate lost what little power it had left. The emperors were in complete control.

Under Diocletian the emperor became a **dominus** or lord, claiming he was the "elect of god" ruling due to divine favor. Diocletian was called Jovius after the god Jupiter, and Maximian called Herculius after Hercules son of a god and mortal woman, indicating the quasi-divine basis of their authority. The foundations of this new regime were traditionally pagan. Diocletian's reforms were enormous. He was successful in restoring the empire that was expiring, but his reforms were not able to eliminate the defects and inefficiencies of Roman government. Diocletian's reorganization transformed the empire by "orientalizing" it in a way that lasted many centuries. First he geographically orientalized the empire by ruling it from the east where the center of its administration was placed because wealth and vitality of the empire was concentrated in this region. Most of his rule was exercised from the city of Nicomedia in Asia Minor or Anatolia (modern-day Turkey), not from Rome. Diocletian's division of the empire into two parts became permanent. Later Constantine and other emperors attempted to unsuccessfully keep the empire together. By the 4th century A.D. the east and west drifted apart and the western section fell in the 5th century A.D. Second, Diocletian wanting to avoid what he viewed as the inevitable result of his predecessors once in power, the lack of sufficient respect, he adopted the title and court ceremonies of an Oriental monarch. Coming forward as an undisguised autocrat that was feared and worshiped, taking on the title of "Dominus" or lord, he hoped to hold on to power with more security; thus abandoning Augustus's policy of appearing to be a constitutional ruler. He wore a crown, purple silk robe, and his subjects had to lie facing down, as in submission or adoration, in an audience with him. Third, an increasing reliance and growth of the imperial bureaucracy. Diocletian's reforms created a need for many new officials. The new bureaucracy kept the empire running but open to corruption and graft, requiring more manpower and expense at a time when the empire was in short supply.

The autocratic regime of Diocletian stifled the cultivation of individual freedom in the arts. Sculpture shows a lack of spontaneity. Roman portrait statuary went from striking naturalism and individuality became impassive and somewhat stiff. Human faces lacked emotions and were symmetrical.

In architecture the style became colossal and pompous. A good example were the baths constructed in Rome covering thirty acres, the largest to that date in 303 A.D.

Diocletian became infamous for his suppression of a new religion on the rise, Christianity. Christianity was seen by the Roman authorities as a threat to the Roman way of life and its security. The Romans believed that there was an unwritten contract between the Roman gods who protected the empire in return for worship. This was highly valued by traditional pagan Roman society as it was believed that stability of the empire depended on this relation. The Romans viewed Christianity as an organized religion that only worshiped one god exclusively. The religious community's monotheism excluded all pagan gods of worship and thus constituted a dangerous threat to the divine pagan blessing of the Roman state, especially in times of crisis when security was at stake. Roman authorities thought that in time of crisis strong repression of this destabilizing monotheistic religion was necessary.

The first persecution of Christians throughout empire was under Emperor Decius who ordered a universal sacrifice in his honor to assure the divine protection of the gods against the Goths threatened the northern borders in 250 A.D. The citizens who participated in these pagan sacrifices received certificates as proof of participation. Christians who refused were tortured and executed as punishment. This persecution ended but the conflict continued among Christians and Roman authorities. Under Diocletian's regime of the four emperors pagan traditions and respect of mythological gods were a major part of Diocletian's reforms and renewal of his empire. The conflict rose up again in 299 A.D. when Diocletian was informed that some pagan priests were unable to get omens from the gods they were inquiring and blamed it on Christian soldiers who had made the sign of the cross. Diocletian ordered a purge of the army and passed an edict to all the empire ordering churches to be destroyed, scriptures burned and to take away offices held by Christians to root out Christianity. Christians were subject to torture and execution, and those who had gained their freedom were to be made slaves again. Diocletian ended the persecutions in 305 because they had no popular support and confirmed how well Christianity had spread throughout the empire.

Diocletian was the first and only Roman emperor to abdicate voluntarily. He decided to retire to his palace by the sea, managing to get Maximian to also retire. Their two Caesars succeeded them in a peaceful manner. He thought that after his authoritarian reform was done he could enjoy the rest of his life without worries. But after his retirement the Tetarchy began to decline because rivalry for power among the emperors continued. Diocletian hoped his Tetarchy would deter the use of force to attain power by establishing a clear and orderly means of succession that did not work in the long run. His successors fought to attain power which began another cycle of civil wars until the rise of Emperor Constantine.

When the former Caesars, Constantinus and Galerius, became the new emperors after Diocletian and Maximian's retirement, Constantine was very disappointed when he was not appointed as one of the new Caesars in 305 A.D. The same disappointment was experienced by Marcus Aurelius Valerius Maxentius, son of Maximian, when he was passed over in favor of Flavius Valerius Severus elected to be the new Caesar in the west. Tension among the east and the west came up with the new successors. Constantinus in the west feared that his son Constantine could become a political hostage of Galerius, and made a request to Galerius to allow his son to join him as he campaigned to put Gaul and Britain again under Roman control. This was not to the likening of Galerius who knew that Constantine at his court was a means to have the upper hand over Constantinus. Galerius for the sake of harmony acceded to the demands but began planning Constantine's demise and instructed Severus to intercept and murder Constantine. Constantine had deep suspicions of the plot and took flight from Galerius to join his father in the west, maiming the horses of the imperial service along the way to avoid being persecuted by potential assassins. He reached his father in Gaul and joined him in his campaign, where he gained great popularity with the army in Britain. He saw how his father paid lip-service to the edict of Diocletian against the Christians and protected them from the brutality practiced in the east. The reason for Constantinus' tolerant policy toward Christianity was for the political reason that persecuting its followers would not help him govern Western Europe. Constantinus died in 306 in England, and before his death appointed his son as Augustus of the West without consulting his fellow emperors. Constantinus's army declared loyalty to the popular Constantine. Now the Tetrarchy was ruined and in crisis.

Galerius had to accept this reality; thus, he recognized Constantine as a junior Caesar and demoted him by promoting Severus to Augustus in the west. The four emperors were in a "cold war" with each other competing for more power and after six years a civil war broke out. First Severus was eliminated when he was captured and executed in 307 A.D. by Maxentius who took over Italy, the Italian islands and North Africa, and Maximian who came out of retirement. For political advantage Constantine had made an alliance with Maxentius marrying his sister Faustina. Maximian, in an attempt to gain imperial power of the west for himself, turned against Constantine and separated from his son. This act forced Constantine to go to war with Maximian, defeating him, and Maximian hanged himself. Now Maxentius wanted revenge for his father's death declaring war on his brother-in-law Constantine. In 311 Galerius died due to an incurable disease after executing the doctors who were not able to cure him, and in his last days repented from his policy of persecuting Christians with his last edict ending the persecutions. With his death the Tetrarchy also died. The final clash between Maxentius and Constantine at the battle of Milvian Bridge would decide the future fate of the empire and change the fate of the world.

Maxentius was a pagan, and even if he did not persecute the Christians he had banished three bishops from Rome and did not restore the property taken from them during Diocletian's persecutions. On the other hand, Constantine at this point a pagan was much more tolerant. Under his rule churches were not destroyed and the right of Christians to worship was restored. Thus high-ranking Christians had a favorable attitude toward Constantine and travelled with him. They wanted to influence him in favoring Christianity. Maxentius in Rome counted on an army of 100,000, that greatly outnumbered Constantine's. Constantine knew this fact but believed his army was superior with the advantage of being veterans of the wars in Gaul and Britain. He had entered Italy through the Alps and defeated the armies Maxentius sent against him and now came close to Rome.

Maxentius was surrounded by pagan priests. The day before the final battle Maxentius was fearful and lacked confidence in his victory, so he asked the priests to read the omens from Rome's pagan gods. The priests then cut open a young animal to put their hands into the body and feel the intestines. The augury pointed to the enemy of Rome would be defeated. Those next to Maxentius insisted that Constantine was the enemy of Rome, and Maxentius agreed. According to Eusebius in his writings Life of Constantine, just before the battle Constantine had a vision at midday. He saw a shining cross in the sky with the inscription "by this sign, you will conquer." Seeking an explanation of his vision Constantine went to the priests who travelled with him. They told him it was the sign of God who had divinely chosen him to defeat the pagan Maxentius. Constantine became convinced this was true and ordered all his soldiers to mark their shields with a Christian symbol in white paint following instructions he had from a dream. This was a gamble because even though some of his soldiers were Christian, the majority were not, and having to confront a large enemy in number under the sign and protection of a new God could have a demoralizing effect.

On October 28, 312, both armies met at the outskirts of Rome on the plain before the Milvian Bridge over the Tiber River. Maxentius planned to do battle in the plain. If he was not victorious then his secondary plan was to retreat across the Milvian Bridge back to Rome and make it his stronghold. To keep his enemy forces from crossing over part of the bridge was destroyed and replaced by a floating bridge that once his army crossed over the bridge the engineers were to unfasten the bolts that would leave the floating structure to float down the river. The battle began and Constantine defeated Maxentius forces which then returned to the bridge to cross over the Tiber. The army was so large the bridge could not support the weight of the stampeding survivors. The engineers released the fastenings too soon and the whole structure collapsed. The panic was great and many fell into the river drowning or were crushed to death in the narrow original bridge. Many bodies littered the banks of the Tiber among them was the body of Maxentius.

THE RISE OF CHRISTIANITY

Constantine's victory gave him complete rule over the western empire under the protection of the Christian God. A converted Constantine emerged that would take steps to make a great change upon the entire Empire by decreeing the freedom to worship any God, and therefore, no longer could Christians be persecuted for their beliefs and practices. Now he had to bring the new religion into Roman politics, into the eastern empire and to the pagan majority of the population in this vast empire (Figure 5.6).

When Constantine entered the city of Rome he was walking through a political tightrope between Christianity and traditional pagan Romans with their main representative the Roman senators. The pagan Romans distrusted this new religion and its followers which they considered out of the mainstream renouncing slavery and Roman entertainments, believing in a heaven after death, embracing a humble and ascetic lifestyle that was considered pleasureless, and upholding to sexual chastity as a virtue. Christians were expecting Constantine who owed his victory to the Christian God to recognize this reality and favor their cause. It would be difficult to please both sides.

Figure 5.6 Statue of the Roman Emperor Constantine. *Image Copyright Andre Nantel, 2009. Used under license from Shutterstock, Inc.*

Following the traditional Roman custom of celebrating military victories with a procession, Constantine surprised the Roman with military standards baring the symbol of Christ, and after taking the symbols of an emperor he refused to perform the traditional sacrifices to Jupiter for his victory. Constantine knew he had to play a delicate political balance keeping both sides content and trusting him as their new sovereign. To gain support of Rome he declared that the authority and responsibility of the Senate would be restored by giving them an active hand in his government. Those who had collaborated with Maxentius were excused with no action taken against them. The senators returned Constantine's trust in them by declaring him sole emperor in the west.

While in Rome, Constantine began to promote his Christian followers to official posts of court advisers. Thus Christians began to gain influence in his government. The balancing act of both groups was done in a successful manner and the emperor left Rome reconciled and consolidated his position in the western half of the empire. Now he wanted to bring peace and unity to the eastern half. The eastern emperor Maximinus Daia was informed of Constantine's status as new emperor of the west and warned him to stop persecuting Christians. Then he had his 18-year-old sister Constantia, also a Christian, for political reasons marry a pagan in his late forties Valerius Lincinianus **Licinius.** The purpose of this wedding was to make an alliance with Licinius for him to rule the east and Constantine the west.

To protect Christians and keep harmony within his domains Constantine insisted on a policy of toleration of all religions in the empire. It placed all religions of the empire on an equal standing. This was a radical new policy for pagan Romans. The result was the **Edict of Milan** of 313 A.D. This was the first document in the world to recognize freedom of religion. It ended the persecutions of Christians, decreed the restoration of all property confiscated from the church, legalized churches, forbade business and servile work on Sundays, which was a holy day for Christians and pagans, and abolished crucifixion as punishment.

Emperor Daia made the first move of aggression invading Licinius' territories in Asia Minor. Thus, war began. In 313 Licinius defeated Daia's larger forces. Daia fled and to avoid the humiliation he took poison as a way out. Licinius settled in Nicomedia, the imperial capital of the east and ordered a purge by murdering all sympathizers, advisers, and family members of Daia, as well as the family members of the former tetrarchs Diocletian, Severus, and Galerius.

Constantine inherited as emperor the title of pontifex maximus or high priest of the Roman gods, a tradition since Augustus. As a Christian he refused to participate in pagan sacrifices, but publically kept a neutral position before pagans and Christians. He began to give Christians a much favored place in the administration of the empire and privileges exempting them from civic public duties and Christians of high rank from taxes. Bishops were given administrative functions in all parts of the empire. Constantine gave generously from the treasury to build churches throughout the empire. He left several basilicas standing in Rome today, making the basilica a model for Christian churches. Constantine's authority extended to acting as arbiter of disputes inside the church. Disunity in the church went against unity of the empire and this Constantine would not tolerate. But the majority of the Roman world was still pagan, and thus, the emperor had to continue to play both sides in public. His reforms favorable to Christians gained many supporters within the domains of Lucinius where most of the Christian of the empire resided. This gave Constantine a base of support in the east.

Both emperors had sons from their wives Constantia and Fausta, creating two new changes of legitimacy. This brought the question to their minds of to whom would the empire belong. Constantine's goal was control of the entire empire. One emperor was Christian the other pagan. All this would lead to rivalry and war of religions.

Lucinius had reasons to have envy and resentment toward Constantine. He thought that part of the empire ruled by Constantine belonged to him. He was jealous of Constantine's popularity in his territories which placed him in second place. Finally Licinius suspected that Constantine's politics were putting obstacles in the way of his newborn son to inherit the throne. He decided to put an end to his alliance and began to plot Constantine's assassination. Licinius needed allies in his plan and found them in the Roman Senate. He can accuse Constantine of breaking the Edict of Milan by favoring Christians over pagans, and when Constantine trespassed his territory in 315 he had another pretext against his rival. By 316 many pagan senators in Rome were dissatisfied with Constantine favoring Christianity and the inner circle made up of Christians. They thought that under Constantine, to rise in his regime you had to be a Christian. It would not be difficult to get accomplices to the assassination plot. Bassianus, a senator married to Constantine's half-sister Anastasia, got involved in the plot and agreed to murder his brother-in-law. Licinius wife's, Constantina, learned of the plot against his brother and through Christian channels of communication was able to inform him of the plot. The night of the assassination attempt was made, Constantine was expecting it and Bassianus was executed instead. Lucinius was angry with his failed plot and had Constantine's statues and busts in his capital smashed. This constituted a declaration of war.

The two emperors fought in 316 with neither of them having a complete victory. Thus, a new alliance was made and Constantine declared that his two sons and Licinius' son were considered Caesars and future emperors. In reality there was no true peace in the heart of the two rivals. Religion became the issue that started the war again.

From 317 to 321 Licinius allowed toleration of Christianity. While Constantine with his speeches demonstrated his Christian fervor and vision for the empire from divine inspiration, there was evidence of the beginning of the slow eradication of pagan cults in the west with the closing of some pagan temples. Christianity kept on the rise with gifts of property to churches, charities to the poor and needy, high profile of bishops and their increased judicial authority, and the legalization of the church. This allowed for the church to become local centers of power and organization in the western empire. The chi-rho, the mark of Christ, appeared on objects that belonged to the wealthy class. This meant that religious conversion had its advantage in this new regime. The upper classes became self-confident that this prosperity would continue as long as Constantine received protection from God, and not from the old pagan divinities. During an Easter speech in the early 320s Constantine declared that God was responsible for his success, and therefore, his obligation was to persuade his subjects to worship God, reform the wicked and liberate the persecuted. At this point, Constantine made clear in public his position that he favored Christianity, and the pluralistic policy of pagan and Christian religions being considered equal was gradually being eradicated.

Lucinius became paranoid of Christians in his own domains. He was suspect of the loyalty of his court officials to his person. He began to interrogate them. Then he imposed tests on his servants like Auxentius, a legal clerk. Liciniuis asked Auxentius to come to a fountain in his palace and cut a cluster of grapes from a vine and offer it to the statue of Dionysus or leave his court forever. The Christian servant chose to leave the pagan emperor. He later became a bishop. Things got worse and Licinius then forced everyone in his government to sacrifice to pagans gods or lose their job. Then the same demand with the army. Later on he imposed it upon civilians, and in 323 he forced the bishops to make sacrifice to pagan gods. Those who refused were punished, and tax exemptions of the clergy were eliminated. Councils and assemblies of bishops were forbidden to keep them from organizing any kind of resistance or protest. These acts were resuming the persecutions of Christianity with the closing of churches, punishment of faithful Christians, and even murder of Christian clergy. Christians urged Constantine to defend their brothers in faith. This would become a war of liberating the oppressed. Constantine made the first move and both emperors renewed the war.

Lucinius had his priests read the omens which promised his victory. Then he made sacrifices to pagan gods with his commanders and made a speech to his troops exclaiming how they were defending their ancestral gods that would lead them to victory. Both armies confronted each other in 324. Constantine had the chi-rho, Christ's sign, to be carried by a special guard in front of his forces. Licinius ordered his men not to get close nor gaze at this sign. When Constantine's forces came under attack many fell but not the standard bearers of the chi-rho. This gave a surge of confidence in victory with God's help through Constantine's ranks. Constantine came out decisively victorious in this battle of Chrysopolis and Licinius lost most of his army. Licinius ran off to his palace at Nicomedia and thought of saving his honor through suicide, the traditional Roman way out. His wife Constantina convinced him to surrender to Constantine and then managed to reach her brother at his headquarters. Begging him to forgive her husband as a Christian, the victorious emperor conceded. Lucinius had to declare Constantine lord and master and beg for forgiveness. Constantine asked Lucinius to convert. Then the defeated emperor and his family were sent off to retirement in peace. But Constantine knew that Licinius had not really changed and to avoid future threats under the charge of treasonable correspondence with the enemies of the empire had him and his son executed a year later in Greece, while Constantina survived and lived out her life in her brother's court.

Constantine as sole emperor of the Roman world restored the persecuted Christians and provided them with the same privileges Christians enjoyed in the west. Constantine urged his subjects to convert to Christianity and his edicts state how the Christian God was supreme, being behind all his successes and brought an end to persecutions. Some traditional pagan temples were closed and sacrifices were forbidden making clear that Christianity was the official favored religion of the Roman Empire. But there were no mass conversions of pagans and paganism would only die slowly. The process of fazing out paganism commenced.

Constantine found the church in the east divided with the heresy of Arianism. A priest called Arius held that Christ, God the son was created by God the father, thus Christ was not eternal and could not be called God. The church for Constantine was a unifying institution and the emperor would not tolerate divisions in his empire. In 335 he called upon all bishops for the first universal council of the church. The **Council of Nicaea,** which he attended in an active manner, rejected Arius' theological arguments. Most bishops supported the decision of the council keeping the unity within the church. When Arius and two of his followers refused approval Constantine exiled them. This treatment of the dissenters as heretics was the first time temporal authority took action in religious matters.

Constantine helped make Jerusalem a holy site for Christians and Jews, and founded Constantinople (modern day Istanbul in Turkey) in 330 which became another imperial center where he spent his last seven years of his life. Toward the end of his life he was baptized and did not wear the robes of imperial purple the emperors wore; he wore only white which was worn by Christians. During his last days he recalled several persons who he had exiled unjustly and his last words were a prayer of praise and thanks to God. This demonstrates the sincerity of his beliefs in his faith when he died in May of 337.

Constantine was succeeded by his three sons who had agreed to share power. Not long after their father's death they began to argue and even rivalry for power was the result that undid the work of unity of the empire achieved by Constantine. Constantine's victories and regime made a very important impact upon western civilization because it established Christianity as one of the major religions of the empire and paganism began to die out slowly. This accomplishment changed the course of western history. Christianity will become the state religion of the Roman Empire and the majority of the Roman world will convert to its faith. It will change the outlook and morality of the ancient world and begin a new one based upon Christian world view, morals, and values. When the Roman Empire fell in the west, the church would be the only standing institution to guide Western Europe's civilization, and an important institution influencing the culture of the Eastern Roman Empire or Byzantium. Therefore, the tremendous influence the church was able to give the world through history was in part able to accomplish it with the contributions of Constantine. The Greek Church and the Roman (Catholic) Church both give this Christian emperor the title of "Great" in virtue for what he did for Christianity and the world. The Greek Church honors him as a saint, and the Roman Church does not see him a model Christian ruler, but as a great one that Christianity is indebted to.

Christianity continued to thrive under the imperial molds that Constantine established. Constantius was Constantine's son who had the longest reign 337–361 A.D. and governed the whole empire during the last ten years of his life. He did with his power all possible to abolish paganism and propagate Christianity. For example, he prohibited all pagan sacrifices under penalty of death in 353, and ordered all pagan temples to be closed or converted to other uses. It did not have the desired effect and made some pagans adhere more to their old ways. He was inconsistent in this antipagan policy by allowing Christianity's intellectual adversaries to teach in Europe's institutions of higher learning. These were the sophists, Neo-Platonic philosophers and pagan rhetoricians. These enemies of Christianity became rivals in faith and seduced the successor of Constantius, Julian who left Christianity and embraced the Neo-Platonic school of philosophers, and during his reign a short pagan reaction took place.

All Roman emperors after Constantine where Christian except for Julian the Apostate who tried to turn back to paganism in 360 to 363. In a general massacre of the younger line of Constantine's family, the Flavian, Julian had been spared due to his very young age. The memory of the murder of his father and brothers caused Julian to hate Christianity, the faith professed by those responsible for the death of his family. Baptized and raised as a Christian, Julian accepted the anti-Christian philosophy of his teacher Mardonios. When he became emperor in 360 he began to promote paganism and persecuted Christianity. He stimulated a literary war against Christianity in which he took an active part, tried to establish a universal pagan church based on the Christian model, and to give infuse life into paganism with the morality and missionary zeal of Christianity. But Julian failed in this attempt to go back to the old ways. Paganism simply had lost its appeal for the masses, and found his converts in those who were looking for imperial favors by abandoning Christianity. Julian's animosity toward Christianity was such that he tried to refute the prophecy of Christ (Matt. 24:2) by rebuilding the Temple of Jerusalem, but he also failed in this endeavor. Julian died in 363 from a wound during a skirmish with the Persian Army, and as he fell from his horse he is said to have exclaimed, "Thou hast conquered, O Galilean." Under Julian's successor, Jovian (363–364) Christianity was reestablished as the religion of all the empire. In 364 a new dynasty was founded under Valentinian I, and the same policy toward Christianity was maintained. Valentinian I decided to divide the empire again between east and west, each half with its own emperor. Emperors that followed took energetic steps to suppress paganism. Under **Theodosius the Great** (379–395), who managed for the last time to unite all the empire under his rule, all pagan sacrifices were forbidden and all pagan temples closed.

Christianity was declared to be the faith of the empire, and no other would be tolerated. In 423 A.D. Emperor Theodosius II declared there were almost no pagans left in his domains. Emperor Justinian the great (527–565 A.D.) took all civil rights from the unbaptized and closed the last stronghold of paganism, the philosophical schools in Athens in 529. The last remains of paganism survived in the remote country-side for another century. The last pagans were converted in the islands of Sardinia and Corsica by the efforts of Pope Gregory the Great (590–604 A.D.). Therefore, by the 7th century A.D. **paganism was completely fazed out** in the territories of the ancient Roman Empire.

THE FALL OF ROME

The Roman Empire in the west fell for many causes. Most were internal causes that gradually weakened the empire. The ultimate cause that brought about its complete downfall was external. It came from the frontiers where Germanic tribes known as **barbarians** were invading the empire across it extensive borders.

The origin of the crisis produced by the barbarian invasions had their origins in the Huns, a nomadic people who came from the Eurasian steppes, from Mongolia to eastern borders of Europe. The Huns pushed the Goths in 376 A.D. from their fertile lands northwest of the Black Sea toward the south into the border of the Roman Empire along the western end of the Danube River. The northern border was not well guarded because the bulk of the Roman army was on the eastern frontier. The pressure of 200,000 Goths made the emperor give permission for one of the Gothic tribes to cross the Danube and settle inside the borders of the empire. The Romans abused these Goths and their reaction was to rebel against Roman authority. This brought about a war between the Gothic tribes and the Roman army between 377 to 382 which resulted in the major battle of Hadrianople, where the Roman army lost over 13,000 troops including 35 military tribunes, its major general and Emperor Valens. It was the greatest defeat the Romans had suffered since Hannibal in the battle of Cannae during the second Punic war. The idea of Roman invincibility was broken sending a shock wave across the empire. In 282 emperor Theodosius I had to make peace with the Goths making a treaty that allowed the Goths to settle in the Balkans. These Goths then came under the leadership of Alaric, who had crossed the Danube into Roman territory as a boy in 376. Alaric demanded long-term recognition of his people, to be treated on equal terms with the Romans, and a food subsidy, to keep part of the agricultural produce of their region.

In 406 to 407 new barbarian invasions took place. The Vandals, Alans, and Suevi crossed the Rhine River in modern Germany sacking and creating havoc through Gaul and crossing the Pyrenees Mountains into Spain. This was the second major breach in the Roman frontier.

An ambitious and unscrupulous senator, Olympius, ended the policy of acclimating the Goth into the empire and persecutions against the Goths began which ignited a war with the Goths under Alaric. In 408 Alaric invaded Italy. Alaric put Rome under siege and Rome paid a great sum of its wealth to have Alaric end the siege. The Roman emperor did not accede to the demands of Alaric, who wanted an agreement to settle permanently in Roman provinces, annual payment in gold, annual supply of grain, and a senior generalship in the Roman army which would secure his influence in the emperor's court and thus be able to defend the interests of the Goths. Therefore, Alaric for the third time marched on Rome and entered it by force in 410. They plundered the ancient city but as a Christian, Alaric respected the basilicas, churches, and treasures of Christians. The Gothic invasion culminating in the sack of Rome, the invasion of other Germanic people in the west and the inability of the western emperor to solve the crisis was a death blow to the Western Roman Empire. The loss of territories to the barbarians meant a loss of income for the empire that had less money to build their army. The provincial landowning elites who collected the taxes for the empire in their regions in exchange for protection from the Roman army were dissatisfied with the emperor for not protecting their property. These local elites thought if it were safer to live under a Gothic or Vandal king, why bother to support the Roman empire that could not protect them? These wealthy Romans owned 80 percent of the land and their disaffection with the empire would be another factor contributing to its downfall.

In 440, the Huns under the leadership of Attila the Hun began to invade and sack the eastern and western empire. Attila was the scourge of the Roman Empire until his death on his bed choked to death by a nosebleed. By 468 The Vandals controlled North Africa and the empire lost one of its richest sources of grain. Only the revenues from Italy and Sicily remained. With few resources there was not enough money to pay for an army strong enough to impose itself over the barbarians that swamped and settled the western empire. The balance of power now lay clearly with the multitude of barbarians, the Goths, Vandals, Burgundians, Franks of Gaul, and Suevi. A reality that the western emperor had to acknowledge and thus he had to make military alliance with a barbarian king. Treaties then were made with the Goths and Vandals recognizing them as legitimate possessors of their territories and partners to govern the west. The different Roman territories in the west broke out of central control held in Italy.

In 476 A.D. the military and financial resources of the central government in Italy were so weak that the government could not maintain itself, much less any invader. Romans and barbarians were fusing together and their differences as people were dissolving with time. Odovacar was a very successful general in the Roman Army who was of barbarian origins from the Germanic tribe of Sciri in the middle of the 5th century A.D. He was able to built up a loyal power base of landowners and soldiers in Italy. He settled his Roman soldiers, who were Germanic mercenaries, paying them with land in Italy. Odovacar became the effective ruler of Italy; he was able to depose the teenage emperor Romulus Augustus who had no effective power. When Odovacar took over the throne instead of proclaiming himself emperor he proclaimed himself a king. Thus Rome was now ruled by a Germanic King who saw no need for the traditional symbols of the Roman emperor; thus, he sent the vestments, diadem, and cloak to the eastern emperor Zeno. Zeno acknowledged that Odovacar had undisputed power. The Western Roman Empire came to an end in 476, while the Eastern Roman Empire or Byzantium continued in existence until it was taken over by the Moslem Turks in 1453 A.D.

GRECO-ROMAN PHILOSOPHY

The Romans obtained their philosophical ideas from the inventors of philosophy, the Greeks. Therefore, Roman philosophy is thoroughly grounded in the traditions of Greek philosophy. Thus, the story of Roman philosophy is of the gradual adoption and adaptation of Greek philosophical doctrines by Roman authors. Interest in the subject was first brought about at Rome in 155 B.C. by an Athenian embassy, consisting of the Academic Skeptic Carneades, the Stoic Diogenes, and the Peripatetic Critolaus. In Rome these three Greek philosophers taught their philosophical ideas to the educated Romans. All this was new and caused a sensation in Rome. The Skeptic Carneades addressed a crowd of thousands on one day and argued that justice was a genuine good in its own right in a convincing manner. The next day he argued against the proposition that it was in an agent's interest to be just in terms that were as convincing. This dazzling display of dialectical skill, together with the deep–seated suspicion of philosophical culture that the more down to earth and practical minded Romans had, generated a conservative backlash against all Greek philosophers led by the censor Marcus Porcius Cato who deported several Greek philosophers from Rome. The conservative Romans considered them a danger to the morals of the citizens, thus a corrupting influence. But as Romans gradually adopted the more sophisticated Greek culture, by 86 B.C. the Romans were ready to receive Greek philosophy with an open mind. A thorough study of Greek philosophy was first introduced in the time of Cicero. Cicero travelled to Athens to study at their philosophical schools and returned to Rome to popularize Greek philosophy making it accessible to Romans who were less educated than himself. Several Greek philosophical schools became popular in Ancient Rome. The most famous are the Stoics, Epicureans, Cynics, Skeptics, and Neo-Platonist.

Stoicism, the most important philosophy in Rome, appealed more to members of the Senate and other political movers and shakers. Its teachings were carried to Rome in 155 B.C. by Diogenes of Babylon. As the Romans admired virtue, many politicians embraced the high moral tone of Stoicism according to which only virtue is a genuine good, while money, health, and even life itself are simply preferred matters of lesser importance. Stoicism became very popular in imperial times along with Epicureanism. Many famous Romans embraced stoic ideas such as Cicero, Seneca, Epictetus, Marcus Brutus, and Emperor Marcus Aurelius. It even influenced Roman culture in general, for example Stoic ideas are found in Rome's greatest work of literature, the *Aeneid,* by the poet Virgil. Stoicism was strong in Rome until the second century A.D., and it will have an influence upon the history of philosophy after the empire. In ethics theories of natural law will go back to Stoicism, and early Christian thinkers, Medieval and Renaissance philosophers will be well acquainted with stoic ideas mainly through the writings of Seneca and Cicero.

The stoics believed that god was fire or active energy and **logos** or reason (rational order) diffused throughout the universe. The logos constitutes the rational order or meaning of the cosmos and it is ordered by god. The law of nature or natural law was god's material presence in the universe. God was providence that ordained all things. Therefore, there was a reason for everything in nature, everything had an explanation. God determined fate, so fate imposed a certain determinism that men could not escape from, and humanity had freedom only within the acceptance of this reality. They believed that all men have a soul which consists of a fragment of the universal divine force.

Their ethics came from their understanding of the cosmos placing emphasis on virtue which was the law that governed the universe. So ethics consisted of practicing virtue by fulfilling one's obligation to god, which is the logos or reason, which leads to justice and satisfies the needs of society. When an individual practices virtue he performs his duty to his family and the community, accepting the law of nature. In the end all will turn out for the good of the individual, his family, and society.

Stoicism was a philosophy that was very compatible with the Roman worldview because it believed in accepting all situations, even the adverse ones, with peace of mind and resignation. This was seen as being in harmony with the Roman highly valued "virtus," or manliness or toughness. It went well with the Roman self-image of duty to state and family, and being destined to rule and civilize the world. The Stoic doctrine that each person is part of God and that all people, because of their capacity to reason, belong to common humanity helped break down national, social, and racial barriers. This view was necessary to help Rome create a vast empire comprising many people of different cultures and ethnicities, and thus the Stoic view of society contributed to this attitude.

Why would the Stoics believe Rome was destined to rule the world? According to this school of thought the meaning of each individual life, action, and situation is determined by its place in a larger whole which is the whole course of history that is fated by god. Therefore, life is progressive, governed for a purpose (teleological), and meaningful. They thought god has his natural law or rational principle to govern mankind. Thus, every event has a place within this larger rational order which is meaningful. This means that all events are part of a larger reason or good. (Christian theologians in the later Roman Empire, like Boethius, will adopt this Stoic idea that historical events are directed by God according to a predetermined plan. This leads to the idea that even from evil actions and situations God lets good come forward in the end.) The Roman Stoics saw this larger good as the spread of law over the entire world. This law was to be established by Roman conquest and it was called the Law of Nations. Therefore, god's grand plan for history was the extension of the Roman Empire and Roman laws over the entire world. So every function a Roman performed for the state in each station of life, whether as a craftsman, engineer, soldier, or government official, constituted a participation in this larger purpose of world history. The main values were duty to the functions an individual has been born to or assigned, and respect for authority. Since god is utilizing the Roman state to further his law and civilization, an individual's prime duty was to the state, and performing this duty to the best of his ability was considered a religious act. As god is utilizing the Roman state and Roman officials to further his will on history, and god is deserving of man's highest respect, then it is logical that respect toward Roman authorities is also respect for god and the logos. All this fitted well with the Roman state that grew through conquest, and a reason why several emperors were Stoics.

Epicureanism was the next important philosophy in Rome and tended to be favored in the ranks in Rome's military. Generals such as Lucius Cornelius Sulla and Julius Caesar were Epicureans. This philosophical school founded by the Greek Epicurus was an ethical philosophy based upon the achievement of pleasure and happiness. Epicurus viewed pleasure as the absence of pain and removal of the fear of death. By avoiding pain you obtained the maximum amount of pleasure in life. His goal was to promote happiness by removing life's pains and fear. The Roman poet Lucretius (96–55 B.C.) helped to popularize Epicureanism in Rome, and the teachings of Epicurus are preserved mainly in Lucretius' philosophical poem *De Rerum Natura* (On the Nature of Things), explaining Epicurean philosophy in Latin for men who couldn't read Greek. Lucretius, like the founder Epicurus, had a negative view of religion because he believed it made people perform evil deeds and caused them to experience anxiety about death and eternal punishment. Thus, he condemned superstition and religion for causing mental distress. He saw nature in purely materialistic terms that left no room for the gods. So mechanical laws governed nature and not the gods. To end the fear of death Lucretius argued that the soul perishes with the body at death. What Lucretius advocated was a simple life without political involvement and excessive passions as the greatest good and the way to peace of mind. The Epicurean rejection of traditional religion, involvement in politics and public service, as well as the quest for power and glory went against the Roman ideal of virtue. But to praise the quiet life enjoying pleasant activities and advice on how to deal with misfortunes in a serene way had great appeal to the Romans of the 1st century B.C. who were disgusted by the civil wars like Lucretius. Thus its popularity among the Romans.

Skepticism was the philosophical school which continued the criticisms of objective knowledge. This school, as the Cynics and Sophists supported, promoted the idea that men cannot arrive at certain truth about anything. They did not deny that certainty did not exist, but human beings could never be certain they could attain knowledge about reality. Thus they challenged the claims of scientists and philosophers to investigate the nature of reality arriving to correct conclusions. Skeptics sustained that it was wise to be aware of one's own ignorance, which was brought up before by the Athenian philosopher Socrates. They concluded that the means to attain happiness was to suspend judgment. By suspending judgment that men have no true knowledge, the skeptics believed it brought tranquility and fulfillment. The Roman Cicero held ideas from Skeptic philosophy and thought that ideas and facts should be questioned, not just accepted at first as truth.

By the 2nd century A.D. the Greco-Roman world no longer held reason as a satisfying guide to life. Both the educated and the masses looked for new meaning to life and what is beyond this earthly life. Greek rationalism never governed completely the mythic religious mentality of the masses that placed emphasis on human emotions rather than reason. Thus the rise of popular attraction to religious forms of ritual mystery, magic, and ecstasy. This non-rational undercurrent prevailed over the rational mind. By the 4th century A.D. people felt anxiety, alienated, impotent, and bored with life. Occult, magic, and astrology became popular. From the Middle East and Egypt came Eastern mystery religions that supplanted the rational and secular classical humanistic values. The Greco-Roman world was going through a cultural transformation. People were looking for a way to overcome life misfortunes and discouragements, with the desire to acquire a sense of belonging to a caring community and to find immortality. This religious tendency came into philosophy that turned away from rational classical humanism. Philosophers lost interest in nature and society, turning their minds toward a union with a higher reality to offer comfort to the individual, such as the mystery religions like the popular cults of Mithra and Isis.

Neo-Platonism will become the popular philosophy of the Late Roman Empire that replaced Stoicism as the dominant school of philosophy and subordinated philosophy to mysticism. Roman philosophers developed a new idea, that after death instead of entering Heaven as yourself, the individual became one with god or a divine force. The divine force was also referred to as the One or the Good, and was the origin of the world. This idea came from Plato's idea of the perfect form. Thus the name Neo-Platonists, that meant New Platonist, which was coined much later in the 19th century.

Plotinus (205–207 A.D.) was a Greco-Egyptian philosopher and the most important promoter of this school of mystical philosophy. Focused on Plato's higher world of reality or the spiritual realm of the perfect forms, Plotinus desired the union with the One or god. As the One transcending all knowledge, man's limited mind could not by itself understand nor describe the One. To become one with god, man needed to rely on mysticism. Mysticism offered the individual the means to purify the soul so it could return to its original source which is the One. For Plotinus and his followers *philosophy became a religious experience* where they contemplated the One in a mystical way, and they lost interest in obtaining knowledge of the physical world and concern for human affairs. Knowledge of the One is what mattered to Plotinus, not the understanding of nature nor making society better. Thus, ecstasy and intuition replace reason, and this meant that ancient rational philosophy became subordinated to religious belief, that is secular values became inferior to religious experience. Plotinus' students continued with Neo-Platonist ideas of uniting with the One after death which mixed with the Gnostic ideas about magic. In the end Neo-Platonism became more about magic than philosophy. Neo-Platonism contains a form of pantheism in that it believes god is found in all beings.

The practical side of this school of philosophy is that it believed that the soul must retrace its steps back to the One it originated from. This is achieved through the practice of *virtue* which tries to be like the One, and leads up to the One or god. Virtue leads to an ascetic life that allows the soul to overcome sensuality, turn to the spiritual, and become free from sin to return and join the One. The soul finally becomes one with god through gradual contemplation, forgetting the surrounding world. Thus life's goal for Plotinus was to purify oneself from dependence and attachment to material comforts because matter is closest to imperfection and evil, and the final goal was to achieve the ecstatic union with god. Here we have the clear influence of Plato's philosophy concerning spiritual dimension or world of perfect ideas or forms, versus the imperfect material copies and that the bodily desires of man are a hindrance to understanding and union with the higher spiritual dimension of ideas or forms. When the soul achieves this end it will enjoy the highest indescribable bliss, an ecstatic union with god. This philosophical contemplation or meditation could bring human perfection and happiness in this life, not just in the afterlife. This ecstatic union with god or the One was not permanent during an individual's life, but temporary. Thus an individual could have this experience more than once. The Neo-Platonist philosopher Porphyry stated that his teacher Plotinus reached this ecstatic union with god four times in a period of six years. Neo-Platonic ideas will have their influence later on Christian thinkers as Saint Augustine of Hippo as well as during the Middle Ages, and later Renaissance thinkers.

During the period of late antiquity in the Greco-Roman world philosophical activity became mainly *recovering the wisdom of the ancient Greek philosophers*. The originality and creativity of the ancient Greek philosophers and philosophical schools is largely not taking place as it did in ancient Greece. The dividing line between ancient Greek and Greco-Roman philosophy begins about 80 B.C. when political and military abrupt changes in Athens drove most philosophers to cultural havens such as Rome and Alexandria, Egypt. This was a blow from which the philosophical institutions of Athens never recovered and even the Roman emperor Marcus Aurelius' attempt to restore them in 176 A.D. did not restore their former philosophical pre-eminence. This decentralized philosophical learning, and for most philosophy was no longer a living activity of the Athenian philosophical schools such as Plato's Academy and Aristotle's Lyceum. What it evolved into was small study groups all over the Greco-Roman world led by professional teachers. New philosophy was not developing as a result, and the goal was now to pursue the correct interpretation of the ancient Greek philosophers by studying their texts. Thus the main activity was systematic cataloguing of philosophical and scientific opinions from about 80 B.C. to 300 A.D., and writing commentaries on classical philosophical texts.

Philosophy was a major influence upon the entire culture of the Greco-Roman world. It was not considered a separate academic discipline, having great political prestige and influencing various other disciplines such as medicine, rhetoric, grammar, history, law, and astrology. Through its mode of discourse it influenced famous ancient scientists such as the doctor Galen of Pergamon and the astronomer Claudius Ptolemy.

During the imperial era of ancient Rome the Hellenistic philosophical creeds (Stoicism, Epicureanism, and Skepticism) gradually declined by the revival of doctrinal Platonism from the study of Plato's texts. These commentaries on Plato and of Aristotle who was seen as going along with his teacher, led to a new age of metaphysical developments culminating in Neo-Platonism and the great influence of original thinkers of which Plotinus was the most famous. In the late Roman Empire philosophical and religious movements had a great impact on the culture competing for the intellectual and spiritual adherence of society. This period coincides with the rise of Christianity which became the main rival to pagan philosophy. This can be seen from the 3rd century A.D. with Christianity's competition with Neo-Platonism and its eventual triumph. Ancient philosophy was considered pagan by the Christian fathers, and some of them, such as Saint Augustine, will incorporate Greco-Roman philosophy at the service of Christianity that will allow for the development of Christian theology during the late Roman Empire and later the Medieval Scholastic theology of thinkers such as Saint Thomas Aquinas. This became the means by which Greco-Roman philosophy was incorporated into Medieval and Renaissance philosophy, thus being preserved through time and influencing Western philosophy to the present date.

ROME'S CONTRIBUTIONS TO WESTERN CIVILIZATION

Rome's most important contributions to Western civilization were law, Greek culture, engineering, and Romanesque languages.

Law

One of Ancient Rome's greatest legacies to the Western civilization was in the field of law. Law was the field in which the Romans saw themselves as achieving excellence and being superior to the Greeks in this respect. It was a product of a long and slow evolution from custom and experience. During the early years of the Roman Republic laws were not written down. Laws were then administered by the offices of the magistrates and priests or pontifices. Both of these offices were monopolized by the patricians, thus this upper class was favored because they could alone interpret laws in their favor. At this early stage Romans did not distinguish between judicial law (court law) or law from the tribunal of a magistrate that on his own issued edicts with legislative effects, and constitutional laws or lex that expressed the will of the people through the Assembly guided by the Senate. In this manner Roman law came before legislation that originated from Roman authority. Due to the conflict of interest between the two social classes, the struggle between patricians versus plebeians, by 451 B.C. a commission of ten patricians wrote down Rome's laws on twelve stone tablets to appease the plebeians. Now the law was in writing for all to read and became known as the **Twelve Tables,** which had the rules of criminal and civil law that applied to all citizens.

Over the next four centuries the tension between patricians and plebeians continued and the plebeians reacted against the iniquities of many laws. To solve these conflicts many law reforms were passed. For example a debtor who did not pay his debt had the risk of falling into slavery to repay his benefactor according to the old laws. This law was abolished in 326 B.C. by the lex Poetelia, a constitutional law named after the individual who proposed it. By 304 B.C. the consul Claudius Appius published a handbook of the correct forms of legal procedure. This was a means to further open law to the public, in general breaking the patrician priestly monopoly of legal knowledge. This allowed for lay jurists who were not professional lawyers to codify and clarify laws, and be able to give legal advice. Thus Roman law was greatly improved due to their revisions, interpretations, and additions of many customary laws that were not in the Twelve Tables.

Roman law developed through two stages. The first stage was the formation of *civil law* (ius civile), first branch of Roman law. The Twelve Tables contained civil law and it expanded over the centuries by the additions of statue laws passed by the assemblies and magistrates' legal decisions, edits from emperors, and the commentaries of lay jurists. The second was the *law of nations* (ius gentium) which came about during the Republic's expansion outside the Italian peninsula coming into contact with Greeks and other people. This second branch of Roman law combined Roman civil law with selected principles of Greek and other people's legal traditions. The law of nations was identified by Roman law experts with *natural law* (ius naturale) of the Stoic philosophical school. What these experts were saying is that Roman law should be in harmony with the rational principles found in nature. Therefore, they recognized that there are uniform and valid laws that apply everywhere and to all nations or peoples that are discerned by rational persons. This central facet of Roman law came out of Stoicism. It consisted of the idea of **natural law**, that is, a higher justice than that made by human beings. In other words, the belief that in nature there are principles of what is right and just that are not created by man nor can man change because all humans are born with it, it is part of human nature. It could be conceived that God created this law and endowed it upon humans. Therefore, a good and just system of law must come to understand this natural law and apply it.

By 242 B.C. the new office of the praetor was created to attend legal cases in which one of the parties was not a Roman citizen, whether a subject of Rome or a foreigner. This was the manner by which Rome united different people together, because the law of nations met the requirements of a vast empire with Stoic ideals. As the Stoic Cicero stated that true law is rational and in agreement with nature, thus it applies universally, and never changes. This one eternal and unchanging law is valid for all nations throughout all history.

It could be said that the great legal genius of the Romans was to develop over time a code of law that, with a pragmatic view to life, observed what different people with their native cultures actually practiced and put those practices into law. *Roman law was based on human nature* and *not on theory*. It focused on facts, how men relate in real life, rather than on abstract notions of what should be the rules of how men relate in society. As Cicero stated, law is founded "not on theory but on nature." Rome used its international experience as a vast empire to develop a body of law based upon consistent human behavior in different environments. Thus it created the legal principles, based on human nature that surpassed nationality, cultures, and time, and are still employed today in the West. Roman law created a notion of justice founded on such ideals as fairness for both citizens and subjects, as well as the presumption of innocence in criminal cases. In other words the accused is innocent until proven guilty. These became the guiding principles of Western legal tradition. This enabled the Romans to have a legal system that was accepted as beneficial among the many peoples that populated and traded with the Roman Empire. The law of nations was applied throughout the entire empire, even though it never supplanted entirely local law. And it went on to thrive even after the Roman Empire fell because it will be reintroduced during the Middle Ages to become the basis of the civil law in Western Europe, except Britain, and also Latin America to the present date.

As the empire grew, legislation became more complicated and this led to the need to harmonize accumulated laws from various sources in what became known as codification of Roman law. The first attempt to codify the law was in 95 B.C. by the Consul Mucius Scaevola. But it was Emperor Hadrian in the 2nd century A.D. that began a serious move to codify the law that continued to the 6th century A.D. The Byzantine Emperor Justinian I in the 6th century A.D. appointed a committee of sixteen lawyers to summarize and put together the entire Roman law into a code known as *Digest of Roman Law or* **Justinian Code**

(*Corpus Juris Civilis*) that took eleven years to accomplish and endured over centuries. It gave Byzantium its laws for the next thousand years, and from 1100 A.D. this code was revived and expanded in Italy to then be adopted by various Western states. In the early 19th century the French Emperor Napoleon Bonaparte created the famous Napoleonic Legal Code that was taken from Roman law becoming the law of almost all continental Europe. Therefore, Roman law is the basis of the legal Continental System of Europe that makes up today the civil law of Italy, France, Spain, and Portugal. Also it is the basis of civil law of Latin America that derived its law from Spain and Portugal. It also has an influence on German law.

In summary, the Romans left us a great legal heritage in use today in many nations due to the fact that the Romans based their laws on principals of natural law that apply universally and over time because human nature does not change. This doctrine of natural law is the basis of the American Declaration of Independence. The belief that all men have the right to life, liberty, and happiness (property rights) as a natural right of man or human nature, and that no individual or government has the right to violate is a basic principle of law and government of the United States and many other Western nations.

Roman Culture, Greek Culture

Romans held fast to their traditional rustic cultural origins but when they came into contact and conquered the Hellenistic world it launched Rome into the heights of ancient civilization. Even though Rome conquered Greece, Greek civilization ended conquering Rome when Greek cultural forms, literature, arts, architecture, philosophy, and its mythology were imported into Rome. The Romans adopted Greek style architecture, art, sculpture, and preserved and transmitted Greek humanism. The Romans coined the term **humanities** to refer to the artistic, literary, and philosophical activities that the Greeks considered basic to any form of civilized life. The humanities were a Greek invention and it was their belief that the study and practice of the humanities is stimulating to the soul and the mind. These great accomplishments in the arts and intellectual fields were preserved and transmitted by the Romans, and this was one of the greatest contributions of the Roman world to the Western civilization. Later on the Christian church will do the same during the Middle Ages.

Engineering

The Romans were the great engineers of the ancient Europe. They had a very pragmatic attitude toward construction. Their strength did not lie in the creative and artistic aspect, where the Greeks were the masters of architecture, but in their engineering skills put to use in building useful and functional public projects such as aqueducts, sewage systems, fountains, indoor plumbing, irrigation systems, central heated buildings, amphitheaters, bridges, paved roads, large heated public baths, running toilets, military hospitals with hygienic facilities, fortifications, domes, palaces, basilicas, etc. This ability made Roman cities the most advanced of their time and Romans could boast that they were cleaner than other people. Their pragmatic attitude can be clearly perceived when the Romans who conquered Egypt exclaimed, "How can one compare Rome's aqueducts and bridges with Egypt's pyramids?" Both the Egyptian and the Roman were great works of engineering, but which one was more useful for society—the Egyptian or the Roman? (Figure 5.7).

Early in Rome's history the Romans learned many lessons from the Etruscans, among them the very important masonry arch. After encountering the Greeks in Magna Graecia, they built Rome along Greek lines. Romans being a very pragmatic people borrowed many ideas from other people and used them to meet their needs, improved them, and employing them on a grand scale. The improvement of mortar by adding a volcanic ash that made it solid and durable without breaking apart, allowed the Romans to

FORUM	Market/Business place
PANTHEON	Temple for all gods
STADIUM/CIRCUS	Race course with tiered seating for presentation of animals and chariot races
BATHHOUSE	Social / recreational / heath facilities
VILLAS	Residences for the wealthy
APARTMENTS	Urban dwellings
THEATER	Large semi-circular building for drama
ODEON	Small semi-circular building for music/poetry readings
AMPHITHEATER	Two Greek theaters joined; for gladiatorial sports
COLOSSEUM	Large (colossal in size) amphitheater
OBELISK	Tall column with relief carving
TRIUMPHAL ARCH	Celebratory gateways to the city
EQUESTRIAN STATUE	Commemorative monuments

Figure 5.7   Roman Buildings and their Functions

build large projects. The concrete and brick did not have a visual appeal so they covered it with slabs of expensive and polished marble and granite from Italy and Greece. From the Greek model the Romans build their chief architectural forms, the Roman temple with its post-beam-triangle construction. The Greek column was also extensively employed with preference given to the Corinthian style over the Doric and Ionic.

The most important innovation was the **rounded arch,** an Etruscan contribution. The Mesopotamians may have invented it, the Greeks knew about it, and the Etruscans used it in their drainage systems. The Romans experimented with it and developed it to be used in many different kinds of construction. The arch's basic round form is created using wedged-shaped stones called voussoirs (Figure 5.8). These voussoirs are then placed forming a semi-circle and at its center a keystone locks the arch in place. Wood beams were used to keep the voussoirs in place until the keystone was placed and the arch was complete, and then the wooden beams were taken off. The stones in the form of an arch would stand by the pressure exerted from both ends of the arch. The installed arch is very strong, diverting the weight of the upper walls both outward and downward onto other supports.

Figure 5.8   Aqueduct of Segovia, Spain. The Romans used the rounded arch in many of their constructions. This aqueduct is a good example of how water was brought from the mountains to the city of Segovia. *Image Copyright kavram, 2009. Used under license from Shutterstock, Inc.*

Employing the rounded arch the Romans invented the **vaults,** a ceiling made from arches (Figure 5.9). The **barrel vault** is constructed by building a series of contiguous arches. It receives its name because it looks like a barrel divided lengthwise. By intersecting two barrel vaults at right angles a **groined,** or **cross vault,** is produced. A original Roman invention was the **dome** made by rotating an arch in a full circle—360 degrees. The Romans used the mathematical ratio 1:2 between the height of an arch and the width of its base to construct the safest arch. Arches were used in the construction of aqueducts, bridges, and buildings. The Romans used the rectilinear temple from the Greeks, and they invented the round temple with their masterpiece the *Pantheon,* a sanctuary dedicated to their deities (Figure 5.10). The Pantheon has three sections, the porch or portico with its columns, the drum housing the sanctuary, and the dome set on top of the drum. It combined a religious with a secular image. The dome symbolized both heaven of the deities and the vastness of the Roman Empire. It was well-decorated in its interior with recessed panel on the dome. It had a hole of 30 feet in diameter, the oculus or eye, at the top of the dome that allowed sunlight and elements to enter. It is the oldest standing dome structure in the world, and the domes in St. Peter's Basilica in Rome and St. Paul's cathedral in London are modeled on the Pantheon's.

Figure 5.9 Sample of Roman rounded vault in Israel. *Image Copyright Yan Vugenfirer, 2009. Used under license from Shutterstock, Inc.*

At the center of Rome was the **forum,** which was the business and government center functioning like the agora of Greek city-states. It was made up of a complex of public buildings, temples, sacred sites, and monuments. The forum became the symbol of Roman power and civilization where the Senate and Pontifex Maximus were located. The main Roman cities in each province had forums. The **triumphal arch** was another symbol of the empire that originated in the 2nd century B.C. The Romans used both the single and the triple arches to celebrate military victories and built them across the empire. These arches had inscribed the dedication to its victorious heroes and reliefs of victorious emperors and army.

Figure 5.10 Exterior of Pantheon, Rome/Interior of Pantheon with oculus. *Image Copyright Pierdelune, 2009. Used under license from Shutterstock, Inc.*

Figure 5.11 The Roman Forum, with the arch of Titus and the Colosseum at the far end. *Image Copyright Oleg Babich, 2009. Used under license from Shutterstock, Inc.*

Figure 5.12 Arch of Constantine at the Forum with the Colosseum in the background. *Image Copyright Jeff Banke, 2009. Used under license from Shutterstock, Inc.*

Emperors had **amphitheaters** built as monuments to themselves and as gifts for the citizens. It was a means to gain popularity and political support. The most famous was the **Colosseum** in Rome (Figures 5.11, 5.12 & 5.13). In these amphitheaters is where the gladiatorial combats and other blood sports, as well as the bloody execution of prisoners took place for the sadistic entertainment of the masses becoming the cornerstone of popular culture in the empire. They were intended to amuse vast crowds, thus Romans invented mass entertainment. *Ludi* or Roman games were held in the Colosseum and the Circus Maximus (famous for its chariot races). Ludi, from which we get

Figure 5.13 Roman paved road at Pompei, Italy. *Image Copyright Danilo Ascione, 2009. Used under license from Shutterstock, Inc.*

the word "ludicrous," were five types of extravaganzas produced for very large arenas, which consisted of chariot races, wild animal hunts, mythological pantomimes, naval battles, and gladiatorial combats. These ludi were not concerned with beauty or style. Gladiatorial contests were of Etruscan origin that began as part of the funeral services of high ranking members of society. The Colosseum was formed by stacking three tiers of rounded arches on top of one another. The arena was made of wood and covered with sand. Water lanes demonstrate that the arena could be flooded for mock naval battles. Then, the hypogeum was constructed under the arena and can be seen today. Hypogeum was a series of underground tunnels under the Colosseum where slaves and animals were kept ready to fight for the gladitorial games. The animals and slaves would be let up through trapdoors under the sand covered arena at any time during a fight. This amphitheater had retractable overhead awnings to provide shade to the spectators. It represented the sordid reality of Roman civilization.

FLAVIAN COLOSSEUM

Ancient Romans were interested in grand engineering and architectural feats that demonstrated the power of their state. Theaters, circuses, and amphitheaters held thousands of people who watched blood sports, gladiatorial fights, and chariot races.

The *Flavian Colosseum* (possibly named after a colossal statue of Nero originally standing nearby) is one of these architectural achievements. The form of the *Colosseum* is an amphitheater—or two Ancient Greek theaters joined together—and it is unique because, unlike the Greek theaters that were built into the sides of hills to save constructions costs, the stands of the *Colosseum* were supported by a vaulting system shown in Figure **5.14**. Aside from the construction of the dome on the *Pantheon*, this was perhaps the most ingenious feat of Roman engineering. It formed the basis of later medieval cathedral design in which central roofs and vaulting were supported by a stacked buttress system. In the *Colosseum*, the buttresses support the seats.

Like Greek theaters where characters were sacrificed at an altar to the gods, doves were released at the opening of the ceremonies in the Colosseum. Sacrificial dramas were enacted and the building was decorated with statues of the gods, and those making a pretense at being gods.

Figure 5.14   Reconstruction (showing direction of forces through buttresses) of the Colosseum, Cross-Section, Jan Goeree (Dutch, 1670–1731), before 1704. *Image copyright © The Metropolitan Museum of Art. Image source: Art Resource, NY*

Figure 5.15   Exterior, Colosseum, Flavian Amphitheater (70–80 C.E.). Rome. *Image Courtesy of Stephen Husarik*

Figure 5.16   Interior,, Colosseum, Flavian Amphitheater (70–80 C.E.). Rome. *Image Courtesy of Stephen Husarik*

THE GRAND TOUR

During the 18th century, graduates of English universities traveled with their tutors on the Grand Tour to see monuments such as the *Colosseum* in Italy. They had been trained in Latin, and were future upper class English landholders. Travel with a tutor was an expensive proposition and, as members of the ruling class, they were able to demonstrate their position in the social order by actually visiting ancient historical monuments.

The Grand Tour evolved over the years and people who were not members of the ruling class went to see these same historical monuments and speculate about their importance and meaning. Of course, the buildings had been picked clean of their decorative marbles, statues, etc. by the time 19th century visitors arrived, and the buildings were so degraded that many visiting artists painted them simply as awesome reminiscences of the past. (see Figures **5.15**, **5.16** and **5.17**)

The modern Grand Tour includes not only this nostalgic attitude to the past, but the addition of curiosity seekers (e.g., those who have seen the blood sports in movies such as *Gladiator*), tourists, and student architects who wish to complete their understanding of past architectural styles with a close-up look at the remains, and perhaps provide help in restoration projects.

The *Colosseum* seated 40,000 people and was designed so that it could be completely emptied in approximately three minutes. A large canopy was hoisted above the arena to protect people from the hot Italian sun and the rain; it is thus the world's first covered stadium.

The militaristic nature of the Roman culture is reflected in gladiatorial combats held in this building. In the early life of the arena (before the floor excavations) the central arena was flooded and gladiators were placed in vessels and pitted against each other in naval battles. The blood from the dead bodies mixing with the water moved some Romans to comment that these were the best games they had ever seen. Each subsequent ruler tried to outdo the previous; Trajan gave one set of games that lasted over one hundred days and killed off thousands of animals.

A day's events at the *Colosseum* were divided into several parts: animals vs. men in the morning; execution of prisoners and enemies of the state at noon; and gladiatorial combats in the afternoons. An enormous support network was involved in preparing the gladiators for battle, maintaining the animals, and providing cleanup of the dead carcasses and the arena. Gladiatorial sports were a major entertainment industry in Rome, and so gladiators were not always condemned to death as quickly as depicted in modern films.

A Greek water organ played during the shows that was supposedly audible up to a quarter mile around the *Colosseum*. Though virtually nothing is known of Roman music today—there are a few scattered mosaics and fresco images that suggest their music was a mix of genres that included Ancient Greek music for tragedies and poetic genres, and brass bands and organ music for ceremonial marches at the gladiatorial shows.

The Romans had a 50,000 mile network of **paved roads** that connected Rome with all parts of the empire. Thus "all roads lead to Rome" was not an inaccurate saying. The roads were built as military highways for the defense of the empire. It carried an efficient postal service. With highway patrols, a stable every 10 miles and inn every 30 miles, and guide-books travel became easier, faster, and safer than any other time until the 19th century. Some of these ancient roads like the Via Apia still exist to this date. Water is indispensible for city life. Rome and other large cities had a very large population for its time that required a large amount of water every day. An elaborate network of **aqueducts,** sluices, and syphons ran by gravity from the water source in nearby hills to the city's reservoirs and fountains. There were underground and elevated aqueducts, and some are still in use today!

ACTIVITY

Fill in the grid below with characteristics of modern America. Do you see any similarities with Ancient Rome?

ANCIENT ROME	TRAITS	MODERN AMERICA
Sewers, roadways, aqueducts	PRACTICALITY	Interstate Highways; Air Traffic Control System; Hoover Dam, etc.
Virgil's *Aeneid*, Greek *Odyssey*	IMITATION	
European and Middle Eastern Conquests	IMPERIALISM	
Identity found in State "*Patras*"	PATRIOTISM	
Large architectural monuments	GRANDEUR	
Senator	TITLES	
Chariot races, gladiatorial fights	SPORTS	
Theaters, circuses, amphitheaters	ARENAS	
Caracalla, Diocletian	BATHS	
Games, street violence	VIOLENCE	
Arch, vault, concrete	ENGINEERING	
State law, *jus gentium*	LAW	
Grid system	CITY PLANNING	
Property, slaves	WEALTH	

Latin

Latin was the language of the Romans. When the Roman Empire fell the different regions of the empire that spoke Latin became isolated and with the centuries that followed the Latin spoken by the population developed into the Romance languages spoken today in Europe and the Americas (Italian, Spanish, French, Portuguese, and Romanian). The English language borrowed many words with a Latin origin. This was due to the Normans, who were French and won over Britain after the battle of Hastings in 1066. The Normans ruled England and they spoke French, so French became the language of the new ruling class. As time passed, the Normans mixed with the local Anglo population and English became the only language in England but many words from French passed to the English language. This is the reason why there are many words in Spanish and French that are similar in English, known as cognates.

Roman Art

Sculpture. Roman sculpture reflected the taste of artists and patrons and their class interests. The patrician class leaned toward the Greek style, and the plebeian toward the local art, known as

Figure 5.17   Roman mural. *Image Copyright Danilo Ascione, 2009. Used under license from Shutterstock, Inc.*

Italo-Roman. Roman portrait sculpture went through three different phases. The first from the 3rd to the 1st century B.C. was influenced by death masks made for the family gallery as part of ancestor worship. This style is reflected in the bust of Lucius Junius Brutus that has a stern look that represents the austerity of early Romans. During the Late Republic 133–31 B.C., sculpture is realistic. The artists make the portrait just as the person looks in real life, with his wrinkles, warts, and aged. It is not the idealistic sculpture of classical Greece. The third phase came under Augustus. Imperial portraiture reverted to the idealism of Hellenic Greece which displaced the realistic art of the late Republic. After Augustus, his successor used sculpture as a symbol of imperial power becoming more propagandistic. The move to symbolic idealism demonstrates the need of later emperors to have a visible means to fill the diversified masses with wonder and reverence toward their persons.

Painting. The most popular type of painting that has survived are **murals** or wall paintings. It was a highly decorative and brightly colored art. They developed fresco painting as the most lasting and practical technique. In frescos paints are mixed and worked into a freshly plastered wall, that later dry into the wall, and the painting is almost indestructible. The subjects of their paintings included landscapes, architectural vistas, religious scenes, Greek and Roman myths, and genre scene.

Mosaics. During the 3rd century B.C. the Romans learned to make mosaics from the Greeks. Mosaics are pictures made by imbedding small-colored stones or pieces of glass into stucco or cement. They can be found on floors as well as walls and ceilings. The most popular subjects were landscapes, still life, Greek and Roman myths, scenes from the circus and amphitheater, philosophers, and orators.

INFLUENCE OF THE LATE GRECO-ROMAN CULTURE IN THE WEST

During the late Roman Empire the Roman civilization created a synthesis of Christian and Greco-Roman values, which became its legacy to the Early Medieval West. Christian intellectuals valued Greco-Roman thought for the support it lent to the spiritual values that were now considered primary. Late Roman art and architecture also blended the two traditions.

This late Roman synthesis of Christian and Greco-Roman values was supremely embodied in the Christian church (Figure 5.18). From the fall of Rome until the 1800s, the church's culture was nearly synonymous with the wider culture; to be Western was to be Christian. Church leaders were now the patrons of culture all through the Middle Ages and continued in the modern era. They commanded artists to create only religious works, using a symbolic, impressionistic style; they commissioned architects to build churches in the form of Roman basilicas adapted to religious needs and baptisteries based on round, or polygonal, designs; they asked composers to write music for the church liturgy; they authorized scholars to harmonize faith with Greco-Roman thought; and they ordered sacred books to be decorated, script illumination, by gifted artist-clergy. Thus, the late Classical World was the womb from which would emerge the next generations of Western institutions as well as Western humanities.

Figure 5.18 Roman mosaic in Lybia, ancient Roman portrait. *Image Copyright Clara, 2009. Used under license from Shutterstock, Inc.*

ROMAN RELIGION

The Romans for most of their history were pagan. During the early Republic Roman had a polytheistic religion of household gods and spirits from nature that were natural for simple agrarian people. This traditional religion remained for the farmers. Urban Romans were not satisfied with an agrarian religion and copied Greek models. They incorporated Greek gods and Greek mythology. Thus Roman mythology was based on the Greek mythology and Romans only made minor changes and changed the names of Greek gods for Roman names such as Aphrodite became the Roman Venus; Athena becomes Minerva, and Poseidon became Neptune, etc.

Emperors were given godly status, thus considered a living god. Emperor worship became the official religion of the empire, which confirmed the famous writer Seneca's observation: "Religion is regarded by the common people as true, by the wise as false, and by the rulers as useful." Emperor worship was a way to promote patriotism. After Caesar Augustus (Octavian) the Senate deified most emperors.

This official religion served the state but did very little for the spiritual needs of the common people. The empire having many diverse cultures resulted in a variety of religions imported to satisfy those needs. *Isis* and *Cybele* were religions imported from Egypt and Asia Minor, respectively. Isis, a female goddess, appealed to Roman women because she was giver of health, beauty, wisdom, and love, and needed priestesses in her cult. Cybele, another goddess, had appeared in Rome since the Second Punic War with Hannibal. In her mythology she castrated the youth Attis who was unfaithful to her after she raised him from the dead. Followers of this religion castrated themselves during their rites and orgies, and Roman authorities had to make periodic attempts to regulate mayhem.

Mystery religions and *Mithraism* were imported from Greece and Persia, respectively. Eleusinian mysteries and Dionysian rites became popular but the vows of silence of both sects were effective enough that little is known about them. Of all the mysteries celebrated in ancient times, Eleusinian mysteries were held to be the ones of greatest importance. These myths and mysteries, begun in the Mycenean period

(c. 1600 B.C.) and lasting 2,000 years, were a major festival during the Hellenic era, later spreading to Rome. The rites, ceremonies, and beliefs were kept secret, as initiation was believed to unite the worshipper with the gods and included promises of divine power and rewards in the afterlife. Since the Mysteries involved visions and conjuring of an afterlife, some scholars believe that the power and longevity of the Eleusinian Mysteries came from psychedelic agents (drugs). Some modern scholars think that these Mysteries were intended to elevate man above the human sphere into the divine and to assure his redemption by making him a god and so conferring immortality upon him. As Christianity gained in popularity in the 4th and 5th centuries, Eleusis' prestige began to fade. Emperor Julian the Apostate was the last emperor to be initiated into the Eleusinian Mysteries. Emperor Theodosius I closed the sanctuaries by decree in 392 A.D. The last remnants of the Mysteries were wiped out in 396 A.D., when Alaric, King of the Goths, invaded, accompanied by Christians bringing Arian Christianity and desecrating the old sacred sites.

Mithraism was a mystery religion which became popular among the military in the Roman Empire, from the 1st to 4th centuries A.D. The Roman religion was a development of a Zoroastrian *cult* of Mithra. Mithraism was an initiatory order, passed from initiate to initiate, like the Eleusinian Mysteries. It was not based on a body of scripture, and hence very little written documentary evidence survives. Religious practice was centered on the mithraeum (Latin, from Greek mithraion), either an adapted natural cave or cavern or an artificial building imitating a cavern. The members of a mithraeum were divided into seven ranks. All members were expected to progress through the first four ranks, while only a few would go on to the three higher ranks. The first four ranks represent spiritual progress. In every Mithraic temple, the place of honor was occupied by a tauroctony, a representation of Mithras killing a sacred bull which was associated with spring. Mithras is depicted as an energetic young man. Mithras grasps the bull so as to force it into submission, with his knee on its back and one hand forcing back its head while he stabs it in the neck with a short sword. A serpent and a dog seem to drink from the bull's open wound which is sometimes depicted as spilling grain rather than blood, and a scorpion (usually interpreted as a sign for autumn) attacks the bull's testicles, sapping the bull's strength. It has been proposed by some scholars that, rather than being derived from Iranian animal sacrifice scene with Iranian precedents, the tauroctony is a symbolic representation of the constellations. Thus, the bull is interpreted as representing the constellation Taurus, the snake the constellation Hydra, the dog Canis Major or Minor. Speculation of the relationship of early Christianity with Mithraism has traditionally been based on the polemical testimonies of the 2nd century church fathers, such as Justin's accusations that the Mithraists were diabolically imitating the Christians. This led to an image of rivalry between the two religions that some scholars have. Not much is known about the decline of the religion. The edict of Emperor Theodosius I in 394 made paganism illegal and Christianity the official state religion. Official recognition of Mithras in the army stopped at this time, but there is no information on what other effect the edict had on Mithraism. Mithraism may have survived in certain remote places into the 5th century.

DECLINE OF THE ROMAN EMPIRE

There are various reasons for the decline of the biggest empire up to that date that lasted over 600 years. First are the *internal causes:*

Political

1. *Lack of clear law of succession.* Once an emperor died or was deposed there was not a well established law or tradition of succession. Violence and use of force had been a traditional way to power since Rome's early history. The legend of Romulus and Remus serves as an example,

with the murder of Remus by his brother Romulus. This lack of peaceful transition of power resulted in civil wars, with a vicious cycle from 235–284 A.D. among the Roman generals fighting to take over the throne. The Roman legions supported any general who offered the greatest benefits to the military for their loyalty. This created a problem of increasing national debt due to military expenses.

2. *Lack of constitutional means for reform,* which lead to civil wars, as a means to overthrow unpopular regimes.

3. *Rome did not involve enough people in the work of government.* The oligarchic Patrician class ruled government. The majority of the Romans were merely subjects who did not participate in government. Hence, the masses were indifferent and even hostile to the government, especially toward its oppressive taxes. Rome lost the loyalty of its population when it needed it most during time of crisis. There was also the disinclination to take public office in other cities because public officers had to pay city taxes to the government, and with increasing rural poverty no one wanted to be bankrupt by holding office. Rome established certain quota for the city to pay in taxes. The governing official had the responsibility to collect this established amount, and if the officer was not able to collect the allocated amount he would have to make it up from his personal income or wealth. Therefore, Rome discouraged its most able and educated citizens from taking office which hindered the empire by not having the most capable governing its provinces and cities.

Economic Causes

1. *Slave system and manpower shortages.* Cities depended on food surpluses from the rural areas. Military conquest had been a major source of slave labor. With conquests halting, less slaves were available and slave labor was not very productive. The economy began to run out of "human fuel." Thus, the countryside produced less food. There was no interest in technology to increase food production because landlords were interested in owning slaves. With the end of foreign conquest, its decline of slavery, more people were needed to stay on the farms, and barbarian invasions increased the need to recruit more manpower for the military. But less men were available to serve in the military, which weakened the Roman security of its empire.

2. *Plagues*—periodical plagues reduced one-third of the population. A decrease in population meant a decrease of labor and military manpower, which hindered the economy and the strength of the Roman army.

3. *Demoralization*—the difficult economic and social condition in the empire discouraged increases in families, so there was a lower birthrate.

All these brought about a condition of insufficient manpower to work the land, causing food shortages, and to defend the empire from foreign invaders.

Lack of Civil Ideals

1. *Few citizens were willing to work for the public good, or defend Roman ideals.* The reasons were many. People throughout the empire did not share the same ideals. Senatorial and republican traditions were obsolete. It could not restore order and peace and property, nor substitute the rule of the emperor as in Republican Rome. The Roman state no longer stood for the beneficial peace (Pax Romana) but fell on repeatedly in civil wars, and oppressive taxation. Regional differences in a very large empire, social classes with the rich and the very poor, and lack of public education were barriers to a unifying public spirit. Finally, disinterest and no trust of the

empire and its leaders, politics, and ideals and concern for the immediate needs and interests and not for the empire as a whole putting the focus on regionalism vs. the welfare of the entire empire.

2. The *division* by emperor Constantine *of the empire into east and west,* resulting in the western Roman Empire with its capital in Rome, and the eastern Roman Empire (Byzantium) with Constantinople as its capital.

3. *Immorality of Roman society and court.* There was a loss of moral fiber in the Roman society that became accustomed to free "bread and circus" with grain handout by the government and the famous sadistic entertainment of the Roman games in the Colosseums. Loss of the traditional discipline and austerity of the Roman character and their main virtue of duty to state and family. Many scandals due to immoral lives of some emperors and members of the court that involved orgies, conspiracies, homosexuality, corruption, etc.

A good example of a scandalous immoral emperor was **Caligula.** As a young child Caligula was taken to the court of Emperor Tiberius after the emperor executed his older brother due to his paranoia. Caligula's life was spared due to his young age. Tiberius lifestyle was notorious for its immorality and orgies, not the best place for an impressionable teenage boy to grow. Caligula never complained and did not express any resentment about the treatment his family received. The lifestyle of Tiberius seemed to suit him and Caligula spoke well of the emperor gaining his sympathy. Caligula binged on food and drink, and sexual pleasures. His taste for sadism is indicated when he enjoyed observing the emperor's enemies being tortured. After Tiberius' death, Caligula became emperor in 37 A.D. To celebrate this event and become popular with the people he had a three-month season of sumptuous shows and games where 160,000 animals were killed for the entertainment of the masses. Six months into his reign he fell ill coming close to death. The frantic activity and his need for non-stop stimulation seem to have burned him out with exhaustion. Maybe his epileptic condition took a severe turn for the worse. He disappears from the public for a while and then returns a changed person.

Out of grief and devotion for the emperor, extravagant gestures were made by Romans of high social status such as the nobleman Atanius Secundus who said publicly that he would go happily to the gladiatorial arena if his emperor would be spared, and another nobleman Publius Afranius Potius remarked that he would gladly give up his own life to save Caligula's. When Caligula returned from his illness he had undergone a dramatic transformation in his personality. Caligula decided to hold them to their promises. Secundus was forced to fight as a gladiator and survived, but Potius was put to death to keep his promise. Then he forced a number of close advisers to commit suicide such as his cousin and father-in-law, due to his paranoia thinking plots were made against his life.

He remarried Livia Orestilla after taking her away when she was to be wedded to another man. Then he divorced her, but as she was still his property according to him and when he suspected she was seeing the man she was going to wed, Caligula sent her in exile. He married another woman and after six months divorced her due to infertility. His three sisters publicly became his concubines. Drusilla was his favorite who divorced two husbands on Caligula's orders. When she died Caligula was very heartbroken, giving her the title of Augusta, the empress, and had her declared a god by order of the Senate. During banquets Caligula would flirt with his sisters and ended up making love in front of everyone, even telling the woman who was his wife at that moment to join in. These banquets became a terrible ordeal for its guests who dared not attend because if they chose not to they might offend the emperor who might have them tortured, put to death, or confiscate the family estate on made up charges. Caligula treated the noble women like cattle, inspecting them and making comments about their looks. Then he would chose a wife and take her to an adjoining room where he enjoyed her and then came back to give his judgment on her sexual performance, while wife and husband endured this humiliation.

Caligula spent lavishly on all sorts of luxuries he had a caprice with. Within a year his extravagances cost the state 2,700,000,000 sesterces that Tiberius had collected. To raise funds to keep up his expenses Caligula invented new arbitrary taxes and tariffs, and invented criminal cases against the rich which required large payment of fines. He became very attached to his favorite horse Incitatus that he had a stable made of marble, with a manger of ebony. Incitatus had a jewel-encrusted collar, and wore blankets of imperial purple. Caligula would send soldiers to enforce strict silence in the streets so his horse's sleep would not be disturbed. He had hopes of appointing Incitatus to the office of consul, behavior which is difficult to determine if it stemmed from insanity or a desire to humiliate his human courtiers. His cruelty was such that he ordered executions to be made not by one stroke but by small wounds giving the victim an agonizing death. To entertain him, prisoners were tortured or executed while he had lunch. Some victims were executed by having wild animals set upon them.

Finally Caligula demanded to be treated as a god. By this time there was a growing opposition as many detested his actions and many did not feel secure with his paranoia. There were several plots that failed to eliminate him. In 41 A.D. a tribune of the Praetorian Guard, Cassius Chaera, and two senators with others involved planned an attempt during the Palatine Games. They knew Caligula would have to pass through a narrow passage to leave the stage for lunch and his bodyguard could not be next to him. This happened as expected and Chaera was able to get close to and stab Caligula while his accomplices came up and stabbed the emperor again. The bodyguards rushed in killing some of the conspirators and innocent bystanders, too. At the same time a separate group of conspirators set to the imperial palace to kill the imperial family with the intent of destroying the Julio-Claudian dynasty and restoring the Republic. But the Praetorian Guard loyal to the family hid and protected Caligula's uncle, Claudius, who survived and became the next emperor.

4. *Disorder and degeneracy.* What made Rome great and allowed it to become a large nation from its beginnings as a small city-state was the qualities of the Roman nobility with their patriotic spirit, devotion to duty and family, and the hardness and tenacity of its citizen-soldier-farmer. But the conquest of the Mediterranean after the Punic Wars (Carthage) and dominion of Greece (Corinth) flooded Rome with riches and slaves that changed the moral nation into a predatory state that lived by war and plunder. The noble officers turned into military adventurer; citizen farmer soldiers into professionals, and at retirement with the inclusion of the poor masses, into the vast urban proletariat that survived on government handouts and bribes of politicians and kept content with "bread and circuses."

External causes: These came by the gradual invasion of Barbarian tribes from northern central Europe into the territories of the vast Roman Empire that could no longer be defended until they were able to take over, settle, and rule over the Western Roman Empire with Rome as its capital. After Rome was sacked in 410 and 455 A.D. it was ruled by the first non-Roman king in 476 A.D., the date taken to be the end of the Roman Empire in the West. The Eastern Roman Empire or Byzantium will last until 1453 when the Islamic Turks conquered Constantinople and renamed it Istanbul.

THE EASTERN ROMAN EMPIRE AND BYZANTINE CIVILIZATION, 476–1453

The end of centralized rule in Rome's western lands in 476 A.D. had little effect on the Eastern Roman Empire, also known as Byzantium. During its 1,000-year existence since the fall of Rome, the empire took its Roman heritage and became an autocratic, static entity in a world of great upheaval and movement of populations. The changing boundaries of the Byzantine world tell the story of an empire under continual siege. Byzantium's borders reached their farthest western limits in the 6th century and then contracted over the next 800 years. The empire lost territory to the Arabs in the east and to the Bulgars and other groups in the west. Finally, no longer able to defend even the city of Constantinople itself, the empire fell to the Ottoman Turks in 1453.

Even though Byzantium was struck by rapid and sometimes catastrophic disasters, its great wealth and economic resources allowed the state to survive. The rulers tightly controlled their subjects' economic affairs, a policy that placed state interest above individual gains. A stimulating urban life developed, centered in Constantinople the capital of the empire and the most important city. Beyond Constantinople, the countryside was dotted by aristocrats and worked by *coloni,* or serfs. Byzantium's economy was based on agriculture, the basic source of wealth.

Although the frontiers of the empire changed over the centuries, its heartland in Greece and Asia Minor remained basically stable. In its heartland, a relatively uniform culture evolved that differed markedly from late Rome and the Medieval West. The Byzantine world gave up its pagan and Latin roots to become a Christian, Greek civilization. The Orthodox Church, led by the patriarch of Constantinople, emerged as a powerful force, but without the independence from secular rulers enjoyed by the Western church and the pope. Greek became the language of church, state, and scholarship, just as Latin served those functions in the West. But, like late Rome and unlike the Medieval West, Byzantium remained characterized by ethnic and racial diversity; new peoples, such as Serbs and the Bulgarians, helped to ensure this diversity as they were slowly assimilated into the Byzantine way of life.

HISTORY OF THE BYZANTINE EMPIRE

Throughout its history, the Byzantine Empire's fortunes fluctuated depending on its relations with its hostile neighbors. From 476 to 641, the Byzantine emperors made a valiant but ultimately futile effort to recover the lost western provinces and revive the empire. Emperor Justinian the Great 527–565 A.D. conquered several of the Germanic kingdoms that had arisen in the former Western Empire and extended the empire's borders to encompass Italy, southern Spain, and North Africa. Justinian's wars exhausted the state treasury, however, leaving his successors unable to maintain the empire.

Between 641 and 867, the second period by Byzantine history, a series of weak rulers lost all the western lands that Justinian had recovered. The emperors were also forced to yield much of Asia Minor to their Arab foes, and in 687 a Bulgarian kingdom was carved out of Byzantine territory in the Balkans. To repel these enemy assaults, Byzantine became more militarized. In the provinces, generals were given vast military and civil powers, and they began to replace the aristocrats as landowners. A style of feudalism, vast estates protected by private armies slowly arose.

With the reign of Basil I 867–886, a new dynasty of capable Macedonian rulers led the Byzantine Empire into the Golden Age from 876–1081. These rulers again expanded the borders of the empire and restored the state to economic health. Orthodox missionaries eventually tied the peoples of Eastern Europe to the religion and civilization of Byzantine, and in the late 10th century they introduced Christianity to Russia. As a result, after the fall of Constantinople in 1453, the Russian state claimed to be the spiritual and cultural heir to Byzantine civilization.

In 1081 general, Alexius Comnenus 1081–1118, seized the throne, and thus began a new period, characterized by increasing pressure from the West from 1081–1261.

The Comneni rulers tried vainly to win allies, but they were surrounded by enemies—Normans, Seljuk Turks, Hungarians, Serbs, Bulgarians, and, after 1095, the European Crusaders on their way to the Holy Land. In 1204 the soldiers of the Fourth Crusade conquered Constantinople and took over the remaining lands. The empire appeared to be finished except for some scattered holdings in Asia Minor. But in 1261 Michael Palaeologus (1261–1282) regained Constantinople and breathed some new life into the feeble empire.

The Palaeologian dynasty ruled over the Byzantine world during the fifth and last phrase of its history from 1261–1453, but eventually it was forced to recognize that the empire was only a diminished Greek state. From 1302 onward, the Ottoman Turks built an empire on the ruins of the Byzantine Empire. By 1330 this new state absorbed Asia Minor, and by 1390 Serbia and Bulgaria were Turkish provinces. In 1453 the Turks took Constantinople, ravaging the city for three days, searching for booty and destroying priceless art treasures. The fall of Constantinople ended the last living vestige of ancient Rome.

BYZANTINE CULTURE

From Rome, Byzantine inherited a legacy of unresolved conflicts between Christian and Classical ideals. In the wider Byzantine culture, this conflict was revealed in the division between secular forms of expression, which showed a playful or humorous side of Byzantine life, and religious forms, which were always deeply serious. However, Byzantine culture, whether secular or religious, tended to stress Classical values of serenity, dignity, and restraint. This timeless and even majestic quality was cultivated, perhaps, in compensation for the besieged circumstances the Byzantine state had to endure from its internal weaknesses and external enemies.

The Orthodox Religion

While the bishop of Rome (the pope) was the head of the Christian church in the West, the bishop (or patriarch) of Constantinople became the spiritual and doctrinal head of the Eastern (Orthodox) Church in Byzantine. The Church in the West and the East had drifted apart since the removal of Rome as the capital of the empire to Constantinople by Emperor Constantine the Great until they became completely separated in 1054. This separation is known as the **Greek** or **Eastern Schism.** Long before this fateful schism there had been misunderstanding and jealousy between East and West. The drift begins with the bishop Eusebius of Nicomedia and his followers in opposition to the Council of Nicaea. This party was behind the organization and establishment of the autonomy of the Byzantine bishops. The Greek Church from its beginnings was in conflict with Christian tradition concerning the divinity of Christ, and in best terms with imperial despotism. This alliance with imperial despotism became known as **Caesaro-Papism.** This Caesaro-Papism became the main cause of the schism in the 11th century (and in the 16th century during the Reformation). The Roman Empire had the pagan tradition that the emperor is supreme in temporal as well as spiritual matters. That means to get involved in religion, and when the empire converted to Christianity, this concept did not disappear. Many emperors wanting to interfere and dictate in doctrinal matters fell into heresies that originated from the East. These emperors who were Arian, Iconoclast, and adherents to other doctrines found the Pope in Rome very irritating to their pride. They wanted a church submissive to their ambitions and passions. They preferred a church where they could be its head, and not the Pope, where they could nominate the bishops who would depend on them. They were looking for councils they could manipulate at their will. They wanted to be the "Pontifex Maximus" just as in pagan times, in other words Caesaro-Papism. The ambition and servility of most bishops in Constantinople prepared the triumph of this imperial despotism in religious matters. Nearly all these bishops owed their positions to the emperor. If the emperors were strong-willed the bishops were completely at their mercy, and religion was at stake. These bishops were at first just simple bishops under the Metropolitan of Heraclea. Then assistant bishops were placed under these bishops and through council of Constantinople in 381 and council of Chalcedon in 451, they became Patriarchs (ecclesiastical heads) that had authority over a large number of bishops. The East came to be under the Patriarchs of Constantinople, in spite of the protest of Rome. The Pope in Rome was too distanced to be able to have an influence upon the East. The difference between East and West kept on increasing as the Eastern Church went into a state of stagnation and rigid adherence to the forms and traditions of the past, and thus became suspicious of the West that made moves forward. The conflict came when the Eastern Church tried to impose her traditions on the West.

A great schism began in 726 when the despotic and heretic Emperor Leo III the Isaurian launched the **Iconoclast heresy** or controversy that lasted until 843. Iconoclasts were the image or icon destroyers. Leo III issued an imperial decree forbidding idolatry, and ordered the destruction of all images of Christ, saints and prophets. Siding with the iconoclastic emperors were bishops, the army, and the civil services; opposed were the monks. In the West, the papacy refused to join the iconoclastic frenzy. This radical position may have been influenced by Islam and Judaism that consider images a form of idolatry prohibited by God. Representations of all sorts were destroyed, including mosaics in Hagia Sophia (Figure 5.19). Entire works of art in Byzantium were lost forever, and thus the world lost a very important artistic legacy, and only very few works of this era were able to survive because they were out of the reach of the image breakers in Byzantine Italy and Mont Sinai. Many people including monks and priests who tried to protect these images were blinded, mutilated, tortured, and even executed. The cause of the conflict was due to politics rather than religious issues, and was mainly a conflict between church and state. The monastic movement had achieved great wealth and power as well as respect from

Figure 5.19   Icon of Christ, Hagia Sophia, Instanbul, Turkey. *Image Copyright PavleMarjanovic, 2009. Used under license from Shutterstock, Inc.*

the people, which the emperors resented. Monasteries were paying very little or no taxes, and diverting revenue from the state. Thus, the monasteries as the main repositories of sacred images were attacked, confiscated, raised to the ground, and their monks martyred. Pope Gregory II condemned Leo III, and the emperor threatened to destroy the image of St. Peter at Rome and imprison the Pope. A fleet was sent to Rome to accomplish the threat but the Italians and Lombards prevented this aggression. By 780 Empress Irene set herself to restore the veneration of images and bring back the peace. A general council was convoked, the Seventh Ecumenical at Nicaea that had Papal legates. The issue of veneration of images was defined by the church declaring that the figure of the cross and holy images are to be retained. The images are not to become objects of adoration in the proper sense, which can only be given to God alone, but are useful because they raise the mind of the faithful to the objects that the images represent. It is right to honor these images because the honor is really given to God and His saints that the images are intended to remind the faithful. A very important event because the belief that images were legitimate in the eyes of God and not against His will resulted in a great religious art production and legacy of the West. During the Middle Ages the church was the main promoter of the arts, and had the iconoclast views prevailed then the advancement of art in the West would have been greatly hampered. The heresy came to an end with Empress Theodora who in 843 brought images back in triumph to the Church of St. Sophia and the traditional faith was reestablished in the East.

Another important event that separated East from West was the **coronation of Charlemagne** in 800 by the Pope. Charlemagne was the king of the Franks, a Germanic people that in Byzantium were considered barbarians. To the Eastern mind that Rome would come under the yoke of barbarians was an issue that national pride would not tolerate. Rome, the ancient capital of the empire should be under Romans, not the Franks, and the Pope was blamed for this unpardonable act. The rivalry among East and West turned into hatred which embittered and complicated the relationship. The Eastern emperors retaliated by taking away provinces from the jurisdiction of Rome to the Patriarchate of Constantinople.

Due to abuses of power in the corrupt court of Byzantium, the patriarch of Constantinople St. Ignatius in 857 was imprisoned and a layman called Photius installed as patriarch which brought the **Photius schism.** Photius was a worldly, crafty, ambitious and unscrupulous individual who acted with arrogance. When the emperor was not able to convince the Pope to acknowledge Photius as the lawful patriarch, Photius went into a rage and proudly addressed the patriarchs and bishops in the East to claim spiritual superiority over the Papacy, and to declare it intolerable because the imperial crown of the West was placed by the Pope on Charlemagne, a Frank barbarian. He accused the Latin church of heresy and for its usages and discipline, such as enforcing the celibacy of the clergy. His hatred finally led him to excommunicate the whole Latin world and Pope. When the eastern decadent emperor Michael the Drunkard was murdered in 867, the next Emperor Basil sent Photius to prison and reinstated St. Ignatius. The Eighth Ecumenical Council at Constantinople in 869 condemned Photius and restored union under the authority of the Apostolic See (authority and jurisdiction of bishops (or Pope) founded by one or more of the Apostles). Photius ascended the patriarchal throne in 877 and acknowledged the Roman Primacy to obtain his approval by the Pope. In 886 Emperor Leo the Philosopher took him off from office and sent him to a monastery in Armenia.

Union among the church continued with the rivalries of East and West until **Patriarch** Michael **Cerularius** began the dissention again. He criticized the West for its practices and closed the Latin churches in Constantinople. The emperor who wanted peace with the West asked Pope St. Leo IX to send legates to Constantinople to come to peaceful terms. Cerularius refused to receive the three legates. Mutual misunderstanding was a main cause of the schism in the church, and each side being ill-informed an understanding was not possible. The Papal Legate **Cardinal Humbert** laid a document containing the excommunication of Cerularius in the church of St. Sophia before the clergy and people and left the city in July **1054**. This document was not well-founded demonstrating misunderstandings. The Pope died in April of 1054 and would not have approved of the excommunication because he had sent Humbert to heal the schism and not to aggravate the matter with the excommunication of the Patriarch. Cerularius' response was excommunicating his rivals. This finalized the schism that has not healed between East and West.

Many differences exist between the two Christian churches. They disagreed over the issue of whether the pope or a patriarch should lead the church; they also differed in language, Latin in the West, Greek in the East, religious practices such as Roman Catholic priests were celibate while Orthodox priests could marry, and fine points of religious doctrine.

Law

As a major contribution of Western culture, Byzantium's greatest accomplishment was the codification of the Roman law made under the emperor Justinian in the 6th century. The **Justinian Code,** which summarized a thousand years of Roman legal developments, not only laid the foundation of Byzantine law but also later furnished the starting point for the revival of Roman law in the West. This law code preserved such legal principles as requiring court proceedings to settle disputes, protecting the individual against unreasonable demands of society, and setting limits to the legitimate power of the sovereign. Through the Justinian Code, these Roman ideals permeated Byzantine society and served as a restraint on the autocratic emperors. When the West revived the study of the Roman law in the Middle Ages, these principles were adopted by the infant European states. Today, in virtually all the Western states, these principles continue to be honored.

Architecture and Mosaics

Architecture was the great achievement of the Byzantine world. Byzantine architecture was committed to glorifying the state and the emperors and to spreading the Christian message. Most of the byzantine palaces and state buildings either were destroyed in the 15th century or have since fallen into ruins, but many churches still survive and attest to the lost grandeur of this civilization.

By the 7th century, the **Byzantine style** had been born, a style that drew from Greek, Roman, and oriental sources. The Greco-Roman tradition supplied the basic elements of Byzantine architecture: columns, arches, vaults, and domes, oriental taste contributed a love of rich ornamentation and riotous color. Christianity fused these ingredients, provided wealthy patrons, and suggested subjects for the interior decorations. The **Greek cross,** which has arms of equal length, came to be the preferred floor plan for later Byzantine churches.

Despite their borrowings, the Byzantines made significant innovation that became fundamental in their architecture: They invented **pendentives,** supports in the shape of inverted concave triangles, that allowed a dome to be suspended over a square base. As a result of this invention, the domed building soon became synonymous with the Byzantine style, notably in churches, like the Hagia Sophia.

The Byzantine obsession with the dome probably stemmed from its central role in the magnificent church Hagia Sophia, or Holy Wisdom, in Constantinople. The dome had been employed in early Christian architecture and in important Roman temples such as the Pantheon. Erected by Justinian, Hagia

Figure 5.20   Exterior of Hagia Sophia. *Image Copyright Mediamix photo, 2009. Used under license from Shutterstock, Inc.*

Sophia was intended to awe the worshiper with the twin majesties of God and the emperor (Figure 5.20). The central dome measures more than 101 feet in diameter and rested on four pendentives that channel the weight to four huge pillars. Half-domes cover the east and west ends of the aisles.

In the vast interior, the architect's goal was not to produce a unified effect but rather to create an illusion of celestial light. Glittering walls covered with polychrome marbles and brilliant mosaics, which have since disappeared or been covered with whitewash, suggested shimmering cloth to early viewers and contributed to the breathtaking effect of this magnificent church.

Mosaic making had experienced a lively flowering in late Rome, and in Byzantium it became a major form of artistic expression. Unlike the Roman mosaics, which were made of stone and laid in floor, the Byzantine mosaics were usually of glass and set into the walls. Of the Byzantine mosaics, the most beautiful and the most perfectly preserved are those in the churches of Ravenna, Italy.

During the Iconoclastic Controversy, the emperors destroyed virtually all figurative religious art that was under their control. After the conclusion of the controversy, a formalized repertory of church decoration evolved that characterized Byzantine art for the rest of its history. The aim of this religious art was strictly theological. For instance, Christ Pantocrator (Ruler of All) dominated each church's dome. In these portraits, Christ was presented as the emperor of the universe and the judge of the world. In that respect, Byzantine art came to picture him with a stern and forceful countenance, in contrast to Western portrayals, which increasingly focused on his suffering.

Art

Byzantine art developed out of the *art of the Roman Empire,* which was itself profoundly influenced by ancient Greek art. Byzantine art never lost sight of this classical heritage. The art produced during the Byzantine Empire, although marked by periodic revivals of a classical aesthetic, was above all marked by the development of a new aesthetic. The most salient feature of this new aesthetic was its "abstract," or anti-naturalistic character. If classical art was marked by the attempt to create representations that mimicked reality as closely as possible, Byzantine art seems to have abandoned this attempt in favor of a more symbolic approach.

Religious art was not, however, limited to the monumental decoration of church interiors (Figure 5.21). One of the most important genres of Byzantine art was the icon, an image of Christ, the Virgin, or a saint, used as an object of veneration in Orthodox churches and private homes alike (Figure 5.22). Icons were more religious than aesthetic in nature: especially after the end of iconoclasm, they were understood to manifest the unique "presence" of the figure depicted by means of a "likeness" to that figure maintained through carefully maintained canons of representation. The illumination of manuscripts was another major genre of Byzantine art. The most commonly illustrated texts were religious, both scripture itself, particularly the Psalms, and devotional or theological texts. Secular texts were also illuminated.

Byzantine style spread to other nations because the Byzantine cultural heritage had been widely diffused, carried by the spread of Orthodox Christianity, to Bulgaria, Serbia, Rumania and, most importantly, to Russia, which became the centre of the Orthodox world following the Ottoman conquest of the Balkans, and even as far west as Sicily and Venice in Italy. Even under Ottoman rule,

Figure 5.21   Interior of Hagia Sophia. *Image Copyright Jarno Gonzalez Zarraonandia, 2009. Used under license from Shutterstock, Inc.*

Figure 5.22   Basilica of St. Marc, Venice, Italy, Byzantine style mosaic depicting the crucifixion of Jesus Christ. *Image © Jupiter Images.*

Byzantine traditions in icon-painting and other small-scale arts survived, especially in the Venetian-ruled Crete and Rhodes, where a "post-Byzantine" style under increasing Western influence survived for a further two centuries, producing El Greco and other significant artists of the 16th century. It strongly influenced some of the western art of the Middle Ages. The influence of Byzantine art in Western Europe, particularly Italy was seen in ecclesiastical architecture, through the development of the Romanesque style in the 10th and 11th centuries.

In conclusion, the Byzantine civilization after the fall of Constantinople left a profound legacy to the West, some of which is still alive today. In Eastern Europe, the Orthodox Church continues to influence the Slavic population. Western law owes a great debt to the Code of Justinian, which became the standard legal text studied in medieval universities. Elements of Byzantine art appeared in Renaissance art in Italy, and the Italian cities of Venice, Genoa, and Pisa became major cultural centers in the 15th century because of the wealth they had accumulated from Byzantine trade.

Byzantine also served conserving functions for the West. The Byzantine Empire acted as a buffer against the Arabs in the 7th century and against the Seljuk Turks in the 12th century. Byzantine scholars preserved ancient Greek texts, many of which were carried to Italy, England, and elsewhere in the mid-15th century. When these works were reintroduced into the West, they intensified the cultural revival already under way during the Renaissance.

SUMMARY

The legendary founding of the ancient city-state of Rome is attributed to the heroes Aeneas and Romulus (Remus was murdered by his twin brother), from Virgil's epic poem *Aeneid* and the legend of Romulus and Remus. The ancient Romans considered these legends to be the historical origins of their state. The Romans believed they were fated to be the grand rulers of the world. These two legends also indicate the Roman traits of hard work, thriftiness, combativeness, loyalty, and dedication to state and family.

Rome's origins are found in the Italic Peninsula. The Etruscans were people who settled in north and central Italy originally from the Greek world and had an advanced culture. They ruled over the city-state of Rome until the Romans overcame the power of the Etruscans in 308 B.C. Rome begins as a small city-state in central Italy upon the seven hills along the Tiber River ruled by kings selected by the council of landowners and then the entire people ratified their choice. This became the origin and model for the later Roman Republic. People participated in government.

In 509 B.C. the Romans overthrew the last Etruscan king and created the Roman Republic because they no longer wanted to be ruled by monarchs. The Republic was an oligarchical form of government run by the patrician upper class. Plebeians constituted the remaining 90% of the population. The Republic was based on a system of representatives with separations of powers. Therefore, the Republic had two heads of state or consuls with the power to veto each other, who kept peace and order, raised armies, and conducted foreign policy. They appointed patricians to the senate. Consuls were senators chosen by the patrician voters in elections. The consuls and Senate submitted laws to the Centuriate Assembly, which passed laws, elected consuls, and elected two censors among the ex-consuls. The censors determined who could be nominated for the Senate, and who could serve in the military. The Republic had a mechanism of checks and balances because all the different governing bodies had to cooperate with one another to govern. The main issue is that power was not in the hands of one person or small group of men. In times of war a dictator was appointed instead of the two consuls for a period of only six months. Eventually the plebeians attained the office of the tribune whose function was to defend the interests and persons of this lower social class. By 287 B.C. the Plebeian Assembly that formed part of the Assembly of the Tribes and made up of plebeians, voted and in that manner participated in the government because the decisions from the Assembly of Tribes had binding force of law for Romans. This allowed the Plebeians to participate in government to a certain extent.

The pragmatic Roman Republic with its checks and balances, its separation of powers, and its government representatives became later the model for which the founding fathers of the United States during the 18th century utilized to create the American democratic republic.

Historically Rome began as a small city-state that later became the greatest empire of ancient times in the Middle East, Europe, and North Africa. As a small city-state in central Italy it had an open door policy to all foreigners to increase its population. This openness to assimilate different people and their cultural contributions played a major role in Rome's progress and empire building through all its history. The Roman Empire was built upon the peoples and their useful contribution that through assimilation or conquest joined to be part of this great idea that is Rome. First by a combination of diplomatic alliances, annexation, and war, all the Italian Peninsula became Roman territory by 275 B.C. Then the three Punic Wars with Carthage from 264–146 B.C. allowed Rome to conquer territories beyond Italy, in three continents extending all across the Mediterranean. Part of the conquest was Greece which provided Rome with its most important contribution, the rich and advanced ancient Greek culture. Thus, Rome absorbed Greek heritage that became a dominant cultural element of what became known as the Greco-Roman world. All this conquest brought society and the city of Rome a great prosperity and the negative consequences of excessive wealth unequally accumulated.

The new wealth and prosperity was not shared by all Roman society, with many landless and jobless. This new empire had a very rich upper class and a large mass of unemployed poor and slaves. This new wealth with its luxurious lifestyles undermined the traditional Roman values that had provided the Romans with the virtues that made them strong and supported the Roman Republic. This brought a moral decline that contributed to the Republic's fall and later the Roman Empire's decline and eventual fall.

The ancient Romans never resolved the issue of land ownership that was the key to Rome's economic and social health of its citizens. By the 1st century B.C. 80% of the population of Rome was either poor or slaves. Two patrician brothers, Tiberius and Gaius Gracchus, attempted to solve this important issue by applying older legislation limiting the amount of land an individual could own, and redistributing public land to landless farmers. This angered the rich senatorial class that responded by murdering both brothers. The senate discarded reason and legal means, using violence as the way to overcome its opposition to the Gracchan revolution. Violence then became a common weapon in Roman politics that led Rome into an era of political violence that ended with the destruction of the Republic in the long run. The Senate became a powerful minority representing a few hundred families whose goal was to retain control over the state and continue to increase their wealth and power, not to serve the greater interests and welfare of Rome and all its citizens. This senatorial self-seeking entrenched oligarchy dragged the Republic with its never ending class struggles between rich and poor into civil wars that brought the decline of the Republic.

This division between two factions, the aristocrats and the Populares, will bring about three civil wars. The first civil war began over a dispute over two military commanders who wanted to lead the Roman forces to put down a revolt in Greece and Asia Minor. The Senate chose Sulla and the Popular Assembly chose Marius. Marius died during the civil war and Sulla was the victor. Sulla purged his populist enemies and then retired. The second civil war was the result of struggle between Julius Caesar, the Roman general that took up the cause of the Roman people, and the Roman general Pompey, who took the side of the Senate. Caesar was victorious, passing legislation to redistribute the land to the citizens and other reforms that angered the rich senatorial class. When Caesar declared himself perpetual dictator, becoming defacto Rome's first emperor, a group of senators stabbed him to death. This violent act did not restore the Republic that was a dying institution. The final civil war between Caesar's heir, Gaius Octavian or Augustus as he is also known, and Mark Anthony came with the breakdown of the

Second Triumvirate due to the struggle between Octavian and Anthony to rule Rome. Octavian won and became the ruler transforming the Roman Republic into an autocracy. Octavian used diplomacy and propaganda to disguise his real intention to rule Rome in an autocratic manner, claiming he was restoring the Republic and the Senate, tired of civil wars, became complacent and rubber-stamped his will. Octavian brought peace and prosperity to Rome inaugurating the Pax Romana 27 B.C.–180 A.D. Octavian's popularity and good administration allowed for Roman society to accept the imperial system of government. The Roman Empire was established with the Roman Emperor as absolute monarch.

After the Pax Romana, incompetent emperors with abusive government and lack of clear laws and tradition of succession brought about a new wave of civil wars as the generals of the Roman legions fought each other to become emperor. The beginnings of the Barbarian invasions took place while the empires' borders were not well protected due to Rome's civil wars. In 284 A.D. Emperor Diocletian put an end to this chaotic period. He made reforms to bring order and progress, and his major reform was a new system of rule, the tetrarchy or rule by four emperors. The empire was divided into West and East, and he ruled from Nicomedia in Asia Minor, not Rome. During his rule, Diocletian imposed a brutal suppression to the new rising religion, Christianity. He was the only emperor to voluntarily abdicate. Civil war broke out once more when the Roman emperors that succeeded Diocletian fought each other to become sole emperor of the Roman Empire. The victor was Constantine who had converted to Christianity.

Emperor Constantine, trying to protect Christians, promulgated the Edict of Milan in 313 A.D. making all religions equal before the law. The new Christian emperor achieved his goal of ending the persecutions of Christians with the edict because no one could be persecuted for being a Christian or a pagan. Constantine ruled the Western Roman Empire and Lucinius the East, but soon they fought to be the sole ruler. Constantine won the war and later had Lucinius executed. To stop religious division of Christianity in his empire, Constantine ordered the Council of Nicaea to resolve the issue of the heresy of Arianism. The council condemned the priest Arius and his doctrine, keeping theological unity within the Church. Christians became larger in numbers and an influence upon the Roman Empire. By 423 A.D. Emperor Theodosius II declared almost no pagans remained. By the 7th century A.D. paganism was phased out in the lands of the ancient Roman Empire. The conversion of the Roman Empire to Christianity was a major event of immense consequence that allowed for Christianity to become an indispensable building block of Western civilization and allowed for the next era of the Middle Ages to evolve.

The fall of the Western Roman Empire by 476 A.D. had many causes. There were political causes: lack of clear law of succession that left the door open for struggle for power after an emperor died or was deposed; lack of constitutional means of reform that made the use of force as a means to change; and Rome did not involve enough people in the work of government, which was a reason why many were indifferent; and there was a lack of loyalty from the masses, and the most able individuals were discouraged to take office. The economic causes were the shortage of manpower due to the decreasing number of slaves and lower demographic of the population due to plagues and difficult conditions throughout the Empire. This shortage was the reason for the food shortages from the farms and not enough military forces to defend the borders. The third major cause was the lack of civil ideals when the many peoples of the Empire did not share the same ideals and the Roman state was not looking after the welfare of its populations with the many civil wars, oppressive taxation, and corruption. The population lost trust in the Roman state and looked after its immediate regional interests. The final cause that destroyed the Western Roman Empire that had fallen into disorder and degeneration were the Barbarians, invasions from northern Europe.

The Eastern Roman Empire known as Byzantium survived the fall of the Western Roman Empire for about one thousand years until its capital Constantinople fell to invaders. The Byzantine emperors tried to retake the Western Empire from 476 to 641 A.D. Emperor Justinian was the most successful regaining lost territories but exhausting the state treasury in the process. Several dynasties ruled the Byzantine Empire throughout its history. In the long run, the Eastern Empire lost territories to European and Arab invaders. Finally Turks that had converted to Islam took over Constantinople in 1453 which was the end of the last vestige of ancient Rome.

The Church became divided into East and West. In the West the Church was headed by the pope in Rome. In the East the bishop or patriarch of Constantinople became the spiritual and doctrinal head of the Eastern (Orthodox) Church. Due to the division of the Roman Empire into East and West, the fall of the Western Roman Empire, the misunderstandings between East and West due to the geographical long distances and different religious traditions, and the alliance of the Eastern Church with imperial despotism known as caesaro-papism, all conspired to bring the Greek or Eastern Schism in 1054 A.D.

The Romans took their philosophical ideas from the Greeks; therefore, their philosophy is based on the traditions of Greek philosophy, which meant adapting to Greek philosophical doctrines. The most famous philosophical schools of ancient Rome were the Stoics, Epicureans, Cynics, Skeptics, and the Neo-Platonists.

The Stoics believed the god's presence in the universe was carried out through natural law. This natural law determined the entire course the world took and men's lives included. Therefore, there was a reason or explanation for everything. God determined man's fate. The Stoics had a deterministic outlook on life, and men could not escape their fate, so mankind could only accept fate or rebel against it, which was entirely futile.

Living ethically consisted in practicing virtue, the only genuine good, which consisted in fulfilling one's duty in life. Another important good was to obtain serenity or tranquility of the mind, which required control over one's inner life even if the external world was in chaos. In the end natural law is in control of the universe and will lead to what is good or god's will. Stoicism as a philosophy was very compatible with Roman values and outlook on civilization and their role in history.

The Epicureans believed in the achievement of pleasure and happiness, avoiding pain as much as possible and removing the fear of death. Their goal was to maintain serenity of mind with life's misfortunes and enjoy pleasant activities.

The skeptics were critical about attaining objective knowledge. They believed human beings could not be certain they could know reality in an objective manner. Therefore, philosophers and scientists could never be completely sure they had arrived at correct conclusions and absolute truths. To obtain happiness man should suspend making judgments that brought tranquility of the mind because the useless search for absolute truth was put aside.

In the late Roman Empire, when society was seeking for a new meaning to life beyond earthly life and placing emphasis on human emotions rather than in reason, philosophers turned toward mysticism. Neo-Platonism will become a popular philosophy during this period with a new idea that after death the individual became one with god, instead of entering Heaven as yourself. To become one with god man needed to rely on mysticism by allowing the soul to become pure so it could unite with god. For Neo-Platonists like the philosopher Plotinus, philosophy becomes a religious experience to contemplate god in a mystical way. They were not concerned with physical reality, science, and human affairs. Religion and magic were of greater concern than rational philosophy. It was pantheistic believing god was found in all beings. To become one with god, virtue must be practiced allowing man to overcome sensual desires and be free of sin. Contemplating god gradually and forgetting the world, the soul finally becomes one with god. Like Plato, the Neo-Platonists value and pursue the spiritual world, despising or devaluing the physical world and human body. Neo-Platonic ideas will later influence Christian thinkers like Saint Augustine of Hippo.

Philosophical activities during the Late Roman Empire became focused on recovering the wisdom of ancient Greek philosophers, and were not original and creative as the Greeks. Greco-Roman philosophy was later incorporated by Christian theologians to serve Christian thought; therefore, in this manner it will be preserved and become an influence upon Western philosophy.

Law was one of Rome's greatest legacies to Western civilization. Roman law was a product of a slow evolution. It was first written down in the Twelve Tables. The first stage was the civil law in the Twelve Tables. The second was the law of nations once Rome expanded overseas out of Italy coming into contact with other people. It combined Roman civil law with principles of legal traditions from the Greeks and other people. The law of nations was identified with the Stoic concept of natural law. Romans recognized there were valid laws founded upon rational human nature that all rational people recognized as legitimate. The pragmatic Romans applied laws they observe that people practiced and accepted across the entire Roman Empire. Application of natural law was considered good and just, universal, and never changed in time. Roman law was based on human nature not on theory. Roman law survived the fall of the Roman Empire because it was reintroduced in the Middle Ages and became the basis of the civil law of many nations in Western Europe and in Latin America to the present date.

Roman culture had its traditional rustic culture when it came into contact with and then conquered the Hellenistic world. They absorbed Greek culture in literature, arts, architecture, sculpture, mythology, and philosophy. The humanities were a Greek invention that elevated soul and mind, and the Romans coined the term humanities, considered a fundamental element of civilized life. One of the great legacies of Rome was the preservation and transmission of the Greco-Roman culture to Western civilization.

Romans were great engineers developing the rounded arch, barrel vault, aqueducts, sewage and indoor plumbing, amphitheaters, stone bridges, and paved roads. These achievements provided a higher standard of living for its urban population never seen before in the ancient world. Many of these structures are still standing today and some are still functional after 2000 years! Roman engineers were problem solvers and their pragmatic engineering achievements attest to this ability. How to get large amounts of water to a city, for example, was solved with the great Roman aqueducts.

Latin was the language of the Romans and became the dominant language of the Western Roman Empire, while Greek was spoken in the Eastern Empire. After the fall of the Western Empire Latin developed into the Romance languages spoken today in Europe and the Americas. It also contributed to the vocabulary of the English language that borrowed many words from Latin.

Roman art was influenced to a great extent by Greek art that the Romans appreciated. Their sculpture was realistic, as most of their works were portraits of real individuals, instead of ideal types of the Greek Classical period. Murals were the most popular type of painting that has survived. From the Greeks the Romans learned the art of making mosaics of stone or glass. It can be summed up that the Greeks can be characterized as the creators while the Romans were content to be the copiers of art. The Romans excelled in copying the world as they saw it.

Byzantine architecture glorified the state and its emperors, and was used to spread the Christian message. The Byzantine style was a combination of the Greek, Roman, and Oriental architecture. They were able to suspend a dome over a square base by inventing pendentive supports. The most obvious features of Byzantine art are its new abstract or anti-naturalistic character. Its goal was to be symbolic, not to closely represent reality. Icons were a religious art form used as objects of veneration in Orthodox churches and homes. This art also had its influence upon Western European art, and especially in Eastern Europe including Russia.

The Justinian Code that consisted in the codification of Roman law under Emperor Justinian, became a starting point for the revival of Roman law in the West and the standard legal texts in medieval universities.

The Romans built the mightiest empire of the world to that point in history. This demonstrates that Roman virtues of duty, honor, and love of country are true values that, combined with practicality and the efficiency of their inventions and technologies, allowed the Romans to make their civilization the dominant way of life on three continents for many centuries.

6

THE MIDDLE AGES

EARLY MEDIEVAL WEST

Late Roman civilization created a synthesis of Christian and Greco-Roman values that the Early Medieval West inherited. Christian intellectuals valued Greco-Roman thought because it had many elements that were in harmony with the spiritual values that were now considered primary. Thus, part of Greco-Roman culture was used to support Christian values and ideas. Therefore, the Early Medieval West preserved the legacy of the ancient world, notably the Christian church, the papacy, the Latin language, the educational ideal of the arts and the sciences, building and artistic methods, Greek thought, and Greco-Roman literary and artistic forms. Most important, this first medieval period added Germanic elements to the Classical and Christian legacy to forge a new civilization centered in Europe rather than in the Mediterranean basin. This new version of Western culture was born in the reign of Charlemagne, and its memory lingered in the monasteries and other isolated outposts. When the barbarian invasions ended, a more-enduring Western culture was born.

PHILOSOPHY—THEOLOGY

Medieval philosophy or scholasticism applied *reason* to *revelation*.

- It explained and classified Christian teachings, the writing of the Bible by means of concept, and logic derived from Greek philosophy.
- Scholastics tried to show that the teachings of faith, derived from revelation and not from reason, were not contrary to reason. They tried to prove through reason what they already accepted as true by faith.
- In their attempt to harmonize faith with reason, medieval thinkers constructed an extraordinary synthesis of Christian revelation and Greek thought.
- The scholastic masters used reason to serve the faith by making it more clear and allowing for a better and deep understanding.
- They were loyal to the central concern of Christianity that is earning God's grace and achieving salvation. This goal could be achieved solely by faith, but scholastic thinkers took the position that philosophy (reason) could assist the Christian in his contemplation of God, nor was it an obstacle to the pursuit of grace (direct relationship with God). They accepted the Christian

beliefs that were embraced through faith and revelation, even those beyond the group of human reason, thus could not be deduced by rational argument. So their truths rested entirely on revelation and were to be accepted on faith.

- To medieval thinkers reason did not exist independently, but ultimately it had to acknowledge a superior and superhuman standard of truth.
- Faith had the final word, because the word of God in the Bible was the ultimate authority; rational thought had to be directed by faith to achieve its Christian end and guided by scriptural and ecclesiastical authority.

The more *cautious Christian* thinkers did not trust Greek philosophy. They considered it pagan, and argued that reason could be used to challenge and reject Christian teachings. Reason could lead men to question their faith.

The more cautious ("conservative") group of Christian thinkers were right to a certain degree in this debate. The reason was, as they cautioned, that philosophy will eventually be used to attack religious teaching and the faith all the way to the 21st century since the end of the Middle Ages. By revitalizing Greek thought, the Medieval Scholastics with its philosophy nurtured a powerful force which eventually challenged and attacked the medieval concepts of nature and society and weakened Christianity from within its society and Church. Since the Renaissance, modern Western thought was created by thinkers who refused to subordinate reason to religious authority or the faith and doctrine of the Church.

Therefore reason proved to be a "double-edged sword." It both ennobled and undermined the medieval world's view. The scholastic with their well intentions by introducing and developing the use of philosophy or reason, unintentionally opened a "Pandora's Box" and gave other men whose spirits were in conflict with the Church's faith and doctrine the intellectual means to attack and undermine the entire beliefs, values, medieval intuitions, and traditions.

This is a very important event that will change the course of the Christian civilization founded during the Middle Ages in the Western world. We will see this development in the Renaissance thinking, the Age of Reason with its main "fruit" the French Revolution, and their different ideological movements of the 19th and 20th centuries.

EARLY SCHOLASTICS

Anselm (1033–1109)

Anselm was a Benedictine monk and abbot of a monastery in Bec, Normandy, France. Anselm used reason to support the faith. Following St. Augustine, Anselm said the faith was a precondition to understand God and his teachings. Without belief there could be no proper knowledge.

He developed philosophical (rational) proof for God's existence:

Anselm believes in God as an established fact because he believes in the Bible and what the church teaches. There he employs logical arguments to demonstrate that God can be known through faith and through reason also.

Anselm's thinking reveals something about the essence of *medieval philosophy*. They assume God exists. He is reality and everything else must fit into this logic.

A modern man of the 1800s–1900s might begin thinking: "If it might be proven that God exists I will adopt Christian belief, if not, I will either doubt God's existence (atheism) or reserve judgment (agnosticism). Totally different attitude than the medieval man who had complete certitude of God, heaven, and hell, and did not bother to waste time questioning these facts.

Recovery of Aristotle

During the early middle Ages, scholars of the Muslim world translated the works of Aristotle into Arabic and wrote commentaries on them. The Islamic civilization made a great contribution to our civilization by preserving ancient Greek thought.

Later during the High Middle Ages, learned Europeans translated these works into *Latin*.

By introducing the Latin translation into Latin Christendom it created a dilemma for religious authorities. The dilemma came from the fact that Aristotle's philosophy was a product of human reason alone. Thus, it conflicted in many points with essential Christian doctrine.

For Aristotle:

- God was an impersonal principle that made *order* and *motion* in the universe, the unmoved mover.
- The universe was eternal, it always existed in time.
- Did not believe in the personal immortality of the soul.
- The soul could not exist independently of the body.

On the other hand, Christianity teaches:

- God is responsible for order in the physical universe, but he is also a personal being, a loving Father who is concerned over his children.
- God created the universe in a specific point in time. It has a beginning.
- The soul is immortal.
- Soul exists independent of the body.

Some of the church officials feared that Aristotle's natural philosophy would endanger the faith. Thus Aristotle's works were forbidden in the University of Paris, but the ban did not apply in all Christendom.

St. Thomas Aquinas (1225–1274) Synthesis of Christian Belief and Reason

Saint Thomas Aquinas was born at Rocca Sicca, near Naples, Italy, son of a very high noble Count Landulf of Aquino, nephew of the Holy Roman (German) Emperor Frederick Barbarossa (Figure 6.1). He was educated by the Benedictines at Monte Cassino and later in Naples. The youngest of the family, he was destined for a career in the church, which from an early age Thomas demonstrated an attraction and vocation for. The goal of the family was that he became the future abbot in charge of the Benedictine monastery that was wealthy with the large estate it owned next to the lands owned by the rich Aquino family. This would increase the family's prestige and wealth to have one of its members in charge of the monastery. The Benedictines was an order whose monks stayed in one place all their life. If Thomas became a Benedictine he would remain always in its monastery near the family estate. After his father's death in 1244 Thomas entered the Dominican order feeling that in it was his religious

Figure 6.1 Saint Thomas Aquinas on the facade of St Nicholas Cathedral in Ljubljana, Slovenia. *Image © Zvonimir Ateltic/Shutterstock, Inc.*

vocation. The Dominican, like the Franciscan order, are known as the mendicant orders and they do not stay in one place but travel to wherever they are needed. Not entering the Benedictines and choosing the Dominicans went against the family's plan and interest. Resenting this choice, his brothers kidnapped Thomas when he was on his way to Paris, France, to finish his studies, and held him prisoner for a year in the family castle at St. Giovanni. They tried all kinds of promises and pressures to make him change his mind about entering the Dominicans, but Thomas held to his decision and vocation. They even ended attempting to tempt him by introducing a attractive woman of ill repute to seduce Thomas, but he threatened to burn her with the burning wood for the fireplace and the women screamed to have the door open to get out of Thomas' "prison." Finally, with his determination and the help of his sister, he managed to regain his liberty and journeyed to Paris to continue his studies and later was ordained a priest. Thomas taught with distinction in Paris, Rome, and Naples. He was so well respected and famous that students flocked to hear his classes to the point that the lecture room could hardly contain all the students. He inspired his students to pursue learning with his synthetic, clear, and intelligible method of lecture. Pope Clement IV offered Thomas the archiepiscopal chair of Naples, but Thomas managed to escape that dignity that was repugnant to his humble character and retired manner of life. He died in 1274 on his way to the General Council of Lyons, France, summoned by Pope Gregory X.

St. Thomas rejected the position of church officials who insisted that philosophy would contaminate faith. He reconciled Aristotelians with Christianity: reason with faith and revelation.

His greatest work *Summa Theologica* is a systematic exposition of Christian thought.

St. Thomas divided revealed truth into two categories:

1. Beliefs whose truth can be demonstrated by reason
2. Beliefs that reason cannot prove to be either true or false

Examples

1. Philosophy (reason) could prove the existence of God and immortality of the soul.
2. Reason could not prove or disprove the doctrine of the Trinity, the incarnation and redemption because these beliefs surpass the capacity of human reason.

Doctrine of faith did not require rational proof to be valid. So reason was not necessary to believe. They were true because these articles of faith originated from God, the ultimate authority.

For St. Thomas Aquinas faith and reason will never be in conflict. Revelation did not contradict reason and reason did not corrupt the purity of faith.

Revelation supplemented and perfected reason. The doctrines of faith are infallible; so if an apparent conflict between philosophy and faith arises, it is certain that reason had erred somewhere.

Because faith and reason came from God, so they are not in competition with each other. They support and form an organic unity when properly understood.

Reason was just another road to God, and no need to fear or distrust. True faith and correct reason go hand in hand. Men must allow faith to guide reason. The wise person will allow the guidance of religion in all matters that relate directly to knowledge needed for salvation.

St. Thomas used correctly Aristotelian thought synthesizing it with the divine revelation of Christianity. An example is the use of Aristotelian logic to give proof of God's existence. St. Thomas argued that an object cannot move itself. Whatever is moved must be moved by something else and by something else again. So one needs to arrive to the first mover, moved by no other, and that only can be God.

St. Thomas agreed with Aristotle's natural system of ethics and politics, but as Aristotle did not know God's revealed truth he was incomplete. Aristotle's ideas about man are accurate and valuable but need to be complemented by revelation. Here, natural reason is not disqualified by revelation, rather it is improved. Reason helps explain revelation and revelation completes where reason is lacking.

St. Thomas held that in nontheological questions about specific things in nature not affecting man's salvation, people can trust only reason and experience. This sufficed, but as St. Thomas was a medieval thinker in that matters of theology and man's salvation, faith must guide reason. Secular knowledge must be supervised and corrected by revealed truths.

St. Thomas, by affirming that knowledge of man and the physical world has its importance and value, altered the tradition of St. Augustine who held a big distinction between the spiritual world and the physical world; that these two realities opposed each other; and that knowledge of the physical or secular world was seen as an obstacle to true knowledge. St. Thomas gave human reason and knowledge of the world (sciences) a new dignity and appreciation. With St. Thomas the "City of Man" became a place worthy of investigation and understanding.

Conclusion

St. Thomas Aquinas brought reason and revelation together, but as *unequal*. This union had to put secular knowledge at the service of faith and church. Faith was above reason and it must guide reason.

MEDIEVAL WESTERN EUROPE

The Establishment of Our Western Cultural Foundations

In this section we will discuss how Latin Christendom (Christianity guided by the Church headed by the Pope in Rome that used the Latin language) established itself in Western Europe and developed a Western Christian culture and civilization, which made the breakthroughs in science, technology, philosophy, economics, and political thought that gave rise to the modern west.

The Rise of Latin Christendom

From the 500–700s (6th to 8th centuries), Western Europe struggled to overcome the decadence, disorder, and chaos brought by the fall of the Roman Empire. In this historic process, a new civilization took ground. It grew from the intermingling of Greco-Roman civilization, Christian religion, and Germanic traditions. Mixing of the Catholic Church's outlook and values, with the ancient Mediterranean and Germanic cultures took place, and centuries later will give many fruits.

The Church: Shaper of Medieval Civilization

The Church, guided by the Pope from Rome, was the dominant institution of the Middle Ages. Society as a whole accepted its teaching and values. By the 900s (10th century) all of society's life (government, laws, customs, religion, education, etc.) was based on the teachings of the church. Church theology and all of society were in harmony. Christianity was the integrating principle; its faith was prevalent and vigorous.

The Church as Unifier

The Church was the unifying and civilizing agent when the Roman Empire collapsed. The Church retained the Roman administrative system, its governmental organization, and preserved elements of Greco-Roman civilization. It gave the people a purpose in life; hope for a better civilized life because it was the only civilizing force. It prevailed over the tradition of the Germanic tribes, so the Christian outlook became the foundations of medieval civilization.

The Church gave the individual a hope for salvation after natural death. The way to salvation required the Church's administration of the sacraments (baptism, confession, communism, absolution, prayers for souls (masses)) as a way to heaven. There was only one truth: God's revelation to humanity taught by the Church. More important than citizen or ethnicity was belonging to the Church, being a Christian.

The Medieval World View

The Christian outlook or Medieval world view changed the understanding of reality and way of thinking of more from antiquity, and unified western European man, because it was universal (crossed ethnic and geographical boundaries).

This outlook differed from both the Greco-Roman and the later modern scientific and secular views of the world. In the Christian (Catholic) view: not the individual, but God the creator determined what made up the good life. As God had revealed the proper rules for the regulation (how to live one's life) of the individual and social life, it was therefore logical that a person whose reason or thinking was *not* illuminated by revelation (teachings from the Bible and traditions of the Church) whether out of ignorance or disregard, or following another religion or philosophy, was either wrong or inadequate.

Ultimately, the good life was not found in this material world, but came from a union with God in a higher world. The good life was to live according to God's laws and will, with peace of conscience (even if this created conflicts with the "world") and to achieve salvation of the soul. Material wealth, comfort, and personal desires were of secondary importance. A good example is Saint Frances of Asia who gave away in public all his possessions, including his clothes back to his father. The medieval belief and attitude was, "What good does it profit a man to gain riches, power and prestige, if in doing so he loses his soul?"

The Christian belief made life and death purposeful and intelligible. Whatever goals, aspiration, lifestyles, struggles, and hardships that men underwent in life made sense and had purpose: to live according to God's will, having a good relationship with God and achieving salvation at the end of life. It determined the thought of the Middle Ages.

The Universe: Higher and Lower Worlds

Medieval thinkers saw a sharp difference between spirit and matter, the realm of grace (God and heaven) and the realm of Earth. They differentiated between a higher world of perfection and a lower world of imperfection.

Christian "Medieval" Order

3 social classes in Medieval Europe:

Clergy: Secular and Regular—Secular clergy are directly under the Bishop and live in parishes. Regular clergy live in convents and make up the different religious orders.

The Church's hierarchy is made up of 3 levels: pope, bishops, parish priests. These ranks have jurisdiction over the institutions and members of the church.

Then there are honorific levels that have leadership, but no jurisdiction: Cardinals, Patriarchs, Primates, and Archbishop in themselves.

The regular clergy also has its hierarchy such as General of the Order, superior of convents, simple priests and brothers. Being a religious society, the clergy has the highest rank and prestige.

Nobility: The second social class in importance in medieval society. Also as with the church it is a highly hierarchical class. With the King as Head of State, Kings were under the Emperor of the Holy Roman Germanic Empire, which was the highest in Christendom, and at the same time under the spiritual authority of the Pope. The nobility or aristocracy had ranks: Duke, Marquise, Count, Viscount, Barons, etc.

Common People: The third social class. These were divided into two categories that were vaguely defined. One category worked with its intellect the other with its hands. Thus a university professor is an intellectual worker, a serf, a manual labor.

Spiritual work had a higher value than material work because the farmer has an intrinsic greater dignity than material work, due to the soul's greater intrinsic dignity than the body.

Justification of this Medieval Order

Proportionality: A balance and harmonious relationship between the different social classes that leads to dignity. We need to see this as the manner and spirit by which the nobility *interacted and valued* with all members of society. This relationship and Christian spirit among the social classes justifies its existence, in addition to the duties or functions each class performed from whose dependence all of society benefited. (Nobility: government, justices, defense; Church: religion, public services of education and health; Common Men: commerce, industry, farming/food.)

Examples of this are found in rituals of antiquity and the Middle Ages.

A good example of the opposite, of disproportionality, can be observed in Ancient Egypt. A surviving text records the meeting between the pharaoh and a Syrian merchant who had the status of a modern consul in our society. The Syrian merchant even having a high social status addresses the pharaoh as being unworthy to kiss the feet of the pharaoh, and not even the hoof of the horse the pharaoh road, so therefore he would bow down and kiss the dirt where the horse of the pharaoh left its footprint. The ancient kings were considered gods and the rest of society was there to venerate and serve them. Thus there existed a great distance between the rulers and their subjects, and those ruled were considered servants in a way that were undignified to medieval and modern Western view. This to some extent continued to exist in Asian monarchies where the Japanese emperor Hirohito (1901–1989) up until World War II was held as divine and the Japanese people had to turn toward the emperor, bow, and face the ground without being able to raise their eyes and make eye contact with the emperor or watch him even if he was just passing by through the streets.

Proportionality in Christendom can be seen from the middle ages to the 18th century where the kings received all members of society whether noble or commoner in audiences or hearings to receive their petitions. An example of this was practiced in Versailles, France, which was visited by all classes of French society. There is an anecdote of the queen Maria Antoinette (1700s) who was sitting on a bench in the gardens of Versailles chatting with her accompanying ladies and saw a commoner who was visiting and observed she was pregnant. Maria Antoinette stood up from the bench and told the lady to sit on it because she had been walking and standing for a long time and needed to rest because of her condition. During the 13th century Saint Ferdinand III king of Castile sat by the window where anyone from the street could talk to him, and Saint Louis IX king of France in the city of Vincennes had a seat under an oak tree to hear his people's petitions. Can we as common citizens just approach our heads of state in the same manner today?

During the French king's ceremony of consecration, after it finished he would go outside the cathedral where those sick with a repugnant skin disease awaited him. The king would say, "The king touches you, that God may cure you," and after touching the skin sores, some were healed. When King John the Good of France was in prison in England, the diseased Englishmen came to his prison to be touched and healed by the king.

These are examples of Christian monarchy, paternalistic, caring, benevolent, and so different in contrast to the overbearing, authoritarian, pagan monarchs of the pharaohs, and other oriental monarchies. The people were considered only servants or slaves to the kings and priest.

Serfs and Former Slaves

The contrast between the slaves of antiquity and the serfs of the Middles Ages demonstrates proportionality of the medieval social classes.

During antiquity slaves were:

- No rights before law
- Considered legally a thing or object to be owned by Roman law
- Sent to death at his master's wish (i.e., used slaves in Roman society to test poisons in case the master wanted to commit suicide)
- Could not have a family or any right over his children
- Separated from his family and sold away from his family
- Due to Christians' influence in the late Roman Empire a form of matrimony was recognized but did not prohibit separation or to be separately sold. Not a true matrimony of free men.
- Where paganism vanished and it was overcome by Christianity in the late Roman Empire (300–400s) due to the Church's influence matrimony was recognized and any rights of life and death over slaves was abolished. It was a gradual progress to eliminate this inhuman practice which society would not let it easily die. But slaves they remained for all other services or labor.

Middle Ages

For the first time in history a continent had no slavery, due to the Christian church. What developed during the medieval era in Europe were the **serfs.** The serfs were common people in a status caught between a free man and a slave. The serf was bound to the land he worked and lived on for life. But the serf had many rights such as:

- To live and farm the land, he could not be driven out of the land "job security or tenure." Security many modern workers do not have.
- Property rights over his home and some of the land he cultivated.
- His "wages" came from the produce he produced on his lord's land or manor; of which the serf had rights over a portion of the produce to maintain his family.
- Contract was hereditary, so it could not be revoked nor could the serf and his family be thrown out of the land and left landless and homeless.
- If the serf was sold or changed lands, the serf remained on the land and could not be reversed by the new lord.
- Right over his family marriage was recognized.
- Could not be put to death, had a right to life.
- As to physical punishments and other penalties, the serf was subject to the penalties established by the law.

Serfdom came out of a free contract between serfs and lords, and some serfs were originally slaves from the old Roman Empire. This was a beneficial situation for both serfs and feudal lords at least until the 11th century with a convenient interdependence of military protection, political authority, and economic security in exchange for food production and menial toil.

When the Middle Ages ended, there were practically no serfs in Western Europe. Therefore, the Middle Ages produced a society of free men in the long run. So freedom became the norm in the end.

The justification of serfdom lies in the historical reality of Europe after the fall of the Roman Empire and the Barbarian and Viking invasions. This led to the rise of local landlords that needed men to defend and farm the land and men who needed protection and land to farm to feed their families. It was not imposed or forced upon society, it arose naturally out of necessity and when its necessity ceased, it gradually ended or faded away.

Corporation (Guilds) were composed by free men, with masters/employers, and apprentice and manual workers. Corporation or guilds were entirely a creation of the Middle Ages, along with the universities, in which artisans with the same crafts such as masons, carpenters, glass, and barrel makers, weavers, cobblers, jewelers, etc., united to promote their trade and create better working conditions for their members and their families.

The guilds were a means by which a specific trade was developed to a more refined stage and transmitted to a new generation of apprentices. It enabled the craftsmen to bargain for better salaries, protected the knowhow of their skills to remain within the guild that reduced external competition, and provided a pension for the sustenance of disabled members or to their families in case of a member's death. They tended to live in specific neighborhoods in the cities, and governed and policed their neighborhoods. In the guilds free men had many rights, such as developing their own labor laws and regulations, having jurisdiction over the neighborhood where the industry took place, plus its own police to control the neighborhood. In some cities the municipal government was exercised by the guilds or corporations. It was a government by common folk.

Conclusion: Thus we can see how medieval society with its hierarchy and social classes was led by a Christian spirit and principles that gave it proportion and harmony with human dignity and respect, the opposite of what had existed before with the authoritarian and inhuman character of pagan monarchies and its societies.

Specialization of Functions, Duties, and Privileges

Church/clergy: This class had functions of spiritual guidance and salvation of souls. Thus the first of social classes with highest ranks and prestige. Any member of society regardless of social origin could enter into the church and many popes came from working class.

The church also provided at its expense education and public health. The church had educated society, and ran the schools. The hospitals were run by feminine religious orders (nuns).

The church preserved written knowledge and works in its convents and monasteries. It educated society by founding schools and universities throughout all of Europe.

When Gutenberg's printing press filled Europe with books it was due to the Church's education and teaching society how to read that enabled people to read these books.

The Church invented the leprosy homes, thus reducing the contacts of the sick with the healthy, and this led to its reduction or even elimination in Europe. It was the Church who took care of the sick, even with contagious disease. Therefore that was the reason why the church did not pay *taxes*.

*The **nobility*** did not pay taxes but paid the "tax of blood," that is, they had to serve in the military and go to war when ordered with all its risks and hardships. (Common men only had to defend their homeland if attacked.)

The nobility had the duty of serving as judges, police, and civil governments over their lands. To hunt wild animals such as boars and bears that were a hindrance to peasants and agriculture, to maintain roads and bridges, and police its territories. Therefore, the reason why the nobility did not pay taxes.

But the nobility paid taxes over the consumer goods they purchased. As they had money they made considerable purchases and paid its taxes.

The **common folk** paid taxes but they received the services from the other two social classes, the clergy and nobility, in education and public health; military defense, police, public works, justice and government. The common people did not have this burden.

The wealthiest occupations were the commercial and industrial ones, where the merchant class became very rich that they were able to lend money to the kings and lords for expenses and to wage war. Thus they were richer than those nobles who won the land, but did not have to govern and go to war. Thus having wealth and receiving the benefits of the nobility's services it was logical they pay taxes.

Judicial Autonomy

As medieval life became more complicated, the judge functions became more complicated and the nobles and kings found educated legal experts to handle the cases in a proper and professional manner. Thus independent tribunals emerge and the judges were independent by having adequate salaries and hereditary positions where his sons, if properly trained, would inherit the father's position if they chose that profession. This avoided a judge to be easily bribed.

Regionalism

Every life and city had its own laws, customs, and traditions. There was a decentralized government, more like a federation. Different traditions and cultures developed in every region of Europe. This is the reason for the vast richness of today's European regional cultures and their traditions, which can be seen today in its varied cuisine, folkloric or regional costumes, regional customs and celebrations, spoken accents and dialects throughout all of Europe.

Common People Made Law

- Customary Law: many laws were not created by a government, but were customs practiced by the people that were made into law.
- Labor Laws: labor, commerce, industry was based on labor relations of common men. The kings simply had them written down in legal codes or compilations.

Cities were largely governed by guilds and free men who voted in municipal and administrative elections (city government). Thus free men who lived in cities govern themselves and had authority. Cities had their own internal elections and authorities. Self government was practiced, and applied the principle of subsidiary, in which the entire group supported the individual members. In medieval society the *universal principal*, from Latin "universes" was applied. Every group was considered a "universe" onto his own and called "universitas." For example, professors from a university governed themselves and elected their authorities. Corporations of merchants such as the merchant of the Seine River (France) included those involved in trade along the Seine River and constituted the universitas mercatorum of Seine.

Medieval monarchies in Western Europe were "organic" because there was a balance and the monarchy and its aristocracy coexisted and governed harmoniously and in cooperation with the local inhabitants and their local democratic governments and laws. There were no autocratic monarchies such as those of antiquity and later European monarchies after the Middle Ages.

Sacred Character of Medieval Civilization

Sacredness means that the order or structure of society is in harmony with God and the teachings of the Church, thus is created to serve religion. It followed the motto of St. Benito: "God be glorified in all things." Therefore, all human organization during the Middle Ages was directed or ordered to give glory to God. All values, philosophy, art, music, fashions, laws, government must conform to God's will and follow the teachings of the Church. The notion was to glorify God now and for all eternity. Thus medieval men made things to last forever as the gothic cathedrals were made to glorify God for all eternity.

Glory to God is to conform to God's will, his law, and the natural order he created in the universe. Therefore civilization must be constructed or structured to this end. That is why for medieval man, whether noble, clergy or commoner, all laws, customs, institutions, art, education, culture, fashions, values, etc., had to lead to this end, the glory of God and salvation of all men, in the present and for future centuries. Thus, the church and the state were responsible for the glory of God and worked together to achieve this end. There was no separation of church and state.

For medieval society when mankind follows God's law (Ten Commandments) in everyone's individual private and public life, when the clergy is faithful to God's law and spirit, then the ideal human order is achieved. With this ideal human order the *true civilization* (no barbarism, decadence, corruption, injustices) and *true progress* is achieved. It is the *only* way. So true civilization consists of disposing of everything in life according to its proper nature that is according to God's law who created the entire universe. True progress is the process by which all things must undergo to perfect themselves in conformity with God's law and the natural order. Thus becoming more perfect and dignified. From this medieval concept is that progress resulted in many fields, even technical ones.

Christendom (Christian Commonwealth) is a family of brotherly people or nations grouped or united around the Church. Christendom became a reality in Western Europe during the Middle Ages. The Catholic Church was seen as a "queen" that all nations or kingdoms tried to serve. This service was achieved in the spiritual as well as temporal fields. So the state (kings/lords) had the obligation to defend the Church and religion against heretics and infidels who threatened Christianity from the outside; or help the Church in its works such as providing resources to build the cathedrals, granting lands to build monasteries and charters for universities.

Thus the highest end of the state was to serve and protect the Church. The state could not interfere in the sovereignty of the church and purely spiritual matters, such as electing popes, naming bishops, interpreting religious doctrine, etc. The state had competence over temporal matters, but could not go against God's laws or church teachings. For example, expropriating property without compensation would be stealing, a sin.

Conclusion

The Middles Age was a time when the philosophy of the gospels governed the states. In this sense it constituted a sacred society.

FEUDALISM

Feudalism was the economic, political, and military system of Europe after the fall of the Roman Empire and invasion of the barbarian tribes. Europe had to find a unique system of organization to meet the needs of a chaotic period with constant invasions and raids of Vikings (Scandinavian seafarers), and the invasion of the Islamic Moors in the Iberian Peninsula. Without strong national governments, economies, and armies, the local lords were the rulers of their territories and had the real power (economical, political, and military). It was based on the feudal contract between the lord and his vassals. The feudal contract originated from the traditions of the barbarian Germanic tribes that settled all over Europe. Every Germanic chieftain had a band of warriors that went along into battle, and every warrior anticipated receiving part of the spoils of war. This is the origin of the bond of **fealty** or loyalty between the warrior and his chieftain. This practice continued and was built into the medieval practice of **feudalism.** The feudal **lord** or king gave land to his warriors or **vassals** in exchange for loyalty and military service. This allowed the vassals to gain land, known as the **fief** or feudum (Germanic word for property) which was the main source of economic wealth of this era, titles of nobility giving the social status or rank, and had domain over the serfs and villages in his granted lands. The feudal lord or king also committed to defend his vassals in case they were attacked and could not overcome their invaders by themselves, and to shelter his vassals in his castle or castles if necessary. The vassals promised loyalty and service to their lord or king, hospitality in their castles, and to come with all their resources to fight with their lord or king when ordered to do so. The **serfs** (free men but bound to the land), or peasant received land to farm and protection from the local lord in exchange for services and part of the agricultural products they produced on the land. This was an agricultural society. This system met the needs of all members of society during this period and all members of society entered into its contracts and obligation freely out of mutual necessity and also became hereditary for future generations.

Feudal contracts between lord and vassal included:

- Lord's provision of a court of justice
- Lord's hospitality for the vassal in his castle
- Lord's protection if vassal was attacked
- Vassal's hospitality for his lord in his castle or fief
- Vassal owed his lord certain number of fighting days during the year (usually 40 days)
- Vassal's contribution for ransom if his lord was captured

Feudalism provided a basic or rudimentary form of local government, while serving the need for security against invasion. Feudal nobility performed the twin responsibilities of military defense and political leadership. This nobility or feudal aristocracy was rather a close social class of men and women into which they were born. Most belonged to this class by inheritance, but it was possible to be elevated to this class by merit or service. It was not a caste system. Lord and vassals made up about 10% of the population. Chevalier or **knights** were the male members of this nobility, raised to serve by arms. **Chivalry** was the strict code of conduct that guided the knight's life and that demanded that he be courageous in battle, loyal to his lord and fellow warriors, reverent toward women, and protector of the weaker members of society. Investiture was the ceremony by which the vassal received his fief and elaborate oaths of fealty were formally exchanged. Jousts were the personal combat between knights on horseback that were used as a means to train for and demonstrate military abilities for battle.

HOW THE CHURCH BUILT WESTERN CIVILIZATION

The Roman Church or Catholic Church had a key role in building Western Civilization and its progress in many fields during the Middle Ages. The Church's tremendous influence had greater weight than antiquity in forming our Western civilization. Unfortunately, in popular culture, that is novels, magazines, television, movies, etc., and even in public schools, the Church's contribution has gone largely unnoticed. In fact, many people have a negative image of the Church during the Middle Ages as responsible for ignorance, repression, and stagnation.

Even though the men of the Church made mistakes, some were corrupt, having their faults or "sins," overall the Church built Western civilization. Its contributions to Western civilization's material progress and to the improvement of mankind, aside from the spiritual guidance to individuals and society, outweighs the negative aspects the Church has been criticized for, be it factual, exaggerated, or false. The church during the Middle Ages was indispensable as a civilizing force and center. It constituted the basis of what later developed into the Scientific Revolution. Most educated men of the time belonged to the clergy, thus many practicing scientists were priests.

As an example among the notable achievements and contributions are:

- Father Giambattista Riccioli was the first to measure the rate of acceleration of a free falling body.
- Father Roger Boscovich is the father of modern atomic theory.
- Father Nicolas Steno is the father of geology.
- The first flight was around 1000 AD by a monk named Eilmer who flew over 600 feet in a glider.
- The first mechanical clock was made in Germany in 996 by a monk who later became pope Sylvester II.
- The Church gave a great amount of financial aid and support to the study of astronomy. Thirty-five craters of the moon were named after Jesuits.
- Monasteries were centers of learning and of production and storage of books. They also cleared the land for agriculture, and introduced new agricultural methods, breeding of cattle, and irrigation that the rest of the inhabitants came to learn and use. They were also the most economically effective centers of production of food, wines, cloths, hides, iron products, glassware, etc. Developed technology such as machines run by water power, adopting mechanization for industrial use on a considerable scale, which was something not done in antiquity which depended on slave labor. Their monks copied manuscripts saving knowledge for future generations. The monasteries served as gratuitous inns for travelers, and built and repaired road and bridges.
- The Church created schools and developed the university system because it was the only institution that showed consistent interest in the preservation and cultivation of knowledge. The papacy established and encouraged the founding of universities. By the 1500s there were 81 universities in Europe. The university was a medieval invention.
- The Church ran the first hospitals for the general population to cure and control the spread of diseases.
- The Church created cannon law, the first modern legal system in Europe. It was a coherent body of law composed of many statutes, traditions, and local customs. The church eliminated superstition based on trial by ordeal of the Germanic legal order. These were the procedures by which the more primitive barbarian tribes that overtook the Roman Empire judged the accused. For example, if the individual accused of a crime picked with his hand a hot stone at the bottom of a large pot with boiling water or oil and his hand healed quickly or did not suffer burnings, then it demonstrated his innocence, if not he was guilty. Another one was the accused be tied and a heavy stone tied to his body and thrown into a river or lake. If the accused floated he was innocent, if not then guilty. The Church introduced rational trial procedures and sophisticated legal concepts.
- The idea of international law was first found in the 1500s in Spanish Universities, and the priest and professor Francisco de Vitoria became the father of international law when faced with the mistreatment of the natives of the New World or the Americas. Vitoria and other Catholic philosophers and theologians began to speculate about human rights and proper relations among nations.

Therefore, the Church was a force of progress that set bases from which the later scientific and industrial revolutions were able to emerge. The positive contributions of the Church outweigh the negative aspects it had during this era due to the faults of the men who ran the church.

DECLINE OF THE MIDDLE AGES

Decline of the Middle Ages began in the 14th century and was over by 1500 A.D. The main cause was the gradual decline of faith and morality within the men of the Church and in society in general, especially the nobility or ruling class and their monarchs. The Church of Rome had many problems due to its great growth of wealth and prestige which brought corruption and lax morals. The monarchs instead of serving the Church and Christendom sought to serve their own personal interests and increase their power.

First there was a power struggle for the papacy that resulted in the *Babylonian Captivity*. The French monarchy was the first to emerge from feudalism as a strong national state. After the Church's struggle with the German monarchy over its supremacy as spiritual and temporal head of Christendom, that was a struggle between the Church and the state, the Pope had allied with the French monarchy which had given its support to the Church. The close alliance between the Papacy and French monarchy was a blessing to the Church as long as the French kings as Christian rulers cooperated with the Popes defending the Christian principles and ideals. The best example of this cooperation was during the reign of King Saint Louis IX (1226–1270). But all this peaceful and harmonious period ceased when the French kings put aside their fidelity to the Church and its head, the Pope, in order to pursue their sole ambition to enhance their power at any cost and to subdue the Church to their interests. Philip the Fair of France (1285–1314) was the first absolute monarch of Europe who wanted control of the Church in his kingdom. He became the creator of absolutism by being the first king to overthrow the medieval system in which no monarch was absolute ruler, and the Papacy in Rome was the ultimate Court of Appeal between the nations and their rulers. The conflict between King Philip and the Pope, Boniface VIII, was over the issue of taxation of the clergy. The doctrine of the time held that the Church belonged to the poor and could not be taxed. The practice had been that the Church contributed to public expense in the form of voluntary donations by giving over to the king one-tenth of its entire revenue or the tithes when the king was in need of money. From 1247 to 1300 the Church paid the monarchy 39 tithes which was one-fifth of all its possessions. Thus the Church's voluntary donations were more burdensome than an obligatory tax.

In 1296 King Philip who was in need of money and greedy for money (his insatiable avarice was the motive for persecuting the wealthy order of the Knights Templar that he was able to suppress in 1311, confiscating their possessions) taxed the Church to finance his war against Edward I of England. Boniface VIII saw this as a threat to the immunities and liberties of the Church, and he wanted to terminate the senseless war between Philip and Edward, therefore he passed a papal bull forbidding the clergy to pay any taxes to layman without papal permission. Philip responded by forbidding money to be taken out of France without his license thus cutting off the papal revenues from the church in France, and even went to the point of publicly casting doubt to the validity of Boniface's election as Pope. Boniface suspended the bull and made concessions to Philip. This suspended the conflict, but Philip's absolute rule over all matters lay and clerical lead Boniface to send a legate to France to protest Philip's interference, and the legate was arrested and imprisoned by Philip. Boniface then enacted his bull against taxing the church and summoned church's hierarchy to discuss the conflict. The Pope also addressed another bull to the king with his grievances and cited the king to appear in Rome to answer for his conduct. Philip refused to submit to the Pope. Boniface then was left with the threat to excommunicate and depose Philip. Two of Philip's accomplices and enemies of Boniface, Nogaret and Colonna, with hired thugs surprised the old pontiff in his palace at Anagni breaking into his bedroom and dragging him out of bed, insulted and mistreated him (Colonna struck the Pope with his iron glove), keeping him under arrest for three days until the citizens of Anagni rescued the Pope and then was taken to Rome. A few weeks later (October 1303) Boniface died of the savage mistreatment and humiliation.

All Europe was indignant with Philip's outrageous act, but no one was ever brought to account for it. The next Pope, Benedict XI, was dead four weeks after excommunicating Nogaret and his accomplices, and it was rumored that Benedict was poisoned. Then King Philip with his great power and influence had the Archbishop of Bordeaux elected as Pope and became Clement V crowned in Lyon, France, not in Rome. Clement V (1305–1314) made France his home and surrounded himself with French cardinals. His rein was one of concessions to the avarice of King Philip, and in 1309 established his residence in the city of Avignon in southeastern France. This all resulted in the influence of French monarchy in the affairs of the church and until 1377, the Popes who all were Frenchmen were under the influence of French kings. These 68 years are known as the "Babylonian Captivity" because the duration of the Papal residence in France was about the same as of the ancient Jews in Babylon. It is clear that by this period the temporal supremacy of the Pope, over monarchs and Christian states, had passed. The Pope still was supreme in spiritual affairs. Many in Europe became critical of the papal court and led to the open resistance of Germany and England. This conflict brought a loss of prestige to the papacy and weakened its allegiance of many in Christendom. The influence of Church policy by the French kings brought the risk of that other kings would want their "Pope" too, which threatened to divide and destroy Christian unity.

Two very pious women made great efforts to solve this long-drawn-out conflict. The famous mystic, Saint Bridget of Sweden wrote letters to the Popes in Avignon urging them to return to Rome to avoid losing their temporal and spiritual authority. She did not live to see the conclusion of the papal exile in France. It was the heroic Saint Catherine of Sienna (Italy) who terminated the exile that Philip the Fair caused. She deplored the sad state that Christendom had fallen under the Babylonian Captivity. In 1376 she went in person to Avignon to urge the Pope, Gregory XI, to return to Rome. Her inspiring words finally convinced the Pope to return to Rome in 1377. That same year Gregory sent her to Florence to urge the citizens to make peace with the Pope after war broke out in 1375. The popular tumult nearly took her life, but peace was made with the new Pope, Urban the VI.

Then the *Great Schism* from 1378 to 1417 was the papal power struggle after the Babylonian Captivity ended. In 1378 a new Pope, Urban VI, is elected in Rome. Rome had decayed during the absence of the Popes. The French Cardinals were not content in Rome wanting to return to Avignon where life was more comfortable and peaceful. Urban VI refused to leave Rome and was resolved to reform the papal court breaking down the luxury of its lifestyle which offended greatly the French cardinals. These rebel cardinals fed up with life in Rome and the violent-tempered Pontiff decided to leave Rome to the kingdom of Naples where they declared Urban VI's election invalid because they claimed that they were pressured by the Roman masses to elect Urban VI, and elected an antipope Clement VII in 1378 which later resided in France. Thus, a struggle between the Roman and the French Popes began, lasting for almost 40 years. Europe became divided with France, Flanders, Spain, and Scotland acknowledging Clement VII, and Germany, England, northern Europe, and the Italian states Urban VI. Clement VII fled Italy and set up court in Avignon. The schism of Christendom was now a reality with two and later three rival Popes claiming to be legitimate and deserving of allegiance. The worst crisis the Church suffered until then, in which both Popes declared a crusade against and excommunicated each other, each created cardinals and confirmed bishops, and attempted to collect all church's revenue. Now there were rival hierarchies claiming to have authority, such as rival bishops in some dioceses, religious orders with rival superiors and each Pope had his college of cardinals.

All over Europe many groups demanded an end to this schism that was tearing up Christendom. A general council in Pisa, Italy, in 1409 attempted to try the rival Popes but neither Popes recognized its authority and obeyed it. Thus the cardinals elected another Pope, now there were three rival Popes. Finally one of the Popes, John XXIII summoned the Council of Constance in 1414 which had great participation of ecclesiastics from all over Europe. The result was the deposition of two Popes, and the true Pope in Rome, Gregory XII, after declaring the council legitimate, abdicated. The council then elected new Pontiff Martin V. This ended the schism. The Roman pope was the legitimate pope recognized by the Catholic Church. This great crisis in the Church and in Western Europe reduced respect and trust for the papacy and much needed reforms in the Church were not done because the Church was consumed in this internal power struggle.

The rise of *nationalism* has a major impact in the decline of the High Middle Ages. Medieval men gave their first loyalty to the Church because Christendom was the most important and main element of identity, and their country came second. Nations and communities were regarded as part of the large whole that was Christendom. Men saw themselves as brothers in Christ and a certain balance existed so no one nation or group had overwhelming power. The different kingdoms and ethnicities that composed all of Western Europe united to defend and fight the external threat to Christendom at the time that was the Islamic invasions in Iberia (Spain and Portugal) and Byzantium that resulted in the Iberian Reconquest and the Crusades. People and monarchies of Europe began to think and act in self-interest and not in the interest of Christendom. The Europeans gradually gave their first loyalty to their national governments, now viewing themselves independent of the Church with no obligation to respect the rights of other nations. War among Christian nations erupted such as the Hundred Years' War between France and England in which Christians of one nationality fought other Christians. These nationalistic wars from the 14th century will continue to plague Europe, affecting the Americas, until the last two worst nationalistic wars in the 20th century, World War I and II.

The *Black Death,* or bubonic plague, was a plague new to Europe that came from the east on board trading ships. These ships were rat-infested and these rats were infested by fleas that carried the bacillus of the bubonic plague. Once these rats got off the ships into European ports the fleas passed onto domestic animals and humans contaminating them with the disease. The plague first appeared in Sicily in 1348 and spread like wild fire in such short time but devastated entire communities bringing sudden death to two-thirds of the population. It is estimated that about one-third of the European population fell to the Black Death. This created a mood among society of despair and bitterness and loss of trust and hope in God and the Church. Also the quality of the clergy was affected in a negative way. Many of the good and morally upright clergy and nuns lost their lives tending the victims of the plague when they themselves contacted the disease and died. The more corrupt and selfish clergy fled the urban areas to the countryside to escape the plague avoiding all contact with the victims. Therefore, after the plague passed the remaining clergy tended to be of lower moral quality (Figure 6.2).

The new *Renaissance* gradually put an end to the spirit and God centered thinking of the High Middle Ages. It began in the middle of the 14th century in Italy and took over all Europe by the 16th century. Renaissance means rebirth, due to the rebirth in the interest of ideas, art and culture of classical civilization. With its spirit and thinking that rejected the teachings and values of the Church and began to admire the Greco-Roman values, art and philosophy, the men of the Renaissance began a secular attitude that gained ground in European society that was man-centered and not God-centered. They coined the term Middle Ages having a negative implication because they regarded Christian culture as inferior to classical civilization. They admired the Greco-Roman world and saw the Age of Faith that came after as the age in the middle of the classical world and their time. Thus the term "Middle Ages" was coined. Christianity was regarded as putting too many limits on the human mind and behavior. They became infatuated with classical literature, philosophy and arts that were products of a pagan culture and thus absorbed the pagan conception of life which the classics embodied. These "Humanists" as they called themselves due to their belief that studying the classical literature alone would form them into perfect beings, looked down with scorn on all that was related to the supernatural and unworldly, in other words to the religious. They rejected the values and beliefs of the high Middle Ages, and even ridiculed the writings of the Scholastics for their use of "bad" Latin. These men became skeptical of Christian teach-

Figure 6.2   Man and woman with the bubonic plague. Medieval painting from a German language bible of 1411. *Image © Everett Historical/Shutterstock.com*

ings and did not want to accept anything on faith. It demonstrated a pride and confidence in the human mind and human achievements rather than in God, just as the Greco-Roman world had done before Christianity changed it toward God. It can be concluded that these secular Humanists developed a pagan spirit because they worshiped the ancient pagan classics they made all efforts to imitate. This spirit and movement lead to the acceptance of immoral ideas and practices of which Niccolo Machiavelli (1469-1527) is a good example. Machiavelli wrote a short book titled *The Prince* in which he states his theory of government declaring that the end justifies the means. In other words the end for the prince or head of state which is to enlarge his power and of the government, and thus overcome his opponents justifies using whatever means are more advantageous regardless of moral ethics. So you can lie, make false promises, go to war, torture, kill if necessary, etc., to achieve your goal. During the High Middle Ages this reasoning would be considered sinful and rejected by society. The church condemned Machiavelli's philosophy as immoral.

Not all aspects of this new intellectual movement of the Renaissance or Humanism were in conflict with the Christian spirit and teachings. Not all of the Renaissance movement was a rejection of the Middle Ages, but it was also a continual development or ripening of the Middle Ages. Thus it also had a Christian aspect along with its pagan one. Men like Dante, Petrarch, Pico della Mirandola, Saint Thomas More, Cardinal Fisher, and others made use of the cultural treasures of antiquity without sacrificing Christian principles. They combined Christian ideals with classical subjects, using the classics only to embellish the teachings of Christ. The Catholic Church did not reject the Renaissance movement, she directed the new movement to serve Christian ideals patronizing the Renaissance literature, art, and architecture in its churches and institutions.

Looking back into history a complete cycle has occurred between secular humanism and Christianity as the philosophy guiding Western society and government. From secular humanism the West during antiquity, then went to Christianity during the late Roman Empire and Middle Agges, and then returned back to a secular mindset and tendencies of the former. The hostility of the early Church during the Roman Empire to humanism and secular thought was but the opening assault in a running battle between two ways of looking at the world. In imperial Rome up to the 3rd century A.D. humanism was triumphant among the people who counted—the aristocrats, the intellectual, and the ruling class. But by the end of the 4th century, the balance had swung over in favor of Christianity, and the non-Christian intellectuals were rapidly disappearing. This state of affairs prevailed until the Italian Renaissance. From this new era that began modern times, artists, writers, and intellectuals challenged the reigning Christian worldview by reviving humanistic learning and the Greco-Roman past. As the modern world has taken shape since 1500s to the present, Christianity has found itself assaulted from many sides and has never regained the preeminence that it held during the Middle Ages, from the time of the fall of Rome to the coming of the Renaissance.

By the late 15th century and in the 16th century the revolt against the Church carried out by the *Reformation* divided Christian Europe into two distinct Religious groups, the Catholic and the new Protestant denominations that rejected the authority of the Pope and had differences with the teachings of the Catholic Church. The one time unity of Christendom in Western Europe was now completely divided, with Catholicism predominately in southern Europe and Protestantism in northern Europe.

MEDIEVAL WESTERN ART AND LITERATURE

Early Medieval West: 500–1000

The culture of the Early Medieval Western Europe was a product of the blending of the Mediterranean centered Greco-Roman world and the Germanic people of Northern Europe into an emerging Christian Europe. This is the period from 500 to approximately 1000 A.D. The Latin Church under the Pope was the guide and light of this new Christian culture that strengthened itself and its hold on society. Pope Gregory the Great (590–604), a very energetic and dedicated pope, became the most successful of the early medieval pontiffs. He made many important and lasting reforms of the clergy and the Church, setting high moral standards. He encouraged the founding of new monasteries among the Germanic peoples and converted Anglo-Saxons in England. During this period the Church found its strength in monasticism. Monasteries followed the guidelines made by Saint Benedict (480–543) which were observed in the Benedictine order's first monastery at Monte Cassino, south of Rome, Italy. By the 10th century nunneries were established for women under an abbess.

The monasteries and nunneries that spread all over Europe served many purposes. They became safe havens for the population during invasions, centers for copying ancient literary and philosophical texts, which made up the libraries only found in these religious institutions. They were centers of learning where the monks established schools for the local young men, and nuns for young women. They were also models of agricultural productivity as well as centers of production of varied goods, and were self-sufficient.

Literature, Learning, and History. During this period writers were more interested in conserving the past than in writing original works. Latin was the language used in writing. Thus, literature became eclectic, that is, blending Christian ideas with Greco-Roman Classical thought. They mixed genres such as theology, philosophy, history, biography, and science.

Boethius (480–524) was the most highly educated scholar of the Early Middle Ages. He was a Roman aristocrat and a courtier of Theodoric, the Ostrogoth king of Italy. Boethius, knowing Greek, translated most of Aristotle's writings into Latin, which made it accessible to those educated as Latin was the written language of Western Europe at that time. During the later Middle Ages, Latin Scholars knew Aristotle from Boethius' translations. Falling from favor in Theodoric's court, before he was executed Boethius wrote *Consolation of Philosophy,* a work very well read throughout the Middle Ages and after. Philosophy is personified as a learned woman with whom Boethius argued many issues in search of the meaning of happiness. In face of near death, he finally concludes that true contentment was reserved for those who combined intellectual inquiry with Christian beliefs. His thought shows ideas in common with Socrates, such as only the examined life is worth living. Thus the blending of the Greco-Roman with the Christian thought.

The writing of historical events or historical chronicles became common. The most famous scholars that can be considered true historians are **Gregory of Tours** and **Saint Bede.** These two scholars, written documents and other sources and to a great extent they generally achieve objectivity and historical accuracy. In his *History of the Franks* Gregory of Tours (538–593) left the single surviving record of the 6th century Merovingian kingdom capturing his times and the characters of the Frankish rulers. St. Bede (673–735), an English monk and scholar, wrote the *A History of the English Church and People,* describing the history of Anglo-Saxon England and the missionary activities that led to the founding of the English church. His *History* is a major source for the chronology of his turbulent age.

During the Early Middle Ages cultural life will achieve its greatest height under Emperor Charlemagne (742–814), king of the Franks. The Carolingian Renaissance was the great achievement of Charlemagne in cultural matters. This famous emperor knew that ignorance was a threat to his regime, and he founded a palace school at his residence in Aachen, West Germany. He gathered there the most learned men of his time to train his own staff and the sons of the nobility. Among these men who came from several countries were Alcuin of York (735–804) and Einhard (770–840) who wrote *The Life of Charlemagne* that became an important literary achievement of the period and gives us today a vivid portrait of Charlemagne and his times. Charlemagne's educational reforms brought about a great rebirth of Classical studies within the context of Christian beliefs.

An important achievement of the palace school was a major innovation in handwriting. The **Carolingian minuscule** was the development of a legible and uniform Latin script used by trained scribes. It consisted mainly of a flowing style of rounded lowercase letters that became the standard form for all later handwriting styles in the West. This allowed educated men to be able to read written texts that before the invention of the printing press were all handwritten using quill and ink, and enable monks who produced these texts to commit fewer errors.

Beowulf

Written in the first half of the 7th century, *Beowulf*, a poem created by storytellers for audiences at royal and aristocratic courts, tells the adventures of a fictional Danish warrior hero. Urged by his loyalty and daring Beowulf kills monsters and brings peace to his inherited kingdom. This poem is considered to be the finest achievement of Old English literature and the most famous surviving epic poem in a European vernacular language, blending superficial Christian values with deep pagan fear of the forces of darkness. **Hrosvitha** was the first German playwright who wrote six plays in Latin, borrowing her style from the Roman dramatist Terence and adding scholarly religious ideas. She did not find Roman comedy in harmony with Christian moral values, so she did not use Roman influence in her plays. Hrosvitha's dramas focused on themes of sinful fall of her characters and their conversion. The plays have a didactic goal of teaching their audience the consequences of sin and benefits of conversion, as in the play *Abraham* that tells the story of a prostitute rescued by a saintly monk. Her plays constituted major works in medieval drama.

Music

During the Early Middle Ages music became an integral part of the church liturgy and kept alive the Greek heritage of music as an art form. This religious foundation was the origin of all the sacred and secular music of the modern West. Pope Gregory the Great standardized the music in the service of worship. Under him the **Gregorian chant** became the official liturgical music of the early church and synonymous with the medieval church. The chants consisted of a single melodic line sung in unison by all in the chorus, without instrumental accompaniment, by male voices. This music had an impersonal, non-emotional quality and served religious purposes rather than aesthetic or emotional. Even with these characteristics the chants cast a spell over their listeners, evoking in them feelings of otherworldliness, peace, and purity. Gregorian chants are monophonic with only the sound of one line of melody.

In the 9th century a very important advancement in the history of music occurred when polyphony was introduced, which consists of two lines of melody sounded at the same time. It gave music a vertical and horizontal quality. But still music had a lot to develop later on.

Painting

Most murals, frescos, and mosaics of this period have disappeared, and most surviving paintings of Early Medieval are the **illuminated manuscripts** (Figure 6.3). This manuscript illumination came out of blending Germanic practice of decorating small objects and Classical fine metalwork from Italy.

Figure 6.3 Opening words of St. Luke's Gospel Quoniam, illuminated manuscripts. *Image © Jupiter Images.*

During this period artists and monks joined these artistic elements to embellish richly illustrated books and bejeweled book covers. Most of these books were employed in the liturgy of the mass. During 300 years in monasteries and abbeys from Ireland to Germany, scribes copied the Bible texts, while their fellow artists adorned the pages of these books with geometric and foliage designs, mythical animals, Christian symbols, and portraits of biblical characters and saints.

The High Middle Ages: 1000–1300

The High Middle Ages was a period in which Western Europe became more stable and society made more advances in many fields. A new foundation was laid that would support the future development of Western civilized life. These great changes in Western Europe's political, social, and economical life were reflected in its culture. Theologians, writers, artists, and architects put their efforts to harmonize the two opposing trends of this period, the spiritual and the secular. Medieval men achieved a short-lived synthesis of this harmony that produced great accomplishments in many fields that made this period the apex of the Middle Ages within society that reached a high point in its cultural balance and stability. Society moved from the rugged warrior values that prevailed between 1000 and 1150, to a more refined, more learned, and increasing secular culture between 1150 and 1300. The first 150 years are associated with monastic and feudal themes in literature and Romanesque style in architecture. In the last half there was a growing trend toward urban and courtly themes in literature and the development of Gothic architecture, whose masterpiece was the Gothic cathedral.

Architecture and Art

During the High Middle Ages artists, artisans, and architects channeled their talents into glorifying the Christian house of worship. Because the dominating physical presence of the church made it a symbol that was present everywhere in both the countryside and the towns, architecture ranked higher than the other arts in medieval life.

In this respect, these art forms conformed to the church's teaching that the purpose of art was to represent Christian truth. Even though the church dominated art and architecture, it did not prevent architects and artists from experimenting with new ideas. In about 1000 an international style called the **Romanesque** emerged. It was the first in a succession of uniform styles to sweep over Western Europe. In England it was introduced by the Normans who conquered England in 1066. The style had been introduced in Normandy, France, and now the Norman bishops and nobles founded abbeys and large churches employing this new style that became known as the *Norman* style in England, and in continental Europe as the Romanesque style. The Romanesque was carried along by the monastic revival until about 1200. But by 1150 the **Gothic** style was developing in Paris. Gothic was to become the reigning style of the towns for the remainder of the Middle Ages, succumbing finally to Renaissance fashion in about 1500.

Romanesque Churches and Arts

The Romanesque style takes its name from "Roman," though based on the architectural language of ancient Rome, was not a pure Roman style but embraced elements inspired by Christianity, along with innovations made by builders, between 1000 and 1200. From Roman architecture, Romanesque builders adapted the basilica plan, rounded arches, vaulted ceilings, and columns for both support and decoration. Inspired by Christian beliefs, they pointed the basilicas toward Jerusalem in the east and curved each building's eastern end into an apse (a semicircle or polygonal building projection of a church) to house the altar. A transept, or crossing arm, was added at the church's eastern end (not at the center) to convert the floor plan into a cruciform shape to symbolize the cross. Christian beliefs also dictated such practices as having three doorways in the western façade—to symbolize the Trinity—and building the baptistery apart from the church to keep the unbaptized out of sacred space. To Roman and Christian elements, Romanesque builders added innovative design features, vaulting techniques, and a wealth of ornamental detail, to create the most expressive and disciplined architectural style since the fall of Rome.

Originally the Romanesque style allowed for great diversity and experiment, which reflected the taste of different regions, communities, and patrons; the types of stone available for building; and the knowledge and historical awareness of the master builders and their workshops.

The general impression made by Romanesque cathedrals and churches is very different from the earlier styles and old Roman basilicas. The overall impression of these building on the outside and inside is one of massive strength. They had few decorations and windows. The buildings were made with firm, unbroken walls and towers which remind the spectator of being securely fixed to their location, and seem to represent a "spiritual medieval fortress" erected by the church in lands where peasants and warriors that had only recently been converted to Christianity from their pagan way of life. This seemed to express the idea of the *Church Militant*, which consisted of the idea that in this temporal earthly life it is the task of the Church to combat the powers of darkness until the

Figure 6.4 Digital photo of the cathedral in Speyer, Germany. The cathedral is the largest preserved Romanesque church in the world. *Image © Jupiter Images.*

hour of triumph arrives. These buildings are more like a physical symbolic representation of an assertive church full of fervor to fight heathenism to convert men to Christ and His church, giving an image of a firm defiant "fortress"-like structure offering shelter against the onslaught of evil (Figure 6.4).

Within this diversity, two stages of development can be identified: the **First Romanesque** about 1000–1080, and the **Second Romanesque,** 1080–1200. The First Romanesque style originated along the Mediterranean, in the Zone ranging from Dalmatia (modern Croatia), across Northern Italy and Provence (Southern France), to Catalonia (Northeast Spain). The First Romanesque churches were simple in design, built of stone rubble which was a Roman technique, and covered with flat, wooden roofs. With high walls and few windows, they resembled fortresses, a trait that came to characterize both Romanesque Styles. The defining exterior features of the first Romanesque churches were a web of vertical bands or buttresses along the sides and a sequence of small arcades (row of arches supported by columns) below the eaves.

The Second Romanesque style is associated with the Cluniac monastic order because the order's mother church at Cluny. The abbey of **Cluny** at Burgundy, France, founded in 910 became the center of an active monastic reform movement of the early 10th century. This movement introduced a splendid and pious religious spirit that many monasteries all over Western Europe joined and looked to Cluny as their mother house. The fast-growing community at Cluny demanded buildings on a large scale. The examples set at Cluny profoundly affected architectural practice in Western Europe from the 10th through the 12th centuries. The three successive churches are conventionally called Cluny I, II, and III; in building the third and final church at Cluny in 1088, the monastery constructed the largest building in Europe before the rebuilding of St. Peter's in Rome in the 16th century The abbey church of Cluny III was constructed in the Romanesque style and was so greatly admired for its vast scale that it had an influence on European construction. Cluny III church was destroyed in the early 1800s after the abbey was sacked and destroyed in 1790 during the French Revolution, and only a small part of the original remains today. The spectacular success of the Cluniac movement in the 11th and 12th centuries led to the spread of the Second Romanesque style over the map of Europe.

These Second Romanesque churches were richly decorated and Earth-hugging, with massive walls and few windows, though they had more and larger windows than in the First Romanesque. They looked like the spiritual fortresses that they indeed were.

Typical of Romanesque architecture, the nave is divided into sections called **bays.** Each bay is framed by a pair of rounded arches. The ceiling of each bay is a groin vault, a Roman Building technique. The support system for the tall nave walls, an arcade, or series of arches resting on clusters of columns, was also taken from Roman architecture. Sculpture was used to provide "sermons in stone" to teach illiterate visitors. Symbolic rather than idealistic, the Romanesque figures are designed to convey religious meanings. For example, instead of copying the ancient Greco-Roman columns, the artisans created their own style of decorated column. The capitals, or tops, of the interior columns are sculptured with religious scenes and motifs, such as one that shows Jacob, one of the Hebrew patriarchs, wrestling with the angel.

Besides church building and church decoration, the Romanesque style was used in manuscript illumination. Originated in late Rome and developed in the Early Middle Ages, this art remained a cloistered activity in this age of monasticism. Perhaps only cloistered painters had the leisure to pursue this painstaking skill. During the High Middle Ages, new local styles arose, inspired by regional tastes and by knowledge of Byzantine painting brought from the East by Crusaders.

Gothic Churches and Art

The word *Gothic* was invented by later Renaissance scholars who preferred Greco-Roman styles. They despised medieval architecture, labeling it *Gothic*—meaning a barbaric creation of the Goths, or the Germanic peoples who invaded and settled in the Western Roman Empire. Modern research, however, has shown that this Renaissance view is false. In fact, the Gothic grew out of the Romanesque and was not a German art. Nevertheless, the term *Gothic* is still used today, although its negative connotation has long since been discarded. Gothic came to represent the pinnacle of Medieval art, engineering, and architectural innovations and achievement.

Gothic architecture sprang from the religious revival of the 12th century, when the clergy wanted to bring God's presence more tangibly to their urban congregations. As a result, clerics began to demand taller churches with more windows than were available in the relatively dark Romanesque churches. To the medieval mind, height and light were symbols of the divine. For Abbot Suger, who initiated the Gothic style, light represented God and heaven, and he wanted that element in the church where the faithful worshiped creating an effect of the "light from heaven" upon the interior of the church. Therefore, Suger wanted very large windows with stained glass to let light in, and height to inspire the faithful to look toward heaven to remind them of God when they saw a cathedral with its tall towers and spires, and when inside the cathedral toward its high ceiling. Another impetus behind the Gothic was the rise of the urban middle class, who wanted churches that reflected their growing economic power. Thus spiritual and economic forces were united in pushing architects to seek a new kind of architecture.

Two problems with the Romanesque stood in the way: The groin vaults were so heavy that the nearly windowless walls had to be extremely thick to support their great weight, and the rounded arches limited the building's height to less than 100 feet. During the early 12th century, builders constantly sought solutions to these problems.

Eventually, between 1137 and 1144, the Gothic style was created by Suger (1081–1151), the abbot of the royal Abbey Church of St. Denis, near Paris. Abbot Suger who was one of the last French abbot-statesmen, an adviser to the French kings, a historian and the influential first patron of Gothic architecture. Suger became abbot of St-Denis, close to Paris, France. Until 1127 he occupied himself at court mainly with the temporal affairs of the kingdom, while during the following decade he devoted himself to the reorganization and reform of St-Denis. Abbot Suger decided in about 1137 to rebuild the great Church of Saint-Denis, attached to an abbey which was also a royal residence. The new structure was finished and dedicated on June 11, 1144, in the presence of the King. The Abbey of Saint-Denis thus became the prototype for further building in the royal domain of northern France. It is often cited as the first building in the Gothic style. A hundred years later, the old nave of Saint-Denis was rebuilt in the Gothic style, gaining, in its transepts, two spectacular rose windows. Through the rule of the Angevin dynasty (that ruled in France, England, and Naples, Italy), the style was introduced to England and spread throughout France, the Low Countries, Germany, Spain, northern Italy, and Sicily.

Suger's approach to architecture grew out of his religious faith, as in his words, "Through the beauty of material thus we come to understand God." The brilliant innovation employed by Suger and the architects and artisans he hired was to change the vaulting problems from one of weight to one of stress. First, they replaced the groin vault with a ribbed vault; this step allowed lighter materials to be placed between the stone ribs, thus reducing the weight.

Next, they abandoned the rounded arch in favor of the Muslim pointed arch. The combination of pointed arch and ribbed vault permitted an increase in the building's height as well as a rechanneling of the ceiling's stresses downward and outward to huge piers internally and, in later buildings, to flying buttresses externally, which formed a bridge between the upper nave walls and the nearby tall pillars. With the support skeleton transferred to the building's exterior, the builders could easily insert stained-glass windows into the non-weight-bearing walls.

Between 1145 and 1500, the Gothic style presented an overwhelming image of God's majesty and the power of the church. A Gothic exterior carried the eye heavenward by impressive vertical spires. A Gothic interior surrounded the daytime worshiper with colored, celestial light; the soaring nave ceiling, sometimes rising to more than 150 feet, was calculated to stir the soul. In its total physicality, the Gothic church stood as a towering symbol of the medieval devotion of the divine.

This new Gothic style gave the faithful a glimpse of a different world than the previous Romanesque style with its heavy and grim structures. From the older churches that in their strength and power tended to convey the idea of the Church Militant, the new Gothic cathedrals seem to convey the idea of the *Church Triumphant* firmly established during the 13th century. Seen from a distance, these miraculous Gothic buildings seemed to proclaim the glories of heaven. The beauty and magnificence was like a vision of heaven had descended from heaven to Earth. A symbol of a church and Christian society that had become firmly established, and all social classes, nobles, clergy, and commoners, were in harmony supporting the church that guided their faith.

During the High Middle Ages, the Gothic style went through two stages, the Early and the High. The Early Gothic style lasted until 1194 and was best represented by Notre Dame Cathedral in Paris. The High Gothic style flourished until 1300 and reached perfection in the cathedral at Amiens, France.

Early Gothic Style, 1145–1194

At first, walls had no special external supports, but as cracks began to appear in the choirs' walls during the 13th century, flying buttresses were added to ensure greater stability, a feature that would later characterize High Gothic churches.

The Gothic sculptures that decorate Notre Dame differ from the exuberant Romanesque style (Figures 6.5, 6.6, 6.7 and 6.8). The Romanesque's animated images of Jesus have given way to the Gothic's more sober figures. In addition, the Gothic figures are modeled in three dimensions and their draperies fall in natural folds.

Figure 6.5 Sculpture detail entrance, arch, and tympanum Notre Dame de Paris, France. *Image © Jupiter Images.*

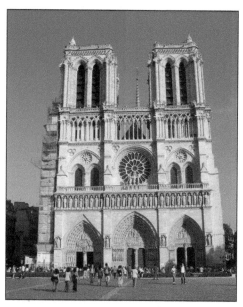

Figure 6.6 Notre Dame, Paris. *Image Copyright Stephen Finn, 2009. Used under license from Shutterstock, Inc.*

Figure 6.7 Back view of Notre Dame cathedral slightly before dusk—Paris, France. Flying buttresses are supporting the high walls. *Image Copyright ErickN, 2009. Used under license from Shutterstock, Inc.*

Figure 6.8 Dome vault with nave and side roof of gothic Dom in Cologne, Germany. *Image Copyright Peter Zurek, 2009. Used under license from Shutterstock, Inc.*

At the same time, the rise of the cult of the Virgin meant an increased number of images of Mary as well as of female saints. The name "Notre Dame" (Our Lady) itself testifies to the appeal of the Virgin cult. Despite these visual differences, however, the Gothic remained true to the symbolic purposes of Romanesque art.

Architects refined the traditional features into a new style, **Rayonnant** or Radiant. The Rayonnant style transformed solid walls by introducing sheets of stain glass framed by elegant **traceries,** or rich intersecting ornamentation made of stone. This radiant effect can be seen in the *rose window,* a large circular window with tracery arranged like the spokes of a wheel, designed to suggest the rays of the sun. With the rose window the cathedral's interior was bathed in constantly shifting colors, giving it a mystical atmosphere.

High Gothic Style, 1194–1300

The High Gothic style is a tribute to the growing confidence of the builders of the 13th century. These builders took the Gothic ingredients and refined them, creating grander churches than had been erected earlier. In comparison with Early Gothic architecture, High Gothic churches were taller and had greater volume; artistic values now stressed wholeness rather than the division of space into harmonious units. Rejecting the restrained decorative ideal used in the Early Gothic style, the High Gothic architects covered the entire surface of their churches; western facades with sculptural and architectural designs (Figure 6.9).

Importance of Medieval Cathedrals. Cathedrals were the church of the bishop, and its name derives from the Latin "cathedra" or throne, referring to the throne of the bishop. They were the largest churches and most took over a century to build and required a great amount of money and resources to build. Those that began a medieval cathedral did not live to see it finished. So one may ask, why were they built? The main reason is because the Middle Ages was an age of faith. Religion was paramount in people's life whether the individual was a

Figure 6.9 Wonderful stained glass in Cologne cathedral church, Germany. *Image Copyright VK, 2009. Used under license from Shutterstock, Inc.*

lowly serf or the king himself. It was an era that valued faith and the church guided everyone from birth with baptism to the last rites in death, with the hope of eternal salvation. Cathedrals were built primarily for the glory of God and to be an inspiration that lead men in this earthly life to salvation. Medieval society demonstrated its sense of love, piety, and duty to God. It was meant to be God's house or palace on Earth. It was a place to celebrate the mass, to worship God and for the individual a place of comfort where man could leave his worldly cares and worries behind and enter into the presence of God. It was seen as a place of union between Heaven and Earth, as a city of God reminding men of God's glory and salvation.

When a cathedral began to be constructed, no one knew when it would be finished, how much would be the total cost, and if all resources needed to complete such a large and ambitious building would be available when the need arose. Medieval society had faith in man's willingness to struggle and his ability to triumph in a project of such magnitude, and faith in God to provide. They believed that God would intervene by inspiring men to overcome obstacles and find a practical way to accomplish this great architectural, engineering, and religious artistic achievement. Cathedrals were meant to be a physical representation of the divine order of things. There represented a microcosm of the universe that was fashioned by the ultimate master builder, God Himself.

The exterior and interior of gothic cathedrals with their large stained glass windows, sculptures of stone and wood, with artistic embellished alters and choirs, were created with a didactic purpose by serving as a three dimensional picture book of religious instruction and a guide to the way of salvation, in a time when few were literate and books were scarce and expensive. Therefore, cathedrals had biblical themes as well as the life of saints, and of the last judgment. The gothic sculptures portray saints and important people with a warm and human attitude and not in a rigid manner (Figure 6.10).

Another reason for the building of cathedrals was to be the houses for holy relics. Relics attracted many pilgrims who came to see them out of devotion and piety, and many were hoping for miracles that would solve their problems, such as cure from disease. By attracting many faithful who came to the cities where the cathedrals were located, they helped the local economy by bringing people to the local market and providing pilgrims with services such as lodging that were paid for. Therefore, cathedrals, even though they were not built for this purpose, play an important role in the economic growth of medieval cities. Important town people and merchants wanted to build large and splendid cathedrals out of pride in their city, which in turn would bring prestige and economic growth to their hometown. The monarchies aided the construction of cathedrals by giving economic support and royal patronage. The church and the common folk also contributed with money and resources to their constructions, which in some cases came to be a heavy burden for parish churches that were instructed to contribute money that would otherwise be spend in the parish's needs, and taxes on commoners. Thus cathedrals symbolized an age when a strong monarchy and church worked together to build a Christian civilization to high standards, and great faith of all the population. It denotes how the High Middle Ages was an age of cultural balance, because religion, church, government, and society in general were in harmony in their beliefs.

Figure 6.10 Gothic church exterior, rose window with tracery. *Image © Jupiter Images.*

Many cathedrals are dedicated to the Virgin Mary and therefore in France have the name "Notre Dame" or Our Lady, such as Notre Dame in Paris, and Notre Dame in Amiens. The Middle Ages is the period in Western history where womanhood is exalted. It is not found in antiquity. During this age chivalric attitude toward women, literature of courtly love, and devotion to the Virgin Mary are good examples of this new attitude. Womanhood comes to be seen with its great virtues of motherhood, love, caring, and femininity (not to be confused with contemporary feminism). Womanhood is highly respected, more than in any other previous era, and its important role as mother and wife is appreciated. Art and sculpture in cathedrals depict the Virgin Mary as queen of heaven and Earth (Figure 6.11).

Cathedrals were built to be the church of the administrative and spiritual center of the diocese with its bishop who had the highest authority. They are still used today for their original purpose, as parish churches

Figure 6.11 Manuscript rendering events of St. Louis IX king of France. It has architectural framing. *Image © Jupiter Images.*

where religious ceremonies are held, storage of baptismal and marriage records, and houses of prayer. During the Middle Ages schools attached to the cathedrals became centers of education. Today both for the faithful and for many tourists that visit them, they serve as "museums" of religious architecture, art, and artifacts. In the end for medieval man and for many faithful today, cathedrals are a spiritual inspiration and reaffirms to the believer that their faith is real, reassuring God's promise of eternal life.

Painting

High Gothic painting serves best in the manuscript illuminations of the late 13th century. By that time, these small paintings were being influenced by developments elsewhere in Gothic art. The Gothic illuminators abandoned the lively draperies of the Romanesque and instead showed gowns hanging in a natural manner. More important, they sometimes allowed the architectural frame to dominate the painting.

Literature

Literature during the High Middle Ages falls into two periods. The first coincides with the Romanesque art from 1000–1150 which was imbued in the feudal and monastic values of the Early Middle Ages. The second period coincides with the Gothic style introducing urban and courtly themes while moving away from the world of the monasteries and rural feudal lords.

The first period from 1000 and 1150 was the period of **monastic and feudal writing.** Most authors were monks writing in Latin hymns, sermons, lives of saints, and historical chronicles. They composed Latin lyric poetry considered the best literary work of the Latin-speaking Middle Ages. These poems were filled with Classical and Christian allusions. The authors wrote for an audience of church intellectuals mainly about themes of religious and moral topics.

Lay poets at the courts of northern feudal France were developing a new literary genre, the **chanson de geste** or song of the brave deed. These were epic poems written in the **vernacular** or popular spoken language. These chansons de geste mainly honored the heroic adventures of warriors who lived in Emperor Charlemagne's France and his Frankish heirs. These medieval epics reflected Christian values but also supernatural and magical elements were a frequent part of their plots. The masterpiece of this genre is the *Song of Roland* becoming the standard of the genre. It was about Charlemagne's favorite warrior, Count Roland who in the end dies defending Charlemagne's rear from the Moors as his army crosses the Pyrenees Mountains, and of Charlemagne's revenge. It contains the values of chivalry, militant Christianity, and primitive nationalism. It was passed down orally for three centuries until it was written down around 1100.

The second period from 1150 to 1300 was the period of **vernacular and courtly writing.** Even though Latin continued to be used and was the dominant language in universities and the church, lay writers were writing in the vernacular and developing new genres that were winning new audiences. An example is the vernacular lyric poetry that began to appear in Provencal tongue of southern France during the 11th century. It reached its apex during the 1200s with the **canzone** or love poem, which influenced all later Western love poetry. These poems were sung by **minstrels** or entertainers at the educated feudal courts of southern France, and the poems were composed by **troubadours** who were often local aristocrats. These sung poems were addressed to court ladies whose identities were thinly disguised in the poem. These songs made devotion to a noble lady the passionate ideal of the chivalrous knight. A matter that would not have been acceptable to the mind of previous feudal warriors who lived rugged lives in their rural castles or had gone to the Crusades. As these Provencal lyrics reached maturity the central theme was adulterous passion and women were idolized and made masters over men. In these poems young noblemen became obsessed with a woman that they idealized, like she was similar to a goddess and her love was difficult or even impossible to consume. She became the focus of his life and desires. Something that would be considered decadent or indecent to pious Christians, the troubadour lyrics now celebrated the worship of women, where previously adoration was reserved for God.

The influence of this poetry spread and changed drastically the status of women in Western literature, when the cult of the Virgin Mary was beginning to flourish in the church. Women in the upper class for the first time were put on a pedestal. For the average medieval women life did not change much. These cultural changes after 1400 encouraged upper class women to play a more prominent role in society, as hostess and as arbiters of social decorum.

After 1150 **romances** rapidly replaced the popularity of feudal chanson de geste. Romances were long narrative of chivalric and sentimental adventures of knights and ladies. These stories derived from legends associated with Troy or Celtic culture from the British Isles, and usually set in feudal times and their themes were centered on licit and illicit love between noble lords and ladies. The best example is the stories of *King Arthur and his knights of the round table.* Their name came from the mistaken belief its authors were imitating a Roman literary form.

Chrétien de Troyes (c. 1148–1190) was the first poet to make King Arthur and his court his subject. His versions set the standard for later romances. The audiences for his romances were the feudal courts of northern France. His treatment of the adulterous love of the knight Lancelot and Arthur's queen, Guinevere, is characteristic of the way romances combined aristocratic, courtly, and religious themes. In Chrétien's version, Lancelot rescues Queen Guinevere after experiencing many adventures and personal humiliations for her sake. The humbling of Lancelot is necessary to teach him to love Guinevere with unquestioning obedience.

Chrétien identifies Lancelot with Christ, so that many episodes echo scenes of Jesus' suffering and death. His literary work does not have the intention of sacrilege and avoids it, but the final effect is unsettling in its mixing of the sacred with the profane. The author describes Lancelot and Guinevere's passion without judging their behavior. Such moral neutrality was unacceptable to other Christian writers, who believed adultery to be a deadly sin. Today the version of King Arthur that is better known is Thomas Malory's *Le Mort d' Arthur* an English prose version of this tale written in 1485. In Malory's version the two lovers are blamed for the collapse of Arthur's court, this being a more judgmental view that the world today tends to agree with.

Dante's *Divine Comedy*. Vernacular writing appeared late in Italy; but, despite its later start, Italy had brought forth by 1300 the greatest literary figure of the High Middle Ages, Dante Alighieri. A native of Florence, in the province of Tuscany, Italy, Dante was the first of a proud tradition that soon made the Tuscan dialect the standard literary speech of Italy.

Born into a minor aristocratic family, Dante was given an excellent education with a thorough grounding in both Greco-Roman and Christian classics. He combined a career in public office with the life of an intellectual, which was a civic duty tradition that came from the ancient Roman republic. When Dante's political allies fell from office in 1301, he was exiled from Florence for the rest of his life. During these years, he composed the Commedia, or Comedy, which stands as the culmination of the literature of the Middle Ages, while he was poor and wandering about Italy.

Divided into three book-length parts, the **Divine Comedy** narrates Dante's fictional travels through three realms of the Christian afterlife. Led first by the ghost of the ancient Roman poet Virgil, Dante descends into hell, where he hears from the damned the nature of their various crimes against God and the moral law. Virgil next leads Dante into purgatory, where the lesser sinners expiate their guilt while awaiting the joys of heaven. At a fixed spot in purgatory, Virgil is forced to relinquish his role to Beatrice, a young Florentine woman and Dante's symbol of the eternal female. With Beatrice's guidance, Dante enters paradise and even has a vision of the almighty God.

The Divine Comedy written as an allegory (a literary or pictorial device in which each character, object, and event symbolically illustrates a moral or religious principle), was meant to be understood on several levels. Read literally, the poem bears witness to the author's personal fears as a moral sinner yet affirms his hope for eternal salvation. Read allegorically, the poem represents a comprehensive synthesis of the opposing tendencies that characterized medieval culture, such as balancing the Classical tradition with the Christian, Aristotle with Aquinas, the ancient with the new, with the proud, with the humble, and the secular with the spiritual.

The Divine Comedy has numerous great cultural symbols. The richest of these symbols in meaning are the central figures of Virgil who represents human reason and Beatrice who represents divine revelation. In the poem, Virgil is made inferior to Beatrice by leading Dante in hell and purgatory that are inferior to heaven, thus revealing Dante's acceptance of a basic idea of Thomas Aquinas that reason can lead only to awareness of sin, and that revelation is necessary to reach God's ultimate truth. Besides this fundamental Christian belief, the two figures convey other meanings. Virgil stands for Classical civilization and the secular literary life; Beatrice (Italian for "blessing") symbolizes spiritualized love and Christianized culture. By turning Beatrice into an image of God's grace, Dante revealed that the High Middle Ages were open to new symbols of Christian truth (Figure 6.12).

Figure 6.12   Statue of Dante Alighieri, Italy. *Image Copyright leigh, 2009. Used under license from Shutterstock, Inc.*

Dante's spiritual odyssey is set during the season of Easter. The author's journey from hell to heaven is synchronized with Jesus' descent into hell and His resurrection during Easter. Therefore, Dante's allegory has the religious aim of forcing his readers to meditate on the fate of their own immortal souls.

Dante's vision of the afterlife underscored his belief that humans have free will. Predestination had no place in his system, as his narration of hell shows. With one exception, all of the damned earned their fate by their deeds on Earth. The exceptions were the people consigned to Limbo (a place where souls are kept from entering into heaven, not suffering but without the joys of heaven), these were the pious pagans who lived before Jesus and thus were denied his message of hope. Moreover, those in Limbo, such as Aristotle and Plato, were not subjected to any punishment other than being removed from God's presence.

The Divine Comedy is a deeply personal poem. Dante rewards and punishes his Florentine friends and foes by the location that he assigns each in the afterlife. He also reveals his private feeling as he enters into discussions with various saints and sinners along the way. Beyond his desire for salvation, the idea he values most is to bring about a harmony between the Church and the secular state on Earth.

DANTE'S COMEDY, A LITERARY PILGRIMAGE

Figure 6.13   *Santiago de Compostela* (1075–1122). With 16th, 17th, and 18th century additions. Galician, Spain. Ninth century location that drew thousands of pilgrims to the alleged remains of Saint James. *Image Copyright* vlad0209/Shutterstock.com

Christians in the Medieval era aspired to do good works. One way in which they satisfied this ambition was to make pilgrimages to important sites containing holy relics. Pilgrimage routes led to churches throughout Europe and eventually converged upon *Santiago de Compostela* (1075–1122) in northwestern Spain where the remains of Saint James supposedly resided (Figure 6.13). Even today one can embark upon a pilgrimage to *Santiago* and receive a certificate (*compostela*) to prove completion of the journey.

Pilgrimage was central to the way of Medieval life and refers to more than just the physical act of travel. Pilgrimage is also a state of mind, reflected in the late Medieval publication of Dante Alighieri (1265–1321) entitled *Il Comedie* (*The Comedy*). Dante embarks upon a pilgrimage in this story that leads him on a journey of purification from Hell to Heaven, and where he ultimately sees the face of God.

Il Comedie (often referred to as *The Divine Comedy*) is a spiritual epic embodying the values of the Israelites/Christians (sin, guilt, redemption, etc.) for the purpose of moral education. The book has the same characteristics as other celebrated epics such as the *Iliad/Odyssey* by Homer, and the *Aeneid* by Virgil. It includes heroes, heroines, and saints, incorporates myth and legend, and takes place outside of real time. New to the literary style of the time, Dante's *Comedy* was written in Tuscan (vernacular Italian). The fact that any literate person could read it thus ensured its popularity.

While the book is a glorification of the life hereafter—in keeping with the theory of a God-centered universe—Dante's *Comedy* is also a contemporary view of politics, theology, and learning: Dante puts all of his enemies in Hell and his friends in Heaven, and alludes to contemporary political situations of his era.

The *Comedy* is organized around a *geo-centric* view of the universe (handed down from the Ancient Greek, Ptolemy) in which the Earth is placed at the center of the universe, with Hell and Satan inside. A track leads out to *Mount Purgatory* on the opposite side of the Earth. The Sun and planets revolve around the Earth with the stars around them. Beyond the stars are the angels and the *Empyrean*, or God. Since the writing of *The Comedy*, scientific writings have of course changed our view of the universe and demonstrated that the sun is at the center of our place in the sky. Thus, we currently hold a *helio-centric* (sun-centered) view of the universe.

Dante's *Comedy* is filled with allegory and symbolism; it is the story of Dante and the people he knew, but it is also the story of man's quest for salvation. It has characters such as Virgil, who represents wisdom and virtue, and a girl named Beatrice, who represents supernatural wisdom. There are of course other characters such as Saint Bernard, Mary, and even God. Full of numerological references to Christian iconography, *Il Comedie* references Medieval numbers such as the perfect number 3 (representing the *Trinity*); the perfect number 10 (as in the *Ten Commandments*), and the perfect number 7 (as in the *Seven Deadly Sins*). The general form of *The Comedy* is organized around the numbers 3 and 10: Hell, Purgatory, and Heaven (the number three) form the canticles (major divisions of the book), while each canticle is subdivided into 33 cantos or songs, and each of the songs or cantos is subdivided into three-line groups called *terza rima*. There are 99 canticles plus an extra one that equals 100, a multiple of 10.

10 commandments × 10 commandments = 100.

Hell   = 9 divisions + 1 = 10

Purgatory   = 9 divisions + 1 = 10

Heaven   = 9 divisions + 1 = 10

9 is a perfect number, which becomes even more perfect when 1 is added and it equals 10. 10 × 10 equals another compound perfect number, 100.

Medieval numerology is not concerned with numeric proportions or ratios as much as symbolic reference to the numbers associated with Christianity. This contrasts sharply with the Ancient Greek Pythagorean worldview where numbers and their proportional relationship to each other have value in themselves

DANTE'S INFERNO (HELL)

Il Comedie covers approximately one week in the life of Dante. The author is having both a mid-life and a spiritual crisis; he has deviated from the straight and narrow path and is confused. Walking along one day, he stumbles into darkness where three apparitions of wild beasts confront him—each representing different kinds of sin. As he proceeds he is confronted by the shadowy figure of Virgil—author of an earlier epic (*Aeneid*) who agrees to serve as his guide through Hell. But Virgil informs him that others will help him continue his journey up through *Purgatory* and on to Heaven in order to regain his full spiritual direction.

Although Virgil was a pagan, he was considered a suitable traveling companion in Hell because the Medieval Christians believed that he, among all the ancients, was the only one qualified to comment on the afterlife. Virgil wrote a series of poems called *Ecologues* in which he predicted the coming of a golden age (*Ecologue No. 4*) signaled by the birth of a child (Christ). The Christians felt that Virgil's premonition of Christ's coming qualified him to be a spiritual guide—at least in Hell.

A sign above the gate of Hell reads: "Give up all hope ye who enter here." Virgil escorts Dante onto the upper rim of Hell where numerous spirits are chased around by wasps and hornets who prod them with pitchforks. On one side of Hell, a hornet waves a colored flag and the demons hurry their victims around to it, but then a hornet on the other side of Hell waves another colored flag and they are bullied over to that side. These spirits are forced to chase flags of different colors in perpetuity around Hell because they are the people who never committed themselves to anything in life. They are the flag chasers of life who run after flags of different colors on the rim of Hell in the afterlife, as well.

As Dante walks along he recognizes some of the sinners, and they tell him about the sins they committed in real life. Many of his descriptions of these repugnant sinners—writhing and twisting in the muck and mire—are so vivid that they have inspired the imaginations of painters and illustrators throughout history such as Eugene Delacroix (Figure 6.14) and William Blake.

Figure 6.14 *Image Copyright Gianni Dagli Orti/The Art Archive at Art Resource, NY*

"And everywhere along that hideous track I saw horned demons with enormous lashes move through those souls, scourging them on the back. Ah, how the stragglers of that long rout stirred their legs quick-march at the first crack of the lash! Certainly no one waited a second, or third. As we went on, one face in that procession caught my eye and I said: "That sinner there: It is certainly not the first time I've seen that one." I stopped, therefore, to study him, and my Guide out of his kindness waited, and even allowed me to walk back a few steps at the sinner's side. And that flayed spirit, seeing me turn around, thought to hide his face, but I called to him: "You there, that walk along with your eyes on the ground—if those are not false features then I know you as Venedico Caccianemico of Bologna: what brings you here among this pretty crew?" [This person actually lived in Florence at the time.] And he replied: "I speak unwillingly, but something in your living voice, in which I hear the world again, stirs and compels me. It was I who brought the fair Ghisola 'round to serve the will and lust of the Marquis, however sordid that old tale may sound."

INFERNO, Canto XVIII*

The man referred to in the excerpt above brought women to satisfy the sexual desires of the Marquis. Dante knew about it and tattled on him in this book. One can understand why Dante developed many political enemies and was eventually banished from his hometown of Florence, Italy.

Dante and Virgil continue their journey down to the pit of Hell where Dante sees Satan himself:

"If he was once as beautiful as now he is hideous, and still turned on his Maker, well may he be the source of every woe! With what a sense of awe I saw his head towering above me! for it had three faces: one was in front, and it was fiery red; the other two, as weirdly wonderful, merged with it from the middle of each shoulder to the point where all converged at the top of the skull. . . .Under each head two wings rose terribly, their span proportioned to so gross a bird; I never saw such sails upon the sea. They were not feathers—their texture and their form were like a bat's wings—and he beat them so that three winds blew form him in one great storm: it is these winds that freeze all of Cocytus. He wept from his six eyes, and down three chins the tears ran mixed with bloody froth and pus."

INFERNO, Canto XXXIV*

Note the use of the holy number three: he kept three people in eternal pain—Brutus, Cassius, and Judas—three people who had turned against their benefactors. Dante felt that the worst sin of all was someone who turned against his own benefactor. Satan turned against God, Judas turned against Christ, and Brutus and Cassius turned against Caesar.

"Judas . . . he who kicks his legs on the fiery chin and has his head inside. Of the other two, who have their heads thrust forward, the one who dangles down from the black face is Brutus: note how he writhes without a word. And there, with the huge and sinewy arms, is the soul of Cassius . . . But the night is coming on and we must go, for we have seen the whole. Then, as he bade, I clasped his neck, and he, watching for a moment when the wings were opened wide, reached over dexterously and seized the shaggy coat of the king demon; then grappling matted hair and frozen crusts from one tuft to another, clambered down."

INFERNO, Canto XXXIV*

It is amusing to read from Dante's catalog of sins in Hell. Hypocrites, thieves, sowers of evil are all here. Fortune-tellers rank very low among the sinners—just above murderers. It is an interesting view of Hell and a popular one from the Medieval viewpoint, but it is not official church dogma.

Dante's account of Heaven is also compelling, but mysterious. In the final page of the book he gives a description of God. (Please note the italicized sentences in the translation below because they reveal what God looked like to Dante.)

"What then I *saw* is more than tongue can say. . . .my vision made one with the Eternal Good. . . . I think I saw the universal form. . . .Within the depthless deep and clear existence of that *abyss of light three circles shown—three in color, one in circumference: the second from the first, rainbow from rainbow; the third, an exhalation of pure fire equally breathed forth by the other two.*

But oh how much my words miss my conception . . . that second aureole which shown forth in Thee, conceived as a reflection of the first—or which appeared so to my scrutiny—seemed in Itself of its own coloration, to be painted with man's image.

I fixed my eyes on that alone in rapturous contemplation. Like a geometer wholly dedicated to squaring the circle, but who cannot find, think as he may, the principle indicated—so did I study the supernal face. I yearned to know just how our image merges into that circle, and how it there finds place; but mine were not the wings for such a flight. Yet, as I wished, the truth I wished for came cleaving my mind in a great flash of light. Here my powers rest from their high fantasy, but already I could feel my being turned—instinct and intellect balanced equally, as in a wheel whose motion nothing jars—by the Love that moves the Sun and the other stars."

PARADISO, Canto XXXIV*

SCULPTURE

The majority of people during the Medieval era saw sculpture in the decorations to portals, piers, and capitals of their city halls, churches, and cathedrals. However, decorative sculpture was also available to members of the nobility in the form of devotional statues such as the carved ivory *Sainte Chapelle Virgin and Child* (Figure 6.11) that belonged to the King of France, Louis IX. This devotional piece was used in a private space in Sainte Chapelle, Paris. Other similar sculptural pieces were available only to the select few who could afford such rare materials and could pay skilled craftsman to work them.

For the Medieval mind, ivory itself connoted purity and chastity, qualities associated with the Mother of God; however, the material was very costly and elephant tusks from Africa were not readily available. A piece of ivory of this quality would be given only to the best artists—especially since the carving was intended for a king.

There are great difficulties in carving elephant tusks because of the hollows and inconsistencies of horned material. This sculptor brilliantly exploited the natural curve of the tusk and inscribed the Virgin within a parabolic arc to create a naturalistic inclination of the Virgin—very much unlike earlier rigid statuary from the previous hundred years. Even the details of the Virgin's stylized hand and face reveal a conscious awareness of naturalism and grace. Her face has bilateral symmetry, and the face of Christ is much less like the head of a man placed upon a child's body than an actual child (as was the practice in the early Middle Ages). The parabolic curve of the Virgin's inclination is picked up in the folds of cloth repeated sequentially down her right leg and the entire piece is tastefully heightened with gold. This is a masterpiece of Medieval art both in terms of its naturalism and mediation between material and image.

Music

The purpose of the High Middle Ages was the glorification of God, as it was with all other arts. At first, the monophonic (single-line) Gregorian chants were still the main form of musical expression, but two innovations, the introduction of tropes and the development of polyphony, led the way to a different sound in the future.

The **tropes,** or turns, were new texts and melodies inserted into the existing Gregorian chants. Added for both poetic and doctrinal reasons, these musical embellishments slowly changed the plainchants into more elaborate songs. Culminating in about 1150, this musical development coincided with the appearance of the richly articulated Gothic churches.

The tropes also gave a powerful impetus to Western drama. From the practice of troping grew a new musical genre, the **liturgical drama,** which at first was sung and performed in the church but gradually moved outdoors. From the 12th century onward, these works were staged in the area in front of the church as sacred dramas or mystery plays (*mystery* is derived from the Latin *ministerium,* "handicraft" or "occupation"). As their popularity increased, they began to be sung in the vernacular instead of Latin. Ultimately, the liturgical drama supplied one of the threads that led to the *revival of the secular theater.*

Gregorian chants were also being modified by the development of **polyphony,** in which two or more lines of melody are sung or played at the same time. In the early 11th century, polyphony was extremely simple and was known as **organum.** It consisted of a main melody, called the *cantus firmus,* accompanied by an identical melody sung four of five tones higher or lower. By about 1150, the second line began to have its own independent melody rather than duplicating the first.

During the 13th century, two-voiced organum gave way to multivoiced songs called **motets,** which employed more complex melodies. In the motets, the main singer used the liturgy as a text while up to five other voices sang either commentaries or vernacular translation of the text. The result was a complex web of separate voices woven into a harmonious tapestry. By about 1250, the *motet composers* had laid the ***foundations of modern musical composition.***

Notwithstanding these developments in sacred music, the church could not stop the rise of secular music any more than it could prevent the spread of courtly love. Indeed, the first secular music was associated with the same feudal courts were the *chansons de geste* and the troubadour songs flourished in the 12th century. At first, France was the center of this musical moment, but in the early 13th century, German poets took the lead. At the same time, music began to be practiced not just by aristocratic poets but also by middle-class minstrels, and new musical instruments—some, such as the **lute** (a multistringed instrument with neck and sound box) and the bagpipe, banned by the church, started to find their way into secular music.

The High Middle Ages also gave rise to some innovations that made modern music possible. Guido of Arezzo (995-1050), an Italian monk, modernized musical notation by this invention of the **music staff,** the set of five horizontal lines and four intermediate spaces on which notes may be drawn. Guido also began the practice of naming the **musical tones by syllables** *ut (or do), re mi, fa, sol,* and *la,* a step that greatly simplified the teaching of music. The music composed according to Guido's system can be reproduced by today's music historians; thus, ***Western music may be said to descend in an unbroken line from the music of this period*** (Figure 6.15).

Figure 6.15   Early written music. *Image Copyright Craig Hanson, 2009. Used under license from Shutterstock, Inc.*

The Legacy of the High Middle Ages

The apex of the Middle Ages, the High Middle Ages, the grandeur of this age of synthesis declined after 1300, when the secular and the spiritual began to go their separate ways. Religious fervor and faith began to lose its hold upon medieval society's heart and mind. But the legacy of the Christian centuries survives, particularly in the writing of Dante, the theology of Thomas Aquinas, and the Gothic cathedrals. Of Dante's works, the Divine Comedy is his most enduring gift to world literature; his poetic style and literary forms influenced Italian writers for centuries. Furthermore, Dante's love for Beatrice has deeply influenced Western literature by encouraging poets to seek inspiration from a living woman.

The Roman Catholic world is the most significant beneficiary of the philosophy of Thomas Aquinas. Since the late 19th century, Thomism has been regarded as the basis of orthodox beliefs. As for the Gothic style, it ceased to be practiced after about 1500, although it was revived in the 19th century as part of the Romantic Movement, and even today universities often adopt Gothic elements in their official architecture.

Besides these great gifts, the Christian centuries have left the modern world other significant cultural legacies. First and foremost was the birth of the courtly love movement that glorified individual romantic affection, the idea that this man loves this woman.

The vernacular writers created one of the richest literary traditions in the west through the stories of King Arthur and the Knights of the Round Table. The basic theoretical system for composing music was developed during this period under the auspices of the church. Outside the church, the ancestor of all Western love songs was invented by the Provencal (French) poets. In Gothic sculpture, artists began to move away from symbolic representation to a more realistic art.

These Christian centuries transmitted many of the legacies that had been received from ancient and other sources. The liberal arts, the Christian religion, the rationalist tradition, Muslim science, and the entire Greco-Roman heritage are only the major ingredients of this invaluable legacy to later ages.

THE LATE MIDDLE AGES: 1300–1500

The 14th century in Western Europe turned into a turbulent time and many of its inhabitants thought that the biblical apocalypse had arrived due to the plague of the *Black Death,* famine, and war. During this time the unique culture of the High Middle Ages began to change in a different direction. The High Middle Ages blended the spiritual with the secular, a time when society in general and its achievements were guided and in harmony with the teachings of the Roman Church, and in the 1300s all this began to break apart. The ideal of a united Christendom which had been achieved to a certain extent in the previous century, now was faced with the reality of warring European states of which the *Hundred Years' War* (1337–1453) between the royal houses of France and England for the French throne was the greatest and longest. The chivalric code began to become obsolete with the new military weapons and tactics. Philosophy and theology that had been integrated by St. Thomas Aquinas, now were being set apart and with contradictions by new intellectual currents in the universities. Secularism was beginning to rise and new technologies and artistic innovation were guiding the Western world into a new direction. Europe entered a disastrous period of economic depression, inflation, and widespread famine. Wars between Christians brought social unrest and armies were looting towns and regions of western Europe. The church did not hold up to a high moral standard and tragically troubled by the Babylonian Captivity and the Great Schism, thus was unable to provide moral and political leadership. As the old stability and certainty unraveled the balance of the Age of Faith, the optimistic mood of the High Middle Ages gave way to a sense of impending doom.

The 14th century was a time that had undergone great changes since the 12th century. During the latter, when the Gothic Style was first developed, Europe was a thinly populated continent of peasants with monasteries and feudal noble's castles as the main centers of learning and power. By the 14th century the towns had grown to become large and prosperous centers of trade that created a new wealth and whose burghers (a prosperous citizen of a town) were increasingly independent of the power of the church and the feudal lords. A new merchant urban class was rising that will achieve great wealth, and in some cases acquire greater wealth than the feudal nobles and even monarchs. Even the nobles no longer wanted to carry on a life withdrawn from the new cultural and economic centers in their grim fortified manors, moving to the cities with their comfort and fashionable luxury, where they could display their wealth in the courts of the high aristocracy and monarchs. The new spirit of society was changing and it was no longer the spirit of the Church Militant and Church Triumphant.

LITERATURE

Culture in general was being reshaped by powerful forces which were the rising new monarchies, the growing national consciousness among diverse peoples, the emerging secularism, and the developing urban environment—were also transforming literature in the late Middle Ages. The rise of literacy produced a growing educated class who learned to read and write the local languages rather than Latin, and a shift to vernacular literature began to occur. The new groups, the monarchs and their courts and the urban middle class, started to supplant the nobility and the churches as patrons and audiences. In the mid-15th century Johann Gutenberg developed a practicable method of using movable type to print books. The invention of the printing press will enable the production of a higher volume and more economical books, which allowed greater dissemination of ideas and literature which fostered a more educated society.

Northern Italian Literature: Petrarch and Boccaccio

New literary forms emerged in the areas were the chivalric and feudal modes were weakest in northern Italy and England. Petrarch and Boccaccio, both Florentines, like Dante, grew up in a Christian world that was rapidly being secularized. These two writers captured the mood of this transition era as Florence and the other Italian city-states shed their medieval outlook. Both authors looked back to the Classical world for inspiration and yet both found in the bustling world of the nearby towns the materials and characters for their stories.

Francesco Petrarch (1304–1374), was Florentine by birth and in spirit, succeeded and prospered in Avignon, France, surrounded by the splendor and learning of the papal court. He was a diplomat for popes and Italian princes performing well, but his reputation arose from his career as a professional man of letters. Rejecting the age's trend toward the vernacular, he dedicated his life to Latin writing and to the recovery of ancient manuscripts, although the work for which he is most renowned, a collection of live lyrics and sonnets called *Canzoniere,* or *Songbook,* is written in Italian. Petrarch shows the typical secular interest of his times. A conventional Christian, he only occasionally addressed religious issues in his works.

Giovanni Boccaccio (1313–1375) was a man of the world, much more so than his lifelong friend Petrarch. The son of a banker, Boccaccio began his literary career by penning prose romances along with poetic pastorals (relating to life in the country and/or shepherds) and sonnets, many of which were dedicated to Fiammetta, a young woman who was both his consuming passion and his literary muse (a source of inspiration). His masterpiece was written about 1351—***The Decameron.*** This work reflects the grim conditions of the Black Death, which had just swept through Florence. In *The Decameron* (from Greek for "ten days"), Boccaccio describes how ten young men and women, in their efforts to escape the plague, flee the city to a country villa, where they pass the time, each telling a story a day for ten days, most of their 100 tales were based on folks stories and the popular legends, although some tales deal lightly with social mores and a few contain moral messages, the majority simply entertain the listener. Boccaccio, speaking through a cross section of urban voices and replying on well-known stories, helped develop a *form of literature that eventually led to the* **modern short story.**

English Literature: Geoffrey Chaucer

English literature rapidly matured into its own forms during the Late Middle Ages.

Geoffrey Chaucer was the son of a wealthy merchant from London, England. He spent his professional life as a courtier, a diplomat, and a public servant of the English crown, and became famous as a poet. English literature was still establishing its own identity and a common language was slowly emerging when Geoffrey Chaucer (c. 1340–1400) appeared on the scene. He wrote in an East Midland dialect of English that became the standard form for his generation as well as the **foundation of modern English.**

Chaucer began composing his most famous work, ***The Canterbury Tales,*** in 1385. He set the tales in the context of a pilgrimage to the tomb of St. Thomas á Becket, a 12th-century martyr and saint. Becket was a friend of the English king Henry II and then he became archbishop of Canterbury. When the king wanted to impose his will and interest upon the church, Becket engaged in conflict with Henry II over the rights and privileges of the Church and was assassinated in 1170 by followers of the king in Canterbury Cathedral where he is buried. Even though the journey has a religious purpose, Chaucer makes it plain that the travelers intend to have a good time along the way. To make the journey from London to Canterbury more interesting, the 31 pilgrims, including Chaucer himself, agree to tell tales, two tales each going and returning, and to award a prize for the best story told.

Chaucer completed only 23 tales and the general Prologue, in which he introduces the pilgrims. Each person on the pilgrimage not only represents an English social type but also is a unique and believable human being. In this poetic narrative about a group of ordinary people, the spiritual is mixed with the temporal and the serious with the comic.

Chaucer drew his pilgrims from nearly all walks of medieval society. Therefore, *Canterbury Tales* gives us a good insight into the people of his time in England, helping the modern reader to better understand the English society of the 14th century. The Knight, in this late stage of feudalism, personified much that was noble and honorable in the chivalric code; his bravery could not be questioned, but he was also a mercenary and cruel to his enemies. Certain representatives of the church are also somewhat skeptically treated. The Prioress, the head of a convent and from the upper class, is more concerned about her refined manners and polished language than the state of her soul. Similarly, the Monk lives a life of the flesh and enjoys good food, fine wine, and expensive clothing. The Friar seems the very opposite of his sworn ideals; he is eager to hear a confession for a fee, and he never goes among the poor or aids the sick. However, in the country Parson, Chaucer portrays a true servant of God who preaches to his parish, looks after the infirm and dying, and never takes more than his share from his religious flock (Figure 6.16).

Figure 6.16 Monk on horseback from *Canterbury Tales,* from medieval manuscript. *Image © Jupiter Images.*

The tales the pilgrims choose to tell, often reflect their own moral values. The worthy Knight tells a chivalric love story, but the Miller, a coarse, rough man well-versed in lying and cheating, related how a young wife took on a lover and deceived her husband, an example of the popular medieval tale known as a fabliau. Thus the pilgrims' stories, based on folk and fairy tales, romance, classical stories, and beast fables, reveal as much about the narrators as they do about late medieval culture.

French Literature: Christine de Pizan

France was also affected by the winds of change blowing through Europe during the Late Middle Ages. Christine de Pizan (c. 1364–1430) was by birth an Italian whose literary gifts blossomed under the patronage of the French kings and dukes of Burgundy. Christine de Pizan, the leading French writer of the day, began to explore in her works the status and role of women. The first known Western woman to earn a living through her writings, de Pizan was a pioneer who blazed the trail for women authors.

De Pizan wrote on diverse topics, working within the well-established literary genres of her day, including love poems, lays (ballads), biography, letters, political tracts, and moral proverbs. There are two themes that dominate her writing: calls for peace and appeals for the recognition of women's contributions of culture and social life.

One of Pizan's famous literary works is **The Book of the City of Ladies** (1405), a book that forcefully tries to raise the status of women and to give them dignity. Offering one of the first histories of women and arguing that women have the right to be educated, based on her premise that women are moral and intellectual equals of men, this book seems at first almost feminist in a modern sense. But a close reading and analysis demonstrates that de Pizan is writing within a medieval framework. Nowhere in this book or any other writings does she advocate that women abandon their traditional roles, such as wives, mothers, and homemakers, and strike out on a new path. It is proper nevertheless to claim that de Pizan is the *first women's rights advocate in society and culture.*

ARCHITECTURE AND ART

The gothic style continued to dominate architecture throughout this period, but the balanced and unified High Gothic of the 13th century was now replaced with the ornate effects of the **Late Gothic style.**

Virtuosity became the chief aesthetic goal, as the architects took basic forms and pushed them to the stylistic limits. This will give architecture an overloaded, heavier, and more complicated look due to the overabundance of decorative features and more elaborate design (Figure 6.17).

Late gothic sculpture and painting also became more virtuosic. Statues and sculptured figures were given willowy, swaying bodies, rendered in exquisite detail and illuminated manuscripts and painted wooden panels became ever more refined. At the same time, *Giotto*, an early 14th-century Florentine painter, was revolutionizing art with a new approach to painting. The trend toward *naturalism* embodied in his works was the most significant new artistic development of this period was destined to be the wave of the future.

Figure 6.17 St. Vitus Cathedral, Prague, Czech Republic. Flying buttresses connected to vertical buttresses support the tall wall with large stained glass windows. *Courtesy of Maria Luisa Elizaondo.*

Late Gothic Architecture

France, the home of the Gothic style, remained a major source of architectural innovation. French architects now abandoned the balanced ideal of the High Gothic and made *extravagance* their guiding principle, creating a Late Gothic style typified by ever greater heights and elaborate decoration. In the 15th century, this tendency culminated in the **Flamboyant style,** so-named for its flame-like effects. French churches built in this style had sky-piercing spires, and their facades were embroidered with lacy or wavy decorations that obscured the buildings' structural components. During the 14th century, the Late Gothic spread to many European countries, becoming an international style. All across Europe, the focus shifted to fanciful designs: The churches were smaller, the roofs and towers taller, the naves wider, and the decorations more luxuriant (Figure 6.18).

In England, the Late Gothic was called **Perpendicular** because of its dramatic emphasis on *verticality*. This Perpendicular style was characterized by an increased use of paneled decorations on the walls and overhead vaults, resulting in a variation of rib vaulting, called *fan vaulting,* in which stone ribs arch out from a single point in the ceiling to form a delicate pattern.

Figure 6.18 Famous Leuven Town Hall, landmark of Flemish Brabant region in Belgium. Architecture in Brabantine Late Gothic style. Built in 1448–1469 on Grote Markt (Main Square). Example of ornate late Gothic style with intricate design. *Image © Jupiter Images.*

This style also increased the number of window openings, which necessitated additional flying buttresses (Figure 6.19).

ARCHITECTURE (CATHEDRALS)

Life revolved around the church in the Medieval era (Figure 6.20). There are well over 100 Christian cathedrals in Europe, and the economy of many towns was boosted by the construction of these edifices. Since most of the funds were donated, construction took anywhere from twenty-five to seventy-five years to complete. A cathedral is the seat of the bishop and, typically, holds important religious relics. The cathedral at Chartres, sixty miles outside of Paris, France is said to have held the tunic worn by Mary, the Mother of Christ. Because of their religious holdings, cathedrals were located on important pilgrim-age routes as explained in the case study given at the end of this chapter.

During the final phase of its construction, one of the important additions to a cathedral was its bells (Figure 6.21). The bells were treated like people; they were conse-crated, covered with vestments, and bap-tized. The power of these bells should not be minimized. Once installed in the cathedrals high up above the town, they were the controlling force for Medieval Europe. If you could hear the bells, you paid the taxes.

Bells decided when people would get up in the morning, when they said prayers, and when they went to sleep at night. Bells were the public timekeepers for workers—an early form of telecommuting for homebound textile workers who gauged their daily lives by them. Bell tolls sounded at public executions and celebrations gives a

Figure 6.19   English perpendicular style, fan vaulting. *Image Copyright Benson HE, 2009. Used under license from Shutterstock, Inc.*

Figure 6.21   *Donald W. Reynolds Tower Carillon.* Bells cast at Paccard, La Fonderie de cloches, Annecy-le vieux, France (1994). University of Arkansas—Fort Smith. *Image Courtesy of Stephen Husarik.*

Figure 6.20   Lincoln Cathedral, England, perpendicular style. *Image © Jupiter Images.*

En ego campana, nunquam de nutnio vana...

Behold, I am a bell,
       never do I announce idle things:

I praise the true God,
       I resound with ringing
I summon the people,
       I resound with ringing
I gather the clergy together,
       I resound with ringing
I bewail death,
       I resound with ringing
I shatter strokes of lightning,
       I resound with ringing
I peal at Sabbath,
       I resound with ringing
I inspire the apathetic,
       I resound with ringing
I disperse the winds,
       I resound with ringing
I bring peace to the blood-stained,
       I resound with ringing

Figure 6.22 *Behold I am a Bell,* Jacob Gallus. Translation by Ernest Cialone. *Image Translation by Ernest Cialone. Used by permission.*

Figure 6.23 April: Planetary figure of Sun in his chariot, Trés Riches Heures du Duc de Berry. *Image © Jupiter Images.*

translation of a poem by Jacob Handl Gallus (1550–1591) that explains the functions of church bells centuries ago (Figure 6.22).

Today, we hold many of the same associations with ringing bells that were held in the Middle Ages. Bells are heard at funerals, weddings, and (early in the 20th century) even heard as warnings (fire bells). When groups of them swing wildly—as in a bell peal—they have a happy sound. When struck repeatedly, as in a bell toll, bells have a mournful sound.

Late Gothic Painting and the Rise of New Trends

Painting underwent the most radical change of all the arts in the Late Middle Ages. No longer was the church the only patron of the arts, now the nobility and wealthy merchant class began to patronize the arts with their more secular interests. Illuminated manuscripts maintained their popularity, but their themes became more secular under the patronage of titled aristocrats and wealthy merchants. At the same time, painters of frescoes and wooden panels introduced new techniques for applying paint and mixing colors. Stylistically, painters preferred to work in the extravagant Late Gothic manner with its elegant refinement and its undulating lines. Nevertheless, as mentioned earlier, Giotto and other Italian painters discovered fresh ways of depicting human figures that started to revolutionize art.

ILLUMINATED MANUSCRIPTS

The Burgundian court played a pivotal role in the production of one of the outstanding illuminated manuscripts of the medieval period, the Trés Riches Heures du Duc de Berry (Figure 6.23). This famous collection of miniatures was painted by the three Limbourg brothers for the duke of Berry, brother of Philip the Bold of Burgundy. These illustrations stand above the others of their time for their exquisite detail, general liveliness, and intricately designed crowd scenes—some of the marks of the Late Gothic style.

THE PRINT

The print, a new artistic medium, developed in the Late Middle Ages in the Austrian-Bavarian regions, eastern France, and the Netherlands. Encouraged by the growth of lay piety, the earliest prints were devotional woodcuts to be used as aids to personal meditation. The prints initially featured scenes from the lives of the Virgin and Christ. For the **woodcut print,** the artist drew an image on a woodblock, which was then cut by a wood-cutter and printed by the artist; some were then hand-tinted by a colorist (Figure 6.24). By 1500 the new techniques of **engraving** (using a sharp tool to draw an image onto a metal plate overlaid with wax dipping the plate in acid, and then printing it) and dry-point (marking an image onto a copper plate with a metal stylus and then printing it) were becoming increasingly popular.

SCULPTURE

The majority of people during the Medieval era saw sculpture in the decorations to portals, piers, and capitals of their city halls, churches, and cathedrals. However, decorative sculpture was also available to members of the nobility in the form of devotional statues such as the carved ivory *Sainte Chapelle Virgin and Child* (Figure 6.25) that belonged to the King of France, Louis IX. This devotional piece was used in a private space in Sainte Chapelle, Paris. Other similar sculptural pieces were available only to the select few who could afford such rare materials and could pay skilled craftsman to work them.

For the Medieval mind, ivory itself connoted purity and chastity, qualities associated with the Mother of God; however, the material was very costly and elephant tusks from Africa were not readily available. A piece of ivory of this quality would be given only to the best artists—especially since the carving was intended for a king.

There are great difficulties in carving elephant tusks because of the hollows and inconsistencies of horned material. This sculptor brilliantly exploited the natural curve of the tusk and inscribed the Virgin within a parabolic arc to create a naturalistic inclination of the Virgin—very much unlike earlier rigid statuary from the previous hundred years. Even the details of the Virgin's stylized hand and face reveal a conscious awareness of naturalism and grace. Her face has bilateral symmetry, and the face of Christ is much less like the head of a man placed upon a child's body than an actual child (as was the practice in the early Middle Ages). The parabolic curve of the Virgin's inclination is picked up in the folds of cloth repeated sequentially down her right leg and the entire piece is tastefully heightened with gold. This is a masterpiece of Medieval art both in terms of its naturalism and mediation between material and image.

GIOTTO: NEW TRENDS IN ITALY

While the illuminated manuscript and the print were popular in northern Europe, a revolution in paining was under way in Italy. The paintings of

Figure 6.24   The Prioress from *The Canterbury Tales* by Geoffrey Chaucer. Woodcut from the Caxton's Edition of 1485. *Image Copyright c., 2009. Used under license from Shutterstock, Inc.*

Figure 6.25   Sainte Chapelle Virgin and Child (ca. 1250–60). Ivory, partially gilded, Musée du Louvre, Paris. © *RMN-Grand Palais /Art Resource, NY.*

Giotto are generally recognized as having established a new direction in Western art, one that led into the Renaissance. In Giotto's own day, Dante praised him and the citizen of Florence honored him. Giotto's revolution in painting was directed against the prevailing Italo-Byzantine style, with its two-dimensional art characterized by naturalism and the full expression of human emotions. Partly through the innovative use of light and shade and the placement of figures so as to create nonmathematical **perspective,** or spatial depth, Giotto was able to paint realistic-looking figures, rather than the flat, ornamental depictions found in most illuminated manuscripts or the Italian alter paintings (Figure 6.26).

Giotto was a prolific artist whose paintings adorned churches in Florence and cities all over Italy. At the Arena Chapel in Padua, Giotto painted his masterpiece, two sets of frescoes, one of the life of the Virgin and the other of the life of Christ. These 38 scenes show Giotto at the height of his powers, rendering space with a sense of depth and organizing figures so as to create dramatic tension. One of Giotto's best scenes from the Arena Chapel frescoes is the *pietá* or *Lamentation* that portrays the grief for the death of Christ. It expresses complete despair through the mourners' faces and gestures, especially from Mary who cradles the body of Christ and St. John who stands with his arms outstretched, to the angles that hover over the scene. Even nature seems to mourn, as in the barren tree symbol of the cross on which Jesus was crucified. After Giotto died in 1337, no painter for the rest of the century was able to match his remarkable treatment of nature and human emotions.

Figure 6.26   Painting of St. Francis of Assisi receiving the stigmata by Giotto. *Image © Jupiter Images.*

FLEMISH PAINTING: JAN VAN EYCK AND HANS MEMLING

Brothers Jan and Hubert van Eyck are the most famous and their religious works and portraits established the Flemish (Belgian) style of art. Little is known of Hubert, but Jan van Eyck (c. 1370–1441) is considered the founder of the Flemish school (Figure 6.27).

As a general principle, Flemish art sought reality through an accumulation of precise and often symbolic details, in contrast to Italian art, which tended to be more concerned with psychological truth, as in Giotto's frescoes in the Arena Chapel. This national style, expressed primarily through painting with oils on wood panels, turned each artwork into a brilliant and precise reproduction of the original scene. The finest details in a patterned carpet, the reflected light on a copper vase, or the wrinkled features of an el-derly patron were laboriously and meticulously recorded. The Flemish style, with its close attention to detail, was widely appreciated and quickly spread to Italy and England.

A second outstanding artist working in Flanders during the Late Middle Ages was Hans **Memling** (c. 1430–1494), the most popular painter of his day in Bruges. Before settling in Bruges, the German-born

Figure 6.27 "Madonna and Child Enthroned" by Jan van Eyck, 1434, Burges. The Virgin Mary and the child Jesus appear with Saint Donatian, Saint George in armor, and the donor, Canon George Van Der Paele. Realism prevails throughout this picture, with no idealization. *Image © Jupiter Images.*

Figure 6.28 The 15th century St. Ursula Shrine, 1489, by Hans Memling. A painting from a reliquary depicting the story of St. Ursula. *Image © Jupiter Images.*

Memling studied painting in Cologne and the Netherlands, where he fully absorbed the northern tradition. Memling's painting style, which borrowed heavily from that of Jan van Eyck and his generation, was characterized by serenity and graceful elegance (Figure 6.28).

MUSIC

The forces of change transforming Europe in the 1300s also had an impact on the field of music. Sacred music began to be overshadowed by secular music, with the rise of new secular forms—such as the ballad and rondeau—based on the **chanson,** a song set to a French text and scored for one or more voices, often with instrumental accompaniment. Polyphony remained the dominant composing style, but composers now wrote **secular polyphonic pieces** that were not based on Gregorian chants. These changes were made possible by innovations that coalesced into what came to be called the *new art* (*ars nova* in Latin), particularly in Paris, the capital of polyphonic music. The innovations included a new system of music notation, along with new rhythmic patterns such as **isorhythm**—the use of a single rhythmic pattern from the beginning to the end of a work, despite changes in the melodic structure. The chief exponent of *ars nova* was the French composer and poet Guillaume de Machaut (c. 1300–1377)

Machaut, who trained as a priest and musician first made his mark as a court official to the King of Bohemia. For his services, he was rewarded with an appointment to the cathedral in Reims (1337), where he worked for much of the rest of his life. His music circulated widely in his day, largely because he made gifts of his music manuscripts to wealthy patrons. Thus, he became one of the first composers whose works have survived. Reflecting the decline in church music, his output consists mainly of secular love themes. In England, his verses influenced the great poet Geoffrey Chaucer.

Although famous for secular music, Machaut's reputation rests on his Notre Dame Mass, the first polyphonic version of the Mass Ordinary by a known composer. "Ordinary" refers to the five parts of the Mass that remain unchanged throughout the liturgical year, namely the Kyrie ("Lord, have mercy"), Gloria ("Glory"), Credo ("The Nicene Creed"), Sanctus and Benedictus ("Holy" and "Blessed"), and Agnus Dei ("Lamb of God"). Written for four voices, some of which may have been performed by instrumentalists, Machaut's Mass made liberal use of isorhythm in most of its parts. Following his lead, composers for more than 600 years made the Mass Ordinary the central point of choral music.

Monks and nuns sang these texts in a melodic style called plainchant that was beautifully adapted to the buildings where it was heard—with reverberation and echoes wafting through the corridors of stone-walled monasteries and convents. The construction of large cathedrals, however, made it necessary to find a contrasting dramatic sound to fill increasingly larger spaces. A new type of music called *organum* was invented to serve this need. It is a kind of polyphonic music based upon an existing plainchant melody that involves multiple voice parts.

One of the great Medieval church music composers, Leonin, created a piece of *organum* called *Viderunt* for the opening of the Cathedral de Notre-Dame in Paris (12th century). Using just a portion of an original plainchant melody, he took single words such as *Viderunt*, and stretched them out over minutes of musical time while adding additional voice parts. This represented quite a break from the past, but the music was grander, more complex, and had much more resonance than plainchant. We have different expectations about how music should sound today and it may not be possible to fully appreciate this dramatic development in musical style.

Legacy of Late Middle Ages

The Late Middle Ages was a turbulent age of change from a Medieval world that began to come to an end and a transition to the new modern world that was the Renaissance. From this period were many of the cultural tensions that defined the history of Europe for the next 400 years.

During the late Middle Ages the most revolutionary change was the rise of a powerful secular spirit that began to impose itself all over western Europe. Philosophy and theology were no longer in complete harmony. A new breed of secular ruler that challenged the church's spiritual and political powers emerged in the victory of the French and English kings over the papacy by securing control over his national church. These were all signs of the breakdown of Christendom. The towns were led by a rising middle class that became wealthy along with its bourgeois citizens. This middle class became a dominant force in society and was able to patronize art. This secular spirit in art was manifested in the rise of vernacular literature, increasing popularity of secular music, and the rise of literary themes that questioned the low status of women. Painting and sculpture began to be liberated from having to be at the service of architecture. Giotto and Italian and Flemish artists began this change. In Italy, painting will be completely free from architecture's tutelage and become the most important artistic genre in the West during the Renaissance.

SUMMARY

Early Medieval Western civilization is a product of the merger between the ancient Greco-Roman culture, with the Christian culture of the Late Roman Empire, and the new addition of the Germanic cultures of the Barbarians from northern Europe. This new civilization will be centered in Europe rather than the Mediterranean basin beginning in the reign of Charlemagne.

Christian medieval philosophy, also known as scholasticism, will apply reason to revelation. It attempted to explain revelation from the Bible using logic derived from Greek philosophy. The scholastics developed a synthesis of Christian revelation with Greek thought. Reason is used to serve the faith that is the ultimate standard of truth and authority. Aristotle's work will be of great influence upon Scholastic thinkers.

The most famous and influential scholastic theologian was Saint Thomas Aquinas (1225–1274) who combined Aristotelian reason with Christian revelation. His greatest work is the *Summa Theologica,* a systematic explanation of Christian thought. Saint Thomas divided revealed truth into two categories that are the beliefs whose truth can be demonstrated by reason, and beliefs that reason cannot prove as true or false. In other words, many truths can be demonstrated to be valid using only rational arguments, but there were some truths that reason could not be used to argue for or against their validity such as that God is eternal with no beginning and no end or that God has three persons, Father, Son, and Holy Spirit. The latter has to be accepted by faith alone and is revealed to man by God because there is no rational explanation to sustain them. For Saint Thomas, faith and reason do not contradict each other, they complement each other. Men have to allow faith to guide reason because the doctrines of faith are infallible. Human reason can make mistakes, and must come into harmony with the teaching of the faith. Saint Thomas used Aristotelian thought with divine revelation in a manner that both complemented each other. He brought reason and faith together, but not as equals because reason had to be in support of faith and Church which are the ultimate authority. Saint Thomas affirmed that knowledge of the Earthly world has value and man should study both nature and man, and religion. Therefore, the great scholastic changed the tradition of Saint Augustine in that the spiritual or the city of Heaven is what had value, and Earth or the city of man was in opposition to the spiritual realm as well as an obstacle to true knowledge. Thus, Plato had an influence upon Saint Augustine and Aristotle upon Saint Thomas Aquinas.

The sixth and seventh centuries were a chaotic period after the fall of the Western Roman Empire. The new civilization that rose, Latin Christendom, was the product of the intermingling of the Greco-Roman civilization, Christian religion, and Germanic traditions. The Church led by the pope in Rome is the only surviving functioning institution after Rome fell and the dominant institution of the Middle Ages. The Church by its teachings shaped the values and outlook of Western Europe. By the 10th century all aspects of Western European culture and institutions were in harmony with the Church's teachings, and its Christian faith was vigorous. The Church was the unifying and civilizing agent. Its monasteries preserved the achievements of the Greco-Roman civilization, patronized the arts and it was the clergy and monks who could read and wrote books in an era when most of the population was illiterate. The medieval worldview was God-centered. The good life focused on the spiritual where salvation had more importance than the material world. Religion gave the individual a hope for salvation, and made life and death purposeful and intelligible. The faith was a central element of life for all of society. By the High Middle Ages a new balance in Western European culture had been achieved based on Christian belief guided by the Church.

Medieval society was made up by three hierarchical classes. The clergy was the highest class because its duty was guiding society in the spiritual life and dispensing the sacraments. The clergy had a hierarchy consisting of three levels, the pope, bishops, and priests. Spiritual guidance and leading souls to their salvation were the functions of this class. They also ran the schools, providing education, and ran the hospitals, providing public health. These services to society exempted the Church from paying taxes. The nobility was the second social class in importance with a hierarchical structure, usually the king as head of state. Their duty was defense of their lands and its population, and served as judges, police, and civil government. These functions exempt this class from paying taxes, but they paid taxes over the goods they purchased. The common folk, or commoners, produced agricultural and industrial goods and was involved in commerce. This class also did intellectual work, for example university professors. This class received the benefits of the service provided by the two upper classes and therefore paid taxes.

Feudalism was an economic, political, and military system that established itself in Western Europe after the fall of the Roman Empire and Barbarian invasions. In an era without strong national governments, economies, and armies, it was local warlords who were able to fill the void and provide for local government and security of the region. It was based on a feudal contract between lord and vassal. The lord or king that owned the land gave it to another warrior that became his vassal in exchange for loyalty and military service to their lord. The lord committed himself to defend his vassals if it became necessary, and vassals to come to the lord's service if called upon. The serfs or peasants bound to the land received land to farm and were able to provide for their families, and received protection from the local lord in exchange for their manual labor of the agricultural lands. This feudal system met the needs of all members of society during this era, because it provided a basic form of local government and security from invasion.

The justification of this medieval order was found in the principle of proportionality that consisted in a harmonious relationship between the different social classes that allowed for the respect of human dignity of all members of society. This is easily understood when medieval society is compared with societies from antiquity. In ancient Egypt and Mesopotamia, for example, kings and pharaohs were considered divine with absolute authority and men were only servile beings to obey and serve these monarchs and their gods. This is disproportionality. In medieval proportionality there is the example of kings such as Saint Ferdinand of Castile who sat by a window where any commoner from the street could come and speak freely to his king and make petitions. Another example is the comparison between Roman slaves during antiquity and feudal serfs. Slaves had no rights and were considered an object, not a person by Roman law. The owner even had a right to life or death of his slaves, and slaves had no right over his family. Medieval Europe was the first in history to eliminate slavery. The serf was not a free man, being bound to the land, but had complete right over his family, right to marriage, right to his home, and enough land to provide for his needs. The serf could only be punished according to the law, not the whims of the lord as it was in antiquity. The slave lacked human dignity, while the serf was treated with dignity and was protected.

With the development of cities, industries, and trade, corporations or guilds were created where craftsmen united within their craft to promote trade and create better working and living conditions for its members. Their members were free men with many rights, their own laws, and ran their neighborhoods.

Common people made law because their customs and practices were made into law. Kings had them written into legal codes. There was judicial autonomy with independent courts and judges. The decentralized governments and the independence that cities had to elect their own authorities and govern themselves allowed regionalism to develop. Regionalism is the development of the customs and traditions of each region and cities. It is the reason why Europe enjoys today a vast cultural richness in each nation. In this manner medieval monarchies were organic, not autocratic, with a balance between the ruling monarchs and the nobility in harmonious cooperation with local inhabitants and their democratic practices and laws.

In this era of Christian faith medieval civilization had a sacred character. Sacredness means that all of society is ordered to be in harmony with God and the teachings of the Church. Human activity was directed toward giving glory to God and thus it is found expressed in the cathedrals and churches, laws, lifestyles, customs and traditions, arts, literature, etc. Western Europe became by the High Middle Ages a family of brotherly people united around the Church led by the pope; this is known as Christendom. The highest end of the state was to serve and protect the Church. The Middle Ages was the era when the philosophy of the Bible governed the states.

The Roman church played a key role in building Western civilization and brought progress in many fields. The clergy made up most of the educated sector of the population, which is the reason why many scientists of the period were priests. These clergymen engaged in scientific practices that contributed to the progress of science with their discoveries. The Church created schools and developed the university system that is a medieval invention. The monasteries were centers of learning and industry, their libraries preserved knowledge, and technology was developed such as machines run by water and wind. This was the beginning of mechanization. These inventions then spread to the rest of society that brought great progress. The Church was the force of progress that set the basis from which later the scientific and industrial revolution emerged. In sum, the positive contributions of the medieval Church outweighed the negative elements due to the flaw of the men who ran this religious institution.

The medieval civilization will begin to decline, its cultural balance will come into crisis beginning in the 14th century. First came a power struggle for the papacy known as the Babylonian Captivity. The French king Philip wanted to tax the Church to finance his war with England and when Pope Boniface VIII prohibited the Church to pay taxes to the crown the French king had the pope kidnapped. After Boniface's death King Philip exerted his influence to have a French Archbishop elected pope, Clement V, who moved to Avignon, France, and governed the Church from France. Rome was the pope's city and governed by the pope. In Avignon he was in French territory governed by the French monarchy. Therefore, the French monarchy influenced the papacy. This conflict brought a loss of prestige to the papacy and weakened the unity of Christendom as other kings would also want to have their "pope."

After the Babylonian Captivity ended, the Great Schism from 1378 to 1417 divided the Church when the French cardinals disgruntled with the new pope who criticized their lavish lifestyle elected a second pope of their liking and moved out of Rome. This created a crisis of two popes claiming to be the legitimate head of the Church, and different monarchs supported both Roman and French popes according to their interests. This crisis reduced the respect and trust of the papacy and the Church's spiritual needs were neglected in the power struggle.

The rise of nationalism shattered the unity of Christendom as men placed their first loyalty to their country and not to the Church. This led to wars among Christian nations against each other as the Hundred Years War between France and England. The Black Death that ravaged Western Europe in the 14th century created a mood of despair with a loss of trust and hope in God and the Church. The Church was weakened with the loss of the morally upright clergy and nuns who died attending the sick. Finally the Renaissance contributed to put an end to the spirit and God-centered thinking of the High Middle Ages. Some men began to admire the Greco-Roman world and with a secular attitude began to reject the teaching and values of the Church. They valued classical culture and were critical of medieval Christian civilization. It shifted the medieval God-centered worldview for a man-centered worldview, regarding Christian cultures as inferior to classical civilization, and placing their trust on human reason, not on faith as the ultimate wisdom and authority. Not all men of the Renaissance held this attitude and they remained faithful to the Christian faith and did not reject medieval culture. These Christians of the Renaissance combined Christian ideals with classical subjects to embellish the former. The Reformation in the 16th century divided Western Europe into two distinct religious groups, and this ended the medieval unity of Christendom.

The one thousand year period known as the Middle Ages can be divided into Early (500–1000), High (1000–1300), and Late Middle Ages (1300–1500). The literature of the early period blended Christian ideas with Greco-Roman classical thought. Writers conserved the past rather than produce original works. Gregorian chants with its monophonic sound became the official liturgical music. Illuminated manuscripts make up most of the paintings that have survived from this period. The art, architecture, and literature of the High Middle Ages reached a very high level of achievement in a spirit of glorifying God and harmony with the Church's teachings. Romanesque and Gothic churches become the architectural achievements of the age. Romanesque buildings give an impression of massive strength, with small windows and fortress-like appearance. Gothic architecture was a development from the Romanesque created by the French abbot Suger. For Suger, light represented God and Heaven and therefore he wanted light to fill in the interior of the church. Large windows with stained glass and very high ceilings were the key features of Gothic architectures that required new innovations such as the external and flying buttresses, pointed arches, and ever higher buildings. These buildings were highly decorated externally and internally with sculpture both of stone and wood, internal woodworks, and large colorful stained glass windows. These gothic cathedrals were built primarily for the glory of God and an inspiration for men to live their faith and attain salvation. It was seen as a place of union between Heaven and Earth. Its artworks were created as a means to teach the faithful who were mostly illiterate and embellish the house of God.

High gothic painting is found in manuscript illuminations. Literature first expressed the feudal and monastic values of the Early Middle Ages during the Romanesque art period. Monks wrote poetry in Latin about themes of religious and moral topics. Lay poets developed a new literary genre, the chanson de geste or song of brave deeds, written in the popular spoken language. The theme was the heroic adventures of warriors like France's Emperor Charlemagne. The second period during the Gothic style introduced urban and courtly themes written in the popular spoken languages of vernacular. Love poems were sung by minstrels in the educated feudal courts addressing court ladies who became the object of chivalrous knight's passionate ideal love. Romances became popular that narrated chivalric and sentimental adventures of knights and ladies. King Arthur and his knights of the round table is a good example. Dante's poem *The Divine Comedy* became one of the most famous literary works of this period and stands as the culmination of literature of the Middle Ages. Dante's main concerns in this poem is salvation and to bring harmony between the Church and the secular state.

In music composers laid the foundations of modern musical composition by combining separate voices in a harmonious manner. Innovations such as the music staff modernized musical notation and is used to the present date.

During the Late Middle Ages there was a trend toward the secular and new groups, the aristocrats of the courts and the urban middle class, began to supplant the nobility and the clergy as patron and audiences for the arts. Books became available to the general public with the invention of the Gutenberg printing press allowing for greater dissemination of ideas and literature in the local language. The printing of a large volume of books with this printing innovation was possible because there was a substantial portion of the population that was literate due to the educational achievements of the Church that created the schools and universities. Gothic style architecture continued to dominate, but the balance of High Gothic was being replaced with a highly ornate and extravagant Late Gothic style. Elaborate and luxuriant decorations are a major characteristic of this style. With new patrons the themes of paintings become more secular. Giotto and other Italian painters discovered new ways to paint human figures in a more realistic manner with dramatic tension. Giotto's paintings established a new direction in Western art.

HOW CHRISTIANITY LED TO FREEDOM, CAPITALISM, AND WESTERN SUCCESS

During the 16th century when Europeans began to explore the globe, they became aware of their own technological superiority over the rest of the world they came into contact with. The Mayan, Aztec, Inca empires, China, India, and the Islamic world were backward compared to 16th-century Europe. How had the nations that had risen out of the fall of the Roman Empire and barbarism greatly advanced surpassing the rest of the world? Why had the Western world excelled in farming, science, metallurgy, shipbuilding, mechanical instruments, and weapons?

Western progress and dominance was due to the rise of **capitalism** that only happened in Europe. This rise of capitalism is due to a great faith in **reason.** This development of reason that gave Europe a unique shape to its culture and institutions occurred within **Christianity.** Only Christianity embraced reason and logic as the primary way to religious truth. Christian faith in reason was the influence from Greek philosophy when Christianity preserved and incorporated the rational Greco-Roman thought. The other world religions put their emphasis on myths, mystery, and intuition, which kept its followers in a frame of mind that depended on logical contradictions and ambiguity that were considered a sacred element. From the early Christian fathers onward the Church taught reason was created by God and given to man, and is what makes man superior to animals. Therefore, mankind was destined to employ human reason and it was a means to progressively increase man's understanding of the Bible. This lead Christianity to be oriented toward the future because its outlook was to use reason to progress in its understanding of God's revelation, and this reasoning could be used in other fields allowing for man to understand his world in a rational manner and use this knowledge to better his earthly life. In contrast, other major religions affirmed the superiority of the past, in that they were oriented toward myth, tradition, meditation, and intellectually examining their thoughts and feelings. In principle Christian doctrine could be developed when it was demonstrated by reason allowing for progress, rather than a purely literal understanding of religious doctrine to be applied as a law which anchors interpretations on the past. The scholastics and the great medieval universities of Europe which were founded by the church fostered faith in the power of reason to penetrate Western culture, which stimulated the pursuit of science and the evolution of democratic theory and practice. Reason inspired by the church led to the rise of capitalism, because capitalism is basically the systematic and sustained application of reason to commerce which first occurred in the medieval monasteries. All this demonstrates that religious ideas played a determining role in the rise of capitalism in Europe that allowed progress to occur.

Theology can be explained as the formal reasoning about God. It focuses on discovering God's nature, intentions, and His will for mankind, and understanding how all this define the relationship between humans and God. God is central, and therefore theology needs a concept of God as a supernatural being, conscious, rational with unlimited power over the universe that cares about humans and imposes a moral code, and responsibilities on men. This results in man asking serious questions that require the use of his intellectual abilities to answer questions such as: Why did God create mankind? What is the purpose of life? Why does God allow evil? When do humans acquire a soul? For centuries theologians have been reasoning what God really meant in scripture. Reason became the means to gain greater understanding in God's revelation and will. An example is astrology and how men should regard it. The Bible does not condemn astrology, and even the birth of Christ has the three wise men or kings following a bright star to find Jesus. This could be understood that astrology is valid. But St. Augustine reasoned that astrology is false because God gave man a free will to determine his life, and if astrology were valid then men's fate would be determined by the stars and planets and not their will. Astrology stands in opposition of God's gift of free will to man. The church did prohibit astrology. What the theologian is achieving is not adding or changing scripture, but by careful deductive reasoning he is developing new doctrines to explain and support scripture. The scholastics and the universities during the Middle Ages ensured that reason ruled in Western man's theology and thought.

As Jesus did not write anything during His life on Earth, from the very beginning the early church fathers were forced to use reason to deduct what the New Testament contained but is not directly expressed. From this time Christian theologians assumed that the use of reason can allow man to have a greater and better understanding of the will of God. St. Augustine believed in theological progress when he said that certain matters of the doctrine of salvation were not grasped during his time, but one day man will be able to do so. He also valued material progress in that he saw as positive the many arts and inventions of man due to necessity as well as to man's creativity, such as weaving, engineering, agriculture and navigation. Here we find a positive attitude to progress in theology as well as science and technology. In St. Thomas Aquinas with his *Summa Theologica* the climax of Christian progress is reached through rationality. Aquinas held the position that due to man's lack of sufficient knowledge to understand completely the essence of things, it is necessary for humans to use reason to attain knowledge, step by step. What the scholastics were achieving was progressively reasoning out the will of God, and this could be done if the Bible is not only to be understood literally. An exclusive literal interpretation does not allow for using reason, and only what the scriptures state word for word must be accepted as definite.

The Christian image of God is that He is a rational being who allows for human progress and reveals himself more fully as humans improve their capacity to understand by the use of reason. Because God is a rational being who created the universe, His universe operates under a rational, lawful and stable structure. Therefore, humans can come to understand the natural laws that govern nature through reason. This is of very great importance because this belief is the key to many intellectual enterprises, among them **science** which is necessary for material progress.

The Western civilization's progress is not possible without **science,** which contains the knowledge to develop technology to meet man's needs and improve life. It is important to understand precisely what is "**real** science" or what we can call a "complete" concept of science. Its definition is that real science is a method used in organized efforts to express in orderly and systematical way explanations of nature that can be modified and corrected through systematical observations. Therefore, real science has two components that are **theory** and **research.** The theory is the explanation of any phenomena, that explains or answers the questions *why* and *how* an aspect of nature fits together and works. Theories are mostly abstract statements. Research is the systematic observations about the definite empirical predictions derived from science's abstract statements. Thus, research is the observation (experiments) to determine if the theory's abstract statements are true or occur as predicted by the theory. Therefore, science is limited to statements about our material reality that can be observed. There are dimensions of life or realities that science is not able to prove or disprove, because they are outside of the material reality, such as who created the universe, the existence of God and the soul, etc. Thus, science has its limits. Science is also an organized effort in that science does not happen by chance, random discovery, or in complete isolation. It is a result of communication of knowledge from different eras, countries, and scientists. Scientists, even when working alone, use previous scientific knowledge and many form a part of networks and institutions.

Science is not only technology. A society can build ships, tools, weapons, porcelain, cloth, etc., but does not have real science unless it develops theory and research. Real science is in a category that requires theorizing and empirical (experimental) observations. The two must be present. It can be called "modern science." Not until the Middle Ages did these two elements coexists to bring about a true science that has continued to progress to our present date. Before this time efforts to explain and control the material world were lacking on all or one of these essential elements. The progress that mankind achieved from ancient times was the result of observation and of trial and error without the theorizing or explanations. And when they came up with theories to explain nature it was non-empirical because they were not observable. Therefore the technical innovations of the Greco-Roman world, of Islam and China can be better defined as knowledge, technologies, techniques, skills, or engineering due to their lack of theory. These ancient peoples made astronomical observations, but not having testable theories to explain these observations they were only facts.

We have stated previously that the intellectual achievements of the Greek philosophers, who taught us how to think rationally, have been described by many as having invented science or rational explanations for natural phenomenon and material reality. But in reality these ingenious thinkers did not invent real science because their empirical achievements were without theoretical explanations, and their theorizing was not empirical or observable through experimentation. Their theories do not qualify as true science because they lack observable consequences. Democritus with his atomic theory is a good example. He proposed that all matter is made of atoms. His theory was mere speculation which was not observable. He had no means at his disposal to conduct experiments to prove that all matter was composed of atoms, nor even to see an atom or what are its components. It was not *scientific* atomic theory without the corresponding research, and the fact that later modern science demonstrated that his theory was correct was just a coincidence. Democritus was only guessing or speculating, with no way to prove his theory. In the same situation was Aristotle who also speculated that all matter was made up of heat, cold, moisture, dryness, and quintessence, and Empedocles who guessed that all matter was composed of fire, air, water, and earth, but it turned out that modern science disproves these statements.

The reason real science only begins in Europe after antiquity is related to the concept that man has of God. Medieval Western Europe infused in Western man the belief that the universe has a secret which can be unveiled, a belief essential to the scientific movement of the West. The medieval theologian and scientist Nicole d'Oresme said that God's creation is similar to a man who makes a clock winding it into motion and the clock continues its own motion by itself. This concept, well-engrained in the mind of Western men, comes from the medieval concept that God is rational and thus created a universe that functions under laws that can be discovered using reason. This faith in the possibility of science, that "science could and should be done" originates from medieval theology. Religion inspired men to attempt to comprehend God's creation which resulted in discovering new knowledge. To achieve full comprehension it is necessary to explain any reality, and only real science can offer this kind of explanation. Therefore, science becomes the spinoff of theology. Science with its rational method becomes the means by which man can unravel the "secrets" that God used to set it in motion or function. The great Western scientists of the 15th and 16th centuries, men like Newton, Kepler, Galileo, and Descartes saw the universe as a book to be read and comprehended (Figures 7.1, 7.2, 7.3). They understood that the universe functioned under natural laws because God its creator is perfect and He acts in a manner that is constant and unchanging, except in the few cases where He intervenes directly violating these natural laws. These exceptions are known as miracles.

Alchemy and the science of chemistry is a good example of how only in the West real or modern science developed. Alchemy was well developed in the Greco-Roman world, in Islam, China, India, Mesopotamia, and Egypt, but only in Europe was it developed into the modern science of chemistry. Alchemy consists of the search to develop certain substances that produced unusual properties such as the creation of a panacea or the elixir of life, a remedy that supposedly would cure all diseases and prolong life indefinitely; the transmutation of common metals into gold and silver; and the discovery of a universal solvent that would dissolve all substances including precious metals. Alchemy is also a part of the occult tradition, which is both a philosophy and a practice with an aim of achieving ultimate wisdom as well as immortality, involving the improvement of the alchemist. Since the Middle Ages Arabic and European alchemists made great efforts to find the philosopher's stone, a legendary substance that was believed to be an essential ingredient or mystic key for creating gold from base metals and the elixir of life for rejuvenation or immortality. The philosopher's stone was believed to mystically amplify the user's knowledge of alchemy so much that anything was attainable. The alchemists were employing metaphysics and theories with no research or experiments to support them such as the theory from the Greeks, India, China, and Japan that matter was composed of the five classical elements: earth, water, air, fire, and aether (a non-material substance), and by the 8th-century Arab alchemist Geber who theorized that every metal was a combination of the four principles or qualities of hotness, coldness, dryness, and moisture. How could alchemy develop into a real science with this kind of approach and belief? It could not unless it was based on rational theories supported by reliable research or observations that demonstrate their validity. Alchemy's metaphysical aspect or spiritual philosophy was out of the scope of science because science can only be employed to explain material realities, and this aspect of alchemy also was in conflict with doctrine of the church during the Middle Ages. The only practical aspect of this discipline was the mundane contributions to the chemical industries of the day such as ore testing and refining, metalworking, ink, dyes, paints, cosmetics, ceramics, glass manufacture, liquors, etc. Due to the rational mind of the Christian man, only in Europe did alchemy develop into the science of chemistry. Chemistry is the scientific study of the composition, structure, properties, and reaction of matter. It is based on theories or explanations validated by observable experiments, and only deals with the physical world, not the metaphysical and spiritual.

To summarize this concept, the development of real or modern science does not derive from Greco-Roman learning, or from other non-Christian civilizations. It is a spinoff of Christian doctrine since the

Figure 7.1   Isaac Newton. *Image Copyright Nicku/Shutterstock.com.*

Figure 7.2   Rene Descartes (1596–1650). *Image Copyright Georgios Kollidas/ Shutterstock.com.*

Middle Ages that believed and understood that nature was created by God. To be able to love and honor God it is necessary to appreciate completely the wonders of the universe, His handiwork. Because Christian men believed that God is perfect, it was logical that they understood that His creation functioned in harmony with unchanging principles. As God had given man the use of reason and the ability to observe nature, making full use of this capacity would make it possible for humans to discover these immutable principles or rational rules. These decisive ideas explain why modern science only was developed in Christian Europe and not in antiquity and nonwestern civilizations.

Freedom is an essential element in the rise of capitalism. Therefore, to have a functioning vigorous capitalism Europeans had to accept the values of **individualism, freedom,** and **human rights.** Western man's belief in individualism was mainly a value originating from Christianity. A basic tenant of Christianity is that sin is a personal matter, thus the individual is responsible for his actions and not anyone else or the community. Christianity upholds the doctrine of free will,

Figure 7.3 Galileo Galilei (1564–1642). *Image Copyright Georgios Kollidas/ Shutterstock.com.*

that God grants man reason to understand and thus to determine his own actions deciding to do God's will or go against it. St. Augustine wrote this clearly that man possesses a will of his own and is free to act accordingly. St. Thomas Aquinas also taught that humans are free to make moral choices and thus are responsible for their decisions. Because the church believed in free will of man, it found the institution of slavery incompatible with Christian doctrine. If men have free will and an immortal soul given by God, and all men were destined to be saved, then it was not morally justifiable that some men were the property of others. Jesus never spoke about or accepted slavery or had any slaves. The Church during the Middle Ages came to the conclusion that slavery is sinful, which is unique in Christianity. Even if the Bible allowed slavery (with humane treatment of slaves) only Christian theologians were able to bring new interpretations of scripture allowing for society to progress. Through the church's influence slavery ended in Western Europe during the Middle Ages.

Capitalism began in the Italian city-states then spread to the cities of medieval Western Europe that offered sufficient freedom from feudal lords. The preexisting feudal system did not provide for founding of cities. Under feudalism life was organized in the rural areas under a network of mutual obligations between lord and vassals and serfs. As trade evolved as an urban activity and towns grew into cities, the merchants who resided in them came to resent the taxes and having to follow the will of the local lords who were of no benefit to trade. They organized into guilds to resist the local rulers. Gradually the towns began to go over the local rulers and appeal to the superior lord who usually was distant from the town or city. The city dwellers offered favors and support to distant lords or the king in exchange for more favorable conditions than the local lords allowed. A good example is in 1073 when Henry IV as emperor of Germany had a conflict with the church, the citizens of Worms went against their bishop and supported the emperor. Henry IV in gratitude made Worms an independent city. With time there were 85 free cities that had control of their government and elected their own council. Thus, the urban population by being able to elect their members to govern were introducing democracy, and feudalism no longer applied in cities where a serf who came to town and lived for a year and a day became free of all feudal obligation to his lord. The free cities paid a fee to the monarch who provided protection from interference of local rulers who could no longer impose taxes and confiscate the wealth of its citizens. In England due to the Magna Charta in 1215 that lords and bishops imposed upon King John, enjoyed freedom in all the land, cities, and rural areas greater that the rest of Europe. The Magna Charta established that the church shall be free of royal dominion, and that London and all the cities, towns, and ports will have their liberties and be free from duties and taxes upon trade. Also all merchants will be free to travel and do business throughout England (Figure 7.4). Thus England enjoyed individual freedom and secure property rights more than any other nation in Europe. Industry was able to establish itself in cities as well as rural areas which made English industries decentralized. This being a major reason why the industrial revolution begins in England, and in reality rather than a revolution it is an evolution of a process that began in the Middle Ages with freedoms and securities, and the technological innovations that were possible and profitable. This freedom to trade and knowing that private property is secure is what attracts commerce and men are willing to invest their resources and money to increase production to attain greater wealth (Figure 7.5). Without this freedom and security of private property capitalism cannot develop and provide the greater wealth and progress.

Capitalism can be defined as an economic system where private well-organized firms operate commercial activities in a stable manner within a free or unregulated market, and then invests and reinvests wealth in productive activities in the expectation to increase wealth or returns in the long run. Thus private initiative, taking the risk to invest capital and resources to attain greater wealth down the road, with the freedom to trade and make decisions, and security that the investment and profits will not be overtaxed or taken away are all essential elements for capitalism to develop and prosper. Free labor is also necessary

Figure 7.4 People at marketplace. With medieval large urban populations and commerce began in Western Europe. *Image © Jupiter Images.*

Figure 7.5 A medieval city of northern Europe. This scene of medieval houses along cobblestone streets became common by the late Middle Ages all over Western Europe. As commerce and trade developed, many people came to live in cities and learn a trade to provide goods and services which rose their standard of living. In these typical houses, they set up shop on the ground floor where they would open a shutter or window to show their goods to the public. The upper floors are where the family of the owner, apprentices, and workers lived. *Image Copyright Andreas Meyer, 2009. Used under license from Shutterstock, Inc.*

to be able to attract the skilled and motivated workers necessary for the highly productive enterprises. The church played a major role in the beginning of capitalism when it began to appear in the 9th century. The monasteries were communities that sustained themselves entirely. They became very efficient centers of production of agricultural and industrial products. The monasteries used and elaborated many innovations that increased their productivity, such as the moldboard plow moved by a horse with proper harness and metal horse shoes, and machinery that employed water or the wind as their source of power. These religious centers of production became large wealthy estates that many came to specialize in one or a few products and generate enough income to purchase all other items that were needed, thus creating a cash economy that supplanted a barter economy. Technological innovations such as the water and wind mill which spread all over Europe were an important element that enabled capitalism to be very productive. Historically, capitalism has been the most productive and progressive of all economical systems that motivates investors and labor to produce more, and explains why the West has attained progress and the highest standard of living in the world.

For capitalism to rise in Europe it was necessary that Christianity allowed theological progress through continuing reappraisal of doctrine and its interpretation, in order to overcome opposition to interests and profits from scripture. **Interest** and **profits** are a central element of capitalism, because without them the motivation to produce, trade, and lend money would be eliminated. The result would be the stifling of the development of capitalism. Deuteronomy 23:19 and Luke 6:34–35 from the Bible were understood as opposition to interest which was also considered usury. By the 13th century Catholic theologians declared that interest and profits were morally legitimate, and therefore established a harmonious relation between religion that govern society's conscience and capitalism. Usury, loans on excessive interest rates, was condemned and defined as sinful. St. Thomas Aquinas supported commercial profits when he declared that the just price of things is based on the buyer's desire to purchase and the seller to sell, as long as there is no misleading of the buyer, no price discrimination (offering different prices to different buyers) and the buyer is not under duress. The theologians are respecting the market forces of supply and demand. Many found situations and exceptions where interest charges were not usury. Money lending was practiced both by religious men and secular capitalists. Thus many monastic houses were able to make profits on their products and lend money at interests according to the market rate. During the high Middle Ages the morality of commerce was well-established due to a theology that was willing to analyze scripture in a way that allowed for progress and capitalism was free from religious restraint that resulted in the medieval Commercial Revolution.

Only in Christian Europe do all these series of essential elements combine to bring progress to the West. A *rational theology* that believes in *human progress* and *individual freedom* of all men, the development of *modern science, freedom of commerce* and security of *private property* from rapacious rulers, *technological innovations,* and rise of *capitalism*. All this put together is not found in other religions and civilizations.

The conditions that allowed Europe to emerge as the most progressive civilization did not exist in antiquity nor in other civilizations that existed after that period. Two of these civilizations, traditional Jews and Muslims, put their emphasis on the law to be understood and applied when following scripture, thus interpreting it on precedent and thus have an outlook anchored it the past, and concerned mainly with the correct practice of law and regulations. Judaism being an exception, the other great world religions conceived history as an endless cycle that repeats itself. Islam sees it as a decline due to Muhammad's statement that the best generation is my generation, then the one that follows it, and then the next and so on. The notion of humanity's progress is absent. Islam sees God as the creator of the universe, but it is not functioning on natural laws laid down by God during its creation, and assumes that the universe is sustained by God's will on a continuing basis. So why put great effort to discover God's natural laws? Muslim philosophers in the 12th century became fixed on Aristotle's ideas, declaring that his physics was complete and infallible, and any contrary observation was wrong. This mindset only allowed the Islamic world to advance in specific knowledge of certain aspects in different fields such as medicine and astronomy, but not in real science. The Qur'an condemns all interest on borrowed money which puts restraints on capitalism. Islam has problems when it comes to theological condemnations of slavery because Muhammad bought, sold, and owned slaves, advising that slaves be treated humanely, which does not foster the freedoms necessary for a complete progress. Buddhists, Confucianists, and Hindus view history as regressive and that later generations are prone to error in relation to their founders and sages. That their founders and sages had limited understanding of religious truths is not acceptable and considered heresy, resulting that no further interpretations can be made and everything must be explained according to what has been established in the past. This leads to a mindset oriented to the past and not to progress into the future. Chinese philosophers think the universe always existed and there is no reason to believe it functions under natural laws and therefore comprehended physically. They try to understand the world mystically searching to be enlightened and not searching for rational and logical explanations. The Chinese did not have a concept of a God that created a universe under operating laws, they rather believe in godless religions in which the supernatural is conceived as an impersonal principle that governs life such as Tao. They do not see science as being possible. It is clear that the progress such as the West developed lacks the fundamental elements in these civilizations. Those civilizations today that have Western progress are because they borrowed it from the West.

Today many Western intellectuals have a negative regard for Christian theology, and many see an inherent conflict between religion and science, as if the Scientific Revolution of 16th-century Europe was the triumph of science over religion when man began to think in secular terms. We have seen that this is far from the truth. The progress and new development in science and technology that came after the Middle Ages was nothing more than the continuation of several centuries of systematic progress by medieval Scholastic theologians, monasteries, universities, and capitalist entrepreneurs, in all aspects of life that included religion, philosophy, art, music, architecture, science, technological innovations, and commerce. During this period of history European technology and science surpassed the rest of the world. It is incorrect to think that since the fall of the Roman Empire European Christian civilization remained backward and since the 16th century all of a sudden man putting gradually aside religion began to make progress to this date. This view of Western history conceives the Middle Ages in Europe as the "Dark Ages" submerged in ignorance, religious fanaticism, superstition, and human misery, until it was miraculously rescued by the 16th-century Renaissance and 18th-century Enlightenment also known as the Illustration. This concept that the Greco-Roman world was superior to what came after the fall or the Roman Empire and then it was revived in the Renaissance period, thus the term Middle Age for the era between (in the middle) the Roman Empire and the new Renaissance, was created by the intellectuals of the 16th-century Renaissance. Then the idea that during the Middle Ages Europe fell into the Dark Ages is a falsehood originated by antireligious and bitterly anti-Catholic intellectuals of the 18th-century Enlightenment who declared the cultural superiority of their own time that only accepted what was explained solely by science in a rational manner, thus the term the "Age of Reason" for this period, and rejected Christian religion and its traditions as superstitions and retrograde. Therefore, the Middle Ages being an age of Christian faith was denigrated and described by one of its most famous philosopher, Voltaire (1694–1778), as an era of barbarism, superstition, and ignorance that covered the world. Voltaire's motto was "Écrasez l'infame!" or "Crush the infamous thing," "thing" referred to the Catholic Church. After the French Revolution, the Western world was influenced by this ideological movement and the myth and term of the Dark Ages was accepted as an historical fact. It is still part of our culture, and even in recent time historians and intellectuals that have done research demonstrating it is a myth, many Western scholars continue to think all the Middle Ages was a "Dark Age."

Western success in all fields is due to firm establishment of reason as a central element of its culture and mindset. The church inspired society in the power of reason and that progress was possible. Its doctrine created a new world based on personal, political, and economic freedom. It can be concluded that the rise of Christianity was the most important single event in European history that led to progress of the Western civilization.

SUMMARY

The rise of capitalism is due to a great faith in **reason**. This development of reason that gave Europe a unique shape to its culture and institutions occurred within **Christianity**. Only Christianity embraced reason and logic as the primary way to religious truth. Christian faith in reason was the influence from Greek philosophy when Christianity preserved and incorporated the rational Greco-Roman thought. God gave man reason, therefore, mankind was destined to employ human reason and it was a means to progressively increase man's understanding of the Bible. This led Christianity to be oriented toward the future because its outlook was to use reason to progress in its understanding of God's revelation, and this reasoning could be used in other fields allowing for man to understand his world in a rational manner and use this knowledge to better his earthly life.

The Christian image of God is that He is a rational being who allows for human progress and reveals himself more fully as humans improve their capacity to understand by the use of reason. Because God is a rational being who created the universe, His universe operates under a rational, lawful, and stable structure. Therefore, humans can come to understand the natural laws that govern nature through reason. This is of very great importance because this belief is the key to many intellectual enterprises, among them **science** which is necessary for material progress.

Western civilization's progress is not possible without **science**, which contains the knowledge to develop technology to meet man's needs and improve life. The development of real or modern science does not derive from Greco-Roman learning, nor from other non-Christian civilizations. It is a spin-off of Christian doctrine since the Middle Ages that believed and understood that nature was created by God. To be able to love and honor God it is necessary to appreciate completely the wonders of the universe, His handiwork. Because Christian men believed that God is perfect, it was logical that they understood that His creation functioned in harmony with unchanging principles. As God had given man the use of reason and the ability to observe nature, making full use of this capacity would make it possible for humans to discover these immutable principles or rational rules. These decisive ideas explain why modern science only was developed in Christian Europe and not in antiquity and nonwestern civilizations.

Freedom is an essential element in the rise of capitalism. Therefore, to have a functioning vigorous capitalism Europeans had to accept the values of **individualism**, **freedom**, and **human rights**. Western man's belief in individualism was mainly a value originating from Christianity.

Capitalism began in the Italian city-states then spread to the cities of medieval Western Europe that offered sufficient freedom from feudal lords. The church played a major role in the beginning of capitalism when it began to appear in the 9th century. The monasteries were communities that sustained themselves entirely. They became very efficient centers of production of agricultural and industrial products. The monasteries used and elaborated many innovations that increased their productivity.

Only in Christian Europe does all these series of essential elements combine to bring progress of the West. A rational theology that believes in human progress and individual freedom of all men, the development of modern science, freedom of commerce, and security of private property from rapacious rulers, technological innovations, and rise of capitalism. All this is not found in other religions and civilizations.

Capitalism can be defined as an economic system where private, well-organized firms operate commercial activities in a stable manner within a free or unregulated market, and they invest and reinvest wealth in productive activities in the expectation to increase wealth or returns in the long run. Thus private initiative, taking the risk to invest capital and resources to attain greater wealth down the road, with the freedom to trade and make decisions, and security that the investment and profits will not be overtaxed or taken away are all essential elements for capitalism to develop and prosper. Free labor is also necessary to be able to attract the skilled and motivated workers necessary for the highly productive enterprises.

THE RENAISSANCE

The **Renaissance** was a cultural movement that spanned roughly the 14th to the 17th century, begin-ning in Italy in the Late Middle Ages and later spreading to the rest of Europe. The term is also used more loosely to refer to the historic era, but since the changes of the Renaissance were not uniform across Europe, this is a general use of the term. The Renaissance profoundly affected European intellectual life in the early modern period. It gradually changed the emphasis of medieval Christendom on eternal sal-vation in the afterlife as the most important purpose of human existence to the idea that life on Earth had its own worth and that the life of each individual was unique and valuable. Man having worth and free will should use their God-given capacities to transform the world. They felt proud that as unique indi-viduals they could create a better new world. They were more individualistic, materialistic, and skepti-cal than their late medieval ancestors. Beginning in Italy (there is a general, but not unchallenged, consensus that the Renaissance began in Tuscany in the 14th century), and spreading to the rest of Europe by the 16th century, its influence affected literature, philosophy, art, politics, science, religion, and other aspects of intellectual enquiry. Most historians agree that the ideas that characterized the Renaissance had their origin in late 13th century Florence, in particular with the writings of Dante Alighieri (1265–1321) and Francesco Petrarch (1304–1374), as well as the painting of Giotto di Bondone (1267–1337).

As a cultural movement, it encompassed a rebellion of learning based on classical sources, the devel-opment of linear perspective in painting, and gradual but widespread educational reform. (In the graphic arts, such as drawing, is an approximate representation, on a flat surface, of an image as it is perceived by the eye. A characteristic feature of perspective is that objects are drawn smaller as their distance from the observer increases.) Traditionally, this intellectual transformation has resulted in the Renaissance being viewed as a bridge between the Middle Ages and the Modern era. Although the Renaissance saw revo-lutions in many intellectual pursuits, as well as social and political upheaval, it is perhaps best known for its artistic developments and the contributions of such extensive learned individuals as Leonardo da Vinci and Michelangelo, who inspired the term "Renaissance man."

Renaissance thinkers sought out learning from ancient texts, typically written in Latin or ancient Greek. Scholars went after Europe's monasteries searching for works of classical antiquity which had fallen into obscurity. In such texts they found a desire to improve and perfect their worldly knowledge; an entirely different sentiment to the transcendental spirituality stressed by medieval Christianity. They did not reject Christianity; quite the contrary, many of the Renaissance's greatest works were devoted to it, and the Church patronized many works of Renaissance art. However, a subtle shift took place in the way that intellectuals approached religion that was reflected in many other areas of cultural life.

In summary, the dominant view of the Renaissance is that it could be viewed as an attempt by intel-lectuals to study and improve the secular and worldly, both through the revival of ideas from antiquity, and through new approaches to thought.

Humanism

The intellectual movement of the Renaissance is **humanism** that began during the first quarter of the 14th century with the purpose the study of the classical authors of antiquity. The Latin classics, and also the Greek, were known in the Early Middle Ages, but their study had been pushed into the background. If they were studied they were valued as a means to an end, as storage of information and models of rhetoric (effective and persuasive speech), and not as live literature to be enjoyed and valued for its ideas and the form they were expressed. In the 1300s reading the classics became common among the educated class. They were studied for their own sake, for the beauty of their style, and the ideas of human life and of the world they contained. Monastic libraries were ransacked for copies of Virgil, Cicero, and Horace. These new intellectuals believed that thorough training in the classical literature of the Greco-Roman world could alone form a *perfect human being,* and they called themselves *"Humanists,"* while the subjects they studied came to be known as *Humanities.* Humanism was not a philosophy per se, but rather a method of learning. In contrast to the medieval scholastic mode, which focused on resolving contradictions between authors, humanists would study ancient texts in the original, and appraise them through a combination of reasoning and empirical evidence. Humanist education was based on the study of poetry, grammar, ethics, and rhetoric. Although it has been difficult for historians to define humanism precisely, most have settled on "a middle of the road definition" that can be summarized as *the movement to recover, interpret, and assimilate the language, literature, learning, and values of ancient Greece and Rome.* Above all, humanists asserted the genius of man, the greatness of human reason, thus putting man on a central plane or pedestal.

The central feature of humanism in this period was the commitment to the idea that the ancient Greco-Roman world was the pinnacle of human achievement, especially intellectual achievement, and should be taken as a model by contemporary Europeans. According to this view of history, the fall of Rome to Germanic invaders, in the 5th century, had led to the dissolution and decline of this remarkable culture; the intellectual heritage of the ancient world had been lost—many of its most important books had been destroyed and dispersed—and a thousand years later Europeans were still living in the ghetto. The only way in which Europeans could expect to pull themselves out of this intellectual catastrophe was to attempt to recover, edit, and make available these lost texts, which included, among others, almost all the works of Plato. This view led these humanists to see the Middle Ages as a period that separated their "modern" time with the world they admired of antiquity, therefore they considered this middle period as backward.

Pagan and Christian Humanism

From the start humanism had both a pagan and a Christian aspect. Men like Dante, Petrarch, and Thomas More made free use of the works of antiquity without sacrificing Christian principles. They combined classical materials with Christian ideals, held to the teachings of the Church and the classics only as a means to embellish those teachings. But other men like Boccaccio and Lorenzo Valla became infatuated with the classics and absorbed the pagan conception of life those classics embodied. They looked down with scorn to what was supernatural and unworldly (characteristic of the medieval world), and ridiculed the writings of the scholastics for their barbarous Latin. Not wanting to accept anything on faith, they became skeptical of Christian teachings. They ended thinking like pagans because the ancients they admired were pagans. Some men who were pious and zealous condemned the whole movement as evil. But the Church did not have this attitude, and on the contrary She was successful to a certain extent in directing this new movement to revive the Christian world. An area where the Church was successful was in art and architecture in the service of religion.

As the Renaissance's Neo-Platonism replaced the Aristotelianism of St. Thomas Aquinas, attempts were made to join the great works of Antiquity with Christian values in a syncretic Christian humanism, such as those by Marsilio Ficino and Pico della Mirandola. Ethics was taught independently of theology, and the authority of the Church was tacitly transferred to the reasoning logic of the educated individual. Thus, humanists were placing human reason above the teachings of the Church, and they constantly skirted the dangers of being branded as heretics.

Although Renaissance humanists were more accepting of pagan philosophy than their Scholastic contemporaries, they did not necessarily object to the idea that Christian understanding should be dominant over other modes of thought. As humanists increasingly opposed the strict Catholic orthodoxy of Scholastic philosophy, some began to intermingle pagan virtues with Christian virtues, and revive religious ideas from the late-classical Greek world, and some risked being declared heretics for distancing themselves from the Church.

Renaissance humanism's divergence from orthodox Christianity was in two broad directions. One introduced new and wide-ranging ideas of supernatural forces, and sometimes came close to constituting a new religion itself. The other, and especially toward the end of the movement, there was the secular world-view of humanist-influenced writers such as **Niccolò Machiavelli** and Francesco Guicciardini, the agnosticism and skepticism of Francis Bacon and Michel Montaigne, and the anti-clerical satire of François Rabelais. Niccolo Machiavelli wrote **"The Prince"** in which a theory of government was developed that held that the prince or lord should use any means regardless if they are dishonest or unjust that best suits his goal of achieving power and overcoming his opponents. Generosity as well as murder were just as valid if they served to reach ones goal, in other words the end justifies the means, with no regard for ethics and morality. These ideas of humanism demonstrated the pride and confidence in the human mind and value on human accomplishments, which was almost like worshiping man and human nature rather than God. Of these two directions, the first mostly dissipated as an intellectual trend, later leading to movements in Western esotericism such as Theosophy and New Age thinking, while the second has had great continuing influence in Western thought.

Arts

With respect to the arts, Renaissance scholars employed the humanist method in study, and searched for realism and human emotion in art. One of the distinguishing features of Renaissance art was its development of highly **realistic linear perspective.** Giotto di Bondone is credited with first treating a painting as a window into space, but it was not until the demonstrations of architect Filippo Brunelleschi (1377–1446) and the subsequent writings of Leon Battista Alberti (1404–1472) that perspective was formalized as an artistic technique. The development of perspective was part of a wider trend toward realism in the arts. To that end, painters also developed other techniques, studying light, shadow, and, famously, in the case of Leonardo da Vinci, human anatomy.

Humanist scholars shaped the intellectual landscape throughout the early modern period. Political philosophers such as Niccolo Machiavelli and Thomas More revived the ideas of Greek and Roman thinkers, and applied them in critiques of contemporary government. Theologians, notably Erasmus and Martin Luther, challenged the Aristotelian status quo, introducing radical new ideas of justification and faith that created the theology of the Reformation.

Painting

The revival of the Greco-Roman past brought about a new world outlook and synthesis of two cultural roots (Greco-Roman and Judeo-Christian) in art, music, literature, and architecture of the period.

Figure 8.1   Detail (lower right), *Last Judgment* (1543), Sistine Chapel, Michelangelo Buonarroti. Vatican, Rome. *Image Copyright David Lees/Corbis.*

This Christian and Greek synthesis is obvious in the iconography of *The Last Judgment* by Michelangelo in the Sistine Chapel, Rome (Figure 8.1). Charon, the River God from Ancient Greek mythology is shown driving souls into Hell at the time of the Last Judgment. Why would Michelangelo put Charon—a god from Ancient Greek mythology—into this Christian scene? The narrative is taken from Dante Alighieri's *Divine Comedy* where Charon and other mythological creatures drag sinners down to Hell on the day of wrath. Despite the fact that it required a special knowledge of people, places, history, and mythology, Dante's book became popular among intelligentsia because it was written in vernacular Italian of the time. Incorporating ancient legends, myths, and contemporary views of the Christian world, characters from antiquity are combined with the Christian view of the world to form a clear cultural synthesis in Michelangelo's painting. Michelangelo took another approach to the synthesis in his Sistine Chapel, where Greco-Roman and Christian figures such as the Libyan Sybil and Delphic Oracle sit amid famous biblical heroes such as Ezekiel and Jonah.

Sculpture

Michelangelo's statue of *David* (Figure 8.2) also presents a synthesis of these cultural roots. If the statue is viewed properly from below (it was originally intended to be seen at the top of the basilica), the sculpture incorporates Golden Section proportions. The artist distorted all of the parts so that the statue would look correct only from below. This is

Figure 8.2   Michelangelo's statue of David. *Image Copyright Shutterstock.com*

sometimes misunderstood when photos of *David* are taken straight on because that view distorts the perspective of the figure and its inherent Golden Section proportions. Michelangelo was not the first Renaissance artist to represent *David* in the nude (Donatello preceded him), but he was the first to ensure that *David* had a Golden Section division at the navel. The fact that *David*, a Hebrew biblical hero, was represented in the nude with Golden Section proportions illustrated the new Renaissance synthesis of Christian subjects with Greco-Roman traits.

Architecture

Much of the information about Greco-Roman architecture was transmitted to Renaissance architects from the ancient Roman architect Vitruvius, who described the façades, moldings, and trim of the ancient buildings in his *Treatise on Architecture* (*De Architectura*, ca.15 B.C.E.). Architects incorporated these ancient motifs into the interiors of Renaissance churches such as *San Lorenzo*, *Pazzi Chapel*, and *San Andrea*. Ancient motifs appeared in the exterior of numerous other buildings, including *Tiempetto*, by Donato Bramante, where one can see the Corinthian capitals and classical shafts with stylobates. The interior of *San Lorenzo* (Florence) has coffered (recessed) ceilings typical of Ancient Greek temples as shown in Figure 8.3.

Perhaps as important as the interior/exterior moldings and shapes of buildings, however, is the fact that architects insisted that church buildings be designed with ancient ideas of mathematical proportion. Filippo Brunelleschi produced a floor plan of *San Lorenzo* designed in *space-block planning*—where one basic unit (a square) was repeated across the floor plan in arithmetic multiples (Figure 8.4). Thus, Brunelleschi was interested not only in Christian architectural traditions, but also in the potential mathematical beauty of buildings. He is also credited with inventing single point perspective—an effective method for representing depth on a flat surface. This three dimensional graphic technique is frequently cited as a principal achievement of the Renaissance.

Andrea Palladio imitated many features of Ancient Roman buildings and used them in numerous villas he built for wealthy patrons in Northern Italy. One of his most celebrated buildings, the *Villa Rotunda*

Figure 8.3 Interior, San Lorenzo (1420–1470), Filippo Brunelleschi. Florence. *Image Copyright Peter Barritt/Robert Harding Picture Library/ SuperStock.*

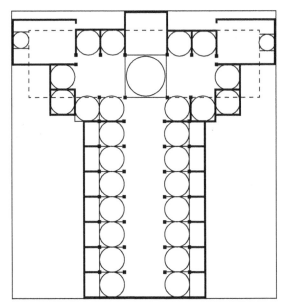

Figure 8.4 Floor plan, San Lorenzo (1420–1470), Fillippo Brunelleschi, Florence. *Image Copyright Kendall Hunt Publishing.*

Figure 8.5 Villa Capra "La Rotonda" (1566–1571), Andrea Palladio. Vicenza, Italy.
Image Copyright Courtesy of Stephen Husarik.

(based upon the *Pantheon*), was a daring achievement for its time because it represented the first time a dome had been mounted upon a secular building (Figure 8.5). Domes had been previously reserved only for churches. Like Brunelleschi before him, Palladio also insisted on the use of *space-block planning*—where a single geometrical unit (such as a square) became the basic shape for all others in the floor plan; it was then repeated in arithmetic multiples.

Music

The Renaissance was a youthful time in which a high value was placed on beauty. Painters made youthful portraits of aristocrats and sometimes painted children holding their deceased favorite pets such as stuffed birds. Even musical scores had a humorous artistic design; some were shaped in the form of hearts (e.g., *Cordiform* manuscript) with notation distributed around the edges. Some composers made music so that the notes would create hidden messages or shapes in the score called *augenmusik* (trans. eye music)— where the notes spelled out words of objects being represented in the music.

As well, the Renaissance produced the first systematic grouping of instruments into families or bands called consorts. There were the *instruments bas* (soft) consisting of flutes, recorders, and other indoor type instruments and *instruments haute* (loud) intended for outdoors, such as the cornet, sackbut, and other brass instruments. These two families of instruments—loud or soft—could be combined to produce a full consort of instruments. Michael Praetorius, one of the well-known composers of the time, composed many compositions in his *Syntagma Musica* (1550) that employed these instrumental combinations. Some of the pieces were "foot stompers"; others were stylized courtly dances. Musicians who otherwise doubled as servants, cooks, valets, and grounds keepers performed the pieces at palace functions.

Composers were no longer anonymous in the Renaissance and a few names stand out: Josquin des Pres, Michael Praetorius, Giovanni Gabrieli, and Giovanni Pierluigi Palestrina. Complicated musical forms evolved; special types of cadences (or chord formulas) were developed to close off sections of music.

A major expressive development occurred when the rhythm of church music was allowed to subdivide into sets of twos, instead of three (the former symbolic reference to the Father, Son, and Holy Spirit). One of the principal features of Renaissance music is the overlapping of voice parts—something akin to singing rounds and referred to as "points of imitation." The voices do not all sing together, but enter at staggered time intervals. The effect is somewhat like the sound of a camp song such as "Row, row, row, your boat. . . ."

Although opera is often construed as an invention of the Baroque, it was actually developed during the late Renaissance as a revival of Ancient Greek theater. Florentine intellectuals met at Count Bardi's palace in Florence to attempt to create a modern counterpart of Ancient Greek music. They succeeded in developing *recitative*—a kind of music that is half sung and/or half spoken. When *recitative* was linked with songs called arias, the stage was set for the production of opera in the late 1500s. *Aria* and *recitative* became the principal pair among the various numbers of opera. Representative of the Greek revival spirit, the earliest operas by Peri, Caccini, and Monteverdi were based upon Ancient Greek mythology, rather than Christian subjects. In opera, one needs songs, *recitative*, instruments, and staging—these were all the invention of the Renaissance and brought together in the 1590s.

Since there were no musical models to imitate from the ancient world, composers had to find ways to create parallel musical styles in the Renaissance. In essence, opera is a Renaissance update of Ancient Greek drama. All of the things one would find in an Ancient Greek drama (course of action, musical delivery of text, instrumental accompaniment, staging, etc.) are found in Renaissance opera. Most of these elements came together in a production of *Oedipus Rex* (1585) at the *Teatro Olympico* in Vincenzo, Italy (Figure 8.6). Combined with the illusory effects provided by the Scammozzi multiple point perspective stage, the total effect on the audience at the time must have been as compelling as the effects experienced by 20th century audiences who attend movies shown in Digital Cinemascope®, 3D or IMAX®.

Figure 8.6 Teatro Olympico, (1580–1585), Andrea Palladio, with Vincenzo Scammozzi perspective stage design. Vicenza, Italy. *Image Copyright Jorg Hackemann/ Shutterstock.com.*

LEONARDO DA VINCI (DESIGNER)

No discussion of the Renaissance would be complete without mention of the most interdisciplinary man of the Renaissance, Leonardo da Vinci (1452–1519): painter, architect, inventor, poet, engineer, sculptor, musician, and author. He is remembered for his famous inventions of the tank, parachute, and bicycle, but he should also be remembered for his medical illustrations since, among many other accomplishments, they were considered classics of American medicine until the early 20th century.

Madonna Lisa, or as it is popularly known, *Mona Lisa*, is the subject of endless research and has probably received more attention than any other European painting (Figure 8.7). Leonardo portrays the sitter with a diffusion of lines called *sfumato* (smoky) that gives a special attractive quality to human flesh in portraits. But there is more to this painting than simply portraiture. Giorgio Vasari, the first art historian, wrote that Leonardo was dissatisfied with the expression on the lips of *La Gioconda (Mona Lisa)* and he hired musicians to perform while he painted in order to get a proper smile on her face.

Much narrative has developed about the enigma of her smile and it has stirred interest in fields as diverse as medicine and computer graphics. If we take Leonardo at his own words, however, the smile seems to be related to geometry in his painting.

As Leonardo wrote: "Let no man who is no mathematician examine the elements of my works." This double negative sentence written on the back of a drawing fully expresses his position that appreciating his work depends upon understanding its underlying mathematical and/or geometrical principles.

Figure 8.7   *Mona Lisa* (1503–1506), Leonardo da Vinci. Louvre, France. *Image Copyright Fine Art Images/SuperStock.*

Description

This painting attributed to Leonardo da Vinci was purchased by Francis I of France and eventually placed in the Louvre, Paris where it remained for centuries until it was stolen and returned in the early 20th century. The painting (on wood) with dimensions of 30" x 21" shows careful working, a smooth surface, and composition using two contrasting warm and cool colors. A seated lady is depicted in three-quarter position on a chair with arms crossed, in front of a window, wearing the costume typical of the Renaissance. Behind the sitter is a rocky landscape with a winding river and a Roman-style bridge. The sitter has very simple facial features and no eyebrows; she is wearing a costume that has very complicated embroidery suggesting a person of some wealth.

Analysis

The painting is closed and painterly. It has a great variety of shapes, a limited color scheme, bi-lateral symmetry, and dominates in the vertical direction. Leonardo wrote "let no man who is no mathematician examine the products of my works" (Richter I, p. 112). Therefore, one way to approach this work is mathematically or geometrically. Leonardo illustrated a book on Euclidean geometry for his colleague Brother Luca Paciloi that discussed conic sections (cone, triangle, parabola, hyperbola, semi-circle, and circle). Parabolas appear widely in Leonardo's paintings and in this one in particular. Parabolic shapes appear over her shoulder, in the mountainous landscape, and even in the smile of Mona Lisa's lips—a smile that can be inscribed perfectly in the vertex of a parabola. Recent X-ray photographs of the painting show that Leonardo expanded the left shoulder of Mona Lisa's garment and enlarged it so that it would fit into a large parabolic curve.

Interpretation

It appears that Leonardo organized his designs around parabolic arcs and other conic sections not only in this painting, but in others such as the Madonna of the *Rocks; Madonna with the Yarnwinder; Lady with the Ermine; Virgin,*

St. John and the Christ Child; and *Virgin St. Anne and the Child*. Repetition of such shapes creates stylistic coherence throughout his paintings and may also serve as a unifying device within the design. Furthermore, the number of these parabolic sequences increases over the years in Leonardo's paintings.

Evaluation

Every age will bring its own meaning to this famous artwork because it has become an icon of European culture. One can tell when an art work becomes an icon because people may poke fun at it, and many twentieth century artists have spoofed the image of Mona Lisa. Giorgio Vasari mentioned that Leonardo had a group of musicians playing to keep a proper expression on the sitter's face. Over the years, this observation has taken on a life of its own. Many fans have ascribed special meaning to the smile of Mona Lisa; people from various disciplines even as far as law and medicine have tried to enter the discussion. One doctor wrote a lengthy article on the smile of Mona Lisa as it relates to the orbicularis muscles of the lips. The conversation about this smile may never end. Should we not take Leonardo at his own words, however, and assume that the importance of the smile of the Mona Lisa, like the smiles of all his Madonnas, relates to geometry? Her smile is inscribed perfectly within the vertex of a parabola.

The geometry in Leonardo's painting style evolved over the course of his career. In the early 1480s, he left Florence to accept a position at the Sforza court in Milan that resulted in a twenty-year investigation of science, mathematics, and art. He was surrounded by distinguished figures in the arts and sciences. Luca Pacioli, the father of modern accounting, asked him to do designs for a book on Euclidian geometry entitled *De divina proportione* (ca. 1497). Leonardo's interest in the formal subject of mathematics increased through their friendship. He devoted much space to geometry in his manuscripts and even dedicated a hundred pages to the study of Euclid's *Elements*.

Because Leonardo read numerous treatises on geometry, collaborated with Pacioli on *De divina proportione*, and delighted in making decorative geometrical designs, one should not be surprised to find an ideal geometrical form in his paintings: the parabola. Parabolas result from slicing or cutting a cone at different angles, just as in the hyperbola and ellipse. All of them are present in Leonardo's paintings, but the parabola has exceptional importance because it became the principal motif for his later paintings.

One of Leonardo's paintings from Milan, *Portrait of the Lady with the Ermine* (Figure 8.8), is a pivotal work because the main motif of the painting, the inclination of the lady, is parabolic. Other curves in the painting such as the body of the animal and the necklace worn by the sitter are also parabolic. These characteristics are not immediately recognizable unless one traces the curves over the figure as shown in Figure 8.9.

Figure 8.8 *Lady with the Ermine* (1489–1490), Leonardo da Vinci. Czartoryski Museum, Kraków, Poland. *Image Copyright Fine Art Images/SuperStock.*

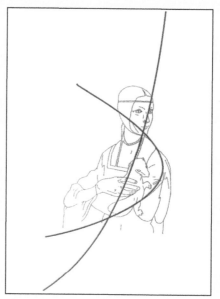

Figure 8.9 *Analysis, Lady with the Ermine*, Leonardo da Vinci. *Image Copyright Courtesy of Stephen Husarik.*

In 1499, after about twenty years of support, Leonardo's longtime patron, Ludovico de Moro, was over-taken by political enemies and Leonardo left Milan, traveling in the company of Luca Pacioli. By this time, he had amassed a considerable body of notes on the subjects of geometry and optics and had even invented a type of compass that could draw parabolas. The trend begun earlier in his paintings—to superimpose conic sections over the contours of natural objects—became much more pronounced, and parabolic curves began to saturate his designs.

A significant work from this period, *Madonna with the Yarnwinder* (ca. 1501), is illustrated in Figure 8.10. This small painting is replete with motifs derived from conic sections. Parabolas are combined into various groups such as strata of rocks upon which the child sits, the right arm of the child, his right leg and hip, vari-ous folds of the Virgin's gown, and the outline of her head. The hand of the Madonna is placed in the air in such a way that a paraboloid (rotated parabola) can be inscribed beneath it as shown in Figure 8.11.

Figure 8.10 *Madonna with the Yarnwinder* (ca. 1501), Leonardo da Vinci. Private Collection, United States. *Image Copyright RMN-Grand Palais/Art Resource, NY.*

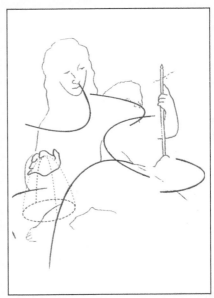

Figure 8.11 Analysis, *Madonna with the Yarnwinder* (ca. 1501), Leonardo da Vinci.. *Image Copyright Courtesy of Stephen Husarik.*

Including sketches and preliminary drawings, it took about ten years for Leonardo to complete his culmi-nating work with sequences of parabolas, *Virgin and Child with St. Anne* (Figure 8.12). Heinrich Wölfflin pointed out that "the inclination of the Virgin forms the main motif of the painting." Sequences of parabolas are sys-tematically developed throughout the painting: the arms and legs of St. Anne and the Virgin, the shapes of the rocky strata beneath them, the winding road to the right of the figure group, and the unrelenting sequences of the mountaintops in the rocky landscape all contribute to the unifying effect (Figure 8.13). As the principal motif of the design, the parabola gives the painting a special unity. Even the major division of the canvas into foreground and background is inscribed on the asymptote of a parabola whose vertex lies somewhere off the edge of the painting (Figure 8.14).

Leonardo's *Virgin and Child with St. Anne* was cleaned in 2011 and the painting was put on public display at the Louvre in 2012. It was a remarkable success; other cleanings have been much more controversial.

Leonardo gained a commission in 1503 to paint a formal portrait, *Mona Lisa*, that he kept until his final days in France. Mona Lisa represents an ideal in paintings precisely because there is a balance between the indi-viduality of the sitter and a prevailing geometrical pattern. Like the *Virgin and Child with St. Anne painting*, Mona Lisa appears to be one in series of paintings directed at geometrical coherence, where every detail of the painting—no matter how small—is geometrically related to the overall pattern. What does the geometrical con-text tell us about the secret of the Mona Lisa's enigmatic smile? Her smile—like the smile of almost all Leonardo Madonnas and angels—gains its unique character because it is inscribed within a parabolic curve.

Parabolic geometry in Leonardo's paintings is an important Renaissance development because it parallels the goals of Ancient Greek artists who sought geometrical solutions to their art. Geometry is as important in an Ancient Greek work as it is in a Leonardo painting. Leonardo's organization of Christian figures (Mary, Christ, etc.) in a design with mathematical coherence is another example of the synthesis of the Greco-Roman and Christian worlds in the art of painting.

Figure 8.12 *Virgin and Child with St. Anne* (ca. 1508), Leonardo da Vinci. Louvre, Paris [before cleaning. *Image Copyright Iberfoto / SuperStock.*

Figure 8.13 Analysis, *Virgin and Child with St. Anne.* Leonardo da Vinci. *Realization: Raechel Martin. Image Copyright Kendall Hunt Publishing.*

Figure 8.14 Analysis, *Virgin and Child with St. Anne.* Leonardo da Vinci. *Realization: Raechel Martin. Image Copyright Kendall Hunt Publishing.*

CLEANING THE SISTINE CHAPEL

In 1983, the Vatican decided to clean Michelangelo's ceiling of the Sistine Chapel. Subjected to centuries of dirt and soot from candles and oil lamps, a thick layer of dirt was encrusted over the painted surface. Restorers over the years had applied layers of glue over the painting in order to hide salts that had filtered down onto the surface in rainwater from a leaking roof. The glue made the paint layers flex with changes in humidity, however, and caused paint to break off the ceiling. As a result, the glue had to be removed in order to save the fresco from further deterioration.

Not everyone was satisfied as the cleaning progressed. Certain art critics said that the Vatican had removed layers of paint that belonged to Michelangelo himself and insisted that the restorers partially destroyed the fresco. You must judge for yourself. Did they or did they not remove Michelangelo's paint from the ceiling? (See Figures 8.15, 8.16, 8.17 and 8.18).

Figure 8.15   Before cleaning. *Fall and Expulsion of Adam and Eve* (1508–1512), Michelangelo Buonarroti. Sistine Chapel. Vatican, Rome. *Image Copyright Album/Prism/Album/SuperStock.*

Figure 8.16   After cleaning. *Fall and Expulsion of Adam and Eve* (1508–1512), Michelangelo Buonarroti. Sistine Chapel. Vatican, Rome. *Image Copyright Album/Oronoz/Album/SuperStock.*

Figure 8.17   Before cleaning, *Creation of Man* (1508–1512), Sistine Chapel. Michelangelo Buonarroti. Vatican, Rome. *Image Copyright Scala/Art Resource, NY.*

Figure 8.18   After cleaning, *Creation of Man* (1508–1512), Sistine Chapel. Michelangelo Buonarroti. Vatican, Rome. *Image Copyright Erich Lessing/Art Resource, NY.*

MICHELANGELO THE ENTREPENEUR

Michelangelo is often misunderstood as a lone, working genius. To the contrary, this sculptor/architect employed as many as two dozen people at a time and kept reliable workers on the payroll for decades. Unable to realize his enormous projects alone, he divided up the work both physically and artistically.

At the stone quarries, he supervised the selection, cutting, and hauling of stones; in his studio, he supervised assistants who chiseled motifs onto his pieces; on site at the Sistine Chapel, he employed numerous assistants to construct the scaffolding, put the plaster on the ceiling, mix paint, and draw outlines on the wet plaster before he painted.

The Last Judgment (on the back wall of the Sistine Chapel), includes work by little-known assistants. Michelangelo's work pattern is a study in how to manage dozens of workers in order to complete major projects.

A team headed by Gian Luigi Colalucci began the arduous task of determining what paint actually belonged to Michelangelo and what did not. A search was launched into the so-called "secret archives" of the Vatican to learn just what the earlier restorers had done. It turned out that some cleanings were accomplished by rubbing Greek wine and bread onto the ceiling. But other work actually involved the repainting of Michelangelo's fresco.

The Vatican investigative team had to decide how to separate Michelangelo's work from the restorer's work. So, they took pin-sized representative samples from across the ceiling, put them into a gel, and made crosssections with a microtome. At least eight significant separate layers were discovered on the ceiling of the Sistine Chapel (which became nine, now that they added their own retouchings), as shown in Figure 8.19.

Michelangelo's fresco technique consisted of having the surface (wall or ceiling) prepared with a

NINE LAYERS ON MICHELANGELO'S CEILING FRESCO

1) vaulting (ceiling)
2) arriccio (the prepared surface—dry plaster)
3) intonaco #1 (a medium dark layer of wet plaster)
4) intonaco #2 (a thin bright white layer of wet plaster)
5) pigment #1 (prepared by assistants for painting by Michelangelo)
6) pigment # 2 "pentimenti" (secco retouchings by Michelangelo)
7) dirt
8) glue layers (put on by restorers)
9) pigment #3 (put on by later restorers)

Figure 8.19   Chart of Paint Layers on the Sistine Chapel Ceiling.

substrate (*arriccio*). On the day of painting he would have a plasterer come in and apply a day's worth of plaster—called a *giornate*—this layer was called the intonaco.

Usually the plasterer added a second extra layer of very white plaster over the *intonaco* in order to help brighten the colors. Michelangelo applied seven colors to the freshly applied plaster (Fresco means fresh—referring to painting in the fresh wet plaster). Once dried, the fresco was complete. The pigment particles combined with the plaster particles to form calcium carbonate—a very hard surface that lasts forever. These steps are given in the first five layers shown below.

Sometimes when Michelangelo got down from the scaffolding and looked up—he reviewed his work and occasionally realized that it needed corrections because the curvature of the ceiling had distorted his drawing. So, there was a sixth step in which he went back the next day to the dried painting and repainted some objects in order to enlarge, foreshorten, or generally change the contour to accommodate visual distortions. These contour corrections (called *pentimenti* or re-thinkings) were done in a different fresco technique called a secco—where pigment is mixed with egg, casein, or some other binder to make the paint stick so that it won't fall off the surface after it dried.

Thus, there are the six layers of paint completed by Michelangelo—all other layers (beginning with step 7 in Figure 8.19) were added by restorers. Some art critics did not understand that Michelangelo's "corrections" were simply altered outlines of figures. They were surprised by the bright appearance of the painting after glue layers were removed and insisted that Michelangelo had put "toning" layers over the entire surface of the ceiling to make his figures look three-dimensional (i.e., *chiaroscuro* effect). They believed that the restorers had removed "toning" layers (not just outlines) thus making the painting look flat and cartoon-like. Indeed, after cleaning portions of the ceiling, the restorers realized that Michelangelo's colors were very bright and that many of the dark values had been removed. Did they remove half-tone layers from the ceiling?

One has to examine the method of the recent restorers in order to answer the question. First, they attempted to decide which layers belonged to Michelangelo and which didn't. They reasoned that everything up to the paint layer (steps 1 through 5 above) belonged to Michelangelo. They further reasoned that the *pentimenti* (step 6) also belonged to Michelangelo because they were applied by him in order to correct visual distortions.

But then they had to sort out layers of over painting, dirt, and glue. The history of the painting helped them to draw their conclusions about how to proceed.

Early in the life of the fresco, the roof leaked and salts in the rainwater leaked out onto the painting. When the salts dried, they left an opaque veil over the painting. In order to correct this defect, early restorers covered the salt-covered painting with glue—which helped to make the painting more visible. This corrected the problem temporarily, but glue is organic—it oxidizes and turns dark. Application of the glue would correct the problem for a while, but then other restorers would have to come back and reapply glue years later in order to correct the same problem of opaqueness. These layers of glue built up with each subsequent retouching and gradually darkened the fresco over the years.

Since a layer of dirt occurs between the glue layers and the original painting, the modern restorers concluded that these correction layers did not belong to Michelangelo and therefore should be removed. In addition, they felt the salts should be removed along with the glue. There were spots where the ceiling had been physically damaged so they were repaired, as well.

Turning to the restoration of the back wall the back wall of the chapel (*The Last Judgment*, also by Michelangelo), modern restorers discovered that Michelangelo used a very expensive pigment made from semi-precious gemstones called *Lapis Lazuli*. Restorers used the same techniques for cleaning the back wall as those they had developed for the ceiling, but a new cleaning technique was developed for this particular type of pigment. It resulted in a stunningly bright painting (Figure 8.20) and contrasting results for the ceiling and back wall.

The restorers began their work in the early 1980s starting on the upper sidewalls of the chapel, working their way upwards to the famous ceiling and finally finishing the back wall of the chapel on which Michelangelo had painted *The Last Judgment*. The restorations took over twenty years to complete. Some art historians claim that during the restoration Michelangelo's original colors have been removed from the surface, even though a team of independent restorers who visited the Sistine Chapel concluded that everything possible had been done to protect the original ceiling. Please view the before and after examples (Figures 8.15 and 8.16) to determine if anything has been lost.

There have been many disasters in the history of restoration, and art critics are rightly concerned about the potential damage that can be done to an artwork. If anything has been taken away from the Sistine Chapel, then it has been lost forever.

Figure 8.20   Interior, *Sistine Chapel (after cleaning, 2007)*, Michelangelo Buonarroti. Vatican, Rome. *Image Copyright Robert Harding Picture Library/SuperStock.*

SUMMARY

The Renaissance was a cultural movement that began in Italy during the 14th century and spread to Europe until the 17th century. Renaissance thinkers were more individualistic, materialistic, and skeptical than their Medieval ancestors. They gradually shifted the emphasis of medieval life from eternal salvation in the afterlife to a human-centered Earthly life. The new Renaissance intellectuals believed that thorough training in the classical literature of the Greco-Roman world could alone form a *perfect human being,* and they called themselves *"Humanists,"* while the subjects they studied came to be known as *Humanities.* Humanism was not a philosophy per se, but rather a method of learning. Humanist education was based on the study of poetry, grammar, ethics, and rhetoric. It has been difficult for historians to define humanism precisely, most have settled on "a middle of the road definition" that can be summarized *as the movement to recover* (rediscover), *interpret, and assimilate the language, literature, learning and values of ancient Greece and Rome.* Above all, humanists asserted the genius of man, the greatness of human reason, thus putting man on a central plane or pedestal. Humanism was a union of love and reason that stressed earthly fulfillment in this life rather than medieval preparation for eternal life in paradise. The central feature of humanism in this period was the commitment to the idea that the ancient Greco-Roman world was the pinnacle of human achievement, especially intellectual achievement, and should be taken as a model by contemporary Europeans. In the arts there is a search for realism and human emotion. Renaissance art developed a highly realistic linear perspective.

The Renaissance humanists were divided into two groups in respect with being in harmony or in conflict with the medieval teachings of the Church. There were those who used freely the works of antiquity remaining loyal to Christian principles, combining classical elements with Christian ideals. The other group became infatuated with the classics and scorned what was supernatural and unworldly which required Christian faith to accept. They placed human reason above the teachings of the Church.

ORIGINAL SOURCE READINGS OF WESTERN CIVILIZATION

DISCUSSION QUESTIONS

The following questions for discussion correspond to the readings from original sources. Read the source and then write your understanding and your personal opinion of the issue utilizing the information from the reading of the original source, the textbook, and any other source. Give *complete explanations* in your answers and opinions.

Epic of Gilgamesh

1. What are the themes of this epic and which do you think is the major theme?
2. Who civilized Enkidu, and what does it mean to be uncivilized and civilized to these Sumerians?
3. What kind of personalities do the gods have and what role do they play in men's lives?
4. What have you learned about the kind of people the Mesopotamians were or their culture from the reading?
5. How does the Epic of Gilgamesh speak to you or how do you relate to the story?

Genesis 1–2:35

1. How does Genesis reflect the concept of the transcendence of God?
2. Where does Genesis place man in God's creation and what does God command man to do?

Exodus 20–21

1. From reading the Ten Commandments do you read that God or Yahweh is declaring he is the only God of mankind, therefore all other gods are false?
2. Do you read any prohibitions that may be an obstacle to the development of art and sculpture?
3. When it comes to the ethical behavior all men must exercise toward other mankind, can you think of a sentence or phrase that includes and summarizes them?

Daniel 7

1. Do you find the Messiah in the Biblical passage, and if so describe His kingdom?
2. How does the Messiah's kingdom compare to the other kingdoms described?

Homer, the Odyssey

1. From reading the passage how does Odysseus represent the uniquely Greek attitude and qualities?
2. What do the Cyclopes tell us about what the ancient Greeks believed the world to be composed of?

Euripides, Medea

1. How does the play portray an ancient Greek woman's point of view of the Greek male and female?
2. This play is a tragedy because in the end Medea decides to take revenge on her husband Jason by killing their children. What is Euripides trying to tell (message) the audience in respect to human reason overcoming human passion?
3. What have you learned about Greek theater in respect to the performers in Greek plays? Is it similar or the same as in modern plays or cinemas you watch?

Aristotle, Politics

1. What idea (influence) of Socrates is expressed by Aristotle in this work?
2. Explain how Aristotle's concept of the state differs from the concept the Sophists had of the state.

A Slave Revolt in Sicily: Diodorus Siculus, Historical Library 34.2

1. From the manner that slaves were treated what kind of people were the Roman masters?
2. What would you assume about Roman labor from this reading?
3. What have you learned about the mind-set and beliefs of these slaves?

Moral Decline During the Republic: Sallust, Conspiracy of Catiline 9–10

1. What is Sallust's opinion of the Roman Republic?
2. How did Rome's victory over Carthage (Punic Wars) change Roman society?
3. Some critics say Western society has become very materialistic and hedonistic, throwing off its traditional values. Do you find any similarities or not between Rome and our society today?

Slave Labor in Spanish Mines: Diodorus Siculus, Historical Library 5.36–38

1. What opinion do you have of Romans in Iberia?
2. What insight do you have of the Roman economy?

Augustus Autocracy: Tacitus, Annals 1.2–4

1. What was Augustus proclaiming in public and what was his goal?
2. Why did many Romans support Augustus?
3. How did Augustus transform permanently the Republic?

4. Could something similar happen today in the USA? Think about the Patriot Act soon after 9/11 under President Bush and the National Defense Authorization Act (NDAA) under President Obama and its effects on our constitutional Bill of Rights. Explain your position.

Caligula and the Jews: Josephus, Jewish War 2.184–7, 192–203

1. What was the policy that the Romans had toward other people it incorporated into its Empire?
2. What was the difference between other pagan cultures of the empire and the Jews of Judea?
3. What kind of people were the Jews according to Josephus?

A Stoic's Views On Slavery: Seneca, Moral Epistles 47

1. From the reading and what is in the textbook, what is the Stoics' view about mankind?
2. How have Romans and slaves changed according to Seneca?
3. Do you think all slaves were treated the same?
4. What have you learned about wealthy Roman's eating habits? Are they healthy or not?

EPIC OF GILGAMESH

The Epic of *Gilgamesh* is the first epic poem in human history. An epic poem is a narration of the achievements, labors, and sometimes the failures of heroes that embodies a people's conception of its own past. Produced by the Sumerians, the *Epic* evolved from five earlier myths, the oldest of which goes back to the third millennium B.C.E. Gilgamesh was the semi-historical king of Uruk whom the Sumerians, Babylonians, and Assyrians considered a hero and a god. The poem recounts the wanderings of Gilgamesh and his companion Enkidu as they pursue immortality and a place among the gods. They attempt to do so by performing wondrous feats against fearsome agents of the gods, who are determined to thwart them. They meet the goddess Ishtar, after which Enkidu dies, and Gilgamesh decides to continue the search for immortality. He seeks out anyone who might tell him how to do so. His journey involves the effort not only to escape from death but also to reach an understanding of the meaning of life.

The human desire to escape the grip of death—to achieve immortality—is one of the oldest wishes of all peoples. The *Epic* of Gilgamesh is the earliest recorded treatment of this topic.

During his search, Gilgamesh learns that life after death is so dreary that he returns to Uruk, where he becomes a good king and ends his life happily. The *Epic* of Gilgamesh is an excellent literary work and an impressive intellectual triumph. It shows the Sumerians grappling with such enduring questions as life and death, humankind and deity, and immortality. Despite its great antiquity, it addresses questions important to people today.

This selection describes Gilgamesh's encounter with Utnapishtim whose story has a remarkable resemblance to that of Noah in the Book of Genesis.

"I will reveal to thee, Gilgamesh, a secret story,
And the decision of the gods I will tell thee.
The city of Shuruppak, a city which thou knowest,
The one that lies on the Euphrates,
That city was old, and the gods thereof
Induced the great gods to bring a cyclone over it;
It was planned by their father Anu,
By their counselor, the warrior Enlil,
By their herald Ninib,
By their leader En-nugi.
The lord of brilliant vision, Ea, was with them.
He repeated their decision to the reed-hut.
'Reed-hut, reed-hut, wall, wall,
Reed-hut, hear! Wall, give ear!
O man of Shuruppak, son of Ubara-tutu,
Break up the house, build a ship,
Abandon your property, seek life!

SOURCE: Charles F. Horne, ed., *The Sacred Books and Early Literature of the East, Vol. I, Babylonia* (New York: Parke, Austin, and Lipscomb, 1917), pp. 208-214.

Throw aside your possession and preserve life!
Bring into the ship seed of all living things!
The ship that thou shalt build,
Let its dimensions be measured, so that
Its breadth and length be made to correspond.
On a level with the deep, provide it with a covering.' "

In another version the name of the hero of the deluge is given as Atrakhasis, signifying "the very clever one." This alternate name is introduced also at the end of our version of the tale, where Ea says that he sent Atrakhasis a dream which the latter correctly understood. Evidently two traditions of the manner in which the hero of the deluge was warned of the coming destruction were current. Both were embodied in our tale, which thus is revealed as itself a composite production. Ut-napishtim continues his narrative:

"I understood and spoke to Ea, my lord:
'The command of my lord which thou hast commanded,
As I have understood it, I will carry out.
But what shall I answer the city, the people, and the elders?'
Ea opened his mouth and spoke:
Spoke to me, his servant.
'As answer thus speak to them:
Know that Enlil has conceived hatred toward me,
So that I can no longer dwell in your city.
On Enlil's territory I dare no longer set my face.
Therefore, I go to the "deep" to dwell with Ea, my lord.
Over you he will cause blessing to rain down.
Catch of bird, catch of fish,'
And . . . rich crops."

At this point the tablet is defective. Ut-napishtim must have told Gilgamesh how he completed the ship, first drawing a plan and building according to it. Thereupon the text proceeds:

"On the fifth day, I designed its outline.
According to the plan, the walls were to be ten *gar* high.
Corresponding, ten *gar* the measure of its width.
I determined upon its shape and drew it.
I weighted it sixfold.
I divided the superstructure into seven parts.
Its interior I divided into nine parts.
Water-plugs I constructed in the interior.
I selected a pole and added accessories.
Six *sar* of asphalt I poured on the outer wall.
Three *sar* of pitch I poured on the inner wall.
Three *sar* the workmen carried away in their baskets. Of oil,
Besides one *sar* of oil which was used for the sacrifices,
The boatman secreted two *sar* of oil."

Ut-napishtim then proceeds:

"All that I had I loaded on her.
All that I had of silver I loaded on her.
All that I had of gold I loaded on her.

All that I had of living beings of all kinds I loaded on her.
I brought to the ship all my family and household;
Cattle of the field, beasts of the field, all the workmen I brought on board."

The ship draws water to two-thirds of its bulk.
The description of the storm which now follows is one of the finest passages in the narrative:

"Shamash had fixed the time,
'When the rulers of darkness at evening-time shall cause a terrific rain-storm,
Step into the ship and close the door!'
The fixed time approached,
When the rulers of darkness at evening-time were to cause a terrific rain-storm.
I recognized the symptoms of such a day,
A day, for the appearance of which I was in terror.
I entered the ship and closed the door.
To steer the ship, to Puzur-Kurgal, the boatman,
I entrusted the palace, together with its cargo.
As morning dawned,
There arose on the firmament of heaven black clouds,
Adad thundered therein;
Nabu and Lugal marched in advance,
Ira tears out the ship's pole.
Ninib marches, commanding the attack,
The Anunnaki lift torches,
Illuminating the land with their sheen,
Adad's roar reaches to heaven,
All light is changed to darkness.

■ ■ ■

One day the hurricane raged . . .
Storming furiously . . .
Coming like a combat over men.
Brother sees not brother:
Those in heaven do not know one another.
The gods are terrified at the cyclone,
They flee and mount to the heaven of Anu;
The gods crouch like dogs in an enclosure.
Ishtar cries aloud like one in birth-throes,
The mistress of the gods howls aloud:
'That day be turned to clay,
When I in the assembly of the gods decreed evil;
That I should have decreed evil in the assembly of the gods!
For the destruction of my people should have ordered a combat!
Did I bring forth my people,
That like fish they should fill the sea?'
All of the Anunnaki weep with her.
The gods sit down, depressed and weeping.
Their lips are closed . . .
Six days and nights
The storm, cyclone, and hurricane continued to sweep over the land.
When the seventh day approached, the hurricane and cyclone ceased the combat,

After having fought like warriors.
The sea grew quiet, the evil storm abated, the cyclone was restrained.
I looked at the day and the roar had quieted down.
And all mankind had turned to clay.
Like an enclosure . . . had become.
I opened a window and light fell on my face,
I bowed down and sat down and wept,
Tears flowed over my face.
I looked in all directions of the sea.
At a distance of twelve miles an island appeared.
At mount Nisir the ship stood still.
Mount Nisir took hold of the ship so that it could not move.
One day, two days, Mount Nisir, etc.
Three days, four days, Mount Nisir, etc.
Five days, six days, Mount Nisir, etc.
When the seventh day arrived,
I sent forth a dove, letting it free.
The dove went hither and thither;
Not finding a resting-place, it came back.
I sent forth a swallow, letting it free.
The swallow went hither and thither.
Not finding a resting-place, it came back.
I sent forth a raven, letting it free.
The raven went and saw the decrease of the waters.
It ate, croaked, but did not turn back.
Then I let all out to the four regions and brought an offering.
I brought a sacrifice on the mountain top.
Seven and seven *adagur* jars I arranged.
Beneath them I strewed reeds, cedar-wood and myrtle.
The gods smelled the odor,
The gods smelled the sweet odor.
The gods, like flies, gathered around the sacrificer."

The gods now realize what havoc had been wrought by their decision and begin to regret it. Ishtar, more particularly as the mother goddess, bitterly laments the destruction of mankind.

"As soon as the mistress of the gods arrived,
She raised on high the large necklace which Anu had made according to his art.
'Ye gods, as surely as I will not forget these precious stones at my neck,
So I will remember these days—never to forget them.
Let the gods come to the sacrifice,
But let Enlil not come to the sacrifice.
Because without reflection he brought on the cyclone,
And decreed destruction for my people.'
As soon as Enlil arrived,
He saw the ship, and Enlil was enraged.
Filled with anger at the Igigi.
'Who now has escaped with his life?
No man was to survive the destruction!'
Ninib opened his mouth and spoke,
Spoke to the warrior Enlil,

'Who except Ea can plan any affair?
Ea indeed knows every order.'
Ea opened his mouth and spoke,
Spoke to the warrior Enlil:
'Thou art the leader and warrior of the gods.
But why didst thou, without reflection, bring on the cyclone?
On the sinner impose his sin,
On the evil-doer impose his evil,
But be merciful not to root out completely; be considerate not to destroy altogether!
Instead of bringing on a cyclone,
Lions might have come and diminished mankind.
Instead of bringing on a cyclone,
Jackals might have come and diminished mankind.
Instead of bringing on a cyclone,
Famine might have come and overwhelmed the land.
Instead of bringing on a cyclone,
Ira might have come and destroyed the land.
I did not reveal the oracle of the great gods,
I sent Atrakhasis a dream and he understood the oracle of the gods.
Now take counsel for him.' "

Enlil is moved by this eloquent appeal and is reconciled. He himself accords immortal life to Ut-napishtim and his wife, and with this act the story ends.

"Enlil mounted the ship,
Took hold of my hand and took me aboard,
Took me and caused my wife to kneel at my side,
Touched our foreheads, stepped between us and blessed us.
'Hitherto Ut-napishtim was a man;
Now Ut-napishtim and his wife shall be on a level with the gods.
Ut-napishtim shall dwell in the distance, at the confluence of the streams.'
Then they took me and placed me at the confluence of the streams."

It is evident that the entire deluge episode has no connection whatsoever with Gilgamesh. It is introduced in accordance with the trait of epics everywhere to embellish the stories of the adventures of the popular hero and to bring him into association with as many of the popular tales and myths as possible. At the close of Ut-napishtim's long recital and thread of the story is again taken up. Ut-napishtim, moved by pity for Gilgamesh, feels inclined to make an effort to secure immortality for Gilgamesh, and this despite the entirely hopeless outlook conveyed by Ut-napishtim's first address. He tells Gilgamesh that if he can ward off sleep for six days and seven nights the secret of immortal life will be revealed to him. Gilgamesh, however, is unable to endure the ordeal, and falls asleep. Ut-napishtim says to his wife:

"Behold the strong one who longed for life;
Sleep has blown upon him like a hurricane."

His wife says to Ut-napishtim, the one dwelling in the distance:

"Touch him, that the man may awake;
May he return safely on the way on which he came;

GENESIS 1–2:35
(NEW INTERNATIONAL VERSION)

GENESIS 1

The Beginning

[1] In the beginning God created the heavens and the earth.

[2] Now the earth was[a] formless and empty, darkness was over the surface of the deep, and the Spirit of God was hovering over the waters.

[3] And God said, "Let there be light," and there was light. [4] God saw that the light was good, and He separated the light from the darkness. [5] God called the light "day," and the darkness he called "night." And there was evening, and there was morning—the first day.

[6] And God said, "Let there be an expanse between the waters to separate water from water." [7] So God made the expanse and separated the water under the expanse from the water above it. And it was so. [8] God called the expanse "sky." And there was evening, and there was morning—the second day.

[9] And God said, "Let the water under the sky be gathered to one place, and let dry ground appear." And it was so. [10] God called the dry ground "land," and the gathered waters he called "seas." And God saw that it was good.

[11] Then God said, "Let the land produce vegetation: seed-bearing plants and trees on the land that bear fruit with seed in it, according to their various kinds." And it was so. [12] The land produced vegetation: plants bearing seed according to their kinds and trees bearing fruit with seed in it according to their kinds. And God saw that it was good. [13] And there was evening, and there was morning—the third day.

[14] And God said, "Let there be lights in the expanse of the sky to separate the day from the night, and let them serve as signs to mark seasons and days and years, [15] and let them be lights in the expanse of the sky to give light on the earth." And it was so. [16] God made two great lights-the greater light to govern the day and the lesser light to govern the night. He also made the stars. [17] God set them in the expanse of the sky to give light on the earth, [18] to govern the day and the night, and to separate light from darkness. And God saw that it was good. [19] And there was evening, and there was morning—the fourth day.

[20] And God said, "Let the water teem with living creatures, and let birds fly above the earth across the expanse of the sky." [21] So God created the great creatures of the sea and every living and moving thing with which the water teems, according to their kinds, and every winged bird according to its kind. And God saw that it was good. [22] God blessed them and said, "Be fruitful and increase in number and fill the water in the seas, and let the birds increase on the earth." [23] And there was evening, and there was morning—the fifth day.

24 And God said, "Let the land produce living creatures according to their kinds: livestock, creatures that move along the ground, and wild animals, each according to its kind." And it was so.25 God made the wild animals according to their kinds, the livestock according to their kinds, and all the creatures that move along the ground according to their kinds. And God saw that it was good.

26 Then God said, "Let us make man in our image, in our likeness, and let them rule over the fish of the sea and the birds of the air, over the livestock, over all the earth,[b] and over all the creatures that move along the ground."

27 So God created man in his own image,
in the image of God he created him;
male and female he created them.

28 God blessed them and said to them, "Be fruitful and increase in number; fill the earth and subdue it. Rule over the fish of the sea and the birds of the air and over every living creature that moves on the ground."

29 Then God said, "I give you every seed-bearing plant on the face of the whole earth and every tree that has fruit with seed in it. They will be yours for food.30 And to all the beasts of the earth and all the birds of the air and all the creatures that move on the ground—everything that has the breath of life in it—I give every green plant for food." And it was so.

31 God saw all that he had made, and it was very good. And there was evening, and there was morning-the sixth day.

GENESIS 2

1 Thus the heavens and the earth were completed in all their vast array.

2 By the seventh day God had finished the work he had been doing; so on the seventh day he rested[c] from all his work.3 And God blessed the seventh day and made it holy, because on it he rested from all the work of creating that he had done.

Adam and Eve

4 This is the account of the heavens and the earth when they were created.

When the LORD God made the earth and the heavens—5and no shrub of the field had yet appeared on the earth[d] and no plant of the field had yet sprung up, for the LORD God had not sent rain on the earth[e] and there was no man to work the ground,6 but streams[f] came up from the earth and watered the whole surface of the ground—7the LORD God formed the man[g] from the dust of the ground and breathed into his nostrils the breath of life, and the man became a living being.

8 Now the LORD God had planted a garden in the east, in Eden; and there he put the man he had formed.9 And the LORD God made all kinds of trees grow out of the ground—trees that were pleasing to the eye and good for food. In the middle of the garden were the tree of life and the tree of the knowledge of good and evil.

10 A river watering the garden flowed from Eden; from there it was separated into four headwaters.11 The name of the first is the Pishon; it winds through the entire land of Havilah, where there is gold.12 (The gold of that land is good; aromatic resin[h] and onyx are also there.)13 The name of the second river is the

Gihon; it winds through the entire land of Cush.[i][14] The name of the third river is the Tigris; it runs along the east side of Asshur. And the fourth river is the Euphrates.

[15] The LORD God took the man and put him in the Garden of Eden to work it and take care of it.[16] And the LORD God commanded the man, "You are free to eat from any tree in the garden;[17] but you must not eat from the tree of the knowledge of good and evil, for when you eat of it you will surely die."

[18] The LORD God said, "It is not good for the man to be alone. I will make a helper suitable for him."

[19] Now the LORD God had formed out of the ground all the beasts of the field and all the birds of the air. He brought them to the man to see what he would name them; and whatever the man called each living creature, that was its name.[20] So the man gave names to all the livestock, the birds of the air and all the beasts of the field.

But for Adam[j] no suitable helper was found.[21] So the LORD God caused the man to fall into a deep sleep; and while he was sleeping, he took one of the man's ribs[k] and closed up the place with flesh.[22] Then the LORD God made a woman from the rib[l] he had taken out of the man, and he brought her to the man.

[23] The man said,

"This is now bone of my bones
and flesh of my flesh;
she shall be called 'woman,[m]'
for she was taken out of man."

[24] For this reason a man will leave his father and mother and be united to his wife, and they will become one flesh.

[25] The man and his wife were both naked, and they felt no shame.

ENDNOTES

a. *Genesis 1:2* Or possibly *became*
b. *Genesis 1:26* Hebrew; Syriac *all the wild animals*
c. *Genesis 2:2* Or *ceased;* also in verse
d. *Genesis 2:5* Or *land;* also in verse
e. *Genesis 2:5* Or *land;* also in verse
f. *Genesis 2:6* Or *mist*
g. *Genesis 2:7* The Hebrew for *man (adam)* sounds like and may be related to the Hebrew for ground (adamah it is also the name Adam (see Gen. 2:20).
h. *Genesis 2:12* Or *good;* pearls
i. *Genesis 2:13* Possibly southeast Mesopotamia
j. *Genesis 2:20* Or *the man*
k. *Genesis 2:21* Or *took part of the man's side*
l. *Genesis 2:22* Or *part*
m. *Genesis 2:23* The Hebrew for *woman* sounds like the Hebrew for *man.*

THE ALLEGORY OF THE CAVE

See website at www.grtep.com for a link to this reading.

WHAT'S THE BEST "PROOF" OF CREATION

See website at www.grtep.com for a link to this reading.

EXODUS 20-21

The following passage lists the Ten Commandments, the core religious rules of the ancient Hebrews. The first several commandments emphasize duties to God, while the later commandments demand proper behavior within the community.

And God spoke all these words, saying,

"I am the LORD your God, who brought you out of the land of Egypt, out of the house of bondage.

"You shall have no other gods before me.

"You shall not make for yourself a graven image, or any likeness of anything that is in heaven above, or that is in the earth beneath, or that is in the water under the earth; you shall not bow down to them or serve them; for I the LORD your God am a jealous God, visiting the iniquity of the fathers upon the children to the third and the fourth generation of those who hate me, but showing steadfast love to thousands of those who love me and keep my commandments.

"You shall not take the name of the LORD your God in vain; for the LORD will not hold him guiltless who takes his name in vain.

"Remember the Sabbath day, to keep it holy. Six days you shall labor, and do all your work; but the seventh day is a Sabbath to the LORD your God: in it you shall not do any work, you or your son, or your daughter, your manservant, or your maidservant, or your cattle, or the sojourner who is within your gates; for in six days the LORD made heaven and earth, the sea, and all that is in them, and rested the seventh day; therefore the LORD blessed the Sabbath day and hallowed it.

"Honor your father and your mother, that your days may be long in the land which the LORD your God gives you.

"You shall not kill.

"You shall not commit adultery.

"You shall not steal.

"You shall not bear false witness against your neighbor.

"You shall not covet your neighbor's house; you shall not covet your neighbor's wife, or his manservant, or his maidservant, or his ox, or his ass, or anything that is your neighbor's."

Now when all the people perceived the thunderings and the lightnings and the sound of the trumpet and the mountain smoking, the people were afraid and trembled; and they stood afar off, and said to Moses, "You speak to us, and we will hear; but let not God speak to us, lest we die." And Moses said to the people, "Do not fear; for God has come to prove you, and that the fear of him may be before your eyes, that you may not sin."

And the people stood afar off while Moses drew near to the thick darkness where God was. And the LORD said to Moses, "Thus you shall say to the people of Israel: 'You have seen for yourselves that I have talked with you from heaven. You shall not make gods of silver to be with me, nor shall you make for yourselves gods of gold. An altar of earth you shall make for me and sacrifice on it your burnt offerings and your peace offerings, your sheep and your oxen; in every place where I cause my name to be remembered I will come to you and bless you. And if you make me an altar of stone, you shall not build it of hewn stones; for if you wield your tool upon it you profane it. And you shall not go up by steps to my altar, that your nakedness be not exposed on it.'

DANIEL 7

The Book of Daniel was probably composed in the second or third centuries B.C.E. The following passage includes an allegorical description of four ancient empires. It also includes an account of the anticipated Messiah.

In the first year of Bel-shaz'zar king of Babylon, Daniel had a dream and visions of his head as he lay in his bed. Then he wrote down the dream, and told the sum of the matter. [2]Daniel said, "I saw in my vision by night, and behold, the four winds of heaven were stirring up the great sea. [3]And four great beasts came up out of the sea, different from one another. [4]The first was like a lion and had eagles' wings. Then as I looked its wings were plucked off, and it was lifted up from the ground and made to stand upon two feet like a man; and the mind of a man was given to it. [5]And behold, another beast, a second one, like a bear. It was raised up on one side; it had three ribs in its mouth between its teeth; and it was told, 'Arise, devour much flesh.' [6]After this I looked, and lo, another, like a leopard, with four wings of a bird on its back; and the beast had four heads; and dominion was given to it. [7]After this I saw in the night visions, and behold, a fourth beast, terrible and dreadful and exceedingly strong; and it had great iron teeth; it devoured and broke in pieces, and stamped the residue with its feet. It was different from all the beasts that were before it; and it had ten horns. [8]I considered the horns, and behold, there came up among them another horn, a little one, before which three of the first horns were plucked up by the roots; and behold, in this horn were eyes like the eyes of a man, and amouth speaking great things. [9]As I looked,

thrones were placed
    and one what was ancient of days took his seat;
his raiment was white as snow,
    and the hair of his head like pure wool;
his throne was fiery flames,
    its wheels were burning fire.
[10]A stream of fire issued
    and came forth from before him;
a thousand thousands served him,
    and ten thousands time ten thousand stood
        before him;
the court sat in judgment,
    and the books were opened.

[11]I looked then because of the sound of the great words which the horn was speaking. And as I looked, the best was slain, and its body destroyed and given over to be burned with fire. [12]As for the rest of the

beasts, their dominion was taken away, but their lives were prolonged for a season and a time. [13]I saw in the night visions,

and behold, with the clouds of heaven
there came one like a son of man,
and he came to the Ancient of Days
and was presented before him.
[14]And to him was given dominion
and glory and kingdom,
that all peoples, nations, and languages
should serve him;
his dominion is an everlasting dominion,
which shall not pass away,
and his kingdom one
that shall not be destroyed.

HOMER, THE ODYSSEY

This next passage from Homer's second poem describes how the hero Odysseus and his men encounter the Cyclopes. One of these creatures nearly puts an end to their odyssey.

We sailed hence, always in much distress, till we came to the land of the lawless and inhuman Cyclopes. Now the Cyclopes neither plant nor plough, but trust in providence, and live on such wheat, barley, and grapes as grow wild without any kind of tillage, and their wild grapes yield them wine as the sun and the rain may grow them. They have no laws nor assemblies of the people, but live in caves on the tops of high mountains; each is lord and master in his family, and they take no account of their neighbours.

"Now off their harbour there lies a wooded and fertile island not quite close to the land of the Cyclopes, but still not far. It is over-run with wild goats, that breed there in great numbers and are never disturbed by foot of man; for sportsmen—who as a rule will suffer so much hardship in forest or among mountain precipices—do not go there, nor yet again is it ever ploughed or fed down, but it lies a wilderness untilled and unsown from year to year, and has no living thing upon it but only goats. For the Cyclopes have no ships, not yet shipwrights who could make ships for them; they cannot therefore go from city to city, or sail over the sea to one another's country as people who have ships can do; if they had had these they would have colonized the island, [78] for it is a very good one, and would yield everything in due season. There are meadows that in some places come right down to the sea shore, well watered and full of luscious grass; grapes would do there excellently; there is level land for ploughing, and it would always yield heavily at harvest time, for the soil is deep. There is a good harbour where no cables are wanted, nor yet anchors, nor need a ship be moored, but all one has to do is to beach one's vessel and stay there till the wind becomes fair for putting out to sea again. At the head of the harbour there is a spring of clear water coming out of a cave, and there are poplars growing all round it.

"Here we entered, but so dark was the night that some god must have brought us in, for there was nothing whatever to be seen. A thick mist hung all round our ships; [79] the moon was hidden behind a mass of clouds so that no one could have seen the island if he had looked for it, nor were there any breakers to tell us we were close in shore before we found ourselves upon the land itself; when, however, we had beached the ships, we took down the sails, went ashore and camped upon the beach till daybreak.

"When the child of morning, rosy-fingered dawn appeared, we admired the island and wandered all over it, while the nymphs Jove's daughters roused the wild goats that we might get some meat for our dinner. On this we fetched our spears and bows and arrows from the ships, and dividing ourselves into three bands began to shoot the goats. Heaven sent us excellent sport; I had twelve ships with me, and each ship got nine goats, while my own ship had ten; thus through the livelong day to the going down of the sun we ate and drank our fill, and we had plenty of wine left, for each one of us had taken many jars full when we sacked the city of the Cicons, and this had not yet run out. While we were feasting we kept turning our eyes toward the land of the Cyclopes, which was hard by, and saw the smoke of their stubble fires. We could almost fancy we heard their voices and the bleating of their sheep and goats, but

Source: From *The Odyssey* by Homer, translated by Samuel Butler, 1900.

227

when the sun went down and it came on dark, we camped down upon the beach, and next morning I called a council.

"Stay here, my brave fellows,' said I, 'all the rest of you, while I go with my ship and exploit there people myself: I want to see if they are uncivilized savages, or a hospital and humane race.'

"I went on board, bidding my men to do so also and loose the hawsers; so they took their places and smote the grey sea with their oars. When we got to the land, which was not far, there, on the face of a cliff near the sea, we saw a great cave overhung with laurels. It was a station for a great many sheep and goats, and outside there was a large yard, with a high wall round it made of stones built into the ground and of trees both pine and oak. This was the abode of a huge monster who was then away from home shepherding his flocks. He would have nothing to do with other people, but led the life of an outlaw. He was a horrid creature, not like a human being at all, but resembling rather some crag that stands out boldly against the sky on the top of a high mountain.

"I told my men to draw the ship ashore, and stay where they were, all but the twelve best among them, who were to go along with myself. I also took a goatskin of sweet black wine which had been given me by Maron, son of Euanthes, who was priest of Apollo the patron god of Ismarus, and lived within the wooded precincts of the temple. When we were sacking the city we respected him, and spared his life, as also his wife and child; so he made me some presents of great value—seven talents of fine gold, and a bowl of silver, with twelve jars of sweet wine, unblended, and of the most exquisite flavour. Not a man nor maid in the house knew about it, but only himself, his wife, and one housekeeper: when he drank it he mixed twenty parts of water to one of wine, and yet the fragrance from the mixing-bowl was so exquisite that it was impossible to refrain from drinking. I filled a large skin with this wine, and took a wallet full of provisions with me, for my mind misgave me that I might have to deal with some savage who would be of great strength, and would respect neither right nor law.

"We soon reached his cave, but he was out shepherding, so we went inside and took stock of all that we could see. His cheese-racks were loaded with cheeses, and had more lambs and kids than his pens could hold. They were kept in separate flocks; first there were the hoggets, then the oldest of the younger lambs and lastly the very young ones [80] all kept apart from one another; as for his dairy, all the vessels, bowls, and milk pails into which he milked, were swimming with whey. When they saw all this, my men begged me to let them first steal some cheeses, and make off with them to the ship; they would then return, drive down the lambs and kids, put them on board and sail away with them. It would have been indeed better if we had done so but I would not listen to them, for I wanted to see the owner himself, in the hope that he might give me a present. When, however, we saw him my poor men found him ill to deal with.

"We lit a fire, offered some of the cheeses in sacrifice, ate others of them, and then sat waiting till the Cyclops should come in with his sheep. When he came, he brought in with him a huge load of dry fire-wood to light the fire for his supper, and this he flung with such a noise on to the floor of his cave that we hid ourselves for fear at the far end of the cavern. Meanwhile he drove all the ewes inside, as well as the she-goats that he was going to milk, leaving the males, both rams and he-goats, outside in the yards. Then he rolled a huge stone to the mouth of the cave—so huge that two and twenty strong four-wheeled wagons would not be enough to draw it from its place against the doorway. When he had so done he sat down and milked his ewes and goats, all in due course, and then let each of them have her own young. He curdled half the milk and set it aside in wicker strainers, but the other half he poured into bowls that he might drink it for his supper. When he had got through with all his work, he lit the fire, and then caught sight of us, whereon he said:

"Strangers, who are you? Where do sail from? Are you traders, or do you said the sea as rovers, with your hands against every man, and every man's hand against you?'

"We were frightened out of our senses by his loud voice and monstrous form, but I managed to say, 'We are Achaeans on our way home from Troy, but by the will of Jove, and stress of weather, we have been driven far out of our course. We are the people of Agamemnon, son of Atreus, who has won infinite renown throughout the whole world, by sacking so great a city and killing so many people. We therefore humbly pray you to show us some hospitality, and otherwise make us such presents as visitors may reasonably expect. May your excellency fear the wrath of heaven, for we are your suppliants, and Jove takes all respectable travelers under his protection, for his is the avenger of all suppliants and foreigners in distress.'

"To this he gave me but a pitiless answer, 'Stranger,' said he, 'you are a fool, or else you know nothing of this country. Talk to me, indeed, about fearing the gods or shunning their anger? We Cyclopes do not care about Jove or any of your blessed gods, for we are ever so much stronger than they. I shall not spare either yourself or your companions out of any regard for Jove, unless I am in the humour for doing so. And now tell me where you made your ship fast when you came on shore. Was it round the point, or is she lying straight off the land?'

"He said this to draw me out, but I was too cunning to be caught in that way, so I answered with a lie; 'Neptune,' said I, 'sent my ship on to the rocks at the far end of your country, and wrecked it. We were driven on to them from the open sea, but I and those who are with me escaped the jaws of death.'

"The cruel wretch vouchsafed me not one word of answer, but with a sudden clutch he gripped up two of my men at once and dashed them down upon the ground as though they had been puppies. Their brains were shed upon the ground, and the earth was wet with their blood. Then he tore them limb from limb and supped upon them. He gobbled them up like a lion in the wilderness, flesh, bones, marrow, and entrails, without leaving anything uneaten. As for us, we wept and lifted up our hands to heaven on seeing such a horrid sight, for we did not know what else to do; but when the Cyclops had filled his huge paunch, and had washed down his meal of human flesh with a drink of neat milk, he stretched himself full length upon the ground among his sheep, and went to sleep. I was at first inclined to seize my sword, draw it, and drive it into his vitals, but I reflected that if I did we should all certainly be lost, for we should never be able to shift the stone which the monster had put in front of the door. So we stayed sobbing and sighing where we were till morning came.

"When the child of morning, rosy-fingered dawn, appeared, he again lit his fire, milked his goats and ewes, all quite rightly, and then let each have her own young one; as soon as he had got through with all his work, he clutched up two more of my men, and began eating them for his morning's meal. Presently, with the utmost ease, he rolled the stone away from the door and drove out his sheep, but he at once put it back again—as easily as though he were merely clapping the lid on to a quiver full of arrows. As soon as he had done so he shouted, and cried 'Shoo, shoo,' after his sheep to drive them on to the mountain; so I was left to scheme some way of taking my revenge and covering myself with glory.

"In the end I deemed it would be the best plan to do as follows: The Cyclops had a great club which was lying near one of the sheep pens; it was of green olive wood, and he had but it intending to use it for a staff as soon as it should be dry. It was so huge that we could only compare it to the mast of a twenty-oared merchant vessel of large burden, and able to venture out into open sea. I went up to this club and cut off about six feet of it; I then gave this piece to the men and told them to fine it evenly off at one end, which they proceeded to do, and lastly I brought it to a point myself, charring the end in the fire to make it harder. When I had done this I hid it under dung, which was lying about all over the cave, and told the men to cast lots which of them should venture along with myself to lift it and bore it into the monster's eye while he was asleep. The lot fell upon the very four whom I should have chosen, and I myself made five. In the evening the wretch came back from shepherding, and drove his flocks into the cave—this time driving them all inside, and not leaving any in the yards; I suppose some fancy must have taken him, or a god must have prompted him to do so. As soon as he had put the stone back to its place against the door, he sat down, milked his ewes and his goats all quite rightly, and then let each have her own young one; when he had got through with all this work, he gripped up two more of my men, and made his supper off them. So I went up to him with an ivy-wood bowl of black wine in my hands:

"'Look here, Cyclops,' said I, you have been eating a great deal of man's flesh, so take this and drink some wine, that you may see what kind of liquor we had on board by ship. I was bringing it to you as a drink-offering, in the hope that you would take compassion upon me and further me on my way home, whereas all you do is to go on ramping and raving most intolerably. You ought to be ashamed of yourself; how can you expect people to come see you any more if you treat them in this way?'

"He then took the cup and drank. He was so delighted with the taste of the wine that he begged me for another bowl full. 'Be so kind,' he said, 'as to give me some more, and tell me your name at once. I want to make you a present that you will be glad to have. We have wine even in this country, for our soil grows grapes and the sun ripens them, but this drinks like Nectar and Ambrosia all in one.'

"I then gave him some more; three times did I fill the bowl for him, and three times did he drain it without thought or heed; then, when I saw that the wine had got into his head, I said to him as plausibly as I could: 'Cyclops, you ask my name and I will tell it you; give me, therefore, the present you promised me; my name is Noman; that is what my father and mother and my friends have always called me.'

"But the cruel wretch said, 'Then I will eat all Noman's comrades before Noman himself, and will keep Noman for the last. This is the present that I will make him.'

EURIPIDES, MEDEA

The playwright Euripides (ca. 480–406 B.C.E.) broke with convention in that his works tended to emphasize emotions and flawed human individuals rather than gods or ill-fated heroes. Euripides also paid more attention to female characters. The following passage is from the tragedy *Medea,* based on the story of the wronged wife of the hero Jason.

MEDEA

Ah, me! The agony I have suffered, deep enough to call for these laments! Curse you and your father too, ye children damned, sons of a doomed mother! Ruin seize the whole family!

Nurse chanting

Ah me! ah me! the pity of it! Why, pray, do the children share their father's crime? Why hatest thou them? Woe is you, poor children, how do I grieve for you lest ye suffer some outrage! Strange are the tempers of princes, and maybe because they seldom have to obey, and mostly lord it over others, change they their moods with difficulty. 'Tis better then to have been trained to live on equal terms. Be it mine to reach old age, not in proud pomp, but in security! Moderation wins the day first as a better word for men to use, and likewise it is far the best course for them to pursue; but greatness that doth o'erreach itself, brings no blessing to mortal men; but pays a penalty of greater ruin whenever fortune is wroth with a family.

The CHORUS enters. The following lines between the NURSE, CHORUS, and MEDEA are sung.

Chorus

I heard the voice, uplifted loud, of our poor Colchian lady, nor yet is she quiet; speak, aged dame, for as I stood by the house with double gates I heard a voice of weeping from within, and I do grieve, lady, for the sorrows of this house, for it hath won my love.

Nurse

'Tis a house no more; all that is passed away long since; a royal bri'e keep Jason at her side, while our mistress pines away in her bower, finding no comfort for her soul in aught her friends can say.

Medea within

Oh, oh! Would that Heaven's levin bolt would cleave this head in twain! What gain is life to me? Woe, woe is me! O, to die and win release, quitting this loathed existence!

Source: *Medea* by Euripides, translated by E.P. Coleridge & G. Bell, 1913.

Chorus

Didst hear, O Zeus, thou earth, and thou, O light, the piteous note of woe the hapless wife is uttering? How shall a yearning for that insatiate resting-place ever hasten for thee, poor reckless one, the end that death alone can bring? Never pray for that. And if thy lord prefers a fresh love, be not angered with him for that; Zeus will judge 'twixt thee and him herein. Then mourn not for thy husband's loss too much, nor waste thyself away.

Medea within

Great Themis, and husband of Themis, behold what I am suffering now, though I did bind that accursed one, my husband, by strong oaths to me! O, to see him and his bride some day brought to utter destruction, they and their house with them, for that they presume to wrong me thus unprovoked. O my father, my country, that I have left to my shame, after slaying my own brother.

Nurse

Do ye hear her words, how loudly she adjures Themis, oft invoked, and Zeus, whom men regard as keeper of their oaths? On no mere trifle surely will our mistress spend her rage.

Chorus

Would that she would come forth for us to see, and listen to the words of counsel we might give, if haply she might lay aside the fierce fury of her wrath, and her temper stern. Never be my zeal at any rate denied my friends! But go thou and bring her hither outside the house, and tell her this our friendly thought; haste thee ere she do some mischief to those inside the house, for this sorrow of hers is mounting high.

Nurse

This will I do; but I doubt whether I shall persuade my mistress; still willingly will I undertake this trouble for you; albeit, she glares upon her servants with the look of a lioness with cubs, whenso anyone draws nigh to speak to her. Wert thou to call the men of old time rude uncultured boors thou wouldst not err, seeing that they devised their hymns for festive occasions, for banquets, and to grace the board, a pleasure to catch the ear, shed o'er our life, but no man hath found a way to allay hated grief by music and the minstrel's varied strain, whence arise slaughters and fell strokes of fate to o'erthrow the home of men. And yet this were surely a gain, to heal men's wounds by music's spell, but why tune they their idle song where rich banquets are spread? For of itself doth the rich banquet, set before them, afford to men delight.

Chorus

I heard a bitter cry of lamentation! loudly, bitterly she calls on the traitor of her marriage bed, her perfidious spouse; by grievous wrongs oppressed she invokes Themis, bride of Zeus, witness of oaths, who brought her unto Hellas, the land that fronts the strand of Asia, o'er the sea by night through ocean's boundless gate.

As the CHORUS finishes its song, MEDIA enters from the house.

Medea

From the house I have come forth, Corinthian ladies, for fear lest you be blaming me; for well I know that amongst men many by showing pride have gotten them an ill name and a reputation for indifference, both those who shun men's gaze and those who move amid the stranger crowd, and likewise they who choose a quiet walk in life. For there is no just discernment in the eyes of men, for they, or ever they have surely learnt their neighbour's heart, loathe him at first sight, though never wronged by him; and so a stranger most of all should adopt a city's views; nor do I commend that citizen, who, in the stubbornness of his heart, from churlishness resents the city's will.

But on me hath fallen this unforeseen disaster, and sapped my life; ruined I am, and long to resign the boon of existence, kind friends, and die. For he who was all the world to me, as well thou knowest, hath turned out the worst of men, my own husband. Of all things that have life and sense we women are the most hapless creatures; first must we buy a husband at a great price, and o'er ourselves a tyrant set which is an evil worse than the first; and herein lies the most important issue, whether our choice be good or bad. For divorce is not honourable to women, nor can we disown our lords. Next must the wife, coming as she does to ways and customs new, since she hath not learnt the lesson in her home, have a diviner's eye to see how best to treat the partner of her life. If haply we perform these tasks with thoroughness and tact, and the husband live with us, without resenting the yoke, our life is a happy one; if not, 'twere best to die. But when a man is vexed with what he finds indoors, he goeth forth and rids his soul of its disgust, betaking him to some friend or comrade of like age; whilst we must needs regard his single self.

And yet they say we live secure at home, while they are at the wars, with their sorry reasoning, for I would gladly take my stand in battle array three times o'er, than once give birth. But enough! this language suits not thee as it does me; thou hast a city here, a father's house, some joy in life, and friends to share thy thoughts, but I am destitute, without a city, and therefore scorned by my husband, a captive I from a foreign shore, with no mother, brother, or kinsman in whom to find a new haven of refuge from this calamity. Wherefore this one boon and only this I wish to win from thee,—thy silence, if haply I can some way or means devise to avenge me on my husband for this cruel treatment, and on the man who gave to him his daughter, and on her who is his wife. For though woman be timorous enough is all else, and as regards courage, a coward at the mere sight of steel, yet in the moment she finds her honour wronged, no heart is filled with deadlier thought than hers.

ARISTOTLE, POLITICS

Plato's student Aristotle (384–322 B.C.E.) took a more empirical approach to the pursuit of truth. He studied a vast range of subjects including biology through the direct dissection of animals. One of his most famous works examined the human institution of politics.

As in other natural compounds the conditions of a composite whole are not necessarily organic parts of it, so in a state or in any other combination forming a unity not everything is a part, which is a necessary condition. The members of an association have necessarily some one thing the same and common to all, in which they share equally or unequally; for example, food or land or any other thing. But where there are two things of which one is a means and the other an end, they have nothing in common except that the one receives what the other produces. Such, for example, is the relation in which workmen and tools stand to their work; the house and the builder have nothing in common, but the art of the builder is for the sake of the house. And so states require property, but property, even though living beings are included in it, is no part of a state; for a state is not a community of living beings only, but a community of equals, aiming at the best life possible. Now, whereas happiness is the highest good, being a realization and perfect practice of virtue, which some can attain, while others have little or none of it, the various qualities of men are clearly the reason why there are various kinds of states and many forms of government; for different men seek after happiness in different ways and by different means, and so make for themselves different modes of life and forms of government. We must see also how many things are indispensable to the existence of a state, for what we call the parts of a state will be found among the indispensables. Let us then enumerate the functions of a state, and we shall easily elicit what we want:

First, there must be food; secondly, arts, for life requires many instruments; thirdly, there must be arms, for the members of a community have need of them, and in their own hands, too, in order to maintain authority both against disobedient subjects and against external assailants; fourthly, there must be a certain amount of revenue, both for internal needs, and for the purposes of war; fifthly, or rather first, there must be a care of religion, which is commonly called worship; sixthly, and most necessary of all, there must be a power of deciding what is for the public interest, and what is just in men's dealings with one another.

These are the services which every state may be said to need. For a state is not a mere aggregate of persons, but a union of them sufficing for the purposes of life; and if any of these things be wanting, it is as we maintain impossible that the community can be absolutely self-sufficing. A state then should be framed with a view to the fulfillment of these functions. There must be husband-men to procure food, and artisans, and a warlike and a wealthy class, and priests, and judges to decide what is necessary and expedient.

Source: From *Politics* by Aristotle, translated by Benjamin Jowett, 1885.

A SLAVE REVOLT IN SICILY: DIODORUS SICULUS, HISTORICAL LIBRARY 34.2

The expansion of Roman territory and influence during the late Republic and early Empire brought thousands of slaves to Rome. These unfortunate victims of Roman imperialism had little to protect them against the cruelty of their masters, and thought some were treated with reasonable civility, many lived lives of unending torment. It is not surprising, then, that Roman slaves occasionally rebelled against their masters. The most famous slave rebellion was led by the Thracian gladiator **Spartacus (73–72 B.C.)**. An earlier rebellion occurred in Sicily in 135–132 B.C. and was described by Diodorus Siculus in his *Library of History*.

. . . The slave revolt in Sicily broke out for the following reasons. The Sicilians, who had become very wealthy, began buying great numbers of slaves. They used to bring great bunches of them from their homelands to Sicily, where they would immediately mark their bodies with brands. They used the young men as shepherds and the rest for all the other jobs that needed to be done. The Sicilians were very hard on their slaves. They made little effort to provide for them the necessities of life, such as food and clothing. As a result, most of the slaves turned to robbery for their needs, and since they were organized into scattered groups, as if they were soldiers, there was bloodshed all over the island. The praetors tried to stop them but did not punish them. They were afraid of the power and influence of the landed gentry who owned the robber-slaves, and so they felt they had no choice but to turn a blind eye to the plundering of the land. The praetors feared the landowners because most of them were Roman equites, and it was the equites who served as judges when provincial magistrates were accused of misconduct.

The slaves, crushed by their hardships and frequently subjected to unreasonably brutal beatings, could not endure their treatment. Meeting whenever they got the chance, they discussed the possibility of a revolt until, in the end, they put their plan into action. Now, there was a certain Syrian slave who belonged to Antigenes of Enna—a man from Apamea [in Syria] who was a magician and wonder-worker. This slave claimed that he could foretell the future (the gods, he said, had commanded him to read it in dreams) and he had cleverly used this skill to take advantage of many people. In addition to giving oracles based on his dreams he also pretended to have visions of the gods while he was awake, and during these he would act as if he was getting his information about the future directly from the gods themselves. Some of his predictions came true and others did not, but since people only paid attention to his successes he quickly earned a reputation as a prophet. He used a certain trick to breathe fire and flame from his mouth, all the while pretending to be possessed by some god and raving about the future. He would put fire and a bit of fuel in a nut, or something like a nut, that had a small hole on both sides. Then he would put this device in his mouth and breathe on it to produce sparks and, finally, a flame. Before the revolt he used to say that the Syrian goddess (Atargatis) appeared to him and told him that he would become king. He told this story to everyone, even to his own master. Everyone treated his claims as a joke, and so Antigenes, who had gotten into the spirit of the wonder-worker's quackery, would introduce Eunus, for that was his name, at his dinner parties and ask him questions about his reign and how he would treat each of his guests. Eunus would answer frankly that he would be moderate in his treatment of masters, and since he was such a marvelously colorful character Antigenes' guests would always break out in laughter. Some of them would give him tasty morsels from the table and ask him as they did so to remember their kindness when he became king. It just so happened that this charlatan did become king, and in return for the tidbits that were given to him in jest at dinner parties he demonstrated his sincere gratitude.

The revolt began in the following way. There was a man named Damophilus from the city of Enna who was at the same time very wealthy and very arrogant. He was extremely cruel to his slaves, and so was his wife, Megallis, who was just as eager as he was to punish them and treat them inhumanely in a hundred ways. Suffering from their abuse, the slaves became like wild animals and conspired to rise up against their master and mistress and murder them. Going to Ennus, they asked him if the gods approved of what they were about to do. Babbling his usual hocus-pocus, he assured them that the gods were on their side and convinced them to put their plan into action without delay. And so they immediately assembled an army of four hundred of their fellow slaves and, after having armed themselves with whatever weapons they could find, they attacked Enna under the leadership of Eunus, who breathed fire in order to inspire them. Whenever they entered a house they spilled blood. They did not even spare tiny babies; instead, they tore them from their mothers' breasts and threw them to the ground. And as for the women, I cannot bring myself to describe the brutal and indecent things they did to them before the very eyes of their husbands. By this time the attacking slaves had been joined by slaves from the city who demonstrated their savagery by first murdering their own masters and then looking for others to slaughter. When Eunus and his men learned that Damophilus and his wife were in a park near the city they sent some men who tied their hands behind them and abused them with insults as they brought them back. The only one who received mercy from the slaves was their daughter, for she was very kind and had always sympathized with the slaves and done what she could to help them. This shows that the slaves were not acting out of some kind of "natural savagery" of slaves but out of a desire to repay their former masters for their cruelty to them.

Now, the men who had been sent to find Damophilus and Megallis brought them back to the city and into the theater, where all of the revels had gathered. Damophilus tried to save their skins by making a well-crafted appeal for mercy to the crowd. But then, when he began winning some of them over, Hermeias and Zeuxis, two men who hated him, denounced him as a liar and, without waiting for the other rebels to pronounce a judgment, one ran a sword through his chest while the other cut off his head with an axe. Eunus was then chosen king, not because he had courage or skill as a military commander, but because he was a wonder-worker and had prompted the revolt, and also because his name [which means "friendly" or "benevolent"] struck them as a good omen suggesting that he would be a kind ruler.

As soon as the rebels had made him their king, he called an assembly and executed all of the citizens of Enna except those who knew how to make weapons. These were bound in chains and put to work. He gave Megallis to the young slave girls, who tortured her and then threw her over a cliff. He himself murdered his own masters, Antigenes and Pytho. Then, after placing a crown on his head and dressing himself like a king, he announced that his wife, who was also from Apamea in Syria, would be queen. Next, he chose a royal council consisting of men who seemed to have the necessary intelligence. One of these was a certain Achaeus (who also happened to be an Achaean by birth), a man who was good both at making plans and carrying them out. Within three days Eunus had armed as best he could a force of more than six thousand men. In addition to these he had others who would fight with axes and hatchets, slings, sickles, stakes and even kitchen skewers. With these men he roamed about, ravaging the entire countryside. And then, when he had recruited many other slaves, he even dared to attack the Roman generals. He defeated them many times because of the size of his army. He had more than ten thousand soldiers. . . .

Soon after, the rebels fought a battle with Lucious Hypsaeus, a general who had arrived from Rome. He commanded eight thousand Sicilian troops, but the slaves numbered twenty thousand and so they were victorious. Before long there were two hundred thousand of them and in their numerous battles with the Romans they had many successes and few defeats. When word of the revolt spread there were other revolts in other places. An uprising of one hundred and fifty slaves occurred in Rome, another thousand revolted in Athens, and there were rebellions in Delos and many other places. But the local magistrates called in the troops so quickly and punished the rebels so severely that the rebellion was put down and those who were considering joining it were deterred. But in Sicily things only got worse. The slaves captured cities, enslaved their inhabitants and cut whole armies to pieces. Finally, however, the Roman commander Repuilius recaptured Tauromenium after subjecting it to a siege so effective that the city was completely sealed off. The rebels inside were trapped under indescribably horrible conditions of suffering and hunger. At first they ate the children, then the women, and finally one another. . . .

In the end a Syrian slave named Sarapion betrayed the citadel. Rupilius seized all of the runaway slaves in the city and, after torturing them, he threw them over a cliff. He then marched against Enna, which he besieged just as he had Tauromenium, causing the revels extreme suffering and dashing all their hopes. Cleon, one of the rebel commanders, came out of the city with a few men, but after a heroic struggle in which he was covered with wounds his dead body was put on display. Rupilius captured Enna by betrayal, for it was too strongly defended to be taken by force of arms alone. Aunus took his thousand bodyguards and fled in a cowardly way. . . .

. . . . He died in a manner befitting such a scoundrel at Morgantina [in central Sicily]. After this Rupilius scoured Sicily with a few picked troops and more quickly than anyone has hoped rid the island of every single robber-slave.

MORAL DECLINE DURING THE REPUBLIC: SALLUST, CONSPIRACY OF CATILINE 9–10

Writing in the difficult years following the assassination of Julius Caesar (44 B.C.), the Roman historian Sallust considered the roots of the evils which plagued his country. In his *Conspiracy of Catiline,* which describes a failed coup d'etat in 63 B.C., Sallust argued that the decline of Rome was due in large part to the abandonment of the civic values and high moral standards which had made Rome great in the past.

[The Romans of the early Republic] considered good morals to be of the utmost importance both in peace and war. Social harmony was the rule and greed was very rare. Justice and goodness were enforced not so much by laws as by nature. These early Romans reserved their quarreling, discord and hostility for the enemies of the state. Citizens vied with each other only for honor. When they made offerings to the gods they spared no expense, while at home they practiced frugality. They were loyal to their friends. By combining courage in war and justice in peacetime they protected themselves and their country. For example, in wartime soldiers were punished more often for attacking the enemy against orders or for being too slow to obey the order to leave the field of battle than for abandoning their standards or giving ground when hard pressed by the enemy. A second example is the fact that the early Romans governed their subjects with generosity rather than fear, and when wronged they sought to forgive the offenders rather than seek vengeance.

But when Rome had grown great through hard work and justice, when mighty kings had been vanquished in war and savage tribes and powerful nations had been brought down, when Carthage, Rome's rival, had been toppled and every land and sea had been opened to us, then Fortune turned against us and brought confusion to all that we did. Those who had found it easy to bear hard work and danger, anxiety and hardship, now discovered that the leisure and wealth which most men find so desirable were a burden and a curse to them. Lust for money grew among them, then the hunger for power, and these two gave rise to every other kind of evil. Greed destroyed honor, honesty and every other virtue, and taught men to be arrogant and cruel, to neglect the gods, and to believe that nothing is too sacred to sell. Ambition made many men false, leading them to say what they knew was not true, to choose friends and make enemies with only personal advancement in mind and to pretend they had good qualities which they did not have. At first these vices grew slowly, and sometimes they were punished. But in the end, when the disease had spread like a plague, Rome changed: a government which had once surpassed all others in justice and excellence now became cruel and unbearable.

SLAVE LABOR IN SPANISH MINES: DIODORUS SICULUS, HISTORICAL LIBRARY 5.36–38

Among the unluckiest of Roman slaves were those who were forced to work in the mines. In the following passage the Greek historian Diodorus Siculus describes the plight of the slaves who labored in the gold and silver mines of Iberia (modern Spain).

Ever since the Romans seized Iberia the greed of the Italians has brought them in droves to the province's mines, from which they have carried away untold wealth. They buy whole lots of slaves and turn them over to those who supervise the miners. The slaves then dig deep shafts in various places in hopes of finding the veins of silver and gold that run through the earth. The shafts they dig are not only very deep, but they also run many stades [a stade is about 607 feet] in length, and tunnels reach out from them at every angle, twisting back and forth under the earth, so that the miners can bring up from the depths the ore which gives their owners the profit they are after. . . .

The slaves who work in the mines produce unbelievable wealth for their masters but they themselves are destroyed by the digging they do day and night in the subterranean shafts. Many of them die because of the extreme suffering that fills their lives. They are given no chance to rest. Instead, under the overseer's lash, they have no choice but to live lives of terrible hardship and misery. Some of them manage to stay alive for quite some time, for they have strong bodies and hardy souls, but their suffering is so great that in their eyes death is more desirable than life.

AUGUSTAN AUTOCRACY: TACITUS, ANNALS 1.2–4

Despite his claims about his accomplishments in the *Res Gestae* and popular support through-out the Empire for his regime, not all Romans approved of Augustus. One of his critics was the historian Tacitus. Writing in the early years of the second century, Tacitus viewed Augustus' assumption of power from the perspective of one who had seen the unhappy consequences of what he regarded as monarchical rule.

When after the deaths of Brutus and Cassius the Republic no longer had an army, when [Sextus] Pompey had been crushed in Sicily, when, after Lepidus had been eliminated and Antony was dead, when even the Julian party had only Caesar left to lead it—it was then that Augustus, giving up the title of triumvir and saying that he was really nothing more than a consul who was content to protect the people with the authority of a tribune, began working to win over the army with gifts, the people with cheap grain and the whole Empire with the blessings of peace. As a result, his power grew steadily and he gradually took into his own hands the functions of the Senate, the magistrates and even the law. No one opposed him. The most spirited men had either fallen in battle or been eliminated during the proscriptions. The rest of the nobles found that accepting slavery without resistance was the quickest route to wealth and political power. They had profited from the revolution, and so now they preferred the security of the new order to the dangerous uncertainties of the past. The new regime was also popular in the provinces where the rule of the Senate and the people had been discredited by the feuding and greed of the government officials. The legal system had offered the provincials very little protection since it had been totally crippled by violence, favoritism and, most of all, bribery.

In order to make his position more secure Augustus made Claudius Marcellus, his sister's son and a mere youth, a priest and an aedile. He honored Marcus Agrippa, a commoner but a fine soldier who had fought with him to many victories, with two successive consulships. When Marcellus died, Augustus chose Agrippa as his son-in-law. He gave imperial titles to his stepsons, Tiberius Nero and Claudius Drusus, even though his own family was still intact, for he had already admitted Agrippa's children, Gaius and Lucius, into the imperial household and, while they were still youths, he had been extremely anxious (though he said he wasn't) to see them become consuls-elect and Princes of the Youth. After Agrippa died either untimely fate or the treachery of their stepmother Livia cut off both of them, Lucius Caesar as he was on his way to our armies in Spain and Gaius Caesar as he was returning from Armenia, suffering from a wound. By that time Drusus had long been dead and so the only remaining stepson was [Tiberius] Nero. Everything centered on him. Augustus adopted him as his son, made him his colleague in ruling the empire, appointed him his partner in exercising his tribunician power and paraded him before the troops—not, as before, because of his mother's schemes and conniving, but at her open suggestion. In fact, she had now gained such control over the aging Augustus that he had sent his only grandson, Agrippa Postumus, into exile on the island of Planasia. It is true that the boy had no good qualities aside from the courage which accompanies brute strength, but he had not been guilty of any serious offense. Curiously, Augustus gave Drusus' son Germanicus the command of eight legions on the Rhine and made Tiberius adopt him, even though Tiberius already had an adult son in his house. He did this to further strengthen and safeguard his position. There was no war at this time apart from a campaign against the Germans which was being fought to make up for the defeat of Quintilius Varus and his army rather than to increase the size of the empire or to gain any other worthwhile benefit. In Rome itself everything was calm and the magistrates continued to use their traditional titles. A new generation had grown up since Actium; most of the older people had been born during the civil wars—how few were left who could remember the Republic!

It was a different world. Not a trace was left of the old Roman morality. The ideal of political equality had been abandoned and everyone watched and waited for the commands of the emperor without the slightest fear for the present so long as Augustus, while he was still vigorous, was able to maintain his own position, that of his house, and the peace.

CALIGULA AND THE JEWS: JOSEPHUS, JEWISH WAR 2.184–7, 192–203

In 39–40 A.D. the emperor Gaius (Caligula) nearly provoked a rebellion of the Jews of Judea by ordering that his statue should be placed in the Temple in Jerusalem. This amounted to a gross offense against the religious sensibilities of the Jews who, as strict monotheists, could not tolerate what the emperor intended. Josephus' account of the matter offers us portraits of a thoughtless emperor, a conscientious Roman governor (Petronius) and a people completely committed to its traditional religious beliefs and values.

The emperor Gaius [Caligula] defied fortune with an arrogance beyond measure. He wanted to be considered a god and to be hailed as such, he destroyed many of the promising young men of the aristocracy, and his impiety reached even as far as Judea. In fact, he sent Petronius to Jerusalem with orders to place statues of himself in the Temple there and, if any of the Jews tried to resist him, to put them to death and sell the entire nation into slavery. But God would have a hand in these matters, as future events would show. Petronius took three legions and a large force of Syrian auxiliaries and marched from Antioch toward Judea. . . .

The Jews gathered with their wives and children on the plain of Ptolemais and pleaded with Petronius to reconsider his intentions out of respect for the laws of their ancestors and, if that did not move him, for their own persons. Giving in for the moment to the pleas of this great multitude, Petronius left the statues and his troops at Ptolemais and went into Galilee where he called upon the people, and especially men of distinction, to meet with him at Tiberias. There he reminded them emphatically of the power of Rome, the emperor's threats and the danger of their request. He told them that there were statues of Caesar in the cities of all the other subject states, along with those of their other gods, and that their resistance amounted to insult and rebellion.

When the Jews claimed that their ancestral law and customs prohibited them from placing an image of God, not to mention the image of a man, not only in their Temple but even in any unconsecrated place in their entire country, Petronius replied, "But I must obey the law of my master; if I disobey him I will be executed, as I should be, and the one who sent me will make war on you. Both of us are under orders." Having heard this the multitude cried out that they were prepared to suffer anything for the sake of their law. Petronius asked for quiet and then asked, "Will you go to war against Caesar?" The Jews answered that they offered two sacrifices each day for Caesar and the Roman people, but that if Caesar truly intended to set up these statues he would first have to sacrifice the entire Jewish nation. They were ready, they said, to present themselves, their wives and their children to be slaughtered. The absolute devotion of these people to their faith and their sincere willingness to die for it filled Petronius with wonder and pity. And so, for the time being, he dismissed them with the issue left undecided.

In the days that followed he met privately with many of the aristocrats and also with the people in public. During these meetings he sometimes begged them, often advised them, but mostly threatened them, remind them of the power of the Romans, the anger of Gaius, and the fact that he would be forced by circumstances to carry out his orders. The Jews, however, were unmoved, and when Petronius saw that the land was in danger of remaining unsown (for it was the sowing season, and the people had spent the last fifty days waiting for his decision and not working) he once again called them together and said, "I will be the one to take the risk. Either, with God's help, I will succeed with Caesar and have the joy of saving all our lives, or, if his fury is aroused, I will sacrifice my own life on behalf of yours." With these words he dismissed the crowd, who praised him profusely, collected his troops and left Ptolemais for Antioch. From there he immediately reported to Caesar about his expedition to Judea, described the pleas of the Jews, and advised the emperor that unless he wanted to destroy the entire country and its people he should respect their law and rescind his order concerning the statues. Gaius replied to this letter in terms which expressed his outrage and warned Petronius that he would be put to death for being so slow to execute his orders. But it just so happened that the bearers of his letter were kept at sea for three months by bad weather, while others, who brought the news that Gaius had died, had a much easier passage. Thus, Petronius learned of the emperor's death twenty-seven days before he received the letter which contained the order for his own execution.

A STOIC'S VIEWS ON SLAVERY: SENECA, MORAL EPISTLES 47

Like other Stoics, the Roman philosopher Seneca maintained that since all human beings are endowed with reason and are governed by the same universal laws they are essentially equal. His belief that slaves possess the same dignity and personal worth as free men and women is evident in the letter he wrote on the subject of slavery to his friend Lucillius.

I am pleased to hear from your associate, Lucilius, that you live on friendly terms with those who serve you. I would expect as much from a man as sensible and well-educated as you. "But they are slaves!" people will say. No, they are men. "Slaves!" No, they are comrades. "Slaves!" No, they are humble friends. "Slaves!" Then so are we, for all men are equally subject to the whims of Fortune.

That is why I laugh at those who think it is degrading for a man to dine with his slave. What is degrading about it? It is only because of our arrogance that the master of the house sits down alone to eat his supper while a throng of slaves stands around him. He stuffs and stretches his belly with such an enormous amount of food that he can barely digest and eliminate it. While he gorges himself the slaves may not so much as move their lips or even speak. The softest murmur brings a beating with the rod, and even an accidental cough, sneeze or hiccup does not go unpunished. There is a severe penalty in store for anyone who causes the slightest interruption of the silence, and so the slaves must stand there, sometimes for an entire night, hungry and wordless.

Slaves such as these speak disrespectfully of their masters behind their backs because they are not permitted to say anything at all in their presence. But in the old days slaves were allowed not only to speak when their masters were in the room, but even with them. In return for the freedom to speak they were willing to risk their own necks for their masters. The saying that a man has as many enemies as he has slaves is true only when slaves are treated with disrespect. They are not naturally our enemies, but we make them such. . . .

We Romans treat our slaves cruelly and arrogantly, but I do not wish to go into this matter more deeply at the moment. Let me just say that you should treat your inferiors as you would have your superiors treat you. And whenever you stop to think of how much power you have over a slave, remember the power that your master has over you. You say, "But I have no master." True. For now you are fortunate. But things change.

JESUS ON ETHICS: GOSPEL OF MATTHEW 13:44–46; 22:34–40; 5:17–48.

See website at www.grtep.com for a link to this reading.

Reference Maps

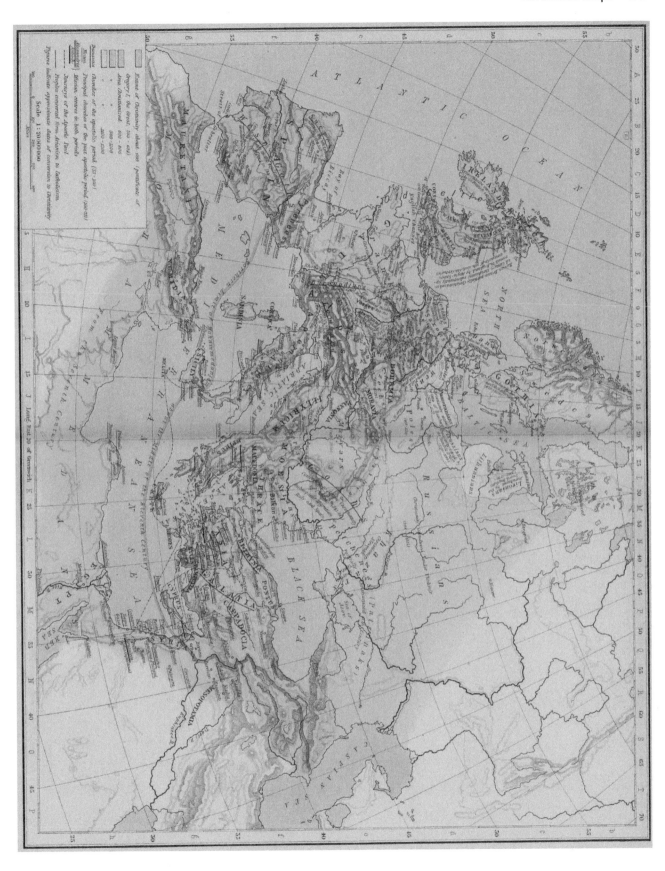

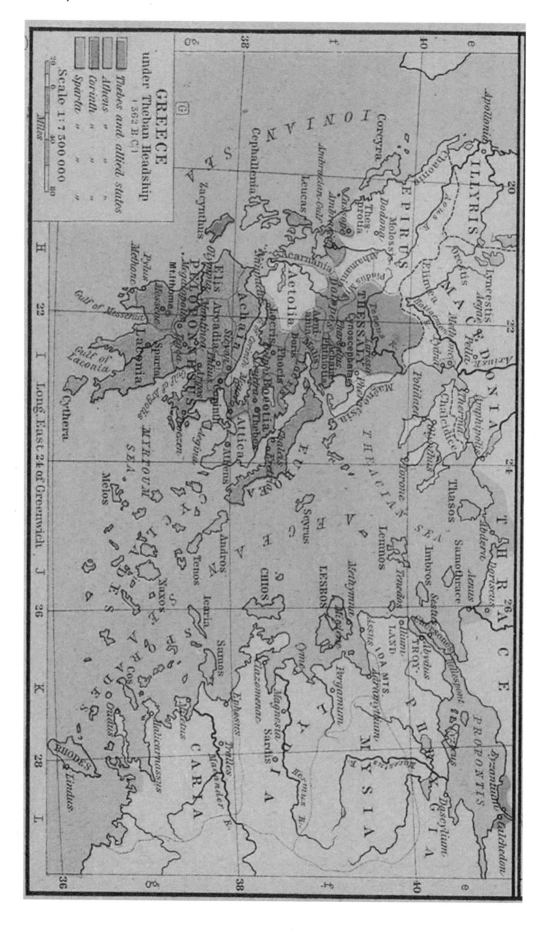

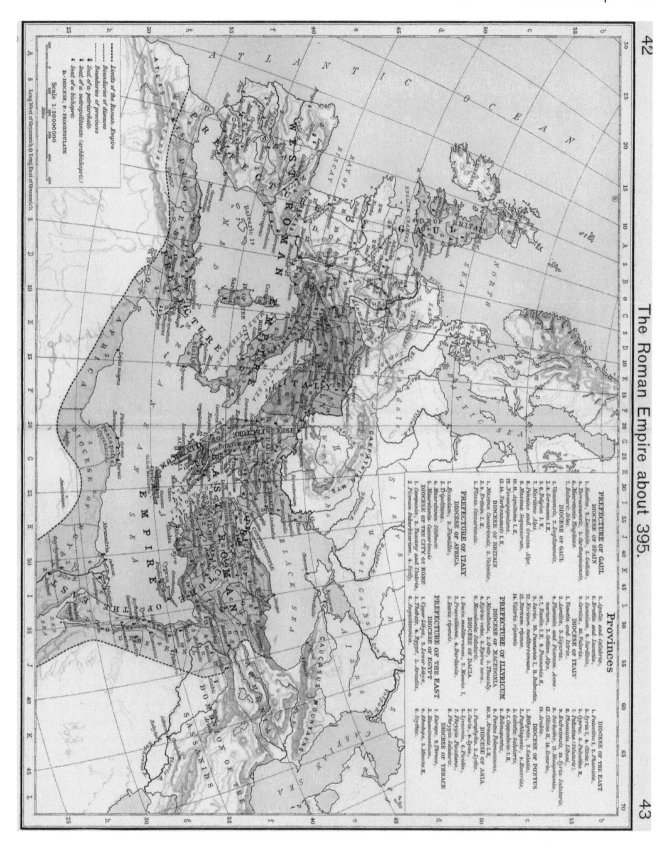

The Roman Empire about 395.

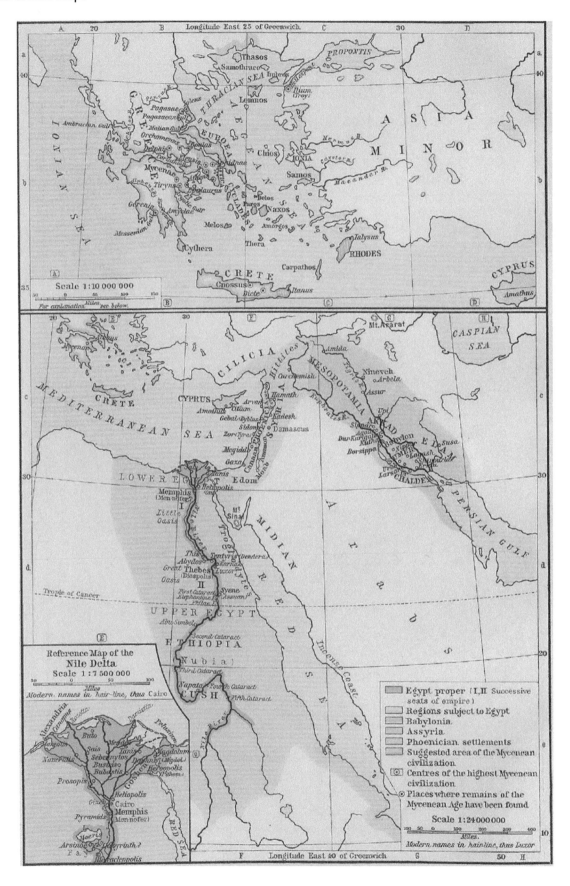

Index